Gunnar Skodbakke
Centralvaskeriet – Kolding

Books by Telford Taylor

Sword and Swastika:
Generals and Nazis in the Third Reich

The March of Conquest:
The German Victories in Western Europe, 1940

The Breaking Wave:
The Second World War in the Summer of 1940

Grand Inquest:
The Story of Congressional Investigations

The Breaking Wave

The German Defeat in the Summer of 1940

by TELFORD TAYLOR

WEIDENFELD AND NICOLSON
5 WINSLEY STREET LONDON W1

To PJC, EMJ, and EJBR

Contents

MAPS

How Hitler Might Have Come to England

IT BURST ON US *with calculated suddenness, and we were just not enough, everywhere where the pressure came. Our ships were good against their ships, our seamen were better than their seamen, but our ships were not able to cope with their ships plus their superiority in aircraft. Our trained men were good against their trained men, but they could not be in several places at once, and the enemy could. Our half-trained men and our untrained men could not master the science of war at a moment's notice, and a moment's notice was all they got. The enemy were a nation apprenticed in arms, we were not even the idle apprentice: we had not deemed apprenticeship worth our while. There was courage enough running loose in the land, but it was like unharnessed electricity, it controlled no forces, it struck no blows. There was no time for the heroism and the devotion which a drawn-out struggle, however hopeless, can produce; the war was over almost as soon as it had begun. . . . One might liken the whole·affair to a snap checkmate early in a game of chess; one side had thought out the moves, and brought the requisite pieces into play, the other side was hampered and helpless, with its resources unavailable, its strategy discounted in advance. That, in·a nutshell, is the history of the war.*

—SAKI, *When William Came* (1913)

Introduction

THE SECOND WORLD WAR, for most of its survivors, has remained the most intense experience of their lives and the source of their most vivid recollections. Still, the very magnitude of the war's geographical and temporal sweep blurs the image of memory. In June of 1942 Manstein was storming Sevastopol, Rommel driving the British out of Libya, and Nimitz routing the Japanese fleet at Midway. A few months later the Germans were simultaneously surrounded in North Africa and at Stalingrad, while the Japanese and the Americans were locked in combat, on land and sea and in the air, in and near the Solomon Islands. The war was truly global, and far too extended for a single field of vision.

There had been a time when things were simpler. After the fall of France only three nations were at war, and of these Italy was not yet seriously committed in combat. The summer of 1940 was one of war between Germany and Britain, and at the time there were many who would not have staked a thruppence on Britain's prospects for national survival, to say nothing of ultimate victory.

During those few weeks of summer sun and clouds, the heat and glare of the war were drawn in focus, as through a lens, on the southeastern corner of England and the opposite mainland shores. There is a consequent unity, and an even painful brightness, about that short period which sets it apart from the war's other and more complicated chapters, as a story which can be told almost by itself.

Throughout the Western Hemisphere, millions of those who watched saw Britain's hope as their own, and the English Channel became the hinge of fate for Western democracy. Alone and against desperate odds

13

Britain fought through under a leader who spoke winged words, and it is both just and poetic that the summer of 1940 is remembered as her finest hour.

It is hardly surprising, therefore, that the summer's tale is usually told in English rather than in German, and is generally known as the Battle of Britain. But, for all the glamour of those encounters in the English skies and for all the heroism of the Few, the German side of the story is the more interesting strategically and significant historically.

For it was the Germans, after all, who selected the theater and set the stage. Their troops and planes had smashed the Allied armies, swept the British Expeditionary Force off the mainland, brought France to her knees at Compiègne, and isolated Britain. It was the Wehrmacht that lined the entire Atlantic coast of Europe north of the Pyrenees and dominated the Continent, and it was Adolf Hitler who held the initiative and could choose when, where, and how to make the next move.

In the early summer of 1940 the British, sorely pressed as they were, had no real strategic worries, because they had no range of choice. To be sure, they confronted desperate and back-breaking problems of organization, mobilization, and training. But not until August, when a modest-sized armored force had been reassembled, did they make a major strategic decision, by sending part of their armor to Egypt, despite the rising threat of invasion of the homeland. Otherwise Britain's task, however difficult of accomplishment, was plain: to defend the island, repulse the looming onslaught, and gather strength for the morrow—in short, to *stay alive* and trust in her only ally, time.

For the Germans, seemingly poised on the brink of triumph, the strategic problems were both crucial and complex. Choked with territorial conquest and militarily impregnable, it was even questionable whether the Reich should continue to seek a solution *vi et armis.* "When at war, prepare for peace!" Conversion of Vegetius' old rubric suggested the possibility of a "peace offensive" that might complete Britain's isolation and gain a triumph without further bloodshed. On the other hand, if victory was to be pursued by the sword, then it was a matter of determining how Germany's superior resources might most effectively be brought to bear in order to break Britain's will to resist.

Could Britain be overwhelmed by immediate assault, before time could be of help to her? In 1913 H. H. Munro (Saki), soon to be killed in France by a German bullet, spun a tale of England defeated and occupied by imperial Germany, an extract from which I have quoted as a sort of nightmare epigraph. *When William Came* is more satire than prophecy, but it is altogether fascinating that the author imagined the German victory as "a snap checkmate early in a game of chess" in which the losing side had no time to bring its resources to bear, for that was precisely the danger that Britain faced in the summer of 1940.

This book is the story of Adolf Hitler and the Wehrmacht during that summer. Herein I have described the strategic alternatives that were open to the Germans during and just after the military conquest of France, the circumstances and considerations leading to the decision to attempt Britain's defeat by direct attack, and the preparations and operations carried out in pursuance of that aim—the Battle of Britain (Eagle), which was executed but never planned, and the invasion of England (Sea Lion), which was planned and prepared, but never executed.

In the skies over Essex, Sussex, and Kent the Luftwaffe was repulsed, and the consequence was the abandonment of Sea Lion and the strategy of direct assault. Thus the wave of German conquest, which had swept over Poland and western Europe, broke on the English shores, and spent its initial force. The historical importance of that failure can hardly be overstated, for it ended Hitler's chances of victory by a "snap checkmate" and required the formulation of a new and wholly different German strategy based on the prospect of an extended war for which the German economy was unprepared and the Wehrmacht ill-designed.

Never again was the Third Reich as close to victory as it was in the summer of 1940. That is why the German effort and its failure were, in a strategic sense, the war's turning point, and must be accounted a crucial episode in the modern history of mankind.

PART I

The Great
Crisis of Strategy

CHAPTER ONE

Ends and Means

ON MAY 20, 1940, the vanguard of Generalleutnant Rudolf Veiel's 2nd Panzer Division reached the French coast at the mouth of the Somme near Abbeville, cutting the Allied armies in two. During the next few days, as the German infantry poured across northern France into the salient, it became apparent that France's military situation was hopeless, and that her immediate fate lay in Adolf Hitler's hands.

Far from simplifying the Fuehrer's problems, however, these stunning victories at once precipitated new strategic riddles of staggering dimension and variety. Across the Channel, Britain lay desperately stricken by the imminent loss of the early flower of her Army in Flanders, but was still battle-worthy in the air and dominant on the sea. For all the Wehrmacht's triumphs, there would be no final victory, and no peace for the Third Reich, unless Britain were brought to terms.

How? The depleted and demoralized French armies south of the Somme and Aisne offered no immediate threat. Nor was there any prospect that they could soon be strengthened; Britain was powerless to reinforce them, and Mussolini was eager to come in on the kill by taking the French in the rear. Should Hitler turn away from a mortally wounded foe that could be finished off at leisure, improvise means of crossing the Channel, and bring the Wehrmacht's power directly to bear on Britain by invasion?

In retrospect, such a course of action was well worth considering, and apparently it was suggested at the time.[1] But however that may be, this strategy found no support in the German High Command. The Army's plan called for a southerly sweep to the Loire and the Swiss

border, that would encircle the Maginot Line and force the French to
capitulate. Hitler and the generals alike were bent on the destruction
of French military power. So complete, indeed, was this preoccupation
that they momentarily relaxed their throttle hold on the Allied forces
cut off in Flanders, and opened the door of opportunity for the Miracle
of Dunkirk. The British Expeditionary Force was stripped of its arms
and driven off the Continent, but nearly a quarter of a million Tommies
were brought safely to home shores.

The Wehrmacht promptly smashed through the French lines on the
Somme and Aisne and rolled on southward. The Pétain government
sued for an armistice, and Hitler danced his famous jig. On June 22 he
had his moment of triumph in the historic *wagon-lit* at Compiègne,
and two days later the fighting ceased. Hitler was the undisputed
master of western Europe, and German troops patrolled the Atlantic
coast from the North Cape to the Pyrenees.

But already a month had passed since the breakthrough on the
Meuse and the armored dash to the Channel—the successes that were
decisive in the Battle of France. When the French laid down their
arms, Britain's home defenses were already measurably stronger than
at the time of Dunkirk. The British ground forces, to be sure, were
desperately insufficient, but the troops evacuated from Dunkirk were
being re-formed, a spirited sort of *levée en masse* had been launched,
and beach and road barriers and other obstacles to invasion in great
variety were mushrooming in southern England. The Royal Air Force
had not suffered much in the second phase of the Battle of France, and
aircraft production was rising rapidly. The first shock of the French
collapse had worn off, and now at least the British did not need to
worry about dividing their forces or aiding an ally whose plight was
beyond redemption, and could concentrate their resources and energies in their own defense.

Hitler, on the contrary, now confronted an eventuality which he had
not foreseen and a problem for which he had made no provision—
essentially the same problem that Napoleon (whose tomb the Fuehrer
visited just before Compiègne) had failed to solve. The question could
be, and was,[2] stated in just two words: *Was nun?* (What now?). This
was the riddle that lay at the root of the great crisis of German strategy
during the summer of 1940.

The Means at Hand

Whatever was to be done had to be done with the means at hand. Powerful as the Wehrmacht was, its resources were not unlimited, and it could not do everything. Indeed, for strife *à l'outrance* with Britain the Wehrmacht was a badly balanced force, largely because it had been designed as an instrument for continental conquest.

This design was reflected in the dominant size and strength of the ground forces. In the summer of 1940 the striking power of the German Army was far greater than that of any other army in the world. The German generals had worked out—as their professional colleagues in other lands, with rare exceptions, had not—principles for the effective employment of mechanized troops *en masse*, supported by ground-attack aircraft. The techniques had been successfully applied and greatly improved in the Polish and Norwegian campaigns and the Battle of France. With such victories under their belts, the German troops were the confident and proven masters of the art of smashing ground defenses and overrunning large areas of enemy territory. No other country as yet had the means or skills to stop them.

The German Army's victories during the first year of the war were not only stunning but cheap. Casualties during the Battle of France did not much exceed 150,000, and in cold military reckoning were far outweighed by the benefits of battle-hardening. Tanks and vehicles had suffered wear and tear, but nothing that could not be put right in a few weeks. Morale was at a peak.

In fact, after the Compiègne armistice the main problem about a German Army of over 150 divisions was whether it was not unnecessarily large. At most forty divisions might be effectively used for an invasion of Britain, and a force of even this size was more than could possibly be put across the Channel. Within striking range, only the Russian Army was of comparable dimension, but the Hitler-Stalin pact, and the Fuehrer's repeated characterizations of the 1914 two-front involvement as a fatal blunder, made the prospect of another Russo-German conflict seem remote if not fanciful. No conceivable adventure in the Mediterranean or the Balkans could possibly absorb a major fraction of the available ground forces.

On the other hand, if the German economy was to be mobilized for protracted hostilities, and the Navy and the Luftwaffe were to be strengthened for long-range strategic employment, too many divisions would be as bad as, if not worse than, too few. The Fatherland was not rich enough in manpower to afford the luxury of surplus soldiery if sailors and airmen were to be multiplied manyfold. Mine and factory managers would be fairly screaming for skilled labor; the harvest season was approaching, and men were needed in the fields. Partial demobilization of the Army was one of the General Staff's principal projects during the summer of 1940, but no program could be adopted until the basic issues of military strategy had been resolved.

If the Army was over strength, the Navy was in reverse case. Grossadmiral Erich Raeder had a handful of assorted warships, but in strategic terms there was no German Navy.

Early in 1939, relying on Hitler's assurance that there would be no war with Britain before 1944, the Navy had embarked on an ambitious plan for the construction of a High Seas Fleet of huge battleships. The first two keels had barely been laid when the invasion of Poland brought about what Raeder had feared. "The surface forces," Raeder noted at the outbreak of war in a gloomy memorandum,[3] "are so inferior in number and strength to the British fleet that, even at full strength, they can do no more than show that they know how to die gallantly . . ."

By the summer of 1940 not many German sailors had been killed, but the Navy had already suffered crippling losses. Raeder had gambled his slender surface strength on the Norwegian venture. It was a brilliant tactical success, but ten destroyers and three cruisers were sunk, and the only two heavy battle cruisers, *Scharnhorst* and *Gneisenau*, were torpedoed and put out of action for many months. Of the three "pocket" battle cruisers, *Luetzow* was also convalescing from torpedo damage, *Admiral Graf Spee* had been lost off Montevideo, and *Admiral Scheer* was laid up for engine repairs. The new battleships *Bismarck* and *Tirpitz* and the heavy cruiser *Prinz Eugen* were not yet battle-ready.

In April 1940 the conquest of Norway had seemed worth the almost certain prospect of heavy naval losses. In June, with command of virtually the entire west coast of Europe, the Navy was far too weak to exploit the enormous advantage of full access to the Atlantic reaches. The hour of strategic decision had struck, but the effective strength of the German surface fleet comprised a single heavy cruiser (*Admiral Hipper*), two light cruisers, half a dozen destroyers, and a scattering of torpedo boats and naval auxiliaries.[4] If an invasion of Britain was to be attempted, the assault force would have to cross the Channel with little or no protection by way of surface escort. If Britain was to be starved into surrender, the blockade would have to be effected primarily by submarines and aircraft, without much help from surface raiders.

Furthermore, the deficiency in surface strength was all but irreparable. The advent of *Bismarck, Tirpitz,* and *Prinz Eugen* would help some, but in terms of war with Britain these ships, powerful as they were, made a pitifully small increment. Conceivably a strategy based on the assumption of five more years of war could have embraced the construction of a high-seas fleet, but only at great detriment to the expansion of the submarine arm and the Luftwaffe, and to other vital armament programs. In fact, and wisely, no such effort was made. Neither the single aircraft carrier *Graf Zeppelin* nor the two battleships whose keels had been laid just before the war were ever completed; indeed, not one German warship larger than a destroyer was launched throughout the war.

As a practical matter, therefore, the German Navy's offensive potential lay with the submarine. In the summer of 1940, however, even this arm—contrary to the popular assumption—was remarkably small. Before the war there had been sharp tactical and technical disagreements among the German naval leaders concerning the size and design of the U-boats. These remained unresolved, with the result that during 1937 and 1938, while the Army and the Luftwaffe were growing rapidly, only ten U-boats were added to the thirty-five previously on hand, and at the outbreak of war there were but fifty-seven.[5]

After the victory in France, Hitler promised Raeder that submarine-building would be given a higher priority, but for months Raeder fought a losing battle for industrial allocations against the indifference or open hostility of Hermann Goering, who was still in direct control of economic mobilization. Throughout 1940, the rate of U-boat production rose only from two to six per month. This was not even enough to cover losses, and in February 1941, as the U-boat chief, Admiral Karl Doenitz, has since written,[6] "the grand total of our operational boats fell to twenty-two."

Even so small a U-boat arm could and did inflict painful losses on the enemy, but it could accomplish nothing of strategic significance. It was not until 1942, when over a hundred and later two hundred U-boats were available, that the Battle of the Atlantic assumed major proportions. In the summer of 1940, accordingly, the U-boat was a weapon of great potential value in a long war, but could contribute little to any strategy directed toward a speedy victory by direct assault on or effective blockade of the British homeland.

Since the Navy was strategically almost nonexistent and the Army could not transport itself across the English Channel, the Luftwaffe was the crucial element of the immediate strategic problem. In the early summer of 1940 it was the strongest air force in the world, and its Commander-in-Chief, Hermann Goering, vowed to Hitler that with it he could crush the British and nail down the final victory. But Goering's optimism was not shared by many of the Luftwaffe generals, who were painfully aware that their arm, despite its power and sensational successes in Poland and western Europe, was unequal to the task which it was about to be given.

In part the deficiency was one of size. Large as the Luftwaffe was, it was not so strong in numbers as it was then thought to be, and its margin of superiority over the Royal Air Force was dwindling rapidly. In April 1940, for the first time, British fighter-aircraft production surpassed the German monthly increment, and during the last six months of 1940 British factories turned out half again as many combat aircraft as did those in Germany.[7]

Nor could the Luftwaffe pulverize England's ports and factories, in line with the teachings of Douhet, for lack of heavy, long-range bombers. In accordance with strategic decisions made several years before the war, the Luftwaffe had been designed primarily to support the Army in the field. Its strength lay in short-range fighters, dive bombers, and twin-engined level-flight bombers of medium weight and range. Four-engined bombers there were none, and there were no satisfactory designs ready for production. In consequence, the Luftwaffe could operate effectively only over the southern part of England, nearest its bases on the Continent.

But while these deficiencies were manifest, in essence if not in full detail, to the initiate in the higher ranks of the Luftwaffe, they were not sufficiently grasped by the German high command. Goering and his entourage consistently overestimated their own and underestimated the British strength. Hitler relied on Goering and did not much concern himself with the conduct of aerial warfare. The Army generals were kept at a distance and in a state of ignorance about the Luftwaffe's independent operations. The inevitable result was that German strategy was based on inflated estimates of the Luftwaffe's potentialities.

A strategy directed toward a speedy victory had to be based on the

Wehrmacht's immediate resources. A long-range strategy would intro-
duce additional and complex factors, economic and diplomatic as well
as military.

For example, if Britain were to be brought to terms not by direct
assault, but by cutting the lifelines of empire in the Mediterranean
and strangling the homeland by blockade, then the Navy and the Luftwaffe would both require great expansion and modification, with the
consequent necessity of precise allocation of raw materials and industrial facilities and drastic restriction of the civilian economy, in order
to mobilize the nation's resources for a long war. Hitler had been
urged to order such a mobilization at the outbreak of the war, but he
had declined to do so, out of reluctance to acknowledge that victory
might not be bought cheaply and swiftly. This lax and overoptimistic
economic strategy was already reflected in the dearth of submarines
and in the deficiencies of the Luftwaffe, and much precious time had
been lost, for British war production was rising, and across the Atlantic
lay the vast and potentially hostile resources of the United States. A
long war meant an economic war for which Germany was poorly
prepared.

The German victory in the west not only knocked France out of the
war but also, by the temptation of cheap conquest, pulled Italy into it.
After Mussolini's declaration of war on June 10, the leaders of the
Wehrmacht found themselves locked in partnership with the Commando Supremo in Rome. It was a situation not altogether to the Germans' liking, even though Italy's military forces thus became directly
engaged in hostilities against Britain.

The Italian forces themselves were not inconsiderable. After mobilization, the Italian Army comprised over seventy divisions.[8] Some of
the infantry and mountain troops were of good quality, but there was
a serious deficiency of armor. The Air Force, numbering some 1,500
combat-ready aircraft, was about half the size of the RAF and one-
third that of the Luftwaffe.[9] The most impressive Italian arm was the
Navy, led by the two new 35,000-ton battleships *Littorio* and *Vittorio
Veneto*. Other surface craft included four old but recently modernized
battleships of 23,600 tons, seven heavy and eleven light cruisers, and
over sixty each of destroyers and torpedo boats. The Italian submarine
fleet was the largest of all the belligerents', with over one hundred
boats, of which eighty-odd were ready for service.[10]

Formidable as these forces were on paper, they were of limited value
for blockading or assailing the British homeland. The Army was of no

use whatever, for Germany already had more divisions that she could possibly use. The Air Force had not been trained or equipped for North Atlantic flying conditions; its assistance was bound, as it proved, to be modest. The Navy's surface craft were locked in the Mediterranean, unless Gibraltar or Suez were captured. Italian submarines could and did run the Straits of Gibraltar and operate from bases on the Atlantic coast of France, but could not be expected to have an immediately decisive impact on the balance of sea power.

Nevertheless, Italy's entry into the war was of great strategic significance, for it turned the Mediterranean into a theater of war. This imposed new burdens on Britain, but it also opened up opportunities for the exploitation of her dominant naval and growing aerial strength. Unless the Italians could at least hold the British at arms' length, Germany might be faced with the danger of attack from the south, and this hazard might suck part of the Wehrmacht into Italy or North Africa.

Furthermore, the Commando Supremo took its orders from Mussolini, not Hitler. Alliance was not subordination, and the Duce was a vain and jealous man. In the event these qualities played havoc with the leadership of the Axis forces. Within a few months after the fall of France, Italy was at war with Greece, and Hitler confronted additional strategic problems which he had not anticipated and did not welcome.

The Diplomatic Setting

In the summer of 1940 the war was not yet a world war. It was not even a general European war, for Russia and the Baltic and Balkan countries, as well as Spain, Portugal, Greece, and Turkey, were neutral or "nonbelligerent."[*] In planning Axis strategy for the defeat of Britain, therefore, diplomatic factors were still of great moment. Furthermore, in eastern Europe and the Mediterranean the diplomatic pot was boiling furiously, and events were shaping which Hitler was powerless to control.

On June 23, 1940, the day after the signing of the Franco-German armistice at Compiègne, Vyacheslav Molotov (then the Soviet Foreign Minister) summoned the German Ambassador, Friedrich Werner Graf

---

[*] Egypt likewise was officially neutral until February, 1945, although Britain undertook the defense of the country pursuant to the Anglo-Egyptian treaty of 1936.

von der Schulenburg, and declared that settlement of the Soviet Union's claim to Bessarabia "brooked no further delay" and that if the Rumanians would not yield peacefully Russia would resort to force.[11] Furthermore, said Molotov, the Soviet claim "extended likewise to Bucovina, which had a Ukrainian population."

On June 28, after strong German pressure, King Carol announced that Rumania would cede Bessarabia and northern Bucovina to the Soviet Union. The world press was still dazed and overwhelmed by the French collapse and the magnitude of the German victories in western Europe, compared to which the fate of Bessarabia seemed a small matter. Yet surely it was remarkable that the Russians ventured to move westward so imperiously, at the very moment of the great German triumph.

To be sure, Soviet "interest in Bessarabia" and Germany's "complete political disinterestedness" in that area had been recognized in the secret protocol annexed to the treaty of nonaggression of August 23, 1939, commonly known as the Hitler-Stalin pact. Under that protocol, as amended on September 28, 1939, the Baltic countries Estonia, Latvia, and Lithuania had also been recognized as within the Soviet "sphere of influence."[12] In the middle of June 1940, while the German armored divisions were cutting through northern France, the Russians exploited these protocols by sending occupation troops into the three Baltic nations and insisting on governmental reorganizations to eliminate anti-Soviet officials.

This was all part of the price Hitler had paid for his pact with Stalin, and the Fuehrer had no grounds for complaint. But Bucovina was not part of the deal, and Schulenburg (on Ribbentrop's instructions) represented to Molotov that it "was formerly an Austrian crown province and is densely populated with Germans." The result of these remonstrances was that the Soviet government limited its claim to the northern part of Bucovina, including Czernowitz, the provincial capital. The concession was a small one, and Molotov was adamant in his insistence that Germany support the Soviet action.[13]

The sudden burst of aggressive diplomacy in the Kremlin irritated and puzzled the Germans,[14] but Hitler thought it best to avoid a breach, and King Carol was told in no uncertain terms that Rumania's future favor in Germany depended on his yielding to the Soviet demands. There was, indeed, nothing else that he could do, and on June 28 Soviet troops moved into the ceded provinces.

A few weeks later the Russians took steps to annex Estonia, Latvia, and Lithuania to the Soviet Union. Their establishment as Soviet republics was formally announced by Molotov to Schulenburg on August 11, together with a request that the German legations and consulates all be "liquidated" by the end of that month.[15]

By that time difficulties had arisen between Berlin and Moscow with respect to the boundary of the "Lithuanian Soviet Republic,"[16] the continued exercise of Lithuania's free port rights in Memel,[17] and division of the nickel output from the Petsamo mines in northern Finland.[18] Whatever might be the motives and fears at work in the Kremlin, the German conquests in the west had not induced a deferential or even a cautious attitude among the Soviet leaders. In planning his over-all strategy, accordingly, Hitler had to reckon with the continued exertion of Russian power, and areas of conflict were already developing.

In the Balkans, the Soviet annexation of Bessarabia precipitated reassertion of the Hungarian and Bulgarian claims to territories that Rumania had gained after the First World War. The Bulgarian demand for return of the Dobrudja was not explosive, for Bulgaria was too weak to resort to war, and Rumania was not unwilling to cede at least part of the disputed area. But Rumania and Hungary were not unevenly matched, and it appeared impossible for them to agree upon a division of the Transylvanian lands that Rumania held and Hungary claimed. A war between them would threaten Germany's access to Rumanian oil and have other consequences, unpredictable but surely damaging to the German economy and Hitler's dominant influence in the Balkans. In coping with this hazard, Hitler had to bear in mind not only Russia's historic interest in southeastern Europe, but Mussolini's ambitions as well.

The Duce's yearning to turn the Mediterranean into an "Italian lake," in fact, was the source of numerous difficulties for Germany. To be sure, German strategy would be supported by any action the Italians might take against Egypt, Malta, or other Mediterranean territories under British dominion or protection, and Hitler repeatedly pressed his fellow dictator to strike the common foe. But Mussolini was looking for easier game. In southeastern Europe both Yugoslavia and Greece were inviting prospects for Italian aggrandizement. To the west France lay beaten, and Mussolini itched for a peace treaty under which Nice, Corsica, and Tunisia might be annexed to Italy.

None of this was in harmony with Germany's immediate interests. Italian adventures against Yugoslavia or Greece would draw off Italian forces that might be used against the British, or even open the door of opportunity for British landings in southeastern Europe. Rumanian oil was still a vital source of supply for the Wehrmacht; Hitler wanted peace in the Balkans to ensure the continued flow of oil, and did not relish the prospect of British bombers based in Greece, close enough to attack the Ploesti oil fields.

Toward the French Hitler had no tender feelings, but he was prudent enough to avoid action which might drive them back into the arms of the British. He himself cherished annexationist designs in Alsace, Lorraine, and Burgundy, and if France were to be carved up Spain would soon be asking for French Morocco. There was simply no way of drawing a peace treaty tolerable to the French and satisfactory to Italy, Spain, and Germany. Accordingly, until the British were brought to terms, it was best not to disturb the precarious balance achieved by the Compiègne armistice. But could the Fuehrer persuade the Duce and the Caudillo of the wisdom of such restraint?

The Russian riddle and Italian imperialism posed these many issues and hazards, but Hitler's worries did not end at the edges of Europe. The expectation of American aid was helping to sustain Britain's determination to continue the struggle. Prolongation of the war might bring in the United States as a belligerent, as in 1917. But the remaining major neutral power, Japan, had since 1937 been linked with Germany and Italy through the Anti-Comintern Pact,[19] and Japanese aggrandizement in southeast Asia was bringing her increasingly into disharmony with the United States and Britain. Could Japan be of help to Germany, by keeping America out of the European conflict? In Hitler's mind Japan and the United States were thus interlocked, and their prime importance lay in the impact of their policies on Britain primarily, and Russia secondarily. Ruminating aloud to the Army chiefs at the Berghof on July 31, 1940, Hitler declared:[20]

"Britain's hope lies in Russia and the United States. If Russia drops out of the picture America too is lost for Britain, because elimination of Russia would tremendously increase Japan's power in the Far East.

"Russia is the Far Eastern sword of Britain and the United States, pointed at Japan. Here an evil wind is blowing for Britain. Japan, like Russia, has her program which she wishes to carry through before the end of the war."

Hitler was not particularly well-tuned to American attitudes about the war. He knew, of course, that President Roosevelt and other political leaders were anti-Nazi and hoped for an Allied victory. But he was inclined to blame "international Jewry" for American hostility, and clung to the view that the United States would pick up the pieces of a disintegrating British Empire rather than intervene openly to shore up an apparently hopeless cause. The Germans found some confirmation for this diagnosis in the bitter "isolationist" debate raging in the United States, and the pessimism about Britain's prospects prevalent in some official quarters.

Reports from the German Embassy in Washington did little to counter these inferences. Many of these came from the military attaché, General Friedrich von Boetticher, whose contacts and judgments were much admired by the chargé d'affaires, Dr. Hans Thomsen.[21] On May 11, 1940, Boetticher reported that the invasion of France and the Low Countries had aroused anti-German feeling, and went on to recount a conversation with Senator Key Pittman (then chairman of the Senate Foreign Relations Committee), in the course of which the Senator observed that the defeat of England was expected "as a consequence of the Fuehrer's genius and the unique organization of the German Wehrmacht."[22] Two weeks later, Boetticher described the United States as "impressed" with the German victories in France, and especially remarked Charles Lindbergh's public expressions and the discomfiture of "Jews and Freemasons."[23]

Impressed the Americans were, and with reason, but tangible support for Britain was forthcoming far more rapidly than Hitler anticipated. After the fall of France, as Britain girded her woefully slender resources to repel invasion, the arsenals of America poured forth quantities of rifles, machine guns, field guns, and ammunition for shipment to the British forces in their homeland. "Tonight the latest convoy of rifles, cannon, and ammunition are coming in," Churchill cabled Roosevelt on July 31. "Special trains are waiting to take them to the troops and Home Guard, who will take a lot of killing before they give them up."[24]

If Berlin was aware of these shipments, they made little impression there.[25] Hermann Goering, to be sure, had taken care to soothe American fears by telling a Hearst newspaper correspondent that the United States could not be invaded, and that the Luftwaffe had no planes of sufficient range for effective transatlantic operations.[26] "Even if you don't like us, give us some credit for common sense and reason," he pleaded. But Hitler remained unconvinced that Britain had much to hope for from America. Discussing the matter with Brauchitsch and Raeder on July 21, the Fuehrer observed that Roosevelt's position was "uncertain," and that "industry does not want to invest" (presumably in

a war), because "America lost $10,000,000,000 in the World War, and got back only $1,400,000,000"; anyhow, the United States was "hoping to become the dominant naval power."[27]

Such was the stuff of Hitler's dreams, while Roosevelt and his aides were mulling over how they might satisfy Churchill's urgent request (first made on May 15) for the Royal Navy's use of some fifty over-age destroyers, to meet the U-boat menace. Legal and policy objections were eventually overcome by transferring the destroyers in return for ninety-nine-year leases to the United States of air and naval bases in Newfoundland, Bermuda, and the British West Indies. The famous destroyers-for-bases "deal"[28] was not publicly announced until September 3, but its general outlines were known in Berlin no later than August 23, for on that day Hasso von Etzdorf (the Foreign Ministry's liaison officer with OKH) told Halder that the United States "will take over a number of British naval bases in Atlantic and Pacific in return for 50-90 old destroyers"—an intelligence item which Halder recorded with the dour reflection that "America's intention to bail out [*aufnehmen*] the British is becoming increasingly obvious."[29]

Others in high places were not so sure about American purposes. A few days after the "deal" was announced, Raeder told Hitler[30] that, while "the delivery of fifty destroyers represents an openly hostile act against Germany," nevertheless it was "not yet clear whether the United States, even in her present policy, is acting selfishly or in Anglo-Saxon interests." Raeder thought that the transaction presaged "a situation which will necessarily lead to closer co-operation between Britain and the U.S.A." Nevertheless: "In the interest of her own position, the United States will hardly support the British motherland with significant amounts of materiel and personnel. Aircraft may be provided after American needs have been satisfied."

In this there was no note of alarm. However, Hitler began to cast about for some means of countering the American trend toward deeper involvement in Britain's military fortunes. The immediate consequence was a closer relation with Japan, reflected in the Tripartite Pact.

The idea of transforming the Anti-Comintern Pact into an outright military alliance was not new. It was much favored by the "military" group in the Japanese government, and in July 1938 such a step was proposed to Ribbentrop by General Hiroshi Oshima, then the military attaché in Berlin. Ribbentrop was sympathetic, and he and Oshima worked out a draft during the summer of 1938. The general idea of a military alliance with the Axis powers was approved by the Japanese

Cabinet in August, and shortly thereafter Oshima was appointed ambassador to Germany and Toshio Shiratori, another spokesman of the "military" view, became ambassador to Italy.[31]

Shortly after the Munich settlement, Ribbentrop broached the project to Mussolini and Galeazzo Ciano.[32] The Duce replied that "this alliance ought to be drawn up," but opined that the Italian people were not yet ready for such a step, and declined to commit himself with respect to "the moment at which the Pact ought to be made."

On New Year's Day of 1939 Mussolini told Ciano that he was now prepared to enter into a military alliance with Germany and Japan, and Ciano promptly informed Ribbentrop. Four days later, however, the Konoye Cabinet resigned, and it soon appeared that there was sharp division of opinion within the new Hiranuma Cabinet with respect to the nature of the proposed pact. Foreign Minister Arita and the "moderates" shrank from a commitment to aid Germany against the Western powers, and wished the alliance to be directed primarily against Russia; War Minister Hagaki and the "militarists" favored a pact without reservation, which of course was what Hitler and Mussolini also desired.

The Japanese were unable to resolve their differences. Fuehrer and Duce waxed impatient, and on May 22 the so-called "Pact of Steel" between Germany and Italy was signed in Berlin. Three months later the Hitler-Stalin pact temporarily undermined the position of the Japanese "military" faction and caused some coolness between Berlin and Tokyo. The Hiranuma Cabinet fell, and the ensuing governments of Abe and Yonai pursued a policy of nonintervention in the European conflict.

Oshima (who returned to Tokyo) and Shiratori, however, were intransigent, and the course of events favored their objectives. Japan's continued exploitation of the "China incident" prevented reconciliation with Britain or the United States. The Wehrmacht's victories in the spring of 1940 greatly enhanced German prestige, and the defeat of France and Holland opened up inviting new prospects for Japanese aggrandizement in southeast Asia. The "military" group regained the initiative, and on July 16, 1940, Yonai resigned, and Prince Konoye formed his second Cabinet, with General Hideki Tojo as war minister and Yosuke Matsuoka as foreign minister.

Matsuoka lost no time in reopening the question of a formal alliance with Germany. On August 1, 1940, he summoned the German Ambassador, General Eugen Ott,[33] and delivered himself of a discourse on

Luftwaffe Redivivus!
Dedicatory ceremonies at Bernau upon the opening of the *Jugendhorst* ("youth eyrie") *Richthofen,* named for Manfred von Richthofen, the leading German fighter ace of the First World War, killed in combat in April 1918. The year is 1935; the Luftwaffe of the Third Reich has just been unveiled. The speaker is Kurt-Bertram von Doering, who had been a pilot in Richthofen's squadron, and in 1935 was a newly-commissioned *Major,* in command of the *Richthofenstaffel* (a fighter aircraft unit named for Richthofen) of the new Luftwaffe. *Ullstein*

1. Air Chief Marshall Sir Hugh C. T. ("Stuffy") Dowding, chief of Fighter Command. *Imperial War Museum*

2. Air Vice Marshall Trafford Leigh-Mallory, in command of No. 12 Group of Fighter Command, covering the Midlands. *Imperial War Museum*

3. Air Vice Marshall Keith Rodney Park, in command of No. 11 Group of Fighter Command, covering London and the "hot" southeastern corner of England. *Imperial War Museum*

4. Squadron Leader (No. 74, Spitfires) Adolph G. ("Sailor") Malan. *Imperial War Museum*

5. Reichsmarschall Hermann Goering, Commander-in-Chief of the German Air Force (Luftwaffe), with the famous fighter aircraft designer and maker, Professor Willy Messerschmitt. *Acme-United Press International*

6. Bad news! Major Werner Moelders—leading ace of the Battle of Britain and commander of JG 51—reports to solemn Goering and (on Moelders' right) General Bruno Loerzer, commander of Fliegerkorps II. *Bundesarchiv*

7. Squadron Leader (No. 257 Squadron, Hurricanes) Roland R. S. Tuck. *Imperial War Museum*

8. Squadron Leader (No. 242 Squadron) Douglas R. S. Bader, standing (on his artificial legs) on the wing of a Hurricane. *Imperial War Museum*

6 ▲

7 ▼

8 ▼

1

2

3

4

5

6

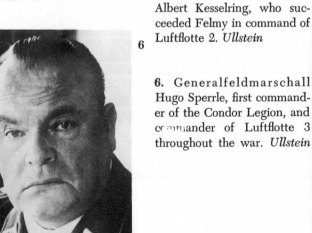

1. Oberst (later General-oberst) Hans Jeschonnek, pictured in 1939, just after his appointment as Chief of the General Staff of the Luftwaffe. *Library of Congress*

2. Otto Hoffmann von Waldau, Chief of the Operations Section of the Luftwaffe General Staff during the Battle of Britain. *Bundesarchiv*

3. Josef ("Beppo") Schmid, Chief of the Intelligence Section of the Luftwaffe General Staff. *Maxwell Air Base*

4. General Helmuth Felmy, commander of Luftflotte 2, whose pessimistic assessments of aerial warfare against Britain incurred Goering's displeasure and led to his dismissal early in 1940. *Bundesarchiv*

5. Generalfeldmarschall Albert Kesselring, who succeeded Felmy in command of Luftflotte 2. *Ullstein*

6. Generalfeldmarschall Hugo Sperrle, first commander of the Condor Legion, and commander of Luftflotte 3 throughout the war. *Ullstein*

General Wolfgang Martini, Chief of Communications of the Luftwaffe, who vainly sought techniques to jam the British coastal radar chain. *Bundesarchiv*

Sir Robert Watson-Watt, first among the scientists who developed British radar detection techniques and equipment. *Imperial War Museum*

Britain's first line of defense against air attack: a typical radar station of the "Chain Home" coastal series. *Imperial War Museum*

1. Generaloberst Ulrich Grauert, commander of Fliegerkorps I, shot down and killed in May 1941. *Ullstein*

2. General Wolfram von Richthofen (younger cousin of Manfred, the "Red Knight" of the First World War), the Luftwaffe's dive-bomber specialist, commander of Fliegerkorps VIII. *Ullstein*

3. General Robert Ritter von Greim, an ardent Nazi and a retread from World War I, commander of Fliegerkorps V. *Bundesarchiv*

4. Oberst Johannes Fink, *Geschwaderkommodore* of KG 2, and commander of the special task force in the July battles over the English Channel. *Ullstein*

5. General Joachim Coeler, specialist in mine-laying and other marine operations, commander of Fliegerkorps IX.

6. Generaloberst Alfred Keller, commander of Fliegerkorps IV, another Nazi retread, who had earned the soubriquet "Bomben-Keller" in the First World War.

From left to right, Kurt-Bertram von Doering, leader of the fighter components of Luftflotte 2 (Jafue 2). *Bundesarchiv.* "Onkel Theo" Osterkamp, Geschwaderkommodore of JG 51 and subsequently von Doering's successor as Jafue 2. *Ullstein.* Werner Junck, their opposite number in Luftflotte 3 (Jafue 3). *Bundesarchiv.* All three were "old eagles" of the First World War who barnstormed, raced, tested, or served foreign military forces until the rebirth of the German Air Force under Goering.

At Goering's headquarters, Werner Moelders is flanked by (left to right) Goering's adjutant, Oberstleutnant von der Osten; Major Walter Storp, commander of a *Kampfgeschwader;* Hauptman Walther Oesau, a leading fighter ace in the Battle of Britain and a *Gruppenkommandur* in JG 2; and Oberstleutnant Oskar Dinort, commander of *Stukageschwader* (St. G) 2. *Ullstein*

With his ever-present black cigar, Major Adolf Galland, *Geschwaderkommodore* of JG 26, is shown with his predecessor, Generalmajor Eduard Ritter von Schleich, famous World War I ace (the "Black Knight") and the first commander of JG 26. *Bundesarchiv*

Hauptman Wilhelm Balthasar, successor to Wick as commander of JG 2, and a leading fighter ace. *Ullstein*

Walking with Generalfeldmarschall Sperrle (center) are (left of picture, on Sperrle's right) Oberleutnant Joachim Muencheberg of JG 26, and (on Sperrle's left) Oberstleutnant Joachim-Friedrich Huth, commander of ZG 26 "Horst Wessel" (Messerschmitt 110s). *Bundesarchiv*

Good news! Goering with officers and men of JG 2, including (second from right on Goering's left) the *Geschwaderkommodore*, Helmuth Wick, at 25 the youngest *Major* in the Wehrmacht, who shared top combat honors with Moelders and Galland. *Ullstein*

Messerschmitt 110s—they were a "bust"—over London. *Ullstein*

The London docks and oil tanks at Purfleet on the Thames east of London, as seen from German bombers on September 7, 1940. *Ullstein*

Rural England near Berwick, on August 19, graced by a crashed Messerschmitt 109. *Wide World Photos*

Hawker Hurricanes of No. 85 Squadron rising to the attack. *Imperial War Museum*

Supermarine Spitfires ready for takeoff. *Imperial War Museum*

Below, the ill-starred Boulton-Paul *Defiant,* which had a brief day of glory at Dunkirk, after which the Germans learned that it could be safely attacked from below, and drove it from the day skies. *Imperial War Museum*

1. Generalfeldmarschall Walther von Brauchitsch, Commander-in-Chief of the German Army.

2. Generaloberst Franz Halder, Chief of the General Staff of the German Army.

3. Generalmajor Hans von Greiffenberg, Chief of the Army General Staff's Operations Section, in which the plans for *Sea Lion* were prepared. *Bundesarchiv*

4. Admiral Otto Schniewind, Chief of the Naval War Staff. *Ullstein*

5. Konteradmiral Kurt Fricke, Chief of the Operations Section of the Naval War Staff. *Bundesarchiv*

6. Generaladmiral Alfred Saalwaechter, Naval Commander-in-Chief in the West. *Ullstein*

Top, Grossadmiral Erich Raeder, Commander-in-Chief of the German Navy (second from left), inspects the conversion of shipping for *Sea Lion* at Duisberg on the Rhine. *Ullstein*

Middle and bottom, at Duisberg, conversion of river barges (prahms) for *Sea Lion. Ullstein*

1.  Admiral Gunther Luetjens, Commander-in-Chief of the High Seas Fleet and the seaborne forces for *Sea Lion*. *Bundesarchiv*

2.  Konteradmiral Hermann von Fischel, commander of Invasion Fleet B. *Bundesarchiv*

3. Generaloberst Ernst Busch, Commander of the 16th Army. *Ullstein*

4. Looking for all the world like *Furor Teutonicus,* Generaloberst Adolf Strauss, commander of the 9th Army. *Ullstein*

5. Generaloberst Eugen Ritter von Schobert, commander of the VIIth Corps. *Ullstein*

6. General Erich v. Lewinsky *gen.* v. Manstein, commander of the XXXVIIIth Corps.

7. General Georg-Hans Reinhardt, commander of the XLIst Armored Corps and of the special staff for training in landing operations. *Ullstein.*

1. Training with prahms for *Sea Lion:* fixing the ramp on the beach. *Ullstein* **2.** Debarking an armored vehicle. *Bundesarchiv* **3.** Debarking personnel. *Bundesarchiv*

Prahms in Dunkirk harbor, a British aerial view.
Imperial War Museum

A prahm under tow from a tug—this is how the Germans
would have crossed the Channel. *Bundesarchiv*

Assault boat training for *Sea Lion* in a French river. *Ullstein*

the wisdom of closer German-Japanese collaboration. The same day, Ambassador Kurusu (who had succeeded Oshima in Berlin) made a similar presentation at the Wilhelmstrasse.

Early in July Kurusu had made preliminary approaches to Ribbentrop, who had responded courteously but conveyed the impression that a German victory in Europe was now assured, and that the project of an alliance was no longer of great importance. During August, however, the Germans became aware of the impending destroyers-for-bases transaction between Britain and the United States, and this intelligence appears to have stimulated Hitler's interest in finally concluding a tripartite alliance. On August 23 Ribbentrop dispatched Heinrich Stahmer* to Tokyo as a special envoy, to work out the details of the treaty.

Upon his arrival in Tokyo, Stahmer informed his hosts that Germany wished to end the European war quickly, that Japanese help was not presently needed, and that the cardinal purpose of the alliance, from the German standpoint, was that Japan should prevent the United States from entering the war. He met with Matsuoka (by German request the Italians were not informed of the negotiations) on September 9, and by September 11 they had agreed upon the text.

On September 19 Ribbentrop arrived in Rome with the draft in his valise and secured Mussolini's agreement without difficulty. The Tripartite Pact was signed in Berlin on September 27, 1940, by Ribbentrop, Ciano, and Kurusu.[34] The signatory governments recognized "the leadership of Germany and Italy in the establishment of a new order in Europe" and of Japan in establishing "a new order in Greater East Asia." The substantive provision was Article 3, in which the parties mutually agreed "to assist one another with all political, economic, and military means, if one . . . is attacked by a Power at present not involved in the European war or in the Chinese-Japanese conflict." However, it was stipulated in Article 5 that the pact did not "in any way affect the political status which exists at present between each of the three Contracting Parties and Soviet Russia."

Thus the Tripartite Pact eventually emerged in a very different form from that which the Japanese had envisaged when they proposed it two years earlier. Then the Japanese had conceived it as aimed pri-

---

* Stahmer was a Foreign Ministry official who had previously undertaken special diplomatic missions in Japan. Aug. 23 was the very day that Halder noted the intelligence concerning the incipient destroyers-for-bases arrangement, and in the same diary entry he recorded: "A special ambassador is on his way to secure Japan's accession to the Tripartite Pact against the event of America's entry into the war. Success doubtful." This expression of pessimism proved unfounded.

marily at the Soviet Union; in the upshot, Russia was expressly excluded from its immediate purview, and the United States (though not mentioned in the text) was recognized as the principal target.

The pact purported to be an instrument for preventing the war from spreading, and apparently Hitler and Ribbentrop believed that it might prevent America from giving the British significant assistance. Yet it was weird diplomacy to seek to avoid conflict with the United States by entering into a military alliance with the one major power whose aims were irreconcilable with American policies. The express exemption of the Soviet Union was likewise illusory (though of this the Japanese and the Italians were unaware), for Hitler was already of more than half a mind to attack Russia the following spring.

In terms of the military problems that confronted Hitler during the summer of 1940, the Tripartite Pact was of little consequence. As Ciano confided to his diary on the day of signature, Japan was distant, and effective mutual assistance very problematical. The possible impact of the agreement in the event of a prolonged war seems not to have been closely analyzed by any of the participants. None of them could have forecast the events of the next fifteen months, during which each of the signatory powers embarked on adventures surprising and more or less unwelcome to the others.

The Strategic Alternatives

This, then, was the situation in which Hitler found himself in the summer of 1940, as the Third Republic crumbled ingloriously into the past. The master of western and central Europe, he confronted a weakened but intransigent insular foe in the west, and a suspicious, demanding continental colossus in the east. His one European ally was of uncertain strength, and the only friendly maritime power was on the other side of the globe. His military resources comprised a peerless army which, for the moment, had no place to go; a powerful and eager air force which was, however, of unproven value for independent strategic employment; and virtually no navy.

Germany's objective was to conclude a victor's peace with Britain. Where, if anywhere, lay the strategic avenues to this end?

One way was to induce the British to stop fighting and negotiate a peace. Obviously, there was much to recommend in a strategy directed toward a prompt conclusion of hostilities. Germany's conquests far exceeded anything Hitler had had in mind only nine months earlier, when the Wehrmacht invaded Poland. Even if national sovereignty were to be restored to most of the lands now occupied by German troops, a treaty could readily be shaped which would establish Germany for years to come as the dominant power of Europe. Hitler could then have emerged as the Great Captain who had wiped out "the shame of Versailles" at small cost to the Fatherland, and the magnanimous statesman who had brought Europe the "peace for our time" of which Neville Chamberlain had rashly spoken after Munich.

However, such a peace could not be counted on merely for the asking. Conceivably the defeat at Dunkirk and the total collapse of their French ally had so demoralized the British that they would snatch at any prospect of peace. But there were no signs of any such hopeless desperation, and Hitler himself had often remarked admiringly on British pride and tenacity. If peace was to be pursued as a *strategy,* then that strategy, like any other, would have to be planned and executed, and the planning would raise problems of temper, terms, and timing.

From the British standpoint, a peaceful settlement immediately after Dunkirk and Compiègne would have involved deep humiliation and a shattering sacrifice of prestige and power. To persuade them to swallow so bitter a dose might well be an altogether hopeless undertaking. If it was to be attempted at all, the offer must be so couched and presented as to offend least and placate most.

Furthermore, London was rapidly becoming a sort of Continental capital-in-exile, with Polish, Norwegian, Belgian, and Dutch émigré governments, and Charles de Gaulle raising the Cross of Lorraine. Thus Britain was not only the seat of her own Empire, but also trustee for the sovereignties of these German-occupied countries. There was little likelihood of arranging a treaty with Britain unless it embraced the terms of peace that would determine the proximate fate of the nations overrun by the Wehrmacht.

Finally, there was the all-important question of timing. In June Britain was at her weakest and Germany at her most victorious. An immediate peace offer could hardly be construed as an admission of uncertainty on Hitler's part. A delay of even a few weeks would give the British opportunity to sort out the Dunkirk evacuees into something resembling an Army, augment and reorganize the Royal Air Force for defensive purposes, and recover from the psychological shock of the disaster on the Continent.

All this argued that if the olive branch was to be extended at all, it ought to be done at once. Nevertheless, Hitler would have to reckon with the possibility—even the probability—that the British would spurn it. In that event, would there have been no alternative to further hostilities? Would there have been any strategic merit in a sustained "peace offensive"?

If so, Hitler would have had to adopt an essentially, if not totally, passive military posture, for he could not convincingly invite a mutual cessation of hostilities and simultaneously turn the Luftwaffe loose over England, or launch an invasion of Britain or attacks on outposts of the Empire such as Gibraltar. Blockade operations with aircraft, submarines, and surface raiders might perhaps have been continued; on this issue possible psychological damage to the peace offer would have had to be weighed against the military and economic benefits that Britain would have reaped from secure sea communications.

If Hitler had followed such a course,[35] it would have enabled the release of several hundred thousand—perhaps over a million—men from the Army to agriculture and industry. National productivity could have been stepped up, and the deficiencies of the Luftwaffe and the Navy at least partly overcome. The Reich would then have been better prepared for a long war, in the event the peace offensive had plainly failed, and full-scale hostilities were then resumed.

On the other hand, the British might have profited equally or even more from a prolonged respite. Especially if the United States should continue as a supporting arsenal, there was little chance that the Luftwaffe could long maintain its superiority over the RAF, and no hope of matching British sea power.

To be sure, a prolonged renewal of the "phony" war (as it was called in the fall and winter of 1939-40) might have caused the British to weary of war with a foe who refused to strike and could not be effectively struck, and thus have sapped Britain's morale and determination to continue the struggle against odds. Italy's entry into the war, however, opened new areas of belligerency. If Germany lay beyond the reach of any British weapons except the RAF's bombers, this was certainly not true of the Italians, with their long, exposed coastline, their African colonies adjacent to Egypt, the Sudan, and Kenya, and their fleet bottled in the Mediterranean. Here were abundant opportunities for the British to relieve their boredom by offensive operations that might eventually suck in German forces, if things went badly for the Italians.

Ultimately, Britain's hopes lay in her ability to fend off the Germans singlehanded, until such time as she might acquire, through alliances, the means of victory. A peace offensive was unlikely to succeed as long as these hopes remained alive. Therefore, a passive German military strategy would have been an unpromising strategy, unless coupled with a diplomacy calculated to isolate the British and destroy their prospects of finding powerful allies.

Such a purpose might perhaps have been accomplished, but only by means of a basic change in the political and economic policies of the Third Reich. Essentially, Hitler would have had to establish peace on the Continent, on terms at least tolerable to the defeated nations. He would have had to restrict Mussolini's and his own annexationist designs, restore national sovereignty in Poland, Czechoslovakia, Norway, and the Low Countries, adopt mild and enlightened occupation policies, and temper if not abandon the Nazi racial policies. As author of a Pax Europa rather than as commandant of a Festung Europa, the Fuehrer might have rendered himself, his regime, and his victories acceptable to European and American opinion, and made British resistance meaningless in appearance if not in actuality.

In theory, such a course was open to the Reich in the summer of 1940, but neither by inclination nor ability were Hitler and his cohorts the men to pursue it. It is probably fair to say that an effective strategy for peace could have been conceived and executed only after revolutionary changes in the German government. But the moment of supreme national triumph is not the right time for revolutionaries, and the practical possibility of a true peace offensive was therefore virtually academic.

If, then, the issue was to be resolved by force of arms, the leaders of the Wehrmacht confronted the task of shaping a strategy within the capabilities of their military establishment and the economic resources of the Reich. Although not mutually exclusive, there were two basic operational patterns to be weighed and considered, either in the alternative or in conjunction. One was to seek the speedy conquest of Britain by a direct assault on the island itself. The other was to prepare for a war of longer duration, and expand the conflict by opening new areas of engagement.

Had the Wehrmacht's air and sea weapons been sufficient for the purpose, Britain might have been laid low by a blockade, without Germany's attempting an invasion or even resorting to air attacks in the interior of the island. No such thing could be accomplished, however, by a Navy comprising only a handful of cruisers and destroyers and less than thirty operational U-boats. Nor could much help be expected from an air arm which had been planned for short-range tactical operations in support of the Army and was virtually destitute of long-range aircraft. Based along the Channel coast, the Luftwaffe could lay mines and attack shipping and ports along England's southeastern shores, but the convoys could then be diverted to the more distant and sheltered western ports, such as Liverpool. Furthermore, the lack of long-range reconnaissance planes would deprive the submarines of the eyes aloft that would have been invaluable for guiding the U-boats to their targets.

Submarines and long-range aircraft could be built much more rapidly than a surface fleet, but a significant increase could certainly not be achieved in less than a year, during which the British could greatly augment their forces for protection of sea lanes and ports. In such a race of construction and technique, Germany would have no advantage and would have to reckon with the possibility of extensive American aid to the British.

Warfare by blockade, therefore, meant a prolonged war of dubious outcome; it offered no prospect of victory in the near future. If the war was to be ended during 1940, or in all probability 1941, the island itself would have to be assaulted.

Could this be successfully accomplished by the Luftwaffe alone, without undertaking an invasion by land forces? "The disintegration of nations . . . will be accomplished directly by . . . aerial forces," wrote the great protagonist of air power Giulio Douhet,[36] and his writings had wide currency in the Luftwaffe, as among professional air soldiers in other countries. Whatever the validity of his doctrine, however, the limitations of the Luftwaffe had to be taken into account. Its bombers and fighters could operate effectively over only the southern part of England. To be sure, this included London and many vital ports and industrial areas, but much of Britain's strength lay beyond the Luftwaffe's radius of action. Conceivably the German planes might sweep the RAF from the air over southern England and make a shambles of much that lay below them. Still, as long as their will to resist held firm, the British would be able to hold out in their island if not in London.

Victory according to the teachings of Douhet, therefore, hung on the possibility of forcing a fatal crack in British morale by air bombardment. This would have been a strategic gamble and, given the limitations of the Luftwaffe, an imprudent one. To ensure success, accordingly, the air attack ought to be part of a larger assault, culminating in an invasion of Britain by ground forces, brought by sea and air. If the Wehrmacht's resources were not sufficient for such a venture, there was at least grave question whether or not the air offensive should be undertaken at all.

In assessing the prospects of an attempted invasion, two factors were of great, if not governing, strategic significance. The first was time. Opportunity would not knock twice. In the early summer of 1940 Britain was at her weakest; with each passing month her power to oppose a landing would increase. Since the German Navy could do very little to protect the passage of troops and supplies across the Channel, the hazards were already very great, if not, indeed, prohibitive. The fall and winter would bring impossible weather, and by 1941 the British would surely have so strengthened their defenses that an invasion could no longer be seriously considered. It was now or never; even the lapse of time between Dunkirk and Compiègne had been costly. If an invasion was to be part of the grand strategy, the decision should be taken at once and preparations made with the utmost vigor and determination.

The other strategic factor was that, for the Germans, considerable risk of failure could justifiably be taken. A successful invasion would ensure enormous, and perhaps immediately decisive, benefits. If the invasion was repulsed, the consequences would probably not be fatal to the Germans' fortunes, and the hazards of not making the attempt were almost as great as those of failure.

What Hitler stood to gain from a successful landing in England is plain enough. It may be, as Churchill declared at the time of Dunkirk,[37] that even if "this island or a large part of it were subjugated and starving, then our Empire beyond the seas, armed and guarded by the British fleet, would carry on the struggle, until in God's good time, the New World, with all its power and might, steps forth to the rescue and the liberation of the Old." Brave were these words, but a Britain overrun by the Wehrmacht and a Royal Navy based in Halifax might have seemed beyond hope of rescue. In any event, the occupation of Britain would have ensured to Hitler several years of virtual immunity from any dangerous military challenge, in the course of which he could have mobilized the sea and long-range air power the lack of which had kept the Wehrmacht musclebound, and consolidated the Reich's economic and political domination of Europe.[38]

Essentially, by the occupation of Britain Hitler would have won a European war, and would have had to fear only that at some future time he might become engaged in a world war. Lacking maritime power and with an economy geared to a short war, Germany's best hope lay in a strategy directed toward a speedy victory. An invasion of Britain was the only avenue to this end, and its successful accomplishment was plainly worth great risk and heavy losses.

The consequences of failure, of course, would have been very serious. The aura of invincibility that surrounded the Wehrmacht after Poland, Norway, Dunkirk, and Compiègne would have been dissipated, along with the myth of the Fuehrer's infallibility. Defeat on the shores of England would have given stimulus and perhaps opportunity to Hitler's domestic opponents, whose distrust and dislike of the Nazi regime had been all but drowned in the tide of victory.

Indeed, these psychological blows would probably have been far more dangerous to the Third Reich than the material and human losses which an unsuccessful invasion attempt would have entailed. There was very little Navy to be lost. The Luftwaffe would have suffered grievously, but at least its resources would have been spent in pursuit of a strategically valid objective, instead of being frittered away to no good purpose, as they were in the Battle of Britain. The Army would have lost a few crack divisions if the invasion forces had been repelled on the beaches, and more if they had been cut off and destroyed after an initial success. But there were divisions to spare, and the losses could have been made good within a year at most.

The strictly military consequences of failing in an attempted invasion, accordingly, would have been tolerable. The diplomatic and political results would have been graver, but some of those unfavorable consequences would flow from not attempting the assault. If the invasion had been repulsed, the losses would not have been so severe or irremediable as to foreclose resort to some other strategy thereafter. If the invasion was not undertaken, Germany would then have to face the dangers, difficulties, and economic dislocations of a long war. All these considerations argued in favor of accepting the risks, and launching the invasion if it appeared to have a reasonable chance of success.

However, the odds against success might appear to be so long that it would be reckless folly to make the attempt. Or, if undertaken, the attempt might fail. In either event, the leaders of the Reich would then be forced to the other and radically different strategy based on the prospect of a longer war. In that event, two decisions should have been

taken with the least possible delay. The first was to determine where
new military operations might most advantageously be undertaken, in
order to weaken Britain's power of resistance and augment Germany's
strength. The second was to mobilize the German economy for a long
war, and plan the strengthening of the Wehrmacht in accordance with
the requirements of future operations.

Italy's declaration of hostilities had already turned the Mediterranean and northern Africa into theaters of war. Britain's shortest sea
route to her resources in the Middle East and southern Asia ran
through the Mediterranean and the Suez Canal; if this route could be
closed, the British "lifelines of empire" would be sharply pinched.
Furthermore, the Reich badly needed additional sources of oil, and
there was an abundance of these at the eastern end of the Mediterranean, in and near the British- and French-mandated territories of the
Near East.

For all these reasons, the Mediterranean littoral was the most promising area for new Axis conquests. Gibraltar and Malta might be attacked,
and the Italians in Libya reinforced for a drive into Egypt, toward
Alexandria, Suez, and Baghdad. The principal obstacle to the success
of such a venture was the British Mediterranean Fleet. There was little
doubt that the German and Italian Armies could overrun Egypt if
problems of transport and supply could be solved. But this was a very
big "if"; the Germans were rightfully distrustful of Italy's military
prowess, and they had no means of strengthening the Italian Navy.

There was another road to the Near East, through the Balkans and
Turkey—the route of the projected Berlin–Baghdad railway that had
symbolized German imperial aspirations a quarter of a century earlier.
The Balkans were Hitler's for the taking, and most of this route lay
beyond the reach of British sea power. But Turkey was no longer the
German ally she had been during the First World War, and to leap the
Bosporus and cross Anatolia, in the face of Turkish and probably British
opposition, would have been no easy task, even for the Wehrmacht of
1940.

If such a drive were to be undertaken, Russia too would have to be
reckoned with. The prospect of German control of the gateway to the
Black Sea was viewed with no pleasure in Moscow, and Soviet occupation of the Baltic countries and Bessarabia had shown that the Kremlin
was far from cowed by the German victories in the west. Yet it was at
least doubtful that the Russians would have ventured to attack the
Germans, even under strong provocation. Britain had been badly

mauled, and the Russians could not have expected much help from that quarter. The Red Army had emerged from the Finnish War with little glory, its soldiers could not be counted on to fight as well on the offensive as in defense of Mother Russia, and its leaders surely would have hesitated to take on the German Army virtually singlehanded.

Even if the Russians had decided otherwise and launched an attack through East Prussia, Poland, and the Balkans, this might well have turned out well for the Germans. In direct encounter, the Red Army of 1940 would have been no match for the Wehrmacht. The German generals would not have been faced with the problem of pursuit into the vast Russian interior; instead, there would have been good opportunities to counterattack, and encircle and destroy the Russian forces. Such a defeat very likely would have had disastrous consequences for the Soviet regime, and Hitler might thus have succeeded in doing what he failed to accomplish in 1941.

In retrospect, and assuming that an invasion of Britain was beyond the realm of reason, it appears that a German campaign directed toward conquest of the Mediterranean lands would have been strategically sound. The only major alternative—and the one Hitler eventually adopted—was to attack the Soviet Union, following the historic German yearning for a *Drang nach Osten,* and Hitler's own preachings in *Mein Kampf.*

The strategic goal of a drive into Russia, according to its proponents of past years, would be to conquer and occupy the Ukraine and the Caucasus, and exploit the fertile plains and extensive coal, ore, and oil deposits of southern Russia. In all probability the German Army would be capable of occupying a large part of this vast area, but the strategic objective of replenishing and augmenting Germany's economic resources could hardly be attained unless military operations were linked with political and administrative policies that would enable the conquerors to pacify the inhabitants and put an end to large-scale hostilities.

Attacking Russia would not weaken Britain, in a military sense. Nevertheless, in Hitler's mind, the hope of eventual support from the Soviet Union was one of the two principal factors (the other being the surer prospect of American aid) sustaining the British will to resist. According to the Fuehrer's analysis, if Russia could be eliminated as a potential ally, and if Japan could draw America's principal strength into the Pacific regions, Britain would soon realize that her situation was hopeless, and sue for peace.[39]

The paradoxical basis of this strategy was, of course, that in order to shatter British hopes of Russian aid, they would first have to be fulfilled. To *defeat* Russia might perhaps have the desired effect on Britain. But to *attack* Russia would bring about the very state of affairs for which the British hoped—a war between the Nazi and Communist colossi that would divert the main weight of the Wehrmacht to the east, lift the threat of invasion, and relieve Axis pressure in the Mediterranean.[40]

Among the several strategic possibilities that presented themselves to the German high command in the summer of 1940, some were mutually exclusive. Obviously, Axis resources were not sufficient to undertake full-scale campaigns simultaneously in the Mediterranean lands and in Russia. Nor would it be possible to build up the Navy and the Luftwaffe for a major effort to blockade Britain while the Army was chewing up huge quantities of oil, steel, and rubber—to say nothing of men—in a drive toward Baku or Baghdad.

Whatever the decision or decisions might be, however, the Germans' fortunes depended on the speed and perspicacity of their taking and the vigor of their prosecution. If there was ever a situation that challenged and tested the decision-making capacities of national leadership to the utmost, it was the situation that confronted the leaders of the Third Reich in June and July of 1940.

CHAPTER TWO

The Course of Decision in the Summer of 1940

T HE SEVERAL STRATEGIC POSSIBILITIES that I have described in retrospect were all—except for the sustained "peace offensive"—perceived and considered by Hitler and the leaders of the Wehrmacht within a few weeks after the fall of France. For example, the major alternatives were set forth with considerable clarity as early as June 30 in a memorandum by Generalmajor Alfred Jodl, chief of the Operations Staff of the Armed Forces High Command (OKW) and Hitler's closest military adviser.[1] "If political measures do not succeed," Jodl wrote, "England's will to resist must be broken by force." This might be accomplished "(a) by making war against the English motherland, (b) by extending the war to the periphery."

Whether these were to be regarded as alternative or conjunctive strategies Jodl did not specify. The first method, he suggested, could be pursued by a naval and air blockade of Britain's maritime commerce, by "terror attacks against English centers of population," or by invasion. The second method would require the co-operation of nations that hoped to see the British Empire disintegrate and to seize part of the "spoils." Jodl regarded Italy, Spain, Russia, and Japan as such countries and remarked on the advantages that would flow from capturing Gibraltar and Suez and thus sealing off the Mediterranean.

In this analysis there was nothing very abstruse. With a good atlas and a bit of common sense, any well-informed armchair strategist could perceive the several choices that were open to the Germans. The difficulties lay in estimating the probable consequences of choice, and in taking pains to arrive at prompt and enlightened decisions. These were the very difficulties with which Hitler and his advisers failed to

44

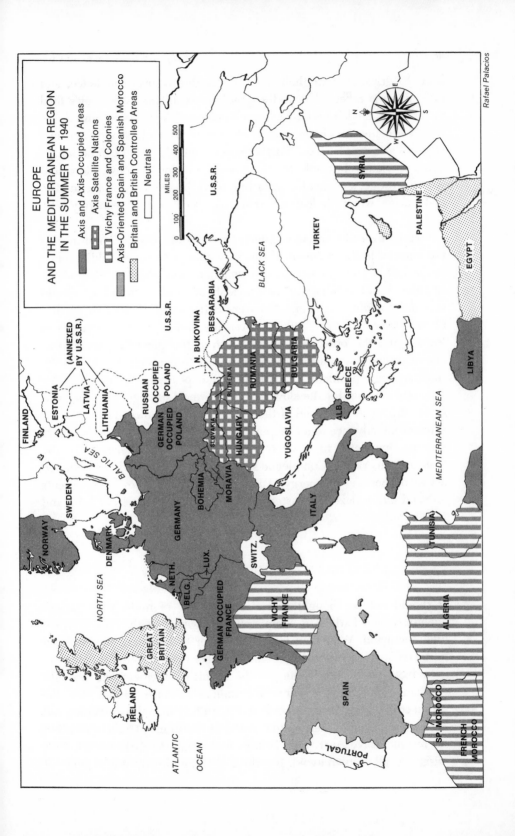

EUROPE
AND THE MEDITERRANEAN REGION
IN THE SUMMER OF 1940

Axis and Axis-Occupied Areas
Axis Satellite Nations
Vichy France and Colonies
Axis-Oriented Spain and Spanish Morocco
Britain and British Controlled Areas
Neutrals

MILES
0   100 200 300 400 500

Rafael Palacios

FINLAND
ESTONIA (ANNEXED BY U.S.S.R.)
LATVIA
LITHUANIA
SWEDEN
NORWAY
DENMARK
BALTIC SEA
NORTH SEA
GREAT BRITAIN
IRELAND
ATLANTIC OCEAN
NETH.
BELG.
LUX.
GERMANY
GERMAN OCCUPIED POLAND
RUSSIAN OCCUPIED POLAND
U.S.S.R.
N. BUKOVINA
BESSARABIA
BOHEMIA
MORAVIA
SLOVAKIA
RUTHENIA
HUNGARY
RUMANIA
BULGARIA
BLACK SEA
U.S.S.R.
SWITZ.
GERMAN OCCUPIED FRANCE
VICHY FRANCE
ITALY
YUGOSLAVIA
ALB.
GREECE
TURKEY
SPAIN
PORTUGAL
SP. MOROCCO
FRENCH MOROCCO
ALGERIA
TUNISIA
MEDITERRANEAN SEA
LIBYA
EGYPT
PALESTINE
SYRIA

N
E
S
W

come to grips. In part their neglect was due to overconfidence, and this failing is reflected in Jodl's same memorandum. "Germany's final victory over England is only a question of time," he declared, and therefore "Germany can choose a form of warfare which husbands her own strength and avoids risks." Furthermore: "Since England can no longer fight for victory but only for the preservation of her possessions and world prestige, she should, according to all predictions, be inclined to make peace when she learns that she can get it now at relatively little cost."

Victory over Britain was indeed "a question of time," but not in the sense of Jodl's comment. If this very able professional soldier, close to the seat of power, could take so confident and relaxed a view of the situation, small wonder that the quondam art student from Linz should succumb to *dolce far niente*. Nor were Hitler and Jodl the only victims of complacent lethargy; alike in Germany and at the headquarters in France and the other occupied countries, the prevailing mood was one of celebration, and few were disposed to concentrate on troublesome strategic problems that the expected peace would brush away.

Another reason for the slow pace of German strategic planning was sheer surprise at the speed of their triumph over France. The swift and exhilarating advance to a cheap and complete victory on the Continent was not conducive to sober reflection on the consequences. For the British, Dunkirk and Compiègne supplied the adrenalin that stimulated a vast outpouring of energy. Among the Germans, these same events induced a rosy daze that lasted through the crucial weeks of June and July.

Peace or Blitz

It should not be thought that the possibility of military operations against Britain had been completely disregarded within the German high command. What had been done prior to Dunkirk, however, lay in the realm of theoretical staff studies rather than purposeful planning.

In 1938, the events leading to the Munich settlement had brought Germany to the brink of war with Britain and France. At that time, the prospect filled the Army General Staff with horror, and its planning did not extend beyond a desperate defense of the Franco-German frontier. As for the Navy, war with Britain was what the German admirals wished at all costs to avoid. But the Luftwaffe already was capable of striking across the Channel, and between February and September Luftwaffe officers prepared several memoranda which explored the elements of an air offensive against Britain.[2]

There were more air-staff studies early in 1939. In May, Hitler informed the military leaders of his decision to attack Poland, and acknowledged the possibility that, if Poland could not be isolated by diplomatic means, there might be war with Britain and France. In that event, as Hitler rightly foresaw, Britain would be the principal enemy. Her defeat could be encompassed, the Fuehrer declared, by occupying the Channel coast, as the basis for a combined air and sea blockade of the ocean lanes, in order to starve the island to the point of surrender.[3]

After the conquest of Poland and the Western Allies' rejection of Hitler's bid for a negotiated peace, formulation of a strategy for war against Britain became a practical and urgent necessity. There is no evidence that Hitler himself then contemplated an invasion of Britain, nor was it given any consideration by OKW. During the last six weeks of 1939, however, Raeder and Brauchitsch directed their respective staffs to examine the possibility of landing troops in England.[4] Studies were duly prepared and interchanged among the three branches of the Wehrmacht. The results were largely negative, and the matter was put aside in January and remained dormant until after the decisively favorable development of the Battle of France, late in May.

In the meanwhile, Hitler's own strategic thoughts about the conduct of hostilities against Britain remained similar to those he had expressed before the outbreak of war. After the victory in Poland, he issued a new "Directive for the Conduct of the War"[5] in which (apart from the defeat of "as strong a contingent of the French Army as is possible") the object of the projected western offensive was described as occupation of "as large an area as possible in Holland, Belgium, and Northern France as a basis for conducting a promising air and sea war against England, and as a protective area for the Ruhr." In an accompanying memorandum,[6] Hitler discussed "Germany's military means of waging a lengthier war" and declared that the Luftwaffe and the U-boat arm of the Navy would be the principal weapons against Britain. Conquest of the Channel coast would greatly increase the striking power of both aircraft and submarines against British shipping and the ports and industrial areas of southern England.

The same thinking pervaded another directive issued by Hitler on November 29, 1939, entitled "Principles for the Conduct of the War against the Enemy's Economy."[7] Therein the Commanders-in-Chief of the Luftwaffe and the Navy (Goering and Raeder) were ordered to submit detailed plans in accordance with the general principles of the directive:

> In the war against the Western Powers, Great Britain is the driving spirit and leading power of our enemies. The conquest of Britain is, therefore, the prerequisite for final victory.
>
> The most effective way to accomplish this is to paralyze Britain's economy through interrupting it at critical points. . . .
>
> As soon as the Army has succeeded in defeating the Anglo-French field army and in occupying and holding a part of the coast facing England, the task of the Navy and Air Force of carrying on warfare against the economic structure of Britain will become of prime importance.

No further directives dealing with warfare against Britain were issued until the last week of May 1940, nearly six months later. There is no evidence that Hitler's strategic thinking, or that of his principal advisers, changed during this time. The directive of November 29, 1939, was still in full force and effect in May, when the western offensive was launched. Britain was to be defeated by the use of military means—aircraft and submarines in the main—to exert intolerable economic pressure, by the cutting off of her foreign commerce and the destruction of her ports and factories. But this could not be undertaken with hope of success until air and naval bases on the Channel coast were available, so there was little point in considering the matter further until the ground forces had cleared the way.

The vanguard of the German armored force reached Abbeville and the ocean shores on May 20. Hitler and Raeder conferred the next day, and the scope of their discussion reflected the Army's sensational success.[8] Raeder asked "how long the Fuehrer believes the war will last," and whether it would be wise to use the U-boats still in training for operational missions, "in the hope that the war will be decided quickly." Hitler did not reply directly to the first question, but they agreed that it would be more prudent to continue the "long-term program for submarine training and construction." After the "main operations in France" were finished, Hitler promised, he would concentrate on the submarine and Junkers-88 (medium bomber) construction programs.

This conference was also notable as the first known occasion at which Hitler discussed an invasion of Britain. But the significance of this talk should not be overestimated. Raeder was then, as later, highly skeptical of any such venture; according to his own account,[9] he raised the question with Hitler only to forestall "irresponsible" suggestions from other quarters, which might lead to "impossible demands" on the Navy. After the meeting, however, Raeder told his staff to resume their studies on the subject, which had been laid aside since January.

Hitler himself was far too deeply concerned with the Battle of France to give continuing consideration to an invasion of Britain. Furthermore, there soon were indications that his mind was turning toward the Luftwaffe as the main weapon against Britain, should additional blows be necessary after the defeat of France. On May 24 (the day of the much-debated order that halted the German armored advance toward Dunkirk),[10] he issued a new directive for the conduct of the war.[11] It was chiefly concerned with the destruction of the Allied forces encircled in Flanders and Artois, but it also prescribed that, "as soon as sufficient forces are available," the Luftwaffe should embark on an independent mission against "the British homeland." Targets were to be selected according to the principles laid down in the directive of November 29, and the operation was "to be started with a crushing attack in retaliation for the British raids in the Ruhr area." Two days later the OKW promulgated a supplement to the November 29 directive, specifying that the British aircraft industry should be the primary target, in order to eliminate "the last potent weapon which could be employed directly against us."

For the time being, the Luftwaffe had its hands full elsewhere. Over Dunkirk it was sharply challenged by the RAF for the first time, and, despite Goering's boasts to Hitler, it failed to prevent the escape of the main British forces. Several Luftwaffe generals suggested immediate pursuit of the British by a speedily contrived invasion. But the high command stuck to its plan for a second offensive to destroy the French Army and knock France out of the war,[12] and the Luftwaffe was regrouped to support the Army's southward attack.

On June 4 (the day before the second offensive was launched) Hitler met with Raeder, who complained that the submarine construction program was being seriously delayed by lack of labor and materials.[13] Hitler replied that it was his intention "to decrease the size of the Army when France has been overthrown and to release all older men and skilled workmen," and promised that then the Navy and the Luftwaffe would have "top priority." In line with these assurances, three days later Keitel told Generalleutnant Georg Thomas, chief of the Military Economy Division of OKW, that the Army would be

reduced to 120 divisions.[14] The mechanized units would be strengthened, but the principal purpose would be to augment the Luftwaffe
and the U-boat arm of the Navy. All of this indicated a future
strategy based on a prolonged blockade of Britain, rather than a quick
knockout blow.

On June 14 these informal advices from on high were given official
form in a new Hitler directive.[15] Halder summarized it in his diary:[16]

It directs immediate initiation of measures to lay the foundation for a reduction of ground forces to 120 divisions, including 20 of armor and 10 of motorized infantry.° The directive is based on the assumption that, since the final
collapse of the enemy is now imminent, the Army will have fulfilled its
mission, and accordingly, while still in enemy country, could comfortably
start on preparations for its projected peacetime organization. Luftwaffe and
Navy alone would be carrying on the war against Britain.

Such was the state of German planning for the future conduct of the
war when, on June 17, the Pétain government's plea for an armistice
was received at Hitler's headquarters. Up to that time the matrix of
German strategy for the defeat of Britain was economic blockade, to
be effected by air and sea. Neither the Luftwaffe nor the Navy was
strong enough to cut off Britain's foreign commerce; therefore they
would have to be greatly augmented, and this meant a considerable
lengthening of the war. Several of Hitler's directives had suggested a
hope that a quicker victory might be obtained by heavy air attacks on
British ports and plants in southern England, but as yet these were but
vague hints of a Douhet strategy. The possibility of an invasion had
been called to Hitler's attention, but he fully shared Raeder's skepticism
of its feasibility, and had not even requested the OKW staff to study
the matter.†

The French request for an armistice turned Hitler's thoughts toward
peace. Meeting with Mussolini at Munich on June 18 to discuss armistice terms, the Fuehrer declared that Britain was a force for world
stability and order, and that her empire should not be destroyed.
Ribbentrop echoed these sentiments to Ciano, and revealed that Eng-

---

° Since the Army was then at a strength of nearly 160 divisions, this represented
a reduction of about 25 per cent. The mechanized forces, however, were to be
approximately doubled in divisional units.

† On June 17 Oberst Walter Warlimont (Jodl's deputy at OKW) told Konteradmiral Kurt Fricke (chief of the Naval War Staff Operations Section) that "with
regard to a landing in Britain, the Fuehrer . . . has not up to now expressed such
an intention, as he fully appreciates the unusual difficulties of such an operation.
Therefore, even at this time, no preparatory work of any kind has been done at
OKW."[17]

land had been informed, through Swedish diplomatic channels, that she could have peace if she would recognize the *fait accompli* and renounce "some of her possessions."[18]

On returning to his headquarters (at Brûly-de-Pesche, near the Franco-Belgian border), Hitler exuded a spirit of *Sieg und Fried*. On June 19 Keitel, in an OKW order, announced the Fuehrer's intention "to stage a big parade in Paris." Hitler himself was working on the armistice terms, and on June 20 there was a great rush to finish the draft and make the necessary translations,[19] in preparation for its presentation to the French. After the triumphant confrontation of the French delegation at Compiègne, Hitler paid a short visit to Paris, and then returned to Brûly-de-Pesche to await the Franco-Italian armistice and the end of hostilities.

While the armistice was absorbing the greater part of his attention, Hitler found time for two military conferences. Raeder was called in on June 20. Much of the conversation concerned the armistice provisions for neutralizing the French fleet, the need for air protection of German naval operations in Norway, and personal friction between Raeder and Goering.[20] In addition, Raeder reported the Navy's developing views on an invasion of Britain, stressing the necessity of "air supremacy" as a prerequisite.

On this occasion, the defeat of France allowed both the Fuehrer and the Commander-in-Chief of the Navy to view a much broader strategic panorama than they ever had before. Raeder spoke of Dakar as a most desirable base for future naval operations, and suggested exchanging Madagascar for "the northern part of Portuguese Angola." Hitler was receptive to these ideas, but disclosed his previous intention "to use Madagascar for settling Jews under French supervision." Raeder also reported unfavorably on a plan (given the fitting cover name "Icarus") for the occupation of Iceland.

In conclusion, Raeder renewed his complaints about delays in the allocation of men and material for the submarine-construction program, and declared that immediate action was necessary "if even the restricted program (January 1, 1942) is to be carried out." Keitel (who was also present) explained "that the demands made by the Navy have been approved at this very moment." Earlier in the meeting Raeder had urged that the Luftwaffe start "vigorous air attacks on British bases in order to destroy ships under construction and repair." Hitler replied that he was contemplating "taking such action soon."

On June 23 Brauchitsch had his turn with the Fuehrer.[21] The con-

versation did not range as widely as it had with Raeder; Britain appears
to have been barely mentioned, though Hitler expressed the view that
she was "coming down a peg." Previous instructions for the reduction
of the Army to 120 divisions and doubling the armored units were
confirmed. British air raids on the Ruhr stimulated a decision that captured French and Czech antiaircraft guns should be sent to Germany
for home defense. Otherwise the discussion centered on occupational
problems. Annexations were already in Hitler's mind, for he directed
that military cordons be thrown around "Strasbourg and other German
towns" in order to "prevent return of the French elements of the
population."

Just before his final departure from Brûly-de-Pesche on June 25,
Hitler informed the Operations Staff of OKW that in a few days he
would want to examine some basic studies for an invasion of Britain.[22]
This request led to OKW's first work on the project (soon to be given
the cover name Seeloewe–"Sea Lion"), but did not as yet indicate any
disposition on Hitler's part to undertake it.

These military consultations at the time of the armistice took place
in an atmosphere which Helmuth Greiner (a civilian historian attached
to the Operations Staff of OKW) described as an "ausgesprochene
Friedenstimmung" (outspoken mood of peace).[23] "The English have
lost the war," Hitler is said[24] to have told Jodl, "but they haven't yet
noticed it; one must give them time, and they will soon come around."
A Luftwaffe staff officer[25] who visited Brûly-de-Pesche at this time
found both Keitel and Hitler's air adjutant "convinced that England
was prepared to sue for peace, and that the war was as good as
finished."

So the week between the French request for an armistice and the end
of hostilities passed without any decision on Hitler's part with respect
to the future conduct of the war. The possibility of invading Britain
had been broached, but nothing more than a preliminary staff study
was ordered. Raeder and Hitler had talked of taking Dakar and
Iceland, but only in a vague and speculative way. The allocations for
submarine construction were approved, as well as the demobilization
of surplus infantry divisions. These measures fell far short of the broad
reorganization of the Wehrmacht and of the war economy that prolonged hostilities against a maritime empire would require, and the
submarine program would not yield substantial operational results for
at least a year.

Only one major order for operations in the near future had been issued—the directive to the Luftwaffe to prepare for a bombing offensive against "the British homeland," in order to destroy Britain's aircraft industry, knock out her seaports, and retaliate for the British raids on the Ruhr. In the optimistic glow of the last few days at Brûly-de-Pesche, peace seemed to be just around the corner, and likely to come as soon as the first bombs were dropped in England, if not sooner. When the armistice with France was signed, Germany's strategy, if such it may be called, was a simple matter of peace or blitz.

The Fuehrer's Vacation

In the early-morning hours of June 25 the armistice became effective, and the fighting in France ended. That same day Hitler closed his headquarters at Brûly-de-Pesche. The Fuehrer had not enjoyed the locale; to conceal his bunker from hostile aircraft, it had been built in a grove of trees, where there were gnats in superabundance. Whether for this or other reasons, the headquarters was now moved to a new location in the Black Forest, between Strasbourg and Freudenstadt, under the cover name "Tannenburg."

Hitler did not accompany the staff of OKW during its transfer to the Black Forest. He departed Brûly-de-Pesche in the company of two comrades of the First World War, and spent several days revisiting old battlefields in Belgium and northern France.[26]

At the end of June the Fuehrer repaired to Tannenburg, but his vacation did not end. To adopt a familiar British term for travel which is ostensibly official but is actually undertaken for pleasure, the Fuehrer was "swanning." Daily he sped up and down the Rhine with a large automobile caravan, stopping to inspect points where the troops of Leeb's army group had broken through the Maginot Line.[27] Albert Speer, official Nazi architect and high in Hitler's favor, was summoned to discuss grandiose plans, stimulated by Hitler's trip to Paris, for new buildings in Berlin, and for a supergauge industrial railway between Berlin and the Ruhr.

No doubt all this was very pleasurable, and Hitler's mood was euphoric. But it was hardly the way to determine complex and urgent questions of strategy and statecraft. Hitler had been what the OKW staff officer von Lossberg called the "motor" of the high command;[28] now, at the critical juncture, the engine was idling. From June 23 to July 11 Hitler did not meet with the Army or Navy Commanders-in-

Chief. On June 30 Dino Alfieri, the Italian Ambassador in Berlin, told Ciano[29] that Hitler was in "one of those periods of isolation that precede his great decisions." Two days later, upon receipt of an urgent message from King Carol of Rumania, Ribbentrop sent word to Bucharest that the Fuehrer was on a trip to the "front" and could not be reached by telephone.[30]

Contrary to Alfieri's impression, Hitler was not making any "great decisions." Nor was he completely inaccessible; on July 1 Alfieri himself was received at Tannenburg. Mussolini, chagrined by Italy's inglorious role in the defeat of France, was pressing Hitler with offers of troops and aircraft for use against England. In this regard, Alfieri was unable to extract any reply from Hitler, who countered with the proposal that the Luftwaffe assist the Italian Air Force in bombing the Suez Canal. Otherwise, Alfieri found the Fuehrer somewhat restless, and weighing many alternatives.[31]

The German record of this interview[32] reflects a very different tone. In the presence of Ribbentrop and Keitel, the Fuehrer told Alfieri that Germany was preparing an air attack against Britain which would be "bloody" and a "horror." The Luftwaffe was refitting and building bases in France, Belgium, and Holland. "These activities had begun immediately after the conclusion of the armistice with France," and now gigantic columns were rolling westward with material "for undertaking the impending tasks."

These strident echoes of Douhet were in line with a memorandum distributed three days earlier by Keitel, in which it was proposed to strike at Britain with the Luftwaffe, which was to be doubled in size by the end of 1940.[33] Invasion was not discussed, nor does Hitler appear to have mentioned that possibility to Alfieri. Invasion was listed in Jodl's memorandum of June 30[34] as one of three means of attacking England, but only as a *coup de grâce* after the Luftwaffe and the Navy had already rendered her virtually defenseless.

However, the OKW staff had been doing some preliminary work on an invasion, in compliance with Hitler's instructions of June 25. At Tannenburg, the only fruit of these studies was a directive issued by Keitel on July 2,[35] which commenced with the announcement: "The Fuehrer and Supreme Commander has decided that a landing in England is possible, providing that air superiority can be attained and certain other necessary conditions fulfilled. The date of commencement is still uncertain. All preparations to be begun immediately." Army, Navy, and Luftwaffe were ordered to supply OKW with basic proposals and estimates, but actual preparations were to be undertaken only "on the basis that the invasion is still only a plan, and has not yet been decided upon."

While Hitler was touring the Rhine front and spinning architectural dreams with Speer, the three service commands were left to their own devices. The Army and the Navy each had a number of individual problems, and both staffs, plagued by the uncertainty of Hitler's strategic intentions, were heavily occupied with invasion studies. The Luftwaffe was almost exclusively engaged in preparations for the coming operations over Britain.

Of the three services, the Army was the worst bedeviled by the lack of an over-all strategy, and had the most numerous and varied problems. By the directive of June 14, the Army leaders had been told that the defeat of France would fulfill the Army's mission and would be followed by reversion to a peacetime footing. Within ten days, however, there was talk of an invasion which, if actually undertaken, would raise difficult and unprecedented tactical problems. At the same time, the Army was responsible for the administration of Belgium and the occupied portion of France—an unfamiliar task for which few preparations had been made. Presumably because the principal business of the moment appeared to lie in France, OKH did not move its operations headquarters back to Berlin after the armistice; instead, it moved (on July 2) to Fontainebleau.

As the fighting in France drew to a close, the first task that the Army confronted was the redeployment of its forces. The eastern frontier had been stripped of first-line troops. Common prudence, and Russian moves in the Baltic States and Rumania, suggested the wisdom of sending troops to East Prussia and occupied Poland. Early in July this was accomplished by transferring fifteen infantry divisions to the east, under the command of General Georg von Kuechler, who established his 18th Army headquarters at Bydgoszcz in Poland.[36] The other armies and the three army groups, with the bulk of the field army, remained in Belgium and occupied France.[37]

A more complicated organizational problem was the deactivation of surplus infantry divisions and the expansion of the mechanized units, as prescribed in the directive of June 14. Late in June, the OKH issued orders specifying thirty-five divisions to be deactivated, and during this period Halder and his subordinates of the Army General Staff were much occupied with these matters, as well as with the structure of the military occupational regime in France.[38] On July 1, for example,

Halder conferred with General Friedrich Fromm (commander of the Replacement and Training Army), who expressed the opinion that the deactivation of thirty-five divisions "will not give any large boost to production," and pointed out that the establishment of fifteen additional mechanized divisions would require so many motor vehicles that the infantry would have to give up some of their motor transport.[39] Five days later the elderly General Alfred von Vollard Bockelberg, military commander in Paris, was in Halder's office[40] to suggest that only crack troops be posted to Paris (so as to ensure good behavior) and to report that the industrial workers in the suburbs were "out-and-out Communists."

These organizational and occupational[41] matters were necessary and important, but contributed nothing to the solution of the basic and pressing strategic problem. Brauchitsch and Halder were aware that this was so; on June 22 the latter noted:[42] "The near future will show whether Britain will do the reasonable thing in the light of our victories, or will try to carry on the war singlehanded. In the latter case, the war will lead to Britain's destruction, and may last a long time."

At the end of June Halder flew to Berlin to celebrate his birthday at home, and took advantage of the occasion to call on his friend Ernst von Weizsaecker, the Ministerial Secretary of the Foreign Office.[43] Weizsaecker declared that there was "no concrete basis for any peace treaty yet," and took the view that "Britain probably still needs one more demonstration of our military might before she gives in and leaves us a free hand in the East."

On the next day Halder met with his "opposite number," Vizeadmiral Otto Schniewind, chief of staff of the Naval War Staff, for a short discussion of the tactical framework for an invasion of England.[44] Immediately after his talk with Schniewind, Halder called upon General Emil Leeb, chief of Army Ordnance, for information on the amphibious capabilities of German tanks.[45] Leeb promptly complained that "he was told all along that invasion of England was not being considered." Halder rejoined that "possibilities have to be examined for, if political command demands a landing, they will want everything done at top speed."

Halder then returned to the OKH operational headquarters (which was in the process of moving to Fontainebleau), and hastened to tell Brauchitsch about his trip to Berlin and to discuss the "basis for a campaign against England."[46] Brauchitsch then went off to Berlin himself, and Halder set about gearing the staff of OKH for serious work on the projected invasion.

The Halder-Schniewind meeting on July 1 was the first high-level Army-Navy discussion of an invasion of Britain. By that time, however, the Navy had already given considerable attention to the problem. Following Raeder's conference with Hitler on May 21, Konteradmiral Kurt Fricke (chief of the Operations Section of the Naval War Staff) drew up a memorandum, entitled "Studie England," as a basis for further work. Throughout June, the staffs of OKM and of the naval commander in France were busy surveying the shipping that might be available and suitable for cross-Channel transportation, studying the southeastern coasts of England, analyzing the use of heavy coastal artillery and mines to protect the invasion fleet, and examining other facets of the project.[47] Consequently, when the OKW directive of July 2 was received, the Navy was already in a position to furnish most of the information requested in the directive, and to point out the difficulties and hazards which an invasion would entail.

The Navy, needless to say, was occupied with a variety of other tasks.[48] Repairs had to be made on the ships damaged during the Norwegian campaign, and the *Bismarck*, the *Tirpitz*, and the *Prinz Eugen* had to be completed, tested, and brought up to operational pitch. The Atlantic ports of France and Norway had to be equipped as U-boat bases. Serious defects in the German torpedoes had been uncovered, and these had to be studied and rectified. Most important of all, the expanded U-boat construction program had to be set in motion. All these matters were essential elements of a long-term strategy of blockade, but none of them could be expected to exert an immediately decisive influence on the course of the war.

Of the three services, the Luftwaffe alone had an immediate and major strategic assignment—to prepare for the air attack against Britain. Consequently, Goering and the staff of OKL were, at this juncture, the least troubled by the uncertainty of Hitler's strategic intentions, and the most deeply occupied with operational problems and undertakings.

After the armistice, Goering took a short holiday in Bad Gastein, and then went to Amsterdam to visit his old friend General der Flieger Friedrich Christiansen, who had been appointed commander of the German forces in the Netherlands. The forward headquarters of OKL was situated near Beauvais (about fifty miles northeast of Paris), and during the preparations for the air offensive Goering divided his time between Beauvais and the numerous Luftwaffe headquarters and bases established along the coast facing England.[49]

Goering's personal arrogance and chronic indifference to the views and needs of the Army and the Navy, as well as the understandable preoccupation of his staff with the coming air assault, resulted in a remarkable and militarily indefensible lack of consultation between the Luftwaffe and the other two services. Likewise, Hitler left the Luftwaffe entirely to Goering's management, and concerned himself very little with the tactics of aerial warfare. During the weeks following the armistice Hitler and Goering seldom were together, and there is no evidence that Goering or any of the Luftwaffe generals was much involved in the formulation of over-all strategy.

Thus the Army, Navy, and Luftwaffe commands each went about its individual tasks, while the Fuehrer relaxed and basked in the warm glow of the victory in France. There were highly competent military technicians in all three services, but there was none with sufficient prestige, initiative, and imagination to supply the driving force for strategic decision-making. When Hitler loosened his grip on the levers of supreme command the machinery ceased to function as a unit, and the Wehrmacht found itself leaderless at the very time that co-ordination, guidance, and a sense of urgency were most needed.

The Thorny Olive Branch

On July 6 Hitler broke up the Tannenburg headquarters and returned in triumph to Berlin. During the ensuing six weeks he divided his time fairly evenly between Berlin and the Berghof, his chalet in the Bavarian Alps near Berchtesgaden. Thus business was mixed with pleasure. A number of highly important military and diplomatic consultations were held at both places, but the Fuehrer's life at the Berghof was tolerably relaxed.

As he departed from Tannenburg, Hitler turned his mind to thoughts of peace and celebration. Peace was indeed a sound strategic objective, and celebration a natural sequel to the sensational victory in France. In the event, however, they proved a poor mixture.

Even before Compiègne, Hitler had started toying with the idea of a mammoth triumphal parade in Paris.[50] Elaborate preparations were made, including the dispatch to Paris of Guderian's panzer-group headquarters, and a large number of tanks. The project soon became a burden and a nuisance to the Army General Staff, because it tied up armored vehicles that should have been sent to repair depots for re-fitting, and because Hitler had had second thoughts about its wisdom and could not make up his mind. In the upshot the Paris parade was called off, and the victory festivities were concentrated in Berlin.[51]

The setting for the Berlin celebration was to be a meeting of the Reichstag. As Brauchitsch (who had just been in Berlin) described the plan to Halder on July 5,[52] the session was to be attended by the Army's field commanders at corps level and above, and by "outstanding troop commanders decorated with the Ritterkreuz." From its first conception, apparently, Hitler envisaged this military-political convocation as the occasion for a "peace offer" to Britain, for on July 8, shortly after Hitler's return to Berlin, Halder was told[53] that the Reichstag session was being postponed "because of probable reshuffle of British Cabinet."

By this time, over two weeks had elapsed since the French had signed the armistice at Compiègne. No white flags were being hoisted in London, and Hitler was beginning to lose hope that the British would take the initiative in seeking peace. A verbal prod, he thought, might help, and at least would be good propaganda. On July 7 he received Ciano at the Chancellery in Berlin:[54]

The Fuehrer began by saying that he has been considering the desirability of making another gesture of psychological and propagandist importance. He has not yet made a decision; however, he considers such a gesture useful in principle, although he is now convinced that the war against England will continue.

Despite his lack of optimism, Hitler appears to have been taking the matter very seriously, for he told Ciano that the speech was being delayed so that every word could be weighed.[55] A few days later, in conference with Raeder, Hitler reiterated his plan "to make a speech before the Reichstag," and inquired whether Raeder thought "this would be effective."[56] The naval chief replied in the affirmative, "because the contents would become known to the British public."

In the meantime, this much-discussed speech was taking shape. Ribbentrop, who saw the text in advance, told Paul Schmidt (the official interpreter) that it would contain "a very magnanimous peace offer to England" and that everyone might soon be "seated at a peace conference."[57] If these expressions reflected Hitler's and Ribbentrop's expectations, both must have completely lost touch with reality.

For, when the great moment arrived, it developed that the triumphal and minatory themes had completely overwhelmed the peace motif. The speech was delivered in the Kroll Opera House on the evening of July 19, at a meeting of the Reichstag attended by the principal commanders and staff officers of the Wehrmacht, as well as by diplomats and high civil officials. "I have summoned you to this meeting," Hitler announced,[58] "firstly, because I consider it imperative to give our own people an insight into the events, unique in history, that lie behind us; secondly, because I wish to express my gratitude to our magnificent soldiers; and thirdly, with the intention of appealing once more, and for the last time, to common sense in general." Thus "common sense" took third place, and the Fuehrer spoke for many minutes before there was any mention of peace.

As domestic political propaganda, Hitler's speech was a masterpiece.[59] With little subtlety but much plausibility, he appropriated to himself the credit for the strategic conceptions that had produced the victories in Norway and France, and he inundated the officers' corps with a flood of promotions that robbed the recipients of individual distinction. Responsibility for the war was laid at the door of "Anglo-French warmongers" who had rejected Mussolini's peace proposals on September 2, 1939, as well as Hitler's own peace offer of October 6, 1939, after the defeat of Poland.

However shrewdly calculated for home consumption, this was a most inauspicious prelude to an appeal addressed to British ears. Worse was to follow. Winston Churchill and Paul Reynaud were condemned as men who could not answer—"neither in this world nor the next"—for all the suffering they had caused. The mere mention of Churchill seemed to enrage Hitler. The British leader was an "unscrupulous politician who wrecks whole nations and states." Furthermore: "Only a few weeks ago Mr. Churchill reiterated his declaration that he wants war. Some six weeks ago he began to wage war in a field where he apparently considers himself very strong, namely air raids on the civil population, although under the pretense that the raids are directed against so-called military objectives." For this a terrible retribution was in store. The German reply would bring "unending suffering and misery," but "of course, not upon Mr. Churchill, for he, no doubt, will already be in Canada, where the money and children of those principally interested in the war have already been sent."

Having thus vilified Churchill and threatened the British with a rain of bombs, Hitler finally laid hold of the olive branch, and with it he slashed his enemy in the face:

"In this hour, I feel it to be my duty before my own conscience to appeal once more to reason and common sense in Great Britain as much as else-where. I consider myself in a position to make this appeal since I am not the vanquished, begging favors, but the victor speaking in the name of reason. I can see no reason why this war must go on. I am grieved to think of the sacrifices which it will claim . . . Possibly, Mr. Churchill will again brush aside this statement of mine by saying that it is merely born of doubt in our final victory. In that case, I shall have relieved my conscience in re-gard to the things to come."

Surrender or face destruction! That was all there was to the "very magnanimous peace offer" which, according to Ribbentrop, would soon gather the diplomats at a peace conference. Small wonder that Paul Schmidt, who read the speech on the radio in English, was "disap-pointed" and subsequently commented[60] that "precision was not a strong point of Hitler's" and that "it was incomprehensible to me that he should believe that such a meaningless, purely rhetorical, observa-tion would have any effect upon the sober British."*

In retrospect, it seems clear that either Hitler had no real desire or hope for peace, or that he had not the slightest notion how to project the issue, either in Britain or in the world as a whole. To be sure, there was little or no prospect that anything Hitler might have said would have elicited a favorable reaction in London. But in other countries, stunned as they were by the magnitude of the German victories, a care-fully contrived and reasonably specific peace proposal would have been eagerly taken up by many who then regarded Britain's plight as hope-less, and it might have laid the basis for a diplomatic strategy directed toward her eventual isolation.

But the formulation and prosecution of such a strategy called for a level of statecraft far beyond the reach of either Hitler or Ribbentrop. If anyone on the Wilhelmstrasse saw the problem more clearly, he did not enunciate it. The Ministerial Secretary of the Foreign Office, Ernst von Weizsaecker—an experienced professional diplomat—has de-scribed his "disappointment" at Churchill's failure to reply to Hitler's speech,[61] but there is no record indicating that he or any of his col-

---

* Galeazzo Ciano, usually a dispassionate observer, seems to have been dazzled by the magnificence (*"solenne e coreografica"*) of the occasion, for he recorded in his diary his impression that Hitler spoke with "unaccustomed humanity" and with a sincere desire for peace.

leagues gave any consideration to the possible terms on which a specific peace offer might be based, or realized the incongruity of launching an appeal for peace with a blast of insulting and threatening denunciation.

Vague and bungling or halfhearted as it was, Hitler's overture was bound to fall on deaf ears in Britain. Press reaction in London was prompt and hostile. Churchill did not dignify it with a personal reply; in a broadcast on July 22 the Foreign Secretary, Lord Halifax, brushed it aside as a mere "summons to capitulate."[62]

Hitler made no effort to renew or particularize the terms of his peace appeal, if such it may be called. On July 20 he told Ciano* that an "understanding" with Britain would have been preferable, but that "the reaction of the English press to yesterday's speech has been such as to allow of no prospect" of peace.[63] Hitler was aware that "the war with the English will be long and bloody" and that "people everywhere are averse to bloodshed." But there was no alternative: "Hitler is therefore preparing to strike the military blow at England." And so ended Hitler's misshapen and short-lived strategy of peace.

The Eagle and Perhaps the Sea Lion

How, then, would "the military blow at England" be delivered? In fact, the Germans' strategic plans had not developed appreciably during the two weeks since Hitler's return to Berlin on July 6. Receiving Ciano the next day, Hitler declared that he had returned to Berlin for military consultations.[64] But the Fuehrer stayed in Berlin only a few days, and then went to the Berghof,† where he conferred with Raeder on July 11 and with Brauchitsch and Halder on July 13.

At the meeting with Ciano on July 7, Hitler admitted that he was "not yet in a position to say in what form the attack against England will develop." The problem was "a very delicate and difficult one" which was "being studied by the General Staff." In the meantime, the Army was reorganizing its mechanized units, and the Luftwaffe was

---

* One man who was not disappointed by Hitler's failure to end the war was Benito Mussolini, who, according to Ciano (*Diario*, July 22), wanted the war to continue, presumably so that Italy could achieve the territorial conquests that had so far eluded her.

† En route to the Berghof, Hitler stopped on July 10 in Munich, where he met with Ribbentrop, Ciano, and the Hungarian Prime Minister, Count Paul Teleki, to discuss Hungary's territorial claims against Rumania.

completing its deployment against England. Ciano then reiterated "the Duce's keen desire to have Italian forces take part in any attack against Great Britain," and offered "a land force up to ten divisions strong and an air contingent up to thirty squadrons strong." Once more Hitler was noncommittal; he "was not in a position to give an answer until the planning stage was over, and the resulting decisions of the German General Staff had been taken." Thereafter it would be possible "to bring about a unified concept as to the continuation of operations," perhaps by means of another meeting with Mussolini at the Brenner Pass.[65]

At luncheon that day, Ciano had opportunity for a long talk[66] with Generaloberst Wilhelm Keitel, Chief of OKW, who rarely took much part in strategic planning, but was no doubt familiar with the views then current in the high command. Keitel confirmed that "at present nothing has been decided by the General Staff," and opined that a landing in England, while "possible," would be "an extremely difficult operation, which must be approached with the utmost caution, in view of the fact that the intelligence available on the military preparedness of the island and on the coastal defenses is meager and not very reliable." But he entertained no such doubts about the coming air assault: "It appears easier, and in any event necessary, to make a large-scale attack on the airfields, factories and principal centers of communication in Britain."

When Raeder appeared at the Berghof on July 11, his main purpose was to impress upon Hitler the difficulties and dangers of attempting an invasion, and win him over to a strategy of economic blockade.[67] The prerequisites for an invasion, he declared, included not only "complete air superiority" but also "the creation of a mine-free area for transports and disembarkation." Whether such an area could be created, and if so how long it would take, it was impossible to foretell. There would be great dislocation of the German economy and inroads on the armament program. Therefore he could not "advocate an invasion of Britain as he did in the case of Norway"; it might be undertaken "only as a last resort to force Britain to sue for peace."

On the other hand, Raeder professed to be "convinced that Britain can be made to ask for peace simply by cutting off her import trade by means of submarine warfare, air attacks on convoys, and heavy air attacks on her main centers, as Liverpool, for instance." He depreciated the current operations of the Luftwaffe as "only pin-pricks, making no impression on the public, and of more inconvenience to ourselves than to them." An "early concentrated attack" was necessary, "so that the whole nation will feel the effect." The only question was "whether such an attack would be more useful before or after the Reichstag speech," and Raeder declared himself strongly in favor of the first alternative.

Hitler agreed that an invasion should be regarded as "a last resort" and that air superiority would be a prerequisite. But he did not comment on Raeder's basic thesis that economic blockade was the best avenue to victory over Britain, and the naval chief's plea for an "early concentrated" air attack, before the Reichstag speech, was not heeded.

At this meeting the discussion ranged far and wide. In Norway, Trondheim was to be developed as a major naval base, and "a beautiful German city," with superhighway connections through Norway and Denmark to Luebeck, was to be built on the Trondheim fiord. Raeder reiterated his yearning for Dakar, and Hitler spoke of acquiring one of the Canary Islands from Spain "in exchange for French Morocco." The construction of several new battleships was authorized, as well as completion of the carrier *Graf Zeppelin*. Most of these projects were pipe dreams, and none of them materialized.

Two days later (July 13) Hitler received Brauchitsch and Halder for a report on the Army's invasion plans.[68] Assuming that the Navy could get the troops across the Channel and the Luftwaffe could protect the beachheads, the Army chiefs were reasonably confident of success. The discussion was specific; Halder was well prepared with maps, tables of organization, intelligence estimates, and time schedules. Hitler approved his recommendations "as the basis for practical preparations," and authorized the "immediate start of invasion preparations."

After all this, the Fuehrer embarked upon a "review of the political situation from a military angle." He wished "to draw Spain into the game in order to build up a front against Britain extending from the North Cape to Morocco"; Ribbentrop would go to Spain to lay the groundwork. The Balkans must be pacified, and to this end "Rumania will have to foot the bill" by territorial cessions to Hungary and Bulgaria. This would not be difficult to arrange, inasmuch as "the King of Rumania has addressed a letter to the Fuehrer, quasi putting himself under his protection." Then, after a few inconclusive comments on the Mediterranean and Africa, came some far more significant observations:

The Fuehrer is greatly puzzled by Britain's persistent unwillingness to make peace. He sees the answer (as we do) in Britain's hope in Russia, and therefore counts on having to compel her by main force to agree to peace. Actually that is much against his grain. The reason is that a military defeat of Britain will bring about the disintegration of the British Empire. This would not be of any benefit to Germany. German blood would be shed to accomplish something that would benefit only Japan, the United States and others.

This little soliloquy revealed Hitler in a much more realistic mood than he had shown with Raeder, and foreshadowed much that was to transpire during the coming year. Hitler did try, though unsuccessfully, to persuade Franco to join "the game"; Rumania did "foot the bill" for a brief peace in the Balkans; German strategy in the Mediterranean remained inconclusive; Hitler prepared for but never undertook an invasion of Britain, the failure of which he feared and the consequences of which he mistrusted. Most important of all, the inferred relation between Britain's hopes and Russia's future alignment was a harbinger of Hitler's hostile designs against the Soviet Union, which became explicit only a few weeks later.

This broadening of the strategic panorama was reflected in a decision, taken at this same conference, with respect to the size of the Army. After the defeat of France was assured, orders had been issued to reduce the Army's strength by thirty-five divisions. Now it was determined that only fifteen divisions would be deactivated, and that the personnel of the other twenty would be furloughed, subject to immediate recall.[69]

The direct assault on Britain, however, was the great matter in hand. The deployment of the Luftwaffe along the Channel coast was nearly finished, and commanders and staff officers were busy with tactical plans. Hitler had by no means decided to invade the enemy island, for he shared most of Raeder's fears. But plans were to be laid and all preparations made, and for the next two months the questions whether and, if so, when and how to invade Britain were the principal subject of his military conferences.

Such was the Fuehrer's preoccupation with coming cross-Channel operations that he neglected to draw Mussolini into the formulation of a unified Axis strategy. On July 13 he finally got around to answering the Duce's repeated offers to send Italian troops and aircraft to join in the assault. In a long letter,[70] Hitler described the great difficulties and hazards that an invasion would involve. To surmount them would require extensive planning and special practice for amphibious operations. To include Italian ground forces would complicate the logistical problems, and therefore the offer must be declined. Possibly Italian ships or aircraft might participate.* But there was no suggestion that this would be necessary, or even desirable. On the contrary, Hitler stressed the strategic breadth of the conflict with England. An Italian invasion of Egypt would be a fine idea,† but, with so many possibilities, "it does not matter in the least, Duce, where these various blows will fall."

Careless, arrogant, and naïve as it was, this comment vividly illustrates Hitler's shortcomings as statesman and strategist. It mattered greatly "where these various blows will fall," and the failure of the two dictators to co-ordinate their plans and operations was to lead, in a few months, to Mussolini's costly blunder in Greece.

While Hitler was conferring with Brauchitsch, Halder, and Raeder and writing to Mussolini, the OKW, OKH and OKM staffs had all been occupied with the specifics of invasion planning. On July 12, Jodl prepared a general memorandum[72] on the operation to which he gave the name *Loewe* ("Lion"), setting forth a tactical program for circumventing Britain's command of the sea by a landing "in the form of a river crossing on a broad front." Part of Jodl's paper was used as the basis for a new Hitler directive (No. 16, dated July 16) for the conduct of the war.[73] Exclusively concerned with the invasion of England, this directive assigned to the projected operation the cover name *Seeloewe* ("Sea Lion"), by which it has since become widely known.

The strategic basis of the new directive was set forth in its opening paragraphs:

As England, in spite of the hopelessness of her military situation, has so far shown herself unwilling to come to any compromise, I have therefore decided to begin to prepare for, and if necessary to carry out, an invasion of England.

This operation is dictated by the necessity of eliminating Great Britain as a basis from which the war against Germany can be fought, and, if necessary, the island will be occupied.

The directive, therefore, was of a provisional nature; there would be an invasion of England "if necessary." In that event, the landing would be "on a broad front extending approximately from Ramsgate to a point west of the Isle of Wight"—a distance of about 150 miles. Prerequisites

---

* According to Ciano, however, Goering had told Alfieri that the Italian Air Force had so important a task in the Mediterranean that it would not be wise to divide it by sending components to other sectors.

† Mussolini replied to Hitler by letter dated July 17, 1940,[71] stating that Italy hoped to attack Egypt at the time of the German assault on England.

of the invasion included elimination of the RAF, clearing mines from the lane of passage, and rendering the lane inaccessible to the British fleet by means of mines and heavy coastal artillery. All this was to be accomplished by August 15!

"During the period of preparation and execution of the landings," the directive continued, the Army "will draft a plan for the crossing and operations of the first wave of the invading force." But the Army was to be little more than a passenger during the opening phase; the real tasks were for the other two services. The Navy was "to provide and safeguard the invasion fleet" and "provide adequate protection on both flanks during the entire Channel crossing." The Luftwaffe was not only to "prevent all enemy air attacks" and engage "approaching naval vessels . . . before they can reach the embarkation and landing points," but also to "destroy coastal defenses covering the landing points, break the initial resistance of the enemy land forces, and annihilate reserves behind the front."

Kesselring and other Luftwaffe officers recognized the gigantic scope of their mission as outlined in the directive.[74] However, Goering and his staff subordinates were deeply engrossed in plans for the air offensive, and were giving little attention to Sea Lion.

Raeder, on the other hand, lacked any such preoccupational protection against impossible demands. How was a navy with only a handful of cruisers, destroyers, and submarines to "provide and safeguard the invasion fleet" against an overpowering and determined Royal Navy? In a memorandum dated July 19,[75] the naval chief lamented that "the task allotted to the Navy in Operation Sea Lion is out of all proportion to the Navy's strength and bears no relation to the tasks that are given to the Army and Luftwaffe"—a complaint that was hardly supportable as applied to the Luftwaffe, but certainly valid with respect to the Navy itself. After rehearsing the problems and the hazards, Raeder concluded that "These reflections cause the Naval Staff to see exceptional difficulties that cannot be assessed individually until a detailed examination of the transport problem has been made."

Seriously alarmed by the form that the invasion plans were assuming, Raeder determined to bring them down to a more realistic level. He had opportunity at a conference with Hitler in Berlin on July 21 (two days after the Reichstag speech), attended also by Brauchitsch and General Hans Jeschonnek, chief of the Luftwaffe General Staff.[76] This was the first top-level military conference following the Reichstag celebration and speech on July 19, and British press reaction had already indicated rejection of the invitation to capitulate. A month had elapsed since the fall of France, but German strategy for the defeat of Britain was still diffuse and tentative. Consequently, while Raeder found Hitler still keenly aware of the hazards of invasion, the project remained very much alive, for lack of a sufficient alternative.

According to the records of this meeting, Hitler did most of the talking. He commenced in a confident vein: Britain's position was "hopeless," the war was already won, and "a reversal in the prospects of success is impossible." But the British were stupid, obstinate, and sustained by hope of assistance from America and Russia. Therefore "preparations for a decision by arms must be completed as quickly as possible," for the Fuehrer "will not let the military-political initiative pass out of his hands."

How to retain it? There was mention of Spain, Rumania, and Japan, and a long discussion of Russia. But at the moment it was "necessary to clear up the question whether a direct operation could bring Britain to her knees, and how long this would take." For his part, the Fuehrer regarded a Channel-crossing operation as "very hazardous." He rehearsed all the difficulties, and concluded that "invasion is to be undertaken only if no other means is left to come to terms with Britain."

These "other means" were "air assaults and submarine warfare," and Hitler declared that "Britain must be reduced by the middle of September." If either the Fuehrer or his listeners took this goal seriously, they must have realized that thirty-odd submarines could make no decisive contribution, and that it was a matter for the Luftwaffe. There is no record of Jeschonnek's comments, if, indeed, he made any. But apparently no one present felt certain that the Luftwaffe could turn the trick unaided, for the discussion turned back to the dangerous but tantalizing prospect of invasion.

Since the weather over the Channel would turn prohibitively bad early in the autumn, the question of timing was crucial. How long would the Navy require for its "technical preparations"? To what extent could it "safeguard the crossing"? The air assault would probably begin early in August; if it was successful, the invasion ought to be launched about August 25. "If it is not certain that preparations can be completed by the beginning of September, other plans must be considered."

Raeder was not ready to answer these questions on the spot, and he took his departure under instructions to study the matter further and report back as soon as possible. The very next day the Naval War Staff informed OKW that preparations for a landing could not possibly be completed by the middle of August (the date specified in the directive of July 16), and that no date could be determined until the Luftwaffe had achieved air supremacy over the Channel.[77]

On July 25 Raeder was again closeted with Hitler,* to report on the "state of preparations."[78] Raeder declared that "every effort is being made to complete preparations by the end of August," but described the prospect as "very uncertain." He indicated that it might be possible to "give a clear picture" the following week, and Hitler (who departed Berlin the next day) thereupon scheduled a conference for July 31 at the Berghof.

The Fuehrer spent the next three days receiving Rumanian, Bulgarian, and Hungarian emissaries *seriatim* at the Berghof, in order to lay the basis for his arbitration of the Bulgarian and Hungarian territorial claims against Rumania.[79] At OKH, OKL, and OKM, however, there was feverish activity, and this last week of July 1940 was the crucial period in the formulation of German military strategy for the ensuing months.

The most significant development was that the Army leaders finally discovered that their invasion plans were based on a completely erroneous conception of the Navy's capabilities. During the evening of July 28 OKH received a memorandum from the Naval War Staff which, as Halder put it, "upsets all draft plans for the Channel crossing."[80] Under the naval estimates it would have taken ten days to put the first assault wave ashore, on a landing front much narrower than the spread which the Army had envisaged as essential to success. The next morning Brauchitsch and Halder reviewed the situation, and agreed that "we cannot carry through our part of the operation on the basis of the resources furnished by the Navy."[81]

Within the Naval War Staff the outlook was even more pessimistic. In a document prepared for Raeder's guidance at the forthcoming Berghof conference, the staff warned that the Navy would be unable to protect the crossing area against attacks by the Royal Navy, and concluded that they "must advise against undertaking the operation this year." Raeder noted his "full agreement," and his chief of staff,

---

* Keitel and Jodl were also there, as well as Dr. Fritz Todt, head of the Ministry of Armaments and Munitions and the Organisation Todt, whose presence was probably connected with the program, discussed at the conference, for the construction of heavy gun emplacements at the Straits of Dover.

Schniewind, expressed grave doubt that an invasion would ever be practicable.[82]

In the meantime the Luftwaffe had completed its redeployment for the air assault, and OKL was drawing up the tactical plans. Disagreement arose between OKL and the commanders (Sperrle and Kesselring) of the two *Luftflotten* that were to carry out the attack, and the resulting delay aroused considerable impatience at the Berghof. On July 30 Hitler sent Goering a brusque message, directing him to put his forces in immediate readiness to begin "the great battle of the Luftwaffe against England" on twelve hours' notice.[83]

Shortly before noon on July 31 Raeder, Brauchitsch, and Halder arrived at the Berghof. Keitel and Jodl were also present, but, as was customary during this period, there was no representative of the Luftwaffe. The Fuehrer, who had been lording it over Balkan diplomats, was in an expansive mood, and the records kept by Raeder and Halder[84] yield a detailed and vivid account of what was perhaps the most remarkable German military conference of the entire war.

It began with Raeder's report on Sea Lion. Preparations were "in full swing," but the barges and other necessary shipping could not be assembled in the Channel harbors until early September, and therefore "15 September, 1940, is the earliest date which can be fixed for the crossing." However, the Army's demand for a landing on a wide front could not be met, and there were other points of disagreement. In view of all the difficulties and dangers, Raeder recommended postponement of the invasion until the following spring: "The best time for the operation, all things considered, would be May 1941."

Hitler scrutinized this proposal courteously but critically. Would not the British Army be much stronger next spring? Would not the weather hazards be just as serious? Would not British naval superiority remain overwhelming? And what other effective action against England, apart from air warfare, could be undertaken in the meantime?

The answers to these questions led Hitler to conclude that "things will become more difficult with the passage of time." Therefore, preparations should be continued for an invasion attempt in the middle of September. The air attack was to be commenced at once, and its results would soon indicate whether or not the crossing should be undertaken: "If we have the impression that the British are crumbling and that the effects will soon begin to tell, we shall proceed to the attack." Otherwise, Sea Lion would be postponed until the following spring.

Raeder then left the meeting, and the remaining participants turned to other matters. The conclusions with respect to Sea Lion were embodied in an OKW directive issued the next day.[85] Its essential points were that preparations were to continue and be completed by September 15, that the air offensive would begin about August 5, that eight to fourteen days thereafter the Fuehrer would "decide whether or not the invasion will take place this year," and that if the decision was against undertaking the operation in September, preparations would continue, "but not to the extent of damaging our economy through the tying up of our inland shipping system."

The decision to launch the air offensive was embodied in a new Fuehrer directive (No. 17), "for the Conduct of Air and Naval Warfare against Britain," also issued on August 1.[86] Its announced purpose was "to establish conditions favorable to the conquest of Britain," by means of intensified air and naval warfare. To this end, the Luftwaffe was ordered "to overcome the British Air Force with all means at its disposal and in the shortest possible time." Once local air superiority was attained, the bombers were to concentrate on British harbors, except those on the southern coast that might be needed for Sea Lion. The assault was to be launched on August 5 or as soon thereafter as the weather might permit.

In execution of the Fuehrer's directive, Goering promptly issued his own basic order to the Luftwaffe setting forth the objectives and governing tactical principles for the air assault, to which he gave the cover name *Adler* ("Eagle").[87] Bad weather caused its postponement to August 13. Thereafter the "Blitz" in the broad sense lasted until the following spring, but the Battle of Britain—the crucial contest between the Luftwaffe and the Royal Air Force—reached its peak in late August and early September. With the approach of fall it became apparent that the Germans could not achieve strategic air superiority, and that Sea Lion, the preparations for which approached completion in the middle of September, would not be undertaken.

Thus, for the latter part of the summer of 1940, German military operations against Britain were governed by the two directives of August 1. For the direct assault and speedy overthrow of the archenemy, it was the Eagle and, perhaps, the Sea Lion. The evolution of this strategy was curious indeed. There never was a considered decision by the high command that the air attack should be launched, and neither Hitler nor the Army and Navy chiefs entered into its planning. Instead, they spent many hours weighing the pros and cons and ways

and means of Sea Lion without benefit of consultation with Goering
or his aides, albeit everyone was relying on the Luftwaffe to establish
the conditions which might make Sea Lion a worth-while venture.
Surely one would have to search far for a more striking example of
shoddy and superficial decision-making on crucial strategic issues.

Berlin to London via Moscow

Conferring at the Berghof on July 13 with Brauchitsch and Halder,[88]
Hitler had diagnosed Britain's puzzling obstinacy as based upon her
"hope in Russia." This passing reference was the first recorded mani-
festation of the trend of thought which was to lead to the invasion
of the Soviet Union a year later.

The matter next arose, in much more specific form, at the Fuehrer's
conference in Berlin on July 21, in the presence of Brauchitsch and
perhaps Jeschonnek.* After the invasion of Britain and several lesser
problems had been canvassed, Hitler announced that:[89]

"Stalin is flirting with Britain to keep her in the war and tie us down,
with a view to gain time and take what he wants, knowing he could not
get it once peace breaks out. He has an interest in not letting Germany
become strong, but there are no indications of any Russian aggressiveness against us."

Despite the lack of any such "indications," Hitler declared, "Our
attention must be turned to tackling the Russian problem. Thoughtful
preparations must be made." A start had already been made for, as
Halder's diary next records:

The Fuehrer is informed—

a) German assembly will take at least 4–6 weeks.

b) Object is to crush Russian Army or slice as much Russian territory as is
necessary to bar enemy air raids on Berlin and Silesian industries. It is
desirable to penetrate far enough to enable the Luftwaffe to smash
Russia's strategic areas.

c) Political aims: Ukrainian State, Federation of Baltic States, White
Russia—Finland. The Baltic area is a thorn in the flesh.

* Raeder was at the meeting, but appears to have departed before the Russian
question arose, as the naval records of the discussion contained no reference to this
subject. The only record of the discussion of Russia is contained in Halder's diary
entry, based on Brauchitsch's oral summary on the following day. This does not
indicate who if anyone, other than Brauchitsch, was with Hitler at the time.

d) Necessary strength 80–100 divisions. The Russians have 50 to 75 good divisions. If we attack Russia this fall, the pressure of the air war against England will be relieved. America can supply both Britain and Russia.

e) Operation: What operational objective can we attain? What strength have we available? Timing and assembly area? Operational gateways: Baltic area, Finland, Ukraine. Protect Berlin and Silesian industrial area. Protect Rumanian oil fields.

This otherwise enlightening entry has several puzzling features. Despite the first few words, much of it—especially the political paragraph—reads more like the Fuehrer's ruminations than information presented to him. As for the military portion, there is no indication whether it embodies information brought to Hitler by Brauchitsch, or whether someone else had given it to Hitler before the meeting. In all probability, however, Brauchitsch came to the meeting equipped with some sort of preliminary memorandum, prepared in response to Hitler's earlier request.*

During the next ten days, Halder consulted with several officers of OKH, and on July 29 Generalmajor Erich Marcks was called in from the field to undertake a special staff study for an invasion of Russia.† The following evening Brauchitsch and Halder had a private conversation[90] about the strategy that should be adopted in the event that "we cannot conduct a successful operation against the British Isles this fall," and they agreed that the Mediterranean would then be the decisive theater and that "we should keep on friendly terms with Russia," a conclusion in line with the strategic outlook of the German General Staff ever since the time of von Seeckt.[91]

The Fuehrer, however, was of a different opinion, and had been pursuing the Russian question at Berchtesgaden with Jodl.[92] At the Berghof conference of July 31, after Raeder had made his report on Sea Lion and had departed,[93] Hitler announced his "skepticism" concerning the "technical feasibility" of invading Britain, and then held forth on the general strategic situation:[94]

---

* The available records do not indicate that Hitler had as yet raised the question of Russia with Keitel or anyone else at OKW, and he would hardly have turned to OKL or OKM for such information. Following the meeting on July 21, Halder's staff promptly went to work on preliminary plans for an invasion of Russia. See also Halder's diary entry for July 18, in which he noted that Koestring, the military attaché in Moscow, "has carried out his mission regarding Russia."

† Marcks was then chief of staff of the 18th Army, which had been transferred to the eastern frontier earlier that month.

In the event that the invasion [of Britain] does not take place, our action must be directed to eliminate all factors that let England hope for a change in the situation. To all intents and purposes the war is won. France has stepped out of the setup protecting British convoys. Italy is pinning down British forces.

Submarine and air warfare may bring about a final decision, but this may be one or two years off.

Britain's hope lies in Russia and the United States. If Russia drops out of the picture America, too, is lost for Britain, because elimination of Russia would tremendously increase *Japan's power* in the Far East.

Russia is the Far Eastern sword of Britain and the United States, pointed at Japan. Here an evil wind is blowing for Britain. Japan, like Russia, has her program which she wants to carry through before the end of the war.

Russia is the factor on which Britain is relying the most. Something must have happened in London.

The British were completely down; now they have perked up again. Intercepted telephone conversations. Russia is painfully shaken by the swift development of the Western European situation.

All that Russia has to do is to hint that she does not care to have a strong Germany, and the British will take hope, like one about to sink, that the situation will undergo a radical change in six or eight months.

With Russia smashed, Britain's last hope would be shattered. Germany will then be master of Europe and the Balkans.

Decision: Russia's destruction must therefore be made a part of this struggle. Spring '41.

The sooner Russia is crushed the better. Attack achieves its purpose only if Russian State can be shattered to its roots with one blow. Holding part of the country alone will not do. Standing still for the following month would be perilous. So it is better to wait a little longer, but with the resolute determination to eliminate Russia. This is necessary also because of contiguity on the Baltic. It would be awkward to have another major power there. If we start in May '41, we would have five months to finish the job. Tackling it this year would have been still better, but unified action would be impossible at this time.

Object is destruction of Russian manpower. . . .

Ultimately: Ukraine, White Russia, Baltic States to us. Finland extended to the White Sea . . .

The conversation then turned to the military aspects. The Army, which had just been reduced in size, would now be increased to 180 divisions. Of these, 120 would be used for the Russian assault, while fifty-three would remain in France and the Low Countries and seven in Norway. Deceptive rumors would be spread to conceal the true intentions, and the eastern deployment would be carried out "in areas safe from aerial incursions."

Thus the conference of July 31 resulted not only in the basic orders

for the operations immediately in prospect against Britain, but also in
the outline of a longer-term strategy based on the destruction of the
Soviet state. At OKW, Jodl's staff promptly went to work on deployment plans under the cover name *Aufbau Ost* ("Eastern Construction"),
and at OKH, on August 5,[95] Generalmajor Marcks submitted to Halder
the first comprehensive plan of attack.[96]

These orders and decisions at the beginning of August marked the
end of the course of strategic decision within the German high command during the crucial summer of 1940. Nevertheless, the relation between the western and eastern programs remained unresolved. As
articulated by Hitler on July 31, *Aufbau Ost* was a fall-back strategy,
contingent on the failure or abandonment of Eagle and Sea Lion. In
consonance with this conception, nothing was done or ordered at the
time which would make the decision to attack Russia irrevocable; there
would still be ample time for a change of mind.

But *Aufbau Ost* was a reincarnation of the old *Drang nach Osten* of
imperial times, and far more in harmony with Hitler's own predilections
as revealed in *Mein Kampf*. Is it possible that in his mind Eagle and
Sea Lion were secondary operations—speculative ventures in the nature
of time-killers, pending the maturation of the eastern plans and
preparations?

On such basic strategic issues Hitler was unstable and indecisive,
and quite possibly he never faced up to this one in his own mind. In
any event, it is from his reactions to events and developments that his
inner motives can best be gauged. As of July 31, he formally committed
the Wehrmacht to a strategy of direct assault against the British homeland. It took about seven weeks—the rest of that fateful summer—for
the failure of this strategy to become apparent, and it is to the course
of events during those weeks that we now turn.

PART II

The Battle
of Britain

CHAPTER THREE

The Opposing Forces

"**N**EVER IN THE FIELD of human conflict was so much owed by so many to so few," said Winston Churchill in the House of Commons on August 20, 1940, as the Battle of Britain approached its climax. His famous and eloquent tribute to the fighter pilots of the Royal Air Force was well-deserved, for their success in blunting, deflecting, and eventually repelling the Luftwaffe's assault was the true turning point of World War II. It changed what Hitler had hoped would be a short war into a long one, to the demands of which the Third Reich was unequal.

However, the popular conception of the Battle of Britain at the time it was waged—a conception which has survived in the memory of those days—is inaccurate in important respects. It is commonly supposed that a heavily outnumbered Royal Air Force, by sheer gallantry and skill, achieved a well-nigh miraculous victory.[1] Gallantry and skill there were, in abundance. Nevertheless, the disparity in numbers was not nearly as great as has been commonly supposed, and the repulse of the Luftwaffe was no miracle, but the logical consequence of its shortcomings in weapons and leadership.

The persistence of these misapprehensions is due, in part, to the failure of military historians to present the Battle adequately from the German standpoint. For the British, the story is one of inspiring success at a moment of dire peril, and not unnaturally most of the English accounts have reflected primarily the viewpoint of the defenders, though a few of them give revealing glimpses of the other side. For the Germans the Battle is no such source of pride, and their works on the subject are generally superficial, or too narrow and personal. It is more

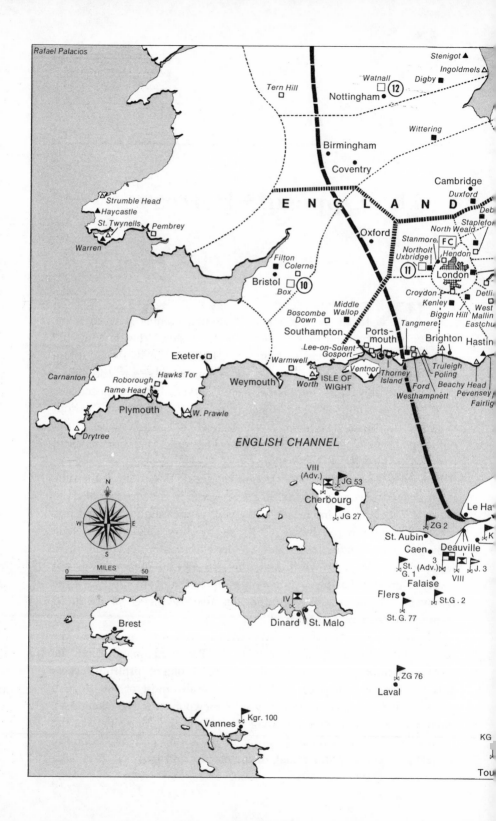

Rafael Palacios

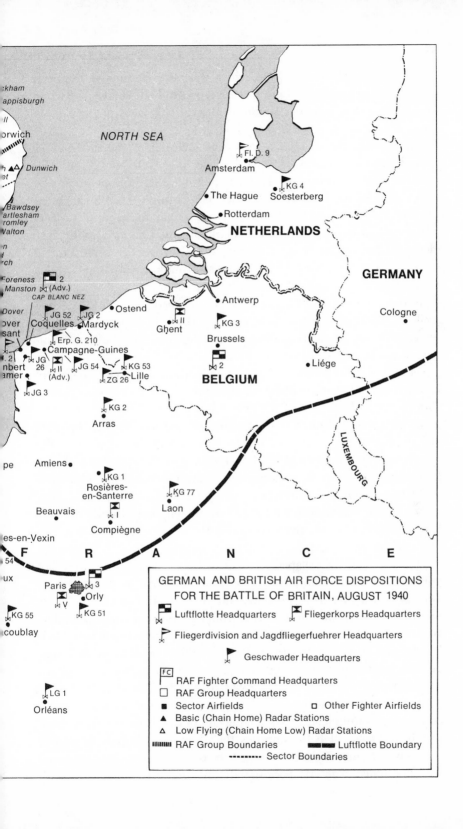

NORTH SEA

ckham
appisburgh
II
orwich
h △△ Dunwich
et
Bawdsey
artlesham
romley
Valton
n
rch

Foreness ▪ 2
Manston ⚐ (Adv.)
CAP BLANC NEZ

Dover
over
sant

F R A N C E

Fl. D. 9
Amsterdam

KG 4
The Hague   Soesterberg

Rotterdam

NETHERLANDS

GERMANY

Antwerp

Cologne

JG 52 JG 2   Ostend
Coquelles Mardyck   II
 Erp. G. 210   Ghent
Campagne-Guines
    KG 3
2 JG   JG 54   KG 53
nbert 26   II   ZG 26 Lille
amer   (Adv.)

Brussels

JG 3   2   Liége

KG 2
Arras   **BELGIUM**

pe   Amiens

KG 1
Rosières-
en-Santerre   KG 77

Beauvais   Laon

es-en-Vexin

54

ux
Paris   3
    V   Orly
KG 55   KG 51

coublay

LG 1
Orléans

LUXEMBOURG

GERMAN AND BRITISH AIR FORCE DISPOSITIONS
FOR THE BATTLE OF BRITAIN, AUGUST 1940

Luftflotte Headquarters   Fliegerkorps Headquarters

Fliegerdivision and Jagdfliegerfuehrer Headquarters

Geschwader Headquarters

FC RAF Fighter Command Headquarters
□ RAF Group Headquarters
▪ Sector Airfields   □ Other Fighter Airfields
▲ Basic (Chain Home) Radar Stations
△ Low Flying (Chain Home Low) Radar Stations
▥▥▥ RAF Group Boundaries   ▬▬▬ Luftflotte Boundary
-------- Sector Boundaries

than a little ironic that Sea Lion, which was never attempted, has been comprehensively examined in excellent works in both languages,[2] while the decisive and dramatic Battle of Britain still lacks a comparable account focused on those who initiated it.[3]

The German air assault known to the attackers as the *Adlerangriff* ("Eagle attack") was the first large-scale use of air power for independent strategic purposes. Again, it is ironic that the operation was undertaken by an air force which had not been designed or intended for long-range, heavy bombardment, but rather for tactical support of the ground forces. Even more remarkable, the Commander-in-Chief of the Luftwaffe, Hermann Goering, seems to have been only dimly aware of this mismating of structure and purpose, and some of his close advisers were no more perceptive than their chief.

As the experience of World War II was to demonstrate, effective strategic bombing, in the then state of the art, required adequate forces of heavy bombers and long-range fighters. The Luftwaffe embarked on the Battle of Britain with neither.

Yet, in historical perspective, Germany's failure to develop the heavy bomber, or fighters of sufficient range to protect them, is not surprising. The theory and practice of air power in the period between the two great wars were both in a state of confusion and uncertainty. Novelists and dramatists had portrayed the frightfulness of the air raids of the future, and the theories of Giulio Douhet and William Mitchell obtained wide currency in military circles.[4] But the technical and tactical problems of strategic air warfare were little explored and less understood, and of all the major military powers only two, Britain and the United States, took the necessary steps for the development of an air arm capable of independent strategic employment at long range.

Thus the men who shaped the Luftwaffe, if shortsighted, were not uniquely so. Neither in France nor in Russia, nor in Japan, nor in Douhet's own homeland of Italy, did the air arm attain the range or striking power that his theories would require for their execution. In France and Russia, as in Germany, the military mind was landlocked, and air power was treated as an adjunct or, at most, as a supporting partner of the ground forces. Except for a greater emphasis on naval air operations, the same was true in Japan and Italy.[5]

Even in Britain and the United States, where events took a different course, the requirements of strategic air power were far from completely foreseen. In both countries the ability of bombers to protect themselves against fighters was greatly overestimated, and the need for long-range fighters correspondingly underestimated. In both countries, and in Britain especially, the accuracy of bomb-aiming at night, in bad weather, and under combat conditions, and the destructive effect of a given weight of bombs, were grossly overestimated. In both cases those misapprehensions required basic changes in tactics during the course of operations.

In both Britain and the United States, however, a basic decision was made during the thirties to create a large force of four-engined bombers capable of carrying heavy bombloads for great distances. The fruits were our Boeing B-17 "Flying Fortresses" and B-24 Consolidated "Liberators," and the RAF Stirlings, Halifaxes, and Lancasters that carried out the great raids over Germany during the last three years of the war.

In Britain, the specifications and plans for the heavy bombers were initially settled on in 1935 and 1936.[6] At that time, under the stimulus of Oberst Wilhelm Wimmer and the first Chief of the Luftwaffe General Staff, General Walther Wever, the Junkers and Dornier aircraft firms were developing a four-engined bomber ("Uralbomber") for the Luftwaffe. But Wever's death in an airplane crash in June 1936 stilled the heavy bomber's strongest advocate, and in April 1937, on the recommendation of Wever's successor, General Albert Kesselring, Goering ordered the developmental work stopped.[7] Later on there were second thoughts and frantic scratching for a suitable four-engined-bomber design, but nothing satisfactory was achieved.[*]

The Luftwaffe entered the war, and remained throughout its course, a force of dive bombers, twin-engined medium bombers, short-range fighters, and assorted transport and reconnaissance aircraft. Nevertheless, in 1940 it was the strongest air force in existence, and the English Channel was only a few flying minutes wide. Across that narrow barrier, the RAF had mustered defensive resources of which the Germans were only partly aware, and the effectiveness of which they greatly underestimated.

The RAF and Fighter Command

The basic advantages which the Royal Air Force[8] enjoyed were maturity and professionalism. It had been established as an independent

---

[*] What price "independence"? An air arm capable of strategic operations was developed in the United States, where the air forces remained part of the Army throughout the war, but was never achieved in Germany, where the Luftwaffe was not only independent organizationally (as was the RAF), but was headed by the ranking officer of the Wehrmacht and second man in the political hierarchy of the Third Reich, Hermann Goering.

arm during the last year of the First World War, so that by the time of the Second it had attained its majority, and its officer corps spanned a generation. In its early years it was at times slighted by the senior services, but in the long run it profited by the patent facts that insular, tightly packed Britain was highly vulnerable to air attack, and that, given her limited manpower, the air likewise offered the most promising means of counterattack against a Continental foe. From these twin realities were born the RAF's two major components, Fighter Command and Bomber Command.

These had both come into existence in 1936, in the course of a general reorganization of the RAF. The commanders-in-chief of these and the other major components* reported directly to the high command of the RAF: the Air Staff, composed of a Chief, a Vice-Chief, and a half-dozen service members, each in charge of a department (personnel, training, supply, research, etc.). Chief of the Air Staff from 1937 to late October 1940, when he reached retirement age, was Marshal of the Royal Air Force Sir Cyril L. N. Newall.

Newall was succeeded by Air Chief Marshal Sir Charles F. A. Portal, who had been the head of Bomber Command since April of 1940.† At the time of the Battle of Britain, Bomber Command disposed of some five hundred aircraft—mostly twin-engined Hampdens, Wellingtons, and Whitleys with performance comparable to that of the German bombers, Blenheims that were faster but inferior in range and load, and some obsolete single-engined Fairey Battles. The heavy four-engined bombers planned in 1936 were now in production, but did not become available for operations until the spring of 1941. In 1940 Bomber Command's night raids over Germany did, upon occasion, influence German operations over England; in general, however, British bombers played a negligible role in the Battle of Britain itself.

For present purposes, accordingly, the key component of the RAF was Fighter Command, established on July 14, 1936, with headquarters at Bentley Priory near Stanmore, on the northwestern side of London. Its first commander (with the title Air Officer Commanding-in-Chief, Fighter Command) was Air Chief Marshal Sir Hugh C. T. Dowding,

---

* Coastal Command and Training Command were also established in 1936, and other home commands less important for present purposes were established in later years. Overseas commands were established in India and the Middle East in 1939, and elsewhere as the war went on. There was also the Fleet Air Arm, which was part of the Royal Navy, not of the RAF.

† Portal had previously been a member of the Air Staff. He was succeeded at Bomber Command by Air Marshal Sir Richard Peirse.

who held that post throughout the crucial period of the Battle and until November 25, 1940. Dowding, fifty-four years old when he took command, was a highly respected career officer who had been the member of the Air Staff for research and development; his unquestioned technical and command competence was not matched by inspirational personal qualities, and an exceedingly reserved manner had drawn upon him the nickname "Stuffy."

Under Fighter Command were four group headquarters, each covering a large geographical area: No. 10 Group in southwest England, No. 11 in the southeast, No. 12 in the Midlands, and No. 13 in the north.* During the Battle, No. 11 was the "hot corner" and bore the brunt of the engagement. Its headquarters were at Uxbridge, just west of London, and its commander was Air Vice-Marshal Keith Rodney Park, a New Zealander and former senior staff officer (the equivalent of a chief of staff) under Dowding at Stanmore. Dowding and Park, therefore, were the commanders most closely involved in and responsible for the direction of Fighter Command's operations during the Battle.

The groups were subdivided into sectors, each under a sector commander. The sectors were the vitals of the fighter-control system, for, once Group had ordered aircraft into the air, Sector handled the radio control of their movements and undertook their direction toward the enemy. In No. 11 Group there were seven sector stations, each bearing a name famous at the time: Northolt west of London and near Uxbridge, and the other six between London and the enemy—from south to north, Tangmere near Portsmouth; Kenley, Biggin Hill, Hornchurch and North Weald around the eastern rim of London; and Debden to the northeast, south of Cambridge.

For the planes themselves, the basic unit was the squadron, which in Fighter Command comprised (if up to strength) sixteen aircraft, of which twelve fought as a unit and four were in reserve. Lying as it did around London and within range of the German fighters deployed in the Pas-de-Calais, No. 11 Group was made the strongest of the four, with twenty-one squadrons.†

Sometimes two or more squadrons were combined and operated as a "wing." This was often so in the case of No. 12 Group, inasmuch as

---

* The lower-numbered groups were in Bomber Command, and the higher-numbered in Coastal and other commands.

† Two of these, however, were equipped with Blenheims—2-engined light bombers converted for fighting—which were used chiefly as night fighters.

the commander, Air Vice-Marshal Trafford Leigh-Mallory, favored the tactical employment of fighter aircraft in large formations. His group comprised fourteen squadrons deployed in six sectors of which the southernmost, with headquarters at Duxford (between Debden and Cambridge), was frequently involved in the Battle. On to the north, the rest of England and Scotland were the preserve of No. 13 Group (Air Vice-Marshal R. E. Saul) with twelve squadrons in six sectors. Newest and smallest was No. 10 (Air Vice-Marshal Sir Quintin Brand) in southwestern England, composed of eight and a half squadrons in four sectors. *

Except for the handful of squadrons equipped with Blenheims and Defiants, Fighter Command was armed with up-to-date aircraft of excellent performance for those times. The basic specifications had been drawn in 1934, and the results were the Hawker Hurricane and the Supermarine Spitfire. The prototype of the Hurricane was flown in November 1935 and that of the Spitfire six months later. In 1936 the Air Ministry adopted a production schedule calling for the delivery of six hundred Hurricanes and three hundred Spitfires by March 1939, and in fact these quantities were achieved in the fall of 1939, shortly after the outbreak of the war.[9] At the beginning of the Battle of Britain, about thirty squadrons were equipped with Hurricanes and nineteen with Spitfires.

The four fighter groups were the principal but by no means the only component of Fighter Command. It included Balloon Command (Nos. 30 to 34 Groups, with about 1,500 balloons for barrages over London and other heavily defended locations) and the Observer Corps, and Dowding, as head of the air defense system, also was given operational control (though not technical command) over General Sir Frederick Pile's Anti-Aircraft Command, with (at the time of the Battle) some 1,300 heavy and 700 light guns.

Perhaps more important than balloons, observers and guns was Fighter Command's No. 60 Group, comprising the fifty-odd stations of the radar chain. These were the product of barely five years of intensive research and development carried on under the aegis of the Committee for the Scientific Survey of Air Defense, established in January 1935, largely in consequence of war games which had shown that "enemy"

---

* Among the squadrons of Groups No. 10, 12, and 13 were four of Blenheims, two of Defiants (a 2-man fighter which proved unsatisfactory and was soon relegated to night fighting), and a flight (half a squadron) of obsolete Gladiator biplanes stationed near Plymouth.

bombers were able to penetrate the island's defenses. The committee, under the chairmanship of Mr. Henry T. Tizard (chairman of the Aeronautical Research Committee), included eminent scientists such as Professors Percy Blackett and A. V. Hill, and the Air Ministry's director of scientific research, Mr. H. E. Wimperis.

Immediately upon its formation the committee consulted Mr. Robert A. Watson-Watt (superintendent of the Radio Department of the National Physical Laboratory) on the possibility of destroying or damaging approaching aircraft by means of electromagnetic radiation, analogous to the "death rays" of comic strips.[10] Watson-Watt threw cold water on that idea, but, drawing on his expertise in the reflection of radio waves by the ionosphere, suggested their use to detect and locate approaching aircraft. On February 26, 1935, Watson-Watt demonstrated the theory of his proposal by displaying on an oscillograph the "echoes" from an aircraft flying a predetermined course overhead. Dowding (then the Air Staff member for research and development) was greatly impressed, and he authorized the construction of an experimental station on the Suffolk coast.

Progress was rapid, and in 1937 it was decided to erect twenty stations along the eastern and southern coasts. Each station required a 250-foot mast, easily visible from a considerable distance, and to conceal the true purpose of the installations they were called RDF ("radio direction-finding") stations; the American term *radar* ("radio direction and ranging") did not come into general use until 1943.

The twenty stations rimming Britain from Cornwall to the Orkneys were called CH ("chain home") stations, and they gave good "visibility" for upwards of fifty miles, except against low or very high aircraft. The risk from low-flying attacks led to the erection of supplemental CHL ("chain home low-flying") stations, of which about thirty were operating by the summer of 1940. Mobile radar stations had also been developed to mitigate the risk from damage to the fixed installations. By the time of the Battle many of the problems of plotting, identification, and communication had been at least partially solved, and the radar chain was ready to play a crucial role in the defense of Britain.*

* On Sept. 3, 1940, as Neville Chamberlain concluded his radio address announcing a state of war with Germany, London had its first air alert. It turned out to be a false alarm, for which the radar chain was responsible. Alarmed by the failure, Watson-Watt carefully investigated the cause. It was learned that the alert had been caused by an approaching private aircraft, unaccounted for by flight plan and unresponsive to the IFF (identification friend or foe) system, which carried a French assistant air attaché who had been on a weekend social trip to Le Touquet.[11]

It might fairly be said that the basic outlines of the RAF as it emerged early in the war had been established by decisions made between 1934 and 1936. Those years saw the basic decision to expand the RAF, made in July 1934; the specifications for the four-engined heavy bombers; and the specifications and initial production of the Hurricanes and Spitfires that fought the Battle and of the light, fast Mosquito bombers that came into service in 1940 and were to prove so versatile and valuable a craft throughout the war; the invention and initial development of the radar chain that eliminated the expensive necessity of standing air patrols and enabled Fighter Command to engage the Luftwaffe before it reached its targets; and the reorganization of the RAF in 1936 that established the unified, functional commands.

At the ministerial level, one important change was made by Churchill when he took office as prime minister in May 1940.[12] This was the withdrawal of production from the Air Ministry's functions, and the establishment of a new Ministry of Aircraft Production under Lord Max Beaverbrook. Top priority was at once given to the production of Hurricanes and Spitfires, and (pending availability of the four-engined heavies) of the proven medium-bomber types. Beaverbrook's drive and ingenuity had a most stimulating effect on aircraft production during the crucial summer and fall of 1940.

Organizationally, the RAF was simple and functional. At Bentley Priory, Dowding had under his command or operational control all the fighters and supporting defensive resources; Bomber Command had all the bombers; both commands were directly responsible to the Air Staff. This simplicity was, to be sure, fostered by Britain's insularity and defensive posture. From British fields fighters would rise to fend off the enemy, and bombers to carry the war to the heart of Germany; the home commands were, for the moment, all-important. When overseas air commands were established, different principles came into play, in order to serve purposes more akin to those for which the Luftwaffe had been designed.

The Luftwaffe: Organization

The Luftwaffe's organization reflected the function for which it was primarily intended: not for home defense nor for launching strategic attacks from fixed home bases, but for tactical support of large and mobile ground forces.[13] This required corresponding mobility on the part of the associated air forces, and led to an organizational system in the traditional Army pattern—the smaller units established on a functional basis with a single type of aircraft, and the higher headquarters commanding a mixture of units and types.

The basic Luftwaffe unit, roughly comparable to the British squadron, but slightly smaller, was the *Staffel,* comprising ten to a dozen aircraft of the same type—fighters, dive bombers, or others as the case might be. The *Staffel* often flew as a formation of ten, with three *Ketten* of three aircraft each, led by the *Staffelkapitaen.*

Three *Staffeln* comprised a *Gruppe,* which approximated a British wing and, at full establishment, would have thirty-nine aircraft.* Three *Gruppen,* in turn, constituted a *Geschwader*—literally, a squadron—the largest homogeneous aircraft unit of the Luftwaffe. Nominally, the *Geschwader* had 120 aircraft,† but under the erosion of combat operations there were rarely as many as a hundred, and during the course of the Battle of Britain there were often as few as eighty.

Gruppen and even *Staffeln* could and did operate independently from widely separated airfields, but during the Battle they were closely concentrated. Administratively, the *Geschwader* headquarters remained the parent even if its components were scattered, except for reconnaissance aircraft and a few other types that were organized in *Gruppen* but not in *Geschwader.*

Each *Geschwader* bore the designation of the type of aircraft of which it was composed. The level-flight bombers, mostly twin-engined Heinkel 111s and Dornier 17s, were in *Kampfgeschwader* (KG). The Junkers-87 dive bombers formed *Sturzkampfgeschwader* (St.G), hence the common appellation "Stuka." The single-engined fighters, virtually all Messerschmitt 109s, comprised the *Jagdgeschwader* (JG), and the twin-engined Messerschmitt 110s were called "destroyers" and, accordingly, *Zerstorergeschwader* (ZG).‡ Many of the *Geschwader* had honorary designations: JG 2 was "Richthofen," JG 26 "Schlageter," KG 1 "Hindenburg," KG 53 "Legion Condor," ZG 26 "Horst Wessel," St.G 2 "Immelmann," and so on.

From the *Geschwader* the upward chain of command normally ran to the *Fliegerkorps,* supposed to include *Geschwader* of different types

---

* Twelve in each of the three *Staffeln* and an additional *Kette* constituting the staff (*Stab*) aircraft of the *Gruppenkommandeur.*
† Thirty-nine planes in each of the 3 *Gruppen,* and the staff *Kette* of the *Geschwaderkommodore.*
‡ There were also *Transportgeschwader* of 3-engined Junkers 52s, and special units of other types, such as night fighters—*Nachtjagdgeschwader.*

and therefore to be able to carry out the various missions of the air arm. During the Battle of Britain there were six *Fliegerkorps* (numbered I, II, IV, V, VIII, and IX*) on the Channel coast, and one (X) in Scandinavia. Although the *Fliegerkorps* was supposed to be a "general" headquarters, in practice some of them became specialized; Fliegerkorps VIII, for example, was almost exclusively composed of *Stukageschwader*, and Fliegerkorps IX specialized in mine laying and other aspects of marine aviation.

Above the *Fliegerkorps* were the Luftwaffe's highest field headquarters, the *Luftflotten* (air fleets). In peacetime there had been four; a fifth was added in Norway in April 1940, in the course of the German conquest of that country. During the Battle of Britain, Luftflotte 1 and Luftflotte 4 remained at their home stations (Berlin and Vienna), virtually stripped of aircraft; the Battle was waged by Luftflotte 2 and Luftflotte 3.

When supporting ground operations, each *Fliegerkorps* would normally be associated with an army, and each *Luftflotte* with one or more army groups, and the fighters and the bombers would be committed as the tactical situation required. The *Adlerangriff*, however, was to be an independent Luftwaffe operation largely carried out from fixed bases along or behind the Channel and North Sea coasts. In these respects the undertaking was more like those for which the RAF home commands were organized, but there was one significant difference, and that was the prospect of joint fighter and bomber operations on a large scale. As long as the RAF defended the island with fighters by day and attacked the Germans on the Continent with bombers by night, there was little need for Fighter and Bomber Commands to work together. But the *Adlerangriff* envisaged daylight bomber attacks under fighter escort, and the consequent need for closely co-ordinated tactics of flight and maneuver. This would require not only good liaison between the KG pilots and commanders and their JG opposites, but also some means of ensuring that the fruits of experience would be passed around in the form of general directives, so that, for example, all the fighter pilots would observe the practices found most effective for protection of the bombers.

For this last purpose, another level of command was established

* These headquarters were originally called *Fliegerdivisionen,* and at the start of the Battle this one was still called Fliegerdivision 9; it was upgraded to Fliegerkorps IX in October 1940. There were no Fliegerkorps numbered III, VI, or VII. Fliegerdivision 7 comprised the parachute and air-landing forces; in 1941 it was upgraded and became Fliegerkorps XI.

over the *Jagdgeschwader* called a *Jagdfliegerfuehrer* (fighter-aircraft leader), abbreviated to *Jafue*. The *Jafue* was to exercise tactical control over all the JGs and be operationally responsible to *Luftflotte* headquarters, but for administration and discipline he was subordinated to a *Fliegerkorps*. Thus the *Jafue* served two masters, and, although the idea of unified fighter command was good, the addition of still another headquarters intermediate between *Geschwader* and *Luftflotte* did nothing to simplify an already complicated situation. In practice, the *Fliegerkorps* tended to become, in an operational sense, a bomber headquarters.

Under the *Luftflotten*, the Luftwaffe's organization was bifurcated, with the combat units under the *Fliegerkorps*, and the ground organization—supply, transport, airfield construction and administration, and all the other noncombat functions*—under the *Luftgaue*, or air districts. The Reich itself was divided into ten such districts, roughly comparable to the *Wehrkreise* (military districts) of German Army home organization, and new ones were created in the various occupied countries. Each *Luftgau* was subordinated to the *Luftflotte* covering its area, and the three established in the Low Countries and northwestern France were thus directly involved in the Battle of Britain.

In Britain, the antiaircraft artillery was put under Fighter Command's control, but remained part of the Army; in Germany, at Goering's insistence and much to the Army's displeasure, the *Flakartillerie*† became part of the Luftwaffe upon its official establishment in 1935. It was organized like Army artillery units in batteries and regiments, and then grouped in still larger units under divisional and corps headquarters. During the Battle of France there were two Flak corps headquarters, one under each of the two *Luftflotten* in the west.

The complexity of the Luftwaffe's field organization, as compared to the RAF, is apparent. Nor were things any simpler at the apex of the pyramid, where the leadership of the Luftwaffe was focused.

The Luftwaffe: Command and Staff

Unlike the RAF, with its Air Staff of career officers, the Luftwaffe was a one-man show. Whatever his faults, and they were many and grave,

---

* Upon occasion, defensive operational units were subordinated to a *Luftgau*.
† The well-known abbreviation "Flak" is derived from *Flugabwehrkanone*—antiaircraft gun.

it was Hermann Goering's ambition, energy, prestige, and unquestioned if spasmodically utilized ability that accounted for the establishment of the Luftwaffe as an independent branch of the Wehrmacht and attracted to its service the men who helped him shape it. He was often indolent or occupied with other matters, but his decisions, when made, were not subject to challenge within the Luftwaffe. In administrative or tactical affairs Hitler never interfered, and, except on matters of major strategic or diplomatic significance, he left Goering free to handle his branch as he saw fit. As will be seen, this autonomy was a very mixed blessing from the standpoint of the Wehrmacht as a whole.

The War Ministry (*Reichskriegsministerium*, successor to the old Defense Ministry of Weimar days) had been abolished when Hitler assumed personal command of the Wehrmacht in February 1938 and established OKW as his staff for the exercise of supreme command. But Goering had clung to the *Reichsluftfahrtministerium* (State Air Travel Ministry, abbreviated RLM), which had been established for him in 1933, before the denunciation of the Versailles Treaty and the unveiling of the Luftwaffe two years later. Accordingly the Luftwaffe, unlike the Army and the Navy, was based on a civilian ministry, and its top organization reflected this complication.

Thus Goering, in his air capacity, wore two hats. He was the Commander-in-Chief of the Luftwaffe (Oberbefehlshaber der Luftwaffe, abbreviated Ob.d.L.) and in this capacity responsible to Hitler at OKW as Commander-in-Chief of the Wehrmacht. But as Reich Minister for Air (RLM) he was responsible to Hitler as Reich Chancellor and head of the civil government.*

A more important consequence was the division of Goering's staff in two parts. Within the RLM remained the basic supporting departments of the Luftwaffe staff—design, procurement, research, training, air defense, and signal communications, to mention the more important. The General Staff of the Luftwaffe, created in 1936 and separated from the RLM in 1939 (largely in order to give it mobility in the event of war), contained the staff sections directly concerned with military operations, and it soon took on the character of a personal operations staff for Goering as Commander-in-Chief.

Shortly before the war, the General Staff moved out of the RLM

---

* It may be that Goering preserved the RLM in order to have an official channel to Hitler that did not go through OKW; on the other hand, he had numerous other such channels in his multiple capacities, so perhaps the reasons may have been administrative rather than personal, or simple inertia.

building in Berlin and established its own headquarters at Wildpark, near Potsdam. Since Goering spent much of his time in Berlin or nearby at his Karinhall estate, command of the Luftwaffe was exercised from the Berlin area during a large part of the Battle. Goering also had a forward headquarters on a special armored railroad train designated "Robinson," and from time to time he and the principal General Staff officers visited the combat units near the coast or his old friend General Friedrich Christiansen, the Wehrmacht commander in occupied Holland. In September of 1940 Goering took "Robinson" to a location near Beauvais, where it remained until the spring of 1941.[14]

"Robinson" and the Wildpark headquarters corresponded roughly to the supreme Army and Navy headquarters, OKH and OKM. Later in the war the Luftwaffe General Staff headquarters became known as OKL, and I will so refer to it hereafter.* Its internal organization was not unlike that of the Army General Staff, with staff sections for operations, intelligence, and training, and a Quartermaster-General responsible for logistics.

Hermann Goering's credentials as a promoter were far more impressive than as Commander-in-Chief. Make it possible for others to build an air force he could, but he was quite unqualified to shape or lead it. As a flyer in the First World War he had shown bravery and leadership capacity,† and he continued to fly professionally in the lean years that followed. But he was hopelessly passé on technical and tactical matters, and lacked the character and judgment for effective delegation of his powers. He set a very bad example for his staff, and often frustrated their efforts to lay the groundwork for considered decisions. Lacking both time and patience for detailed operation analyses or intelligence estimates, he hated to be contradicted, especially with unwelcome information. His frequent preoccupation with political matters, aggravated by irresponsible and self-indulgent personal habits, destroyed the sequence and logic of Luftwaffe policy, which all too often was determined by impulse, emotion, or wishful thinking.

Second man in the Luftwaffe, and the only one other than Goering who straddled the top of RLM and OKL, was Generalfeldmarschall

---

* Officially, the designation OKL (Oberkommando der Luftwaffe) was not applied until 1944; up to then the official designation was simply "Ob.d.L.," for "Oberbefehlshaber der Luftwaffe" (Commander-in-Chief of the Air Force).

† Goering stood 46th on the list of First World War German "aces," credited with 22 victories. In July 1918 he was appointed commander of Geschwader No. 1, the famous "Flying Circus" that Manfred von Richthofen had led until his death in April 1918.

Erhard Milch, who was *Staatsekretaer*° in the RLM, Inspector General of the Luftwaffe, and deputy to Goering as Commander-in-Chief. Milch had been an airman in the First World War and had then gone into civil aviation. He became managing director of Lufthansa, and likewise a friend of Goering's and closely connected with the Nazi Party. Although he came to the Luftwaffe on Goering's invitation, Milch had other contacts in the upper reaches of the Third Reich. He was an able, ruthless administrator and, unlike Goering, was capable of sustained concentration, but he was by no means expert in military aviation, and was egocentric to a degree that his colleagues and subordinates found painful and often intolerable.

Milch had as much to do as anyone with shaping the Luftwaffe that fought the Battle and the Blitz, but not much connection with its leadership in the field.† Primary responsibility here lay with the Chief of the Luftwaffe General Staff, the young (born in 1900) General der Flieger Hans Jeschonnek. Barely old enough to have flown a little at the end of the First World War, Jeschonnek then went into the Reichswehr as a cavalryman, discharged staff duties with distinction, and in 1933 was one of the group of Army officers with flying experience who were transferred to the RLM as the nucleus of an officer corps for the Luftwaffe-to-be. He found great favor with his seniors, and in February 1939, his older predecessors Kesselring and Stumpff having found it impossible to get along with Milch, Goering appointed him Chief of Staff at the age of thirty-nine, with the rank of *Oberst*. Rapid advancement continued, and Jeschonnek was made *General der Flieger* on the big Reichstag promotion day, July 19, 1940. His ability was undeniable, but he was primarily interested in tactical air support of ground forces, and knew little of independent strategic operations. He was a devoted supporter of Hitler and Nazism, and this worship, coupled with his youth, greatly restricted his inclination and ability to challenge Goering's methods or decisions.

In the RLM was one other major figure—Generaloberst Ernst Udet, in charge of design and procurement of aircraft, with the resounding title "Generalluftzeugmeister." A war hero‡ and stunt flyer with a real

---

° In German official nomenclature the principal subordinate of a Cabinet minister, equivalent to an undersecretary.

† At the time of the invasion of Denmark and Norway, Milch left his desk at RLM and spent a few weeks as the commander of the newly created Luftflotte 5, comprising the air units in those countries.

‡ Udet was second only to Manfred von Richthofen among the World War I aces, with 62 victories to Richthofen's eighty.

gift for design, Udet was a wit and *bon vivant* with no stomach for
intrigue, and was utterly lacking in the hardness, precision, and
capacity for in-fighting which should have characterized the incumbent
of his position. As might be expected from a fighter pilot and aerial
acrobat, Udet was keen on speed and maneuverability and fascinated
with dive-bombing, but was out of his element in long-range bombing
and transport problems.

Goering, Milch, and Udet shaped the Luftwaffe, Goering and
Jeschonnek led it into the Battle, and the records of these four men
are eloquent indications of its leadership weaknesses. Not one of the
four was a truly professional military aviator; Goering and Udet were
both touched with dilettantism; in Udet's case the weakness was ami-
able, but that did not weigh in the scales of battle.

To be sure, a number of Army officers senior to Jeschonnek were
brought into the Luftwaffe—men like Kesselring, Sperrle, Stumpff,
Wever (killed in 1936), Felmy, Wolfram von Richthofen (younger
cousin of Manfred), and Grauert. Some of them had had flying experience in the First World War, others none. Many of them had real
ability and staff experience, and they gave the Luftwaffe the elements
of a professional military structure. But they too (with a few exceptions,
such as Wever) tended to think of the Luftwaffe as aerial artillery
supporting the Army, and slighted its strategic potential.

Throughout the Luftwaffe officer corps, the Army men were mixed
with others of whom Udet was the prototype—so-called "old eagles"
(*alten Adler*) from the First World War who stayed in aviation as
barnstormers, stunters, company executives, advisers to foreign governments, or in other capacities. Gifted as many of them were, they found
it difficult to satisfy the disciplines and meet the demands of military
service, and they were often temperamentally at odds with their colleagues who had made careers in the Army.

In a sense, the true professionals of the Luftwaffe were the officer
cadets of 1933 to 1935, with five years or more of training under
their belts and combat experience in Spain, Poland, or France. From
their ranks emerged the leading "aces" of the Battle of Britain, and
some, who displayed ability beyond the gymnastics of air combat, soon
rose to important command or staff assignments. But they were too
young and inexperienced in high-command problems to make much of
a contribution to the Battle's generalship.

And so, despite the conscientious efforts of the abler officers transferred from the Army, the Luftwaffe's staff work was often slipshod

and hasty; the intelligence sections were especially weak.[15] A persistent odor of amateurishness pervaded the entire establishment, and this is hardly surprising, for the officer corps of the Luftwaffe was, in the large, an aggregation of "retreads," hastily converted ground soldiers, and youngsters.

Some Comparisons

There are so many ways of measuring the effective strength of an air force, or the comparative strengths of two or more air forces, that tabular presentations may be dangerously misleading. Aircraft are of no use without the crews to fly them, or if their quality is so poor or so unsuited to the task in hand that they are unable to damage the enemy. Planes which are used for training or other nonoperational purposes, or are under repair or sitting in supply depots or factories awaiting delivery, are of no use for immediate operational requirements. But if all the aircraft and crews are assigned to combat units, there will be no means of training new crews, and neither planes nor pilots will be in reserve to replace those lost in operations. And even if the immediate reserves are adequate, an air force will be a rapidly wasting asset unless it is supported by an industrial establishment capable of turning out planes in sufficient volume to cover losses, and new equipment to meet new needs.

Likewise, in any contest between two reasonably well-matched air forces, many elements other than the number and the quality of planes and crews will count heavily. These will include geographical factors, the caliber of staff work, strength of the ground defenses such as radar and antiaircraft artillery, and the morale of the civilian population, to mention only a few.

Finally, an air force may or may not be able to invest its entire strength in a given operation. In the Battle of Britain, for example, the British decided not to undertake bombing attacks under fighter cover against German airfields and other targets, and thus were able to utilize their entire fighter force for defense against German attacks. But the Germans were obliged to hold back some of their fighters from the fray, for defense against Bomber Command's unescorted raids and to guard against the possibility of escorted attacks. Some eighty-five fighter aircraft were based in Norway[16] and a larger number in the Reich itself (particularly in the northwestern section from the Ruhr to

Berlin) for defensive purposes, and of course these played no part in the Battle of Britain.

It is important to bear all these qualifications in mind in assaying the comparative strengths of Luftwaffe and RAF as they squared off against each other in August 1940. Thus it has been said that on August 1, 1940, the Luftwaffe had a strength of 4,549 first-line aircraft, as compared with 2,913 for the RAF.[17] In a literal sense these figures are accurate enough,[18] but each included many aircraft that were not or could not have been engaged in the Battle of Britain, such as transport, liaison, and short-range reconnaissance planes.

For all practical purposes, the Luftwaffe aircraft used in the Battle were those of Luftflotten 2, 3 and 5, the combined strength of which has often been given as 3,500 planes.[19] But this figure can be supported, if at all, only by using "establishment" rather than serviceable aircraft on hand as the basis of the calculation. Since the number of serviceable planes on any given day varies according to recent combat and other operational loss or damage, mechanical failures, and other factors, it is fallacious to attempt an exact specification. Early in August the effective strength of the three *Luftflotten* lay in the range between 2,400 and 2,600 aircraft.[20]

As for the RAF, on August 7 Fighter Command and Bomber Command had some 1,200 aircraft on their operational fields.[21] It would be neat and easy to say, therefore, that the odds in favor of the Luftwaffe were about two to one. But in fact the problem is not so simple, and a true assessment requires a breakdown by aircraft types, as well as consideration of reserves and aircraft production.

For bombing the British airfields, air-armaments plants, and other installations, the Germans relied principally on their level-flight two-engined bombers (Dornier 17s, Heinkel 111s, and Junkers 88s), of which the three *Luftflotten* could muster nearly a thousand. In addition, there were some three hundred single-engined dive bombers ("Stukas," all Junkers 87s), which were slow, short-ranged, and so vulnerable to fighter attack that they were soon withdrawn from the Battle. A few twin-engined "destroyers" (Messerschmitt 110s) were also used as "fighter-bombers." These 1,300-odd planes—soon to be fewer than a thousand, after the withdrawal of the Stukas—were the Luftwaffe's Sunday punch.

To escort the bombers and to destroy the RAF in the air, the two *Luftflotten* on the Channel coast disposed of about eight hundred single-engined pursuit planes, all Messerschmitt 109s. They were excellent fighters, but their effective radius of action was so short that they could cover only the southeastern corner of England and were quite useless for operations from Norway or Denmark, where Luftflotte 5 was based. The longer-ranged fighter was the Messerschmitt 110, of which there were over 250 distributed among the three *Luftflotten*.[22] The aircraft was a disappointment; too heavy and unmaneuverable, it was soon found unsatisfactory as a daytime escort plane and was relegated to night-fighter and light-bomber employment.

Of the RAF's planes available for the Battle, some five hundred were bombers. Their normal mission would have been to attack the Luftwaffe's airfields along the Channel and the aircraft industrial plants in the Reich—to do exactly what the German bombers were undertaking in Britain. Bomber Command attempted to do just this, but it was soon found that daylight raids were suicidal without fighter escort, and there were no fighters to spare for such tasks.

Throughout July and August, the British bombers continued to peck away at the German airfields and factories at night or out of heavy cloud cover by day, but little damage was done.[23] It is probably fair to say that the damage inflicted by Bomber Command played no substantial part in the Battle of Britain, though the noise of its raids on Berlin did, as we shall see, have a surprising and highly significant effect on the Luftwaffe's own operations.[24] The British Air Ministry's decision not to undertake escorted raids against the German airfields was certainly necessary under the circumstances, but the consequence was that Fighter Command had to operate from fields that were under attack against an enemy whose own fields were virtually undisturbed.

The crucial component of the RAF during the Battle was, of course, Fighter Command. Apart from a few squadrons of second-line aircraft, on August 8 there were some forty-six squadrons with a normal strength of over eight hundred Hurricanes and Spitfires and an actual operating strength of something over six hundred serviceable aircraft with crews.[25] The greater part of these were Hurricanes, which were not quite so fast as either the Spitfire or the Messerschmitt 109, but were sturdy, steady planes with (for those times) great fire power.[26]

Eliminating the British bombers and the German dive bombers and twin-engined "destroyers"—none of which proved able to participate effectively—the Battle of Britain, in its essential elements, became a contest between the seven-hundred-odd aircraft and supporting installations of Fighter Command, and the Luftwaffe's thousand bombers and eight hundred single-engined fighters. Once again it is tempting to say—as it has been said[27]—that the RAF faced odds of at least two to one. But in terms of fighter power the antagonists were not far apart.

Indeed, if one looks behind the front-line fighter strengths, the British were in the stronger position. Goering shared Hitler's predilection for the quick victory by a knockout blow. In line with its chief's propensity, the Luftwaffe put most of its strength into the operational units and held very little in reserve.[28] The British policy was much more conservative; on August 11, for example, there were 289 Hurricanes and Spitfires—over a third of Fighter Command's operational strength —available for issue as replacement aircraft.[29]

The reserve cushion reflected the even more important fact that by the summer of 1940 British aircraft production was averaging some 1,600 aircraft a month, or double the German rate. Five hundred Hurricanes and Spitfires were being turned out each month, as compared with an output of 140 Messerschmitt 109s and 90 Messerschmitt 110s in Germany.[30] Furthermore, the British trend was upward, with new types of aircraft, including the four-engined heavy bombers, soon to be available, while the German production, both in quantity and quality, was virtually static.

In terms of aircraft, therefore, the British were much the better equipped for a protracted struggle and continuing losses. But their situation with respect to pilots was far less favorable. Nearly three hundred fighter pilots had been lost during the Battle of France,[31] and early in July Fighter Command faced a deficiency of nearly two hundred pilots out of 1,450 in its authorized establishment. A month later, on the eve of the main Battle, there was still a deficiency of 160 pilots, and the flow of trained replacements was only about fifty per week.[32] This rate was less than half that at which their aircraft were being produced, and was plainly insufficient to make good the losses that sustained, heavy combat would entail.

The Germans were in a much better situation; more than ten thousand pilots had come out of the flying schools in 1939, and during the first two years of the war there was no shortage of recruits.[33] Yet training, however rigorous, was no substitute for operational experience, and the Luftwaffe suffered painful losses among its best pilots and crews, which seriously affected its performance in the air as the Battle wore on.

For the conservation of both aircraft and aviators, the British enjoyed the great advantage of fighting over their own territory. The RAF fighters could stay aloft in the combat zone much longer than their German opponents, who had to use more than half of their flying time crossing and recrossing the Channel. A damaged Hurricane or Spitfire could make an emergency landing in short order; a German plane in similar straits was lost unless it could survive the return flight across the Channel. RAF pilots who parachuted safely or walked away from a crash landing might fly again in a few hours, while the Germans became prisoners.*

The Luftwaffe, however, had the great advantage of initiative. Its leaders could choose the time and place of attack, and if the British reaction was too slow the German bombers would reach their targets unopposed. Therefore early detection of the German formations and a correct anticipation of their line of flight were all-important.

Fortunately for the British, they were far ahead of the Germans in the development and use of radar. By 1940, as we have seen, the east and south coasts of England and Scotland were pretty well covered, and the necessary communications had been installed so that Fighter Command could make immediate use of their observations. The Germans had a few radar scanners (known as "Freya" and "Wuerzburg") along the North Sea and Channel coasts, but they had not devised any jamming or other effective countermeasures against the British chain.[34] It is not too much to say that lacking these stations the RAF would have been fighing more than half blind, and the Battle might have had a very different outcome.

The scope of the Luftwaffe's initiative was much restricted by its lack of an effective long-range escort plane. The Messerschmitt 110 had been intended for this purpose; had it been a success, German bombers could have launched daylight attacks en masse anywhere in the United Kingdom and thus forced a comparable diffusion of Fighter Command's forces. But the 110 itself needed escort and was quite unable to protect the bombers. Consequently, the daytime attacks could be undertaken only within the Messerschmitt 109's radius of action, which was about 125 miles. Penetration by day much beyond London was thus impossible, and most of the fighting took place over the city and the neighboring counties of Surrey, Essex, and Kent, where the RAF's defenses were concentrated.[35]

---

* Airmen who ditched their planes in the Channel or the North Sea, or parachuted into the water, were fished out by the air-sea rescue units. The Germans were much better organized for this task, but the advantage was small compared to the factors favoring the British in the fighting over their own homeland.

In terms of the skill and morale of the pilots and crews, there was probably little to choose between the two forces. The German pilots had had a year or more of basic military and flying training;[36] some of them had flown in Spain, and many of them in Poland or Norway or during the Battle of France. On the average they were more experienced than their opponents, but this advantage wore off rapidly in the course of battle. On both sides there were bravery and determination in abundance; beyond doubt, however, the "few" were stimulated and inspired by their homeland's desperate need, even more than were their opponents by ambition, pride, or devotion to their Fuehrer's cause.

There remains the vital factor of command. It is another of the ironies of the Battle of Britain that Germany, the storied land of military prestige and expertise, entered the fray with an air arm led by amateurs, whereas the British, who muddle through and lose every battle but the last, had an air force the leadership of which, as we have seen, was highly professional.

It is true that professionalism, military or otherwise, carries its own hazards and disadvantages. Especially in a military career service, invention and imagination may be smothered under bureaucratic rigidity and a stifling technical conservatism. The German Army itself was afflicted with some of these ills, which especially plagued Heinz Guderian and his colleagues in the development of new methods of mechanized warfare. The senior levels of the RAF have been sharply criticized for their slowness in recognizing the shift from wood-and-fabric biplanes to metal monoplanes, and held responsible for the consequent and dangerous delays in production of the Hurricane, Spitfire, Mosquito, and other successful RAF aircraft of those times.*

But neither is inexperience a guarantee of imaginativeness, and if military professionalism is internally competitive and principled, it generally pays high dividends. The principal commanders and higher staff officers had made their careers in the RAF; they were experienced, energetic, and steadfast. And if their tactical problems were grave and difficult, there was no problem of choice of strategies. Their mission was to stay in business and keep Britain in business—to survive the onslaught of the heavier Luftwaffe, and to blunt the attack sufficiently for the basic economy of Britain to continue to function. War production was rising rapidly, heavy bombers would soon be available for retaliation, and accordingly the leaders of the "few" could reasonably

* Such criticism is cogently expressed in David Divine's recent work *The Broken Wing—A Study in the British Exercise of Air Power* (London: Hutchinson & Co., 1966), *e.g.* pp. 174–98.

expect that, if the initial assault could be withstood, the peril would diminish with time.

It was in the quality of its leadership that the Luftwaffe's inferiority to the RAF was most marked. Staff and command alike lacked the homogeneity and sheer professionalism of the RAF; in this sense the restrictions of the Treaty of Versailles had accomplished their purpose. If Goering and all his men had been as conscientious and devoted as their British opponents, still the Germans could not in six years have made up for the loss of the nearly fifteen years after 1919, during which military aviation in Germany was at a virtual* standstill.

Of the three western *Luftflotten* commanders, for example, only Sperrle had had any air experience before transferring from the Army to the Luftwaffe after Hitler came to power; even Sperrle, who had flown in the First World War, had served in routine Army assignments during the Weimar years. Indeed, none of the Luftwaffe's senior officers had had an uninterrupted career in military aviation. Despite these handicaps, some of them—Richthofen, Grauert, Coeler, and a number of the staff officers—had achieved a high degree of professional competence. But through the higher circles of the Luftwaffe, the indelible streak of amateurishness was coupled with an ugly taint of favoritism.

Had Goering been a better commander, some of these defects might have been less glaring. At the higher levels, the trouble was not so much that things were done wrong as that they were not done at all. Opportunities and obstacles alike were overlooked for lack of care and imagination. *Adlerangriff's* strategic aim remained foggy and shifting, and thus tactics became the master rather than the servant of strategy. Goering was unable to put matters right and unwilling to delegate his authority.

It is interesting to speculate on the probable consequences if Adolf Hitler had taken personal charge of *Adlerangriff,* as he did of the Norwegian and French campaigns. Probably the operation would have been much more carefully planned and its aims more clearly defined. But after the Battle was joined, Hitler's participation might have been more of a hindrance than a help, for twice already the Fuehrer had shown a tendency to panic in the clutch of hazard or adversity.†

---

* Virtual but not total. Hidden air-staff sections and secret use of Russian air bases during the Weimar period helped to bridge the gap, as did civil aviation.[37]

† During the Norwegian campaign, when Dietl's forces were cut off at Narvik, and during the Battle of France soon after the breakthrough on the Meuse, when Hitler sought to slow down the armored troops' advance toward the coast, because he feared a French counterattack from the south.[38]

However that might have worked out, in fact Hitler was present neither in flesh nor in spirit. Except for occasional visits to Berlin, the Fuehrer remained at the Berghof, where he weighed the chances for and against *Seeloewe*, carved pieces off Rumania for the benefit of Bulgaria and Hungary, and fixed his sights on Russia. Goering came to none of his military conferences, and Hitler did not go near OKL.

According to Goering,[39] Hitler understood nothing of air tactics and "could not think in the third dimension." Right he was; the Fuehrer was unable to grasp even the enormous folly of leaving the Luftwaffe in Goering's charge. Despite Hitler's deep concern with military matters generally, and his extraordinary capacity for absorbing detailed information, he took very little interest in aeronautical matters.[40] He even seems to have been somewhat hostile to the Luftwaffe officers; could it have been the resentment of an old *Frontschwein* against the cavaliers of the empyrean?

Hitler doubted, and with reason, that the Luftwaffe alone could bring Britain to the point of surrender;[41] that is why he toyed with *Seeloewe*. Yet he knew and repeatedly declared that *Seeloewe* could not prudently be launched unless the RAF had first been driven from the skies and Britain so far reduced that the invasion forces could not be strongly opposed. What chance was there that the Luftwaffe could bring things to this point? If the likelihood of such a sweeping success was not great, why should there be an *Adlerangriff*?

Such questions Hitler never faced. Except for the German Navy's pitifully few submarines, the Luftwaffe was the only weapon that could be used to strike England. The pigheaded British would not make peace, and Goering said that he could knock them about and bring them to their senses. Well and good, let him try. But there was no reason for the Fuehrer to be personally associated with a venture for which he had neither talent nor inclination, and in the success of which he felt no real confidence.

These, or something like these, must have been Hitler's thoughts about *Adlerangriff* as he looked down from his mountain retreat at a Europe that he dominated as no one had since Napoleon. The thoughts were in character, but they were not the thoughts of a Great Captain, for Hitler had neither selected a strategy that held good promise of success nor taken into account the cost of failure.

CHAPTER FOUR

Conception and Inception

N O CONTEMPORANEOUS RECORDS have come to light which set forth the reasons why Goering and his aides decided to forgo the creation of a long-range heavy-bomber force. Testifying at the Nuremberg trials, Goering assumed personal responsibility for the decision, which he said was based on lack of aluminum and of satisfactory designs.[1] Kesselring, who was Chief of Staff early in 1937, when the decision was made, gave much the same reasons, adding that at the time he and others in the Luftwaffe "had a low opinion of the four-engine bomber."[2] Milch, on the other hand, testified that the early designs were "technically perfect," and that their production was abandoned because Goering and Kesselring thought the heavy bombers too costly.[3] General Paul Deichmann, who in 1937 was chief of the Operations Section under Kesselring, has subsequently written an account putting the "blame" squarely on the shoulders of Milch.[4]

Despite the conflict of testimony, the governing considerations are readily inferrable: the death in 1936 of the heavy bombers' principal advocate, General Walther Wever; the preoccupation of Army-trained officers with air support of the ground forces, at the expense of strategic operations; the shortage of raw materials. Germany's resources were sharply strained in the prewar years, and a program for the construction of heavy bombers would have required large allocations of metals, rubber, and oil. Within the Luftwaffe, partisans of the dive bomber questioned the possibility of accurate bombing in level flight at high altitudes.

Had the possibility of long-range operations been foreseen, these obstacles might have been overcome. Goering, however, held fast to the view that war with Britain was both undesirable and unnecessary, and until 1939 nothing occurred to shake his assumption that Hitler would manage to avoid so dangerous an involvement. Like their Army colleagues, the Luftwaffe leaders thought in terms of Continental warfare, in which the air arm would work in co-operation with the ground forces.

True to this theory, during the prewar period the Luftwaffe General Staff developed no plans for taking the initiative against Britain by means of an air attack. In 1938, however, when Hitler began his expansionist policy in central Europe, the possibility of British intervention became a matter of real concern. This danger, to which the cover name *Fall Blau* ("Case Blue") was given,* precipitated the first Luftwaffe staff studies—"plans" would be too strong a word—of air warfare between Britain and Germany.

Prewar Studies: Fall Blau

The matter appears to have first arisen in February 1938, in the midst of the campaign of diplomatic pressure that led, the following month, to the absorption of Austria into the Reich. On February 18 the Chief of the Luftwaffe General Staff, General Hans-Juergen Stumpff, instructed the commander of Luftflotte 2, General Helmuth Felmy, to prepare air operational plans for use in the event of military intervention by Britain. Major emphasis was to be placed on raids on the factories in and near London and on the southeastern ports. The assignment of a staff duty of this sort to a field commander was unusual, but apparently Stumpff's staff was overburdened, and Felmy's air fleet, with its headquarters at Braunschweig, was nearest the Channel coast and would have been most heavily involved in case of hostilities.[5]

The tensions generated by the Anschluss were soon dissipated, and there is no record of Felmy's reply to the inquiry. Six months later, however, the burgeoning crisis over the Sudetenland led to a second and more urgent demand from Stumpff, transmitted to Felmy on August 23. Felmy replied on September 22, when Neville Chamberlain was conferring with Hitler at Bad Godesberg. As targets for his bombers, Felmy suggested factories at London and Kingston, and

---

* Using a color as the cover name was in line with prevailing staff practice—e.g., *Fall Rot* (the possibility of a French attack on the western frontier), *Fall Gruen* (the plan of attack against Czechoslovakia), *Fall Weiss* (Poland), and *Fall Gelb* (France and the Low Countries).

RAF ground installations in southeastern England. The Royal Navy, he observed, was the most important target, but probably the ships would be moved out of range. The tone of his memorandum was pessimistic. Lacking bases in the Low Countries, the Luftwaffe would have to operate from Germany, and the maximum range of German bombers with a half-ton load was only 425 miles. Under these circumstances, a war of annihilation à la Douhet would be impossible.*

These lugubrious pronouncements did not please Hermann Goering, who penned an angry note on Felmy's report:

I have not asked for a memorandum weighing the existing possibilities of success and pointing out our weaknesses; these things I myself know best of all. What I requested is information on the manner in which you expect to obtain maximum effect with the projected strengths, and what conditions you require for this purpose.

Felmy's loss of favor with Goering was permanent,† but the Munich settlement ended the Sudeten crisis, and for another six months the matter of air operations against England was quiescent. Then, in April 1939, Hitler issued the directive (*Fall Weiss*) for a plan of attack against Poland, shortly after the Anglo-French guaranty of assistance in the event of "any action which clearly threatened Polish independence." The danger of hostilities with Britain at once emerged, much more sharply than before. Early in May the new Chief of the Luftwaffe General Staff, Generalmajor Hans Jeschonnek, told Felmy that in such an event the mission of Luftflotte 2 would be to support Army operations in Holland and Belgium, and to attack England.

The result was a spate of staff studies and conferences. Felmy's staff held a "map exercise" to determine the technical requirements for air operations over Britain. On May 22 the Operations Section of OKL produced an estimate of the prospects, and concluded that Luftflotte 2 lacked the necessary strength for a decisive victory, since western and southwestern England would be out of range. Small attacks against armament factories might be feasible, but terror raids against London would be of doubtful value, and indeed might even stiffen

---

* These views were generally parallel with those expressed in a Luftwaffe General Staff memorandum of Aug. 25, which pointed out that in the event of British intervention the Luftwaffe would be unable to achieve an effective blockade, since it would be needed to support the Army in Czechoslovakia and, perhaps, to attack France.

† In January 1940 Goering seized upon the loss of a courier plane in Belgium to dismiss Felmy from the Luftwaffe. Kesselring replaced him in command of Luftflotte 2, and Felmy was retired to civil life. He was recalled to active duty in the east during the spring of 1941.[6]

British resistance. In July the intelligence officer of OKL, Oberst Josef Schmid, submitted a memorandum advising that Britain could not be defeated by air attack alone, and that for a decisive success an invasion would be necessary.*

Pessimism at OKL in 1939 did not have such disastrous consequences for its exponents as Felmy was to suffer for having expressed similar views the previous fall. Indeed, the Fuehrer himself was of a like mind. Addressing the military chiefs at the Reich Chancellery on May 23, 1939, Hitler declared that a country could not "be brought to defeat by an air force," and that victory over Britain would require a long war and "the unrestricted use of all resources."

Such were the intramural reflections of the Luftwaffe during the year preceding the war. If the French and British military leaders had rightly appreciated the jaundiced views on the other side of the hill, would they perhaps have stiffened Neville Chamberlain's spine at the time of Munich? It is a fascinating matter for speculation, since unquestionably it was fear of the Luftwaffe, above all, that pushed the British government toward appeasement and stimulated the shouts of "Good old Neville!" when Chamberlain returned from Munich bearing what he proclaimed as "peace for our time."

However that might have been, these prewar studies of Felmy, Schmid, and others go far to explain the dearth of aerial activity in the west during the first seven months of the war—the period of "phony" war. The Luftwaffe did not attack during these months because its leaders saw no prospect of decisive results.

After the defeat of Poland the bulk of the German Air Force was moved to the western front, under Felmy's Luftflotte 2 in the north and Sperrle's Luftflotte 3 in the south. But the Luftwaffe's mission remained purely defensive, except for mine laying and occasional attacks on British ships.[7] Except for one insignificant accident, not a single German bomb fell on British soil until June 5, 1940, just after the Dunkirk evacuation, when the great German victory was already assured and the fall of France was imminent.

The Unconsidered Decision

If the prewar views within the Luftwaffe were so conservative, and its operations against Britain during the early part of the war so limited

---

* This appears to be the earliest reference to invasion in the German records, but it was a purely hypothetical one.

and cautious, why was the Battle of Britain undertaken at all? The Luftwaffe was not significantly stronger in an absolute sense in the summer of 1940 than it had been in the fall of 1939. Indeed, the Royal Air Force was greatly strengthened during the quiet months of the *drôle de guerre,* so that in terms of comparative size the German position had worsened.

Now, in historical perspective, the most extraordinary thing about the Battle of Britain is that the German attack—the *Adlerangriff*—was not the product of deliberation. There appears to have been no staff study, no high-level conference at which the pros and cons were weighed.* In the crisp and categorical phrase of Lord Tedder,[8] the German air assault on Britain "was not a considered operation."

It is fair, I believe, to say that the Battle of Britain came about not by decision but by assumption. The assumption developed during the period from October 1939 to May 1940, and it is now possible to trace the circumstances from which it emerged.

The concepts which ultimately inspired the *Adlerangriff* were closely connected, in their origin, with Hitler's desire to launch an attack in the west in the fall of 1940, after the conquest of Poland. He was frustrated in that desire by a combination of circumstances—the weather, tactical difficulties, and the opposition of the Army generals.[9] But Hitler's vigorous efforts to force the issue, punctuated by bitter controversy with Brauchitsch, Halder, and others, involved close scrutiny of the strategic benefits which such an attack might secure, and it is in his directives and memoranda in October 1939 that the first suggestions of an air attack against Britain are to be found.

Hitler's first order for a western offensive was embodied in his Directive No. 6 for the Conduct of the War,[10] issued on October 9. Apart from the general purpose of inflicting a defeat on the Anglo-French armies, the more specific objective was to gain control of the Low Countries and northern France, in order to protect the Ruhr and obtain "a base for conducting a promising air and sea war against England." In a discursive memorandum circulated the same day,[11] Hitler enlarged on this theme. In the event of a long war, Germany's main weapon against England would be an air and sea blockade. However, as long as the Channel coast was in enemy or neutral hands, the Luftwaffe and the Navy would labor under extreme disadvantages, since their bases

---

* No records of such studies or conferences have come to light since the war, and none of the surviving participants has spoken or written of any such deliberation or reasoned decision.

would be too far from the target for effective operations. So far as the air was concerned:

> The Luftwaffe cannot succeed in efficient operations against the industrial center of England and her . . . ports . . . until it is no longer compelled to operate offensively from our present small North Sea coast, by extremely devious routes involving long flights. . . . If we come in possession of Holland, Belgium, or even the Straits of Dover as jumping-off bases for German aircraft, then, no doubt, Great Britain could be struck a mortal blow. . . .
> Such a shortening of routes would be all the more important to Germany because of our difficulties in fuel supply. Every 1,000 kilograms of fuel saved is not only an asset to our national economy, but means that 1,000 kilograms more of explosives can be carried in the aircraft. . . . And this also leads to economy in aircraft, in mechanical wear-and-tear of the machine, and above all in valuable airmen's lives. . . .
> . . . the destruction of the Anglo-French forces is the main objective, the attainment of which will offer suitable conditions for later and successful employment of the Luftwaffe. The brutal employment of the Luftwaffe against the heart of the British will-to-resist can and will follow at the proper time.

Hitler's analysis of the advantages was entirely correct; deployed along the Channel coast, the Luftwaffe would be in a far better position for operations against Britain. The question remained whether, given the size of the Luftwaffe and the range and capacity of its planes, the advantage gained would be *sufficient* to justify strategic air attack. In the fall of 1939, however, this issue did not have to be faced, for the Low Countries and France were not yet in German hands.

Thus the prospect of air warfare against England, in the event the Channel coast was reached, became a built-in part of the strategic concept on which the plan of attack in the West (*Fall Gelb*, as it was called) was based. In one important respect this purpose affected the scope of the offensive. The ground forces' tactical plan did not require an invasion of the Netherlands, except for the Maastricht appendix just north of Liège, and at the outset it was thought that perhaps that country could otherwise be left untouched. The Luftwaffe generals, however, feared that the British might then come into Holland, and in November the plan was modified so as to include the invasion and occupation of "as much Dutch territory as possible."[12]

As the autumn of 1939 passed and the western offensive was repeatedly postponed, the OKL apparently became restive under the strict limitations that Hitler had imposed on Luftwaffe activities. On November 22 the Operations Section of OKL submitted a memorandum on the possibility of attacking British military and economic targets, and suggested that this might cause the English to bring some of their aircraft in France back to the homeland. Six days later Goering went to the Fuehrer with a request that the Luftwaffe be given a freer hand for operations against England.[13] But Hitler would have none of the idea and forbade any change, at least until after the ground offensive had been launched. The next day he issued Directive No. 9 for the Conduct of the War,[14] in which he declared that an economic blockade was the most promising strategy for the defeat of Britain, and ordered the Luftwaffe and the Navy to prepare for "warfare against the economic structure of Britain," to be launched "as soon as the Army has succeeded in defeating the Anglo-French field army and in occupying and holding a part of the coast facing England."

Six months passed before the desired state of affairs was achieved, and during this time the Luftwaffe leaders were thoroughly occupied with plans for the Norwegian venture and for the western offensive itself. So far as appears from the available records, no further attention was paid to air operations against England until the last week of May 1940, after the Allied armies had been cut in two by Guderian's thrust to the coast at Abbeville.

Then, on May 24, Hitler issued his Directive No. 13,[15] in which a new note was struck. This directive was principally concerned with the destruction of the Allied forces encircled in Belgium and northern France, but it also called for a large-scale air attack against England "as soon as sufficient forces are available," to be initiated with "a crushing attack in retaliation for the British raids in the Ruhr area." Two days later, a supplemental OKW order specified the British aircraft industry as the primary target, the destruction of which would remove "the last potent weapon which could be employed directly against us."

The contrast between these orders and the directive (No. 9) of the previous November is most significant. The earlier directive had envisaged a sustained economic blockade, in which the Luftwaffe and the Navy would co-operate in sinking British ships, sealing off Britain's harbors, and destroying port installations and factories. This would have been strategic air and sea warfare, but not an all-out air assault against the British homeland.

In the May 1940 directives, on the other hand, the evident purpose is "crushing" retaliation for British raids, and prevention of their continuation by eliminating the enemy aircraft industry. This is a remarkable reflection of the uncertainty and sensitivity with which both sides regarded the prospect of bombing operations in heavily populated areas. The British had adopted the concept of strategic bombing and were rushing the construction of a large force of heavy bombers, but Bomber Command was restricted to leaflet raids throughout the "phony war," and even when the Germans launched the western offensive the British at first confined their attacks behind the German lines to bridges and railroad yards, hoping to check the flow of enemy troops and supplies. Only after the German bombing of Rotterdam on May 14 did the War Cabinet give Bomber Command permission to attack industrial targets in the Ruhr.

The result was a series of raids—the first on the night of May 15— directed chiefly against oil plants. Bomb loads were light, aim was poor, the attacks did only negligible damage, and the British soon realized that these early efforts were a failure.[16] But these were the first raids on the German homeland, and their remarkable psychological effect on Hitler is vividly reflected in the directive of May 24. It was issued just as the Battle of France approached its climax and when it was of the utmost strategic importance to exploit the Army's success and destroy the encircled Allied armies. Compared to these matters of the greatest consequence and portent, the paltry British raids on the Ruhr were utterly insignificant. Yet they were sufficient to divert Hitler's attention from the main battlefield and draw him into a snap decision that completely altered the nature and the purpose of future air operations against Britain. It was a behavior pattern which Hitler was to repeat a few months later,[17] with far more serious consequences for the Germans' fortunes.

The directive of May 24, impulsive and ill-considered as it was, embodied the decision that there should be a large-scale air attack against Britain, with strategic objectives transcending those of long-term economic blockade. Like the directives of October and November 1939, it was the product of Hitler's emotional and dialectical reaction to events or problems that were basically irrelevant to the issue of the Luftwaffe's capacity to conduct independent strategic operations. In the fall of 1939, improved opportunity for economic blockade was put forward as justification for a ground offensive which Hitler wished to launch, despite the opposition of the Army leaders. In May of 1940, the order for "crushing" retaliation resulted from annoyance and alarm generated by the British raids and, in all probability, from Goering's desire to assume a leading role in a war which had thus far been dominated by the Army. On neither occasion did these directives develop from staff studies or recommendations from within the Luftwaffe. The pessimistic studies by Felmy and Schmid were still in the files.

When the directive of May 24 was issued, occupation of the Channel coast by the German Army was a virtual certainty, and soon it would be possible to deploy the Luftwaffe at bases in Holland, Belgium, and northwestern France, only a few miles from Dover and less than thirty minutes' flying time from London. These were conditions far more favorable to the attackers than those which Felmy and Schmid had considered. Nevertheless, most of the United Kingdom still lay outside the Luftwaffe fighter planes' radius of effective action, and in a few days the air battles over Dunkirk would disclose the RAF as a most dangerous and determined antagonist.

Under these circumstances, did an all-out air assault by the Luftwaffe offer sufficient prospects of a major strategic success to justify the hazard of sacrificing the flower of its strength to no avail? So far as the records disclose, no one ever stopped to consider this crucial issue. The French were crushed, the British fleeing across the Channel. The Wehrmacht was in the full flush of triumph, and the Fuehrer had ordered the Luftwaffe to prepare for crushing retaliation against the British.

Who was to question his wisdom? Certainly not Hermann Goering or the Luftwaffe's young and impressionable Chief of Staff, Hans Jeschonnek, who was completely under Hitler's spell. Immediately after Dunkirk the Luftwaffe commenced a series of probing attacks along the southern coast of England, and the staff officers at OKL and the principal field commands began to draw up the plans and orders for the operation. When the fighting in France came to an end, OKL concentrated its attention on the redeployment of the Luftwaffe at its new bases along the Channel.

Thus the lines were drawn, and the Luftwaffe stumbled, enthusiastically but unthinkingly, into the first great air battle in history.

Terror Bombing and the "Freiburg Massacre"

In the light of the subsequent history of aerial warfare, it is noteworthy that none of the German directives and staff studies, prior to the Battle of Britain, envisaged concentrated bombing attacks on the residential sections of London or other British cities.* From this it should not be inferred that the writings of Douhet were unknown to or disregarded by the Luftwaffe staffs; on the contrary, General Wever and other officers of the newborn Luftwaffe were strongly influenced by his teachings.[18] But, as has been seen,[19] after Wever's death the German air arm followed a different course of development, with major emphasis on tactical bombing to support the advance of the ground forces.

Even in Britain and the United States—the only powers that were building heavy bombers in large numbers—the concept of "area" or "terror" bombing to destroy civilian morale was by no means dominant. It was recognized, of course, that high-level bombing attacks on factories, railroads, or docks in or near thickly settled areas would inevitably result in residential destruction and civilian casualties. But these consequences were widely regarded as the incidental and unfortunate concomitant of operations directed against the "material sources of military power," and in the United States "precision bombing by daylight" was the method to the perfection of which the American air generals directed their principal efforts.[20]

British Air Staff doctrine was ambivalent, and there was a strong school of thought that "the principal object of air forces was to create destruction" by bombing "towns and centers of production."[21] Nevertheless, the Air Ministry's prewar plans contemplated attacks aimed specifically at manufacturing and transportation resources, especially oil depots and refineries, rather than at populated areas in general.[22]

In June of 1940, when Goering and his aides set about their planning of the *Adlerangriff*, the theories of Douhet were still untested by practical application. The Japanese had heavily bombed Canton in 1938 and Chungking in 1939;[23] civilian casualties were high, but conditions in China were not such as Douhet had envisaged. Barcelona suffered heavily from air attacks during the Spanish Civil War, and the Condor Legion's raid on Guernica was widely condemned as an outrage. The famous German fighter ace Adolf Galland has described this episode as the accidental accomplishment of inexperienced air crews.†

---

* The expressions "crushing attack" and "retaliation" in the directive of May 24 might be read to imply such a threat, but the context makes it clear that aircraft factories and other industrial plants and port installations were to be the primary targets. Jodl's memorandum of June 30, 1940 (*supra*, p. 44), mentioned "terror attacks against English centers of population" as a means of breaking Britain's will to resist, and suggested that they be described as "reprisal actions."

† Galland, then a lieutenant, arrived in Spain shortly before the Guernica bombing. In his postwar book of memoirs he declares that the Condor Legion was under orders to spare civilians so far as possible, and that the destruction of the town "caused great depression among the members of the Legion."[24]

However that may be, the Spanish Civil War, despite its many other harbingers of the Second World War, shed no real light on the military efficacy of "area" bombing. Nor did the German raids on Warsaw and Rotterdam, which, though tragically destructive, were tactical operations in support of assault by ground forces.

The restraints which Hitler imposed on the Luftwaffe during the first year were primarily motivated by political considerations and were not based on a sound understanding of air power. Neither he nor Goering was sufficiently aware that their decision to forgo the construction of heavy bombers had left their air arm inadequately equipped for warfare of the type envisaged by Douhet against a well-defended country, much of which lay beyond the reach of the German fighter planes.

As events were soon to prove, neither Hitler nor the Luftwaffe leaders had any moral compunctions about terror bombing. Nevertheless, Hitler was well aware that whichever side first embarked on raids specifically directed against civilians would incur widespread condemnation. Accordingly he was alert to all opportunities to shift the blame for commencing so lethal a game, so that terror attacks by the Luftwaffe, should they be undertaken, would appear to be in retaliation for outrages already inflicted by the Allies on the cities of the Reich.

On the very first day of the German invasion of France and the Low Countries, such an opportunity arose. In southwest Germany, over the old university city of Freiburg-im-Breisgau, there was a heavy but broken cloud cover. Just before four o'clock in the afternoon of May 10 there came a roar of airplane engines and a hail of bombs over the airfield and near the railroad station. There had been no air-raid warning, and no one had time to take cover. The fifty-seven dead included twenty-two children and thirteen women; the wounded numbered over a hundred.

During the attack aircraft were seen overhead streaking through the clouds, but visibility was so poor and the onslaught so unexpected and brief that none of the inhabitants of the city could accurately estimate their number, much less identify their type or nationality. It was generally assumed that they were enemy and probably French, particularly since Freiburg, situated only fifteen miles from the French border on the Rhine, was one of the few German cities bombed during the First World War. Press and radio denounced the enemy raid on an open city, and the official OKW communiqué of May 11[25] reported it as an "enemy attack."

Nevertheless, there was something very strange about the affair. How had enemy planes so easily penetrated the German air defenses, and why was there no warning? The next day the responsible Army and air district commanders visited Freiburg to express their regrets to the city authorities. But neither General Friedrich Dollman of the 7th Army nor Generalleutnant Emil Zenetti of Luftgau VII offered any satisfactory explanation.

There was reason for the generals' reticence. An air warning unit stationed on the Lorettoberg overlooking Freiburg had had a good look at the planes as they approached from the south. On the underside of the wings the German Balkankreuz was plainly visible, and the watchers correctly identified the aircraft as three Heinkel-111 bombers. As they passed over Freiburg in V-formation, the bomb detonations in their wake were clustered near the railroad station.

The Lorettoberg unit promptly reported its observations through the proper channels. Luftgau VII immediately ordered an examination of the bomb fragments, and treatment of the results as strictly secret. The fragments proved to be of German origin, and within a few hours after the raid the chief of staff of Luftgau VII was satisfied that Freiburg had been hit with German bombs dropped from German planes. The following day the chief of staff of the 7th Army, Generalleutnant Walter Fischer von Weikersthal, reported to higher headquarters (Army Group C) that "investigation of the bomb fragments after yesterday's air attack disclosed that the bombs dropped were of German origin."[26]

In the meantime inquiries were also under way at the nearby Luftwaffe airfields, all of which lay within the area of General Hugo Sperrle's Luftflotte 3 and the next-lower headquarters, Fliegerkorps V, commanded by Generalleutnant Robert Ritter von Greim. His bombers were operating from various fields in southwestern Germany and, at the start of the western offensive, had the mission of attacking the French airfields on the other side of the Rhine. On the afternoon of May 10 about ten Heinkel 111s, forming part of Oberst Josef Kammhuber's* Kampfgeschwader 51, had taken off from the airfield at Landsberg to bomb the French air base at Dijon.

The formation, a *Staffel*,† rose through heavy clouds, and when they emerged the *Staffelkapitaen* noticed that a *Kette*—three aircraft—was missing. The remaining planes proceeded to attack Dijon and returned

---

* Future commander of the West German Luftwaffe.
† This particular unit was the 8th *Staffel* in the 3rd *Gruppe* of KG 51.

to Landsberg, to find that the missing *Kette* had come in some minutes earlier. The leader of the wandering *Kette*** explained that he had lost the rest of the formation in the clouds, and that he and the other two planes of his *Kette* had carried out the mission independently. Further questioning revealed, however, that the time between the bomb drop and his return to Landsberg was far too short to cover the distance between Dijon and Landsberg, but matched the flying time from Freiburg to Landsberg. The Landsberg planes had all carried 50-kilogram explosive bombs identical to those that were found in Freiburg. These had missed their intended target at Dijon by nearly 150 miles!

When Hitler was informed that Freiburg had been bombed, he immediately ordered Goering to investigate the circumstances. Goering soon suspected what proved to be the truth, and wondered aloud how such a thing could ever be explained to the German people. As the reports came in, however, a cloak of strict secrecy was laid over the affair. In the press and on the radio the Freiburg bombing continued to be described as a cowardly and wanton enemy attack on an open city, and in 1943 Joseph Goebbels dubbed it the *"Kindermord in Freiburg."* So successful was this mendacious propaganda that a distinguished British military historian, Major General J. F. C. Fuller, was led to write in 1949 that Freiburg was bombed by the Royal Air Force, and that "there can be little doubt that the bombing of Freiburg and the subsequent attacks on German cities pushed him [Hitler] into his assault on Britain."[27] This, of course, was precisely the inference that Hitler and Goering wished to be drawn.

There is a striking parallel between the bombing of Freiburg and the sinking of the British passenger liner *Athenia* on the very first day of the war at sea.[28] In both cases the Germans were responsible, and both catastrophes were due to errors of identification, caused by inexperience and the excitement and confusion accompanying the opening of an offensive. In both cases the facts soon became known to the German authorities, but Nazi propaganda continued to belabor the enemy with false accusations.

The truth about the *Athenia* was publicly revealed soon after the end of the war, but the myth of Allied responsibility for the bombing of Freiburg lasted for years longer, despite the many senior officers who knew all or a good part of the truth. Ugly rumors began to circu-

---

* The available records refer to the errant leader (*Kettenfuehrer*) as "Leutnant S.," and state that he was lost in an attack on the harbor of Portsmouth in August 1940.

late as early as 1946,* but not until 1956 was the matter finally and publicly resolved.[30] The legend of Allied responsibility dies hard, and was given renewed currency in a book published in the United States as late as 1960.[31]

The suppression of the truth about the Freiburg bombing was motivated in part by Goering's desire to avoid the necessity of confessing so tragic and humiliating an error. But he and Hitler had another and more important purpose in their repeated charges that it was an enemy raid on an open city—the very purpose that led some to suspect that the Heinkels had attacked Freiburg not by accident, but under orders. The Nazi chiefs wished, as has already been indicated, to fasten on the Allies the guilt for starting the terror bombing of urban areas.

All the resources of the Reich Propaganda Ministry were at once mobilized to exploit the opportunity. "This is not war, this is murder!" thundered the press. On May 11 Hans Fritzsche, in his radio commentary for foreign transmission, spoke of French aircraft, but soon the blame was shifted to the Royal Air Force. Lord Haw Haw referred to "this perfectly substantiated atrocity," and the German propaganda organ in New York City denounced the "Allied raid" and cited the American Red Cross representative Wayne Chatfield Taylor as a witness to the slaughter.[32]

Then the Fuehrer himself spoke, using the Freiburg bombing as a focal point of his address in the Reichstag on July 19, 1940. Mr. Churchill, he declared, had embarked on "air raids on the civil population, although under the pretense that the raids are directed against so-called military objectives." However: "Since the bombardment of Freiburg, these objectives are open towns, market places and villages, burning houses, hospitals, schools, kindergartens and whatever else may come their way. Until now I have ordered hardly any reprisals, but that does not mean that this is, or will be, my only reply."[33]

The threatened "reply" came in less than two months, when the

---

* General Franz Halder, the former Chief of the Army General Staff, was the source of a story, first publicized in 1946,[29] that Freiburg had been bombed by German planes under secret orders from Hitler, who wished thereby to lay the basis for accusing the Allies of commencing the bombing of open cities. This account appears to have originated with an officer who knew that the bombs were German, but was unaware of the facts about the flight from Landsberg. Subsequent investigation disclosed no credible basis for this version of the episode, and it is inconceivable that Hitler and Goering, had they in fact undertaken so risky a project, would have used German planes marked with the Balkankreuz, and German bombs, to simulate an enemy bombing.

Luftwaffe began its daytime raids over London. Hitler and Goering had used the Freiburg bombing to create, at least in the eyes of the German public, the image of injured innocence, so that at such time as they might desire to turn loose the Luftwaffe against the British people it could be plausibly justified as a well-merited reprisal for the atrocities already perpetrated by the Royal Air Force.

Plans and Probing Attacks

At dawn on June 5, 1940, the second phase of the Battle of France began, when von Bock's army group in western France attacked the French defensive line along the Somme and started its drive south to the Seine. That night the Luftwaffe launched its first bombing attack against land targets in the United Kingdom. Some fifty Heinkel 111s ranged widely over the countryside, and in many British cities and towns air-raid sirens roused the sleeping inhabitants. Most of the bombs were aimed at airfields, but many fell in the open, and little damage was done.

The following two nights there were similar attacks,[34] but then they ceased until June 18, after the French had asked for an armistice. During the interim the Luftwaffe was fully committed in France, and these first few nights of light and scattered bombardment were more a source of puzzlement than of alarm in London. What had the Germans been up to?

The answer is still obscure. It was surmised at the time that the Germans were trying out navigational aids and techniques, but in retrospect it seems unlikely that this would have been undertaken when the Luftwaffe was still preoccupied with the fighting in France. Very possibly the purpose of these raids was simply to alarm the British and thus discourage them from sending reinforcements to the French.

However that may be, it is clear that the small raids in early June were in no sense part of what was soon to become known as the Battle of Britain. Hitler's directive of May 24 had called for a crushing air attack "as soon as sufficient forces are available," and this was not yet the case, for the bulk of the Luftwaffe was deployed behind the German Army and helping it administer the *coup de grâce* in France. There was as yet no OKL order, or any tactical plan, for an air assault against Britain.

The Battle of Britain was given its name by Winston Churchill him-self, in his speech in Parliament on June 18, immediately after Pétain's armistice plea. "What General Weygand called the Battle of France," said Churchill, "is over. I expect that the Battle of Britain is about to begin." His prediction was borne out within a few hours, when German bombers reappeared in the night sky. From that night on, Luftwaffe operations against Britain continued without interruption* save for the weather, and with increasing intensity, until the issue was joined and resolved.

The attacking forces in the ensuing June night raids never exceeded seventy bombers, and the physical damage inflicted was negligible.[36] Their main importance, on both sides, was experimental. The British soon discovered that if one or a few aircraft were allowed to touch off alerts the protracted alarms would interrupt production and cause great inconvenience; it was better to risk an occasional unheralded bomb and sound the siren only under the imminent risk of heavier attacks. The Germans, for their part, learned that their bombers were flying in too low and were suffering unnecessary losses at altitudes where searchlights could illuminate them for the night fighters.[†] A few thousand more feet took the bombers out of the effective reach of the beams, and then there was little that the defenders could do with the means then available.

The most significant aspect of these preliminary raids, however, was navigational and electronic, and the scientists on each side were more heavily engaged than the handful of pilots and bombardiers. Night bombers might be safe as long as they stayed high, but they were woe-fully inept at finding and hitting their targets. A night raid was like a boxing match between two blind men, and was bound to remain so as long as it was primarily a visual operation. The future lay in radio and radar aids to navigation and interception.

During these June raids the German bombers were testing a new device—crude enough by present standards—to which they had given the cover name *Knickebein*. This was a simple matter of two radio navigational beams intersecting over the target area. Its existence was suspected by a brilliant Air Ministry scientist, Dr. R. V. Jones, and was confirmed by airborne radio monitors on June 21. Radio counter-

---

* An attack on Southampton with some 220 bombers, scheduled for the night of June 21, was canceled "for political reasons," no doubt in pursuance of Hitler's hope that the British might soon sue for peace.[35]

† During June, 12 German night bombers were brought down from altitudes of less than 12,000 feet.

measures were rapidly devised, which obscured, diffused, or "bent" the German beams. The early detection and partial frustration of *Knickebein*—a feat then known only to a few—was an early and major British victory in the Battle of Britain.[37] What Winston Churchill called the "wizards' war" had begun in good earnest.

The late-June raids were carried out in accordance with Hitler's directive of May 24, in preparation for the large-scale attacks which the Fuehrer had called for.* Still there was no OKL directive or other order from higher headquarters setting forth the strategic objectives or tactical methods for the forthcoming encounter. As Goering's intelligence chief, Oberst Josef "Beppo" Schmid, later declared: "The German military leadership had no plan for the Battle of Britain."[39]

On June 30, Goering finally issued his first general directive for the Battle of Britain,[40] addressed to the three *Luftflotten* that were to carry out the assault. His order laid down a dual mission for the Luftwaffe: to destroy the enemy air force, and to cut Britain off from its overseas supplies. Strategically, therefore, the directive reflected the same mixture of purposes that characterized Hitler's preceding directives, which Goering was now seeking to implement. However, Goering put primary emphasis on the necessity of engaging the RAF at every opportunity, and his directive as a whole reflects a short-term "destructive" rather than a long-term "blockade" strategy.

The directive's immediate purpose was to authorize the Luftwaffe's redeployment, and the establishment of its principal forces at bases along the Channel and North Sea coasts, suitably located for operations against Britain. Ammunition was to be stockpiled, antiaircraft defenses were to be installed, and the supply and communications channels of the three air fleets were to be integrated. While all this was being done, and until the Luftwaffe had attained full readiness for the large-scale assault, harassing raids over Britain and attacks on convoys and other sea targets were to be continued.

Deployment and Order of Battle

During the first half of July, this redeployment was the Luftwaffe's primary concern. Its general nature was largely determined by the configuration of the Continental Channel coast. Closest to England is

* An implementing OKL order of June 22 specified airfields and aircraft factories as priority targets, and directed that systematic reconnaissance of British airfields be carried out beginning June 27.[38]

the area around Calais, the Pas-de-Calais, so the largest concentration of fighter aircraft was there. But the Normandy peninsula is the closest part of France to the ports on England's southern coast, and accordingly there were other fighter units near Cherbourg and Le Havre. The Pas-de-Calais and Normandy were, in fact, the only Continental locations near enough to England to support operations by the Messerschmitt 109s, with their 125-mile radius of action.

The Stukas and the Messerschmitt-110 "destroyers" had greater range, but were still short-winded enough to benefit from proximity to their targets, and were therefore based near the coast, behind the fighter fields. The level-flight bombers, on the other hand, had ample range for most of their intended missions. There was no need to crowd them near the shore; better to have them a bit inland, as a measure of security against counterattack by RAF bombers.

Over-all command of all these units lay with Luftflotte 2 in the northern and Luftflotte 3 in the southern portions of the operational area. The line of territorial demarcation between the two *Luftflotten* ran from Le Havre up the Seine, passed north of Paris, and then ran northeast to the vicinity of Cologne. The projected dividing line for operational purposes ran from Le Havre north across the Channel to the English coast just east of Portsmouth, and on to Oxford and Manchester. For the Battle of Britain, therefore, the leading role fell to Luftflotte 2; its fighter bases were nearest to the enemy, and London and eastern England lay within its zone of operations. The main headquarters of Luftflotte 2 were at Brussels, with a forward "combat" headquarters at Cap Blanc-Nez.

The two *Luftflotten* commanders, Albert Kesselring and Hugo Sperrle, were regular Army officers who had transferred to the Luftwaffe in 1933. Kesselring, at Luftflotte 2, had had no prior experience in military aviation, but had learned to fly and studied his new trade assiduously. Because of a perhaps excessively cordial manner he was known as "smiling Albert," and some thought him an overoptimistic diagnostician, but he was a gifted commander and administrator and was as well equipped as anyone else in the Luftwaffe to lead large forces into battle. Sperrle, gigantic of body and brooding of mien, kept his rear headquarters at Paris and his forward at Deauville. He had flown a bit in the First World War, but for purposes of 1940 his experience as commander of the Condor Legion in Spain was certainly more meaningful.

Subordinate to each *Luftflotte* were four *Luftgauen** and three *Fliegerkorps*. At the beginning of the Battle, Fliegerkorps I, II, and IX were under Kesselring, and Fliegerkorps IV, V, and VIII under Sperrle; during its course Fliegerkorps I went to Sperrle and VIII to Kesselring. The latter also had command over the night fighters (Nachtjagddivision), and each *Fliegerkorps* had two *Staffeln* of long-range reconnaissance aircraft and other special units.

Fliegerkorps I, II, and V were much alike, with three *Kampfgeschwader* (some three hundred bombers) each. Their commanders, however, were not so similar. Generaloberst Ulrich Grauert, at Fliegerkorps I (headquarters near Compiègne), had flown in the First World War and then served as an artillery officer in the Reichswehr until his transfer to the Luftwaffe in 1935.† Commanding Fliegerkorps II (south of Calais) was General der Flieger Bruno Loerzer, an "old eagle"‡ who had spent the between-war years in various business activities connected with aviation. He was perhaps Goering's closest friend in the Luftwaffe and is reputed to have saved Goering's life on one or more occasions during the First World War. Another such was the commander of Fliegerkorps V, General der Flieger Robert Ritter von Greim, a Bavarian and a fiery Nazi (not an aristocrat; his "von" was the perquisite of the Militaer-Max-Joseph order for bravery) who after the war had stunted with Udet, trained Chinese flyers in Canton, and then gone into German civil aviation.§

All three of these commands also included reconnaissance planes, and Loerzer had a few Stukas as well. Fliegerkorps IV, with its headquarters in Brittany near St.-Malo, was a much more mixed bag, with a *Geschwader* each of bombers and Stukas, an elite mixed *Geschwader*,‖

---

* Less important than the *Fliegerkorps* for present purposes were Luftgauen VI (Muenster), XI (Hamburg), Holland, and Belgium–North France, all under Luftflotte 2, and Luftgauen VII (Munich), XII (Wiesbaden), XIII (Nuremberg), and West France, under Luftflotte 3.

† Grauert was killed in May 1941, when a British aircraft shot down the transport plane in which he was flying along the Channel coast.

‡ Loerzer, with 44 victories, was in a triple tie for seventh place on the First World War list of aces. Von Greim, with 28 victories, was quadruply tied in 32nd place.

§ In April 1945, a few days before the final collapse of the Third Reich, Hitler, believing Goering to have betrayed him, summoned von Greim to Berlin. Faithful to the last and at great personal risk, Greim flew in with the famous aviatrix Hanna Reitsch. In the bunker, Hitler promoted Greim to *Generalfeldmarschall* and appointed him to succeed Goering as Commander-in-Chief of the Luftwaffe. A few days after the war ended, Greim committed suicide.

‖ This was Lehrgeschwader 1 (LG 1), originally formed for demonstration and instructional purposes, with one *Staffel* for each of the major aircraft types—fighters, bombers, and dive bombers.

two *Gruppen* of long-range reconnaissance aircraft, and a special *Gruppe* for coastal operations. Generaloberst Alfred Keller was the oldest (fifty-eight) of the top Luftwaffe commanders. He had entered the Army in 1902 and taken pilot training in 1913, and his exploits as leader of Kampfgeschwader 1 in the First World War earned him the sobriquet "Bomben-Keller." Between the wars he had a successful career in civil aviation (Junkers, A.E.G., Deutsche Luftreederei), and in 1934 he joined the Luftwaffe as an *Oberst* and bomber specialist. Like Greim, Keller was an ardent Nazi; in 1943, when he retired from field command, he became head of the National Socialist Flying Corps (NSFK).

At the north end of the "front," with headquarters in Holland between Amsterdam and the coast, was Fliegerkorps IX, with the equivalent of two *Kampfgeschwader* and a coastal *Gruppe*. These units (a few of which were based in Brittany) were specially trained and equipped for marine aviation, especially mine laying and attacking shipping. Their commander, Generalleutnant Joachim Coeler, had been a naval flyer in the First World War and had transferred from the Navy to the Luftwaffe in 1933.

Fliegerkorps VIII was the most specialized, with three *Geschwader* of Stukas, and reconnaissance planes. Its headquarters were at Deauville, and its commander, General der Flieger Wolfram von Richthofen, was the Luftwaffe's outstanding "close-support" commander. A younger cousin of the famed Manfred, he had himself been a junior member of the "Flying Circus," had studied engineering after the war, re-entered the Army in 1923, served as attaché in Rome—where he was befriended by the famous Italian aviator Italo Balbo—and been transferred to the RLM in 1933. He had been chief of staff and later commander of the Condor Legion, and had led his Stuka forces with great success in Poland and France.

Operational control of the fighter *Geschwader*, as already indicated, was in the *Jagdfliegerfuehrer*. At the beginning of the Battle there was one for each *Luftflotte*, and both were "old eagles." Jagdfliegerfuehrer 2, under Kesselring, was Generalmajor Kurt-Bertram von Doering, an alumnus of the Richthofen squadron who had carried his aerial skills to Argentina, Peru, and China during the twenties and early thirties. Jagdfliegerfuehrer 3, Oberst Werner Junck, under Sperrle, had been chief test pilot for Heinkel and an assistant to Udet at the RLM.[41]

Luftflotte 5, offspring of the Norwegian campaign, was also expected to take part in the Battle. Its commander, Generaloberst Hans-Juergen Stumpff, was of the same vintage and Army background as Kesselring and Sperrle. His operational aircraft* were in Fliegerkorps X, commanded by a veteran naval aviator, General der Flieger Hans Geisler. The planes, based at Stavanger in Norway and Aalborg in Denmark, included two *Kampfgeschwader* and a *Gruppe* of Messerschmitt 110s, as well as another *Geschwader* of 109s which, because of their short range, were useful only for defense.

As it turned out, Luftflotte 5 engaged in one day of highly unsuccessful operations early in the Battle, which abundantly demonstrated that it could not participate effectively from Scandinavian bases. Stukas and Messerschmitt 110s would likewise be found wanting, and it was therefore the level-flight bombers and single-engined fighters of Luftflotten 2 and 3 on which the great issue would turn.

The Battle of the Channel

While the redeployment was being carried out, the units already fit and placed for operations continued their harassing actions over Britain and the adjacent waters, with increased intensity and variety. The month of July was ushered in by the first sizable daylight raids, along the south coast of England at Plymouth, Weymouth, Falmouth, Portland, and Dover. Most of these were carried out by fifteen or twenty bombers, escorted by a like number of fighters. The scattered night attacks continued; the German bomber crews now flew higher, and the defense was correspondingly ineffective.[42]

As more of the Luftwaffe units settled into their new bases and became operational, the pace of battle quickened. In the afternoon of July 10 some twenty German bombers, protected by about twice as many fighters, attacked a convoy off Dover. The Germans were met by twenty-odd British fighters; the ensuing engagement was described that evening to the House of Commons[43] as "one of the greatest air battles of the war." In retrospect this description seems an absurd hyperbole, and the day carried no special significance for the German airmen, many of whom were still busy with redeployment. But the encounter off Dover was much the largest since Dunkirk, and for that

* The two principal subordinate commands of Luftflotte 5 were Fleigerkorps X and Luftgau Norway.

reason July 10 has been taken by many, including Sir Winston Church-ill, as the "opening" of the Battle of Britain.[44]

The following day the heavy fighting was renewed, as the Germans launched three attacks from the Cherbourg area against Portsmouth, Portland, and a convoy off the southwest coast. July 11 is more truly noteworthy, however, as the date of the second OKL general order, governing the operations preliminary to the main assault. Entitled "Directive for the Intensified Air Warfare against England,"[45] it reiterated the familiar theme that destruction of the enemy air force and air armaments industry was a "prerequisite condition of a success-ful air war against England." Much of it was devoted to technical problems such as pinpointing landmarks in the combat zone, allocating targets, and training crews for the new tasks. The next few weeks were to be devoted to indoctrination and tactical experimentation, and during this interim period operations were to be directed principally against British convoys in coastal waters, though the harassing attacks on land were also to be continued.

There ensued a full month of limited aerial warfare, concentrated over the Channel and the southern coast of England, which became known to the German participants as the *Kanalkampf*. The commander of the bomber *Geschwader* KG 2, Oberst Johannes Fink, was desig-nated *"Kanalkampffuehrer,"* with the mission of "attacking English shipping in the Channel and the mouth of the Thames." For this purpose a *Geschwader* each of Stukas and two-engined "destroyers" (Messerschmitt 110s) were subordinated to Fink, and still another *Geschwader* (JG 51) of Messerschmitt 109s, under Oberst Theo Oster-kamp, was assigned to provide fighter cover. Osterkamp, an "old eagle" of the First World War, was an unusually observant and reflec-tive commander, who learned much from these early encounters with the "Lords," as his men called their English opponents.[46]

The material damage inflicted during the *Kanalkampf* was not, on either side, of much importance. At most forty thousand tons of ship-ping was sunk in the daylight attacks on the Channel convoys.[47] There were a few days of heavy engagements such as those of July 10 and 11, but otherwise losses in the air were light on both sides during July and the first week of August. The German losses were more than double those of the British, but that is hardly surprising, since the Luftwaffe was attacking with vulnerable bombers and dive bombers under fighter cover, while British bomber operations were negligible. During the four weeks from July 10 to August 6 the RAF lost seventy and the Luftwaffe about 180 aircraft, but of these latter more than half were bombers, so that the fighter losses on each side were not far apart.[48]

Small as they were, compared to what was soon to follow, these early encounters precipitated many of the tactical problems that endured throughout the Battle of Britain. On the British side, it became apparent that quite as much would depend on the accuracy of the radar operators and the judgment of the group commanders and controllers as on the skill and bravery of the pilots. Fighter Command could not keep its planes constantly aloft. Aircraft had to be serviced and pilots changed and rested, and it took several minutes for the fighters to climb from their fields to combat altitudes. An effective defense, therefore, depended in very large measure on prompt radar detection of the German planes assembling over the French coast, and accurate estimates of their strength and the probable direction of attack. Otherwise the German flights would be unopposed or met only by weak patrols, as frequently happened in the early stages.

The Germans, on the other hand, needed to devise aerial tactics for the protection of their relatively defenseless bombers and for the destruction of the British fighter forces without suffering crippling losses of their own. Osterkamp at first essayed a policy of prudence, by dispatching his fighters in large numbers and close formation, under orders not to attack except when the odds were favorable. He also tried using the two-engined Messerschmitt 110s as "bait" to draw up the British fighters as victims for a closely following force of Messerschmitt 109s. On the whole these tactics met with little success, partly because the British, to conserve their resources, generally refrained from attacking the German fighters and concentrated their efforts on the bombers, and partly because the British fighter forces, when engaged, proved a match for the Germans.[49]

Other German fighter commanders tried different tactics. Major Adolf Galland, soon to become famous as one of the Luftwaffe's leading aces, commanded a *Gruppe* of JG 26 based near Calais, which commenced operations on July 24.[50] Galland's pilots did not fly in close formation, but pursued their Spanish Civil War practice of a "wide-open combat formation" which, they believed, afforded better opportunity to the individual fighter pilot in terms of initiative and field of vision. But Galland and his men soon met the same difficulties that had frustrated Osterkamp, and they achieved no decisive results.

Thus the German pilots and their field commanders soon realized that the Royal Air Force would be no soft touch and German "air superiority" would be far from easy to achieve. They also learned a great deal about the structure and workings of the British air defenses and the strength and distribution of the British fighter forces.

But these educational benefits did not rise to the higher levels of the Luftwaffe, pervaded as they were with false optimism. On July 11 the Army liaison officer at OKL, Generalmajor Otto Stapf, reported to Halder the OKL's estimate that it would take from two to four weeks to "beat down" (*niederschlagen*) the enemy air force.[51] There were many in the Luftwaffe who knew better, and soon there would be more; nevertheless, three weeks later Goering was making preposterous predictions of even speedier victory.

The Fat One, during this crucial period of preparation, was setting a very bad example. Neither in the field nor in staff conference was he furnishing the leadership that the Luftwaffe so badly needed at this moment of its supreme test. After the Compiègne armistice, Goering indulged in vacation and travel until about the middle of July, when he returned to his beloved hunting lodge Karinhall, north of Berlin.[52] It was there, on July 18, that he held his first (so far as the available records show)[53] General Staff conference on the developing conflict.*

Hitler's victory speech in the Reichstag was made the following evening, and on July 20 there was a general gathering of senior Luftwaffe officers at Karinhall to celebrate the promotions which the Fuehrer had distributed with so lavish a hand. On the next day, July 21, Goering conferred with his three western *Luftflotte* commanders, Kesselring, Sperrle, and Stumpff. The main purpose of the meeting was to specify a new and important target for the Luftwaffe bombers—to wit, the British fleet.

What had stimulated this order, involving so radical a departure from the primary goal of air superiority? Plainly, it had some connection with the plans for Sea Lion, with which the Army and Navy were so heavily occupied. It is quite possible that Raeder, alarmed at Hitler's growing interest in the possibility of invading England despite the enormous superiority of the Royal Navy, had suggested to the Fuehrer that the Luftwaffe be called on to lend a hand. However that may be, the prospect of Sea Lion must have been on Goering's mind,[54]

* The conference does not appear to have dealt with any of the basic strategic or tactical problems. The attacks on convoys were to be used as a means of training aircraft crews, and to develop close co-operation between the bombers and the fighters. The need for an adequate sea rescue service, to save crews shot down over the Channel and the North Sea, was also stressed.

for he also instructed his commanders that, in attacking the southern English coast, the docks should be spared.[55]

The conferees' chief concern, however, was the main air assault, the appointed time for which was drawing near. Nevertheless, little if any preparatory staff work seems to have been done. There was a nervous note, betraying an uncomfortable apprehension of bomber and dive-bomber losses, in Goering's suggestion that the fighter cover should try to drive off the British forces before the arrival of the massed bombers.

The *Luftflotte* commanders departed, with instructions to submit their detailed plans for the coming offensive within a few days. Under these circumstances, the final planning of the air offensive was necessarily hurried, as well as contentious and superficial.

Adlertag

The *Luftflotte* and *Fliegerkorps* staff memoranda embodying their ideas for the conduct of the *Adlerangriff* were submitted to OKL during the last week of July—a full month later than they would have been in hand had the Luftwaffe's staff work been up to Army standards. Two of these studies have survived, and the general burden of a third has been described by the staff officer who prepared it. The paper from Richthofen's Fliegerkorps VIII merely recommended that the Stukas be used to attack the RAF's ground installations and is otherwise of little interest.[56]

The document submitted by Fliegerkorps II has not survived, but according to its author, Chief of Staff Oberstleutnant (later General) Paul Deichmann, great stress was laid upon attacking London.[57] His study recognized the impossibility of sending the bombers into the interior of England, beyond the range of the German fighters, until the British fighter force had been greatly weakened. Attacking London, Deichmann thought, would bring up the British fighters in defense of the city, and thus enable the Luftwaffe so to reduce Fighter Command that thereafter the German bombers could sweep inland unchecked. According to Deichmann, Goering's staff was prepared to adopt these tactics. However that may be, Hitler's refusal to allow attacks on London prevented their execution during the first month of the Battle.

The memorandum sent to Luftflotte 2 on July 24 by Generaloberst

Grauert of Fliegerkorps I will repay fuller examination.[58] Entitled "Thoughts on the Direction of the Air War against England," it was only four pages long. "England must defend herself with fighter planes and antiaircraft artillery," he declared, and he then listed four objectives of the assault: (1) to achieve air superiority (*Luftueberlegenheit*) by destroying the RAF and its sources of strength, especially the aircraft motor industry; (2) to protect the Army's passage across the Channel, and the airborne troops, by striking the British fleet and the RAF, and by ground support for the Army once it was landed; (3) to blockade and "throttle" England by rendering the harbors unusable; and (4) "independently of these tasks, consideration may be given to ruthless terror attacks as reprisals [*als Vergeltung ruecksichtlos Terrorangriffe*] against the big cities."

Grauert's list combined, in brief compass, all three of the basic strategies to which the Luftwaffe's efforts might be dedicated—blockade, conquest by terror à la Douhet, and invasion.* But which one was governing? If anyone had decided this question, apparently Grauert had not been told, and it can only be described as extraordinary that the strategic thinking of a leading (and able) Luftwaffe commander could be so diffuse, so short a time before the operation.

The OKL staff considered the memoranda from the field and sent back its comments on July 29. The *Luftflotten* replied on August 1.[59] In the meantime there was increasing impatience at the Berghof, and on July 30 a peremptory message from Hitler interrupted the shuffling of staff papers.[60] "The Fuehrer has ordered," it read, "that the preparations for the Luftwaffe's great attack against England should immediately and with great dispatch be completed, so that it can be commenced within twelve hours after the Fuehrer so orders."

Hard on the heels of this rocket from on high came the new Fuehrer Directive No. 17, "For the Conduct of Air and Naval Warfare against Britain," issued the day after Hitler's conference with the Army and Navy chiefs at the Berghof on July 31.[61] This order fixed August 5 (weather permitting) as the opening day, but failed to specify the operation's strategic goals any more precisely than theretofore. The RAF was to be overcome by direct attack in the air and on the ground,

* Following the list of objectives, Grauert considered the tactical problem of winning air superiority. He thought that this could not be done by attacking the RAF's bases and ground organization, but must be accomplished in the air. To this end he suggested a two-wave attack—the first by forces only large enough to bring up the British fighters and get them embroiled, and the second by massed fighter aircraft (*Masse der Jagdkraefte*).

and then harbors were to become the primary target, in order to cut off Britain's food supplies. But the south-coast ports were to be spared, and the Luftwaffe was to remain in readiness to support Sea Lion, as well as naval operations generally. Thus the blockade and invasion strategies were still mixed. Douhet, however, was to be held in leash: "I reserve for myself the decision on retaliatory terror attacks."

The OKL, however, was not yet ready to turn the Eagle loose. On July 31 the OKL liaison officer at OKW, Major Freiherr von Falkenstein, reported to Jodl that Goering had not yet made a decision as between the conflicting tactical recommendations of Sperrle and Kesselring.* This dispute had delayed completion of preparations for the assault, but Goering had assumed, from Hitler's comments, that about eight days still remained before the attack. Now Goering had decided to open the operation with a feint attack on London, under cover of which the main blow would fall on the RAF's fighter organization. It would take five or six days of exhaustive conferences with the Luftwaffe's *Gruppenkommandeure*, and map exercises with the crews, to acquaint everyone with the new tactics.

On the same day (August 1) that Hitler issued Directive No. 17, Goering held a great conclave of Luftwaffe commanders at The Hague. Osterkamp's account† is extraordinarily vivid and revealing:[63]

A big conference of the Luftwaffe command with its Supreme Commander Hermann Goering. Place of action—The Hague, at the headquarters of General Christiansen, the commander in Holland. I have the honor to join this illustrious company as the representative of the fighter forces.

Everybody of rank and name is present. Because of the good weather the festival takes place in the garden. The "Iron One" [Goering] appears in a new white gala uniform.

At first he praised extravagantly the lion's share of the Luftwaffe in the defeat of France. "And now, gentlemen, the Fuehrer has ordered me to crush Britain with my Luftwaffe. By means of hard blows I plan to have this enemy, who has already suffered a decisive moral defeat, down on his knees in the nearest future, so that an occupation of the island by our troops can proceed without any risk!"

Then the matter of orders and directives for the execution of the plan was taken up. According to the information of the intelligence service, Britain disposed in its southern sector—the only one which came into question for us—of at the most 400 to 500 fighters. Their destruction in the air and on

---

* Quite possibly it was this report[62] of Goering's leisurely pace that aroused Hitler's impatience and prompted the peremptory message from him to Goering dispatched that same day.

† The subtitle of this section of Osterkamp's book is "Utopien," signifying the excessive optimism at OKL to which he took such strong exception.

land was to be carried out in three phases: during the first five days in a semi-circle starting in the west and proceeding south and then east, within a radius of 150 to 100 kilometers south of London; in the next three days within 50 to 100 kilometers; and during the last five days within the 50-kilometer circle around London. That would irrevocably gain an absolute air superiority over England and fulfill the Fuehrer's mission!

I think that I must have made a terribly stupid face, but in my case that should scarcely attract any attention. Udet told me later that I shook my head in shock, but I do not remember.

At any rate I saw Udet leaning down to Goering and whispering something to him. Goering looked up, saw me and said, "Well, Osterkamp, have you got a question?"

I explained to him that during the time when I alone was in combat over England with my *Geschwader* I counted, on the basis of continuous monitoring of the British radio and of air battles during which the distinctive marks of the units [to which the British fighters belonged] were ascertained, that at that time about 500 to 700 British fighters were concentrated in the area around London. Their numbers had increased considerably if compared with the number of planes available at the beginning of the battle. All new units were equipped with Spitfires, which I considered of a quality equal to our fighters.

I wanted to say more, but Goering cut me off angrily: "This is nonsense, our information is excellent, and I am perfectly aware of the situation. Besides, the Messerschmitt is much better than the Spitfire, because as you yourself reported the British are too cowardly to engage your fighters!"

"I shall permit myself to remark that I reported only that the British fighters were ordered to avoid battles with our fighters—" "That is the same thing," Hermann shouted; "if they were as strong and good as you maintain, I would have to send my *Luftzeugmeister* [Udet] before the firing squad."

Udet smiled and touched his neck with his hand. I still could not hold back and said, "May I ask how many fighters will be used in the combat against Britain?" Hermann answered, "Naturally, all our fighter squadrons will be used in the struggle." I now knew as much as I had known before and thought, after a careful appraisal, to be able to count on some 1,200 to 1,500 fighters. In this too I was to be bitterly disappointed.

The disappointment with the bombers came sooner. Both of the *Luftflottenchefs*, General Sperrle and General Kesselring, hesitated to stage bomber attacks before the destruction of the British fighter force.

They proposed, with reason, first to destroy, with continuous night bomber attacks, the ground organization, the airfields, etc., of the fighters, as well as the fighter-producing industry centers. Only after the British fighter force had been decisively weakened should mass [day bomber] attacks on the fighter fields around London take place. Goering declared that these objections were ridiculous. "Jagdgeschwader 51, which alone is at the Channel, has downed over 150 planes. That is enough of a weakening. And besides, considering the number of the bombers of both *Luftflotten*, the few British fighters will be of no consequence!"

Goering's assertion to the effect that my *Geschwader* had downed over 150 planes was correct, to be sure, but he forgot that that number included also all planes which we had destroyed both in the air and on land during the French campaign.

But he was already continuing: "Count how many bombers alone we can put into the sky for this campaign!"

On the basis of the fact that our industry had concentrated on bomber production for a long time, and having deducted the losses suffered in France, I was counting on at least 1,500 to 2,000 bombers. Goering often spoke publicly of 4,500, but I considered that his estimates were exaggerated about one hundred per cent. Therefore I was completely staggered when the two *Luftflotten* reported that they had not even 700 bombers ready for combat duty. But Goering too was sitting there completely staggered, and his consternation seemed genuine. Looking around, shocked and as if in search of help, he murmured, "Is this my Luftwaffe?"

Other sources[64] record the tactical instructions issued for *Adlertag*. There were to be three major attacks, the first of which would be made in three waves. The first (in line with Grauert's ideas) would be a small group of fighters, Stukas, and level-flight bombers. The second wave of massed fighters would follow ten or fifteen minutes later, and then would come the main bomber flight, escorted by Messerschmitt 110s. Later in the day there would be two more attacks in waves, and at night the bombers and mine layers of Fliegerdivision 9 would operate.

What was the nature of the disagreement between Sperrle and Kesselring? Seemingly it cannot have been of great importance,* for it is mentioned only in Falkenstein's report. Whatever it may have been, apparently it was resolved by OKL promptly upon the receipt of Hitler's directive. On August 2 Goering issued to Luftflotten 2, 3, and 5 his own basic order for the *Adlerangriff*.[65] But this was no earth-shaking document; it did little more than reiterate that the objectives of the attack were the achievement of air supremacy and the destruction of nearby naval units. Until the signal for the big blow was given (no date was fixed in the order), harassing attacks were to continue against ports, communications, factories, and airfields all over the United Kingdom.

This general directive was tactically supplemented by oral instructions from OKL to the *Luftflotten,* transmitted by telephone the next day.[66] The escort fighters were admonished to stick close to the

---

* There is no reference to any dispute with Sperrle in Kesselring's memoirs, and Osterkamp portrays them as of one mind at the conference at The Hague.

bombers, and were cautioned to break off the engagement soon enough to avoid running out of gasoline on the return flight. Special aircraft of the first wave were to attack the British radar installations.

There was good flying weather during the first few days of August, but the major assault was still not fully prepared. The Navy grumbled that the Luftwaffe was missing favorable opportunities,[67] and also expressed dissatisfaction with Goering's directive insofar as it gave only second priority to attacks against the Royal Navy.[68]

On August 6, Goering called a last preoperational conference at Karinhall.[69] Presumably everything was now in readiness for *Adlertag*, but the weather turned bad, and on August 7 Major von Falkenstein had to report to OKW that, for this reason, no date for the offensive had yet been fixed.[70] No immediate improvement was promised by the meteorologists, and the next day Hitler (who had come to Berlin on August 3 to observe the results of the assault) returned to the Berghof, intending to stay there until the offensive could be launched.[71]

As Goering and his staff waited impatiently for a change in the weather, their frame of mind was highly optimistic. On July 29 Generalmajor Otto Stapf (the OKH liaison officer at OKL), reporting to Halder on the progress of preparations, summed up the official Luftwaffe viewpoint:[72] "Our Air Force on the whole feels that they have the edge on the British in equipment, leadership, skill, and with respect to the geographic factors. Decisive results will be forthcoming before the close of the year."

At OKW, Major von Falkenstein painted the same rosy picture. Bemoaning the bad weather on August 7, he reassured his listeners that "the prospects of success" were "definitely favorable." But his description of the intended tactics would hardly have satisfied a precise staff officer, for he declared that a particular plan had been adopted only for the first day, and that thereafter things would be governed by the developing situation. Furthermore, there was concern that Goering might break off the attack prematurely in the not unlikely event that the Luftwaffe's own losses were considerable and if there was no clear evidence that the assault was inflicting heavy damage.[73]

From all these conferences and discussions on the eve of the great engagement the conclusion emerges that the *Adlerangriff* had no sound strategic foundation, and that its tactical planning was superficial and slipshod. If Goering and his entourage were confident of success, there

were many others, like Osterkamp, who had grave misgivings. Kesselring himself has written:[74]

I was even left in the dark about the relation of the current air raids on
England and the invasion plan; no orders were issued to the *Luftflotten* . . .
I found this the more disheartening because in the light of verbal instructions given me on August 6, 1940 [the last pre-*Adler* conference at Karin-
hall], I could presume that the air offensive which started two days later*
was intended to be the prelude to Sea Lion. But in the very first days of the
offensive it was conducted on lines quite at variance with those instructions
and never harmonized with the requirements of an invasion. . . . It was clear
to every discerning person, including Hitler, that England could not be
brought to her knees by the Luftwaffe alone. . . . No doubt economic warfare
against targets on or off the island was an essential part of the strategic war
in the air which could have satisfactory results if target-setting was carefully
planned, but to begin it as a substitute for a worked-out operation [Sea
Lion] of a very much vaster scope without special preparation of all serviceable means was a bad makeshift with many drawbacks.

Kesselring's reference to "target-setting" is especially significant. The
heaviest bombs and the most accurate bombsights are wasted unless
the targets are well chosen. Target selection for strategic air warfare
is the responsibility of both the intelligence staff, to provide the necessary information about location and protection, and the combined
command, to determine what will hurt the enemy most in terms of the
war as a whole. The selective process is a function of strategy, and
from the German standpoint the targets of attack in 1940 should have
been chosen quite differently depending on whether the primary
strategic objective was to strangle Britain by blockade, to prepare the
way for an invasion, or to crush her will to resist by air attack alone.

Since the *Adlerangriff* was launched without making a definite choice
among these alternatives, there could be no target plan geared to a
specific strategic objective. This was bad enough, but it might not
have been fatal if the target studies had been sufficient in terms of the
immediate tactical objective—local air superiority over southeastern
England and the Channel. Even in this narrower frame of reference,
however, the target analysis was defective.

If the *Adlerangriff* was to succeed in beating down the RAF, the
Luftwaffe's operational commanders should have received target instructions from OKL based upon the decisive tactical factors. Which

---

* A good example of the divergent opinions about the opening date of the
Adlerangriff; in the eyes of OKL it did not begin before Aug. 13 or 15.

factories were essential for the immediate production of Spitfires and Hurricanes? Which airfields were most important for the defense of southern England? How valuable were the coastal radar stations, and if once destroyed could they be speedily rebuilt? In attacking airfields, was it more important to destroy hangers and buildings or planes on the ground, or to tear up the runways? Would it be worth while to attack antiaircraft artillery emplacements and barrage balloons? And each of these questions suggests numerous subsidiary problems.

Scanty as they are, the contemporaneous Luftwaffe records are sufficient to disclose that none of these questions was adequately studied or thought through. In part this seems to have been the fault of the OKL intelligence chief, Oberst Josef "Beppo" Schmid, whose performance has been sharply criticized in postwar writings.[75] In part it may be explained by the difficulties and hazards of aerial reconnaissance over England in 1940* and the Luftwaffe's failure to develop a practical plan for the employment of its reconnaissance units.[77] But these shortcomings were but the symptoms of the Luftwaffe's chronic and, in the end, fatal disease. Competent, professional airmen would not have tolerated poor intelligence and the lack of a carefully prepared target plan, and would have insisted on a precise definition of the strategic goal, to the achievement of which the tactics could be fitted. But Goering and his cronies did not think in these terms.

The confusion of Luftwaffe planning extended even to the launching of the main assault. It had been envisaged that *Adlertag* would be signalized by a sudden, crushing blow, but in the upshot it proved very difficult even to determine which day was *Adlertag*. On August 8—the day after Falkenstein had reported to OKW that no date could be fixed because of unfavorable weather forecasts—some four hundred German planes, mostly Stukas and Messerschmidt 109s, attacked convoys off Dover and the Isle of Wight. By the end of the day four ships had been sunk and six were damaged, and the RAF and the Luftwaffe had lost twenty and thirty aircraft respectively.[78]

To the airmen on both sides this looked like a major operation, and no doubt this is why Kesselring and Galland regarded August 8 as the first day of the main assault.[79] But Hitler left Berlin for the Berghof that very day, as OKL had not yet given the order for *Adlertag* and

---

* In 1939, before the war, a special Luftwaffe unit had carried out high-altitude photographic flights over England. This interesting antecedent of the U-2 episode of 1960 was the work of Bildstaffel Rowehl, named after its commander, Hauptmann Theodor Rowehl.[76]

the weather forecasts were unpromising. The meteorologists were right; the next two days were unsuitable for large-scale operations, and they passed quietly.

But August 11, despite cloudy weather, was a day of heavy fighting. Sperrle sent over 850 aircraft of Luftflotte 3. The bombers attacked Portland and Weymouth, and the fighters tangled with the "Lords." Thirty-two British and thirty-eight German planes were lost.[80]

Late in the morning of August 12, Falkenstein reported to OKW that "the weather forecast is favorable and the order for a major attack is therefore to be expected." The *Adlertag* order was not given, but the attacks that day began to assume the pattern of the Battle itself, since for the first time the RAF's own airfields were struck, as well as the harbor of Portsmouth and shipping on the Thames. The Luftwaffe committed to battle some 300 bombers and 1,100 Messerschmitt 109s and 110s.[81] This was very nearly the entire fighter force, and the total of 1,400 was more than half of the Luftwaffe's combat-ready aircraft. In view of the size of the effort, August 12 may well be taken as the first day of the Battle's crucial phase.[82]

Portsmouth was attacked by Stukas from Luftflotte 3, with little effect despite a concentration of shipping that offered a fine target.[83] The three fighter airfields attacked—Manston, Hawkinge, and Lympne —were all on the coast of the Straits of Dover, between Folkestone and Margate. Because of their exposed position, these fields were used mainly as forward daytime landing fields and were not of major importance. All three were badly hit and were temporarily out of action from cratered runways, but they were serviceable again by the next day.[84]

Losses in aerial combat were heavy on both sides,* in about the same ratio as in the heavy attacks of August 8 and 11. But August 12 was chiefly noteworthy in that it was the only day of the entire Battle on which the Germans directed heavy raids against the British radar stations. Six stations on the southeast coast were attacked; at five of these the damage was of little consequence, but the sixth, Ventnor, on the Isle of Wight, was put out of action for some days, chiefly because of delayed-action bombs.[85] The failure to continue to attack the British radar chain was one of the Luftwaffe's worst blunders.

Late in the afternoon of August 12, OKW was informed that Goering had resolved to issue the order for *Adlertag* on the morrow, as the

* The RAF lost 22 planes, the Luftwaffe 31.

weather prospects for the next few days were favorable.* Hitler, duly notified, left the Berghof; he arrived in Berlin at about noon on the thirteenth. But he appears not to have paid much attention to *Adler;* Raeder and Jodl were closeted with him that same afternoon, and the Fuehrer's attention was focused on the plans for Sea Lion rather than the exploits of Luftwaffe pilots and bombardiers.

Adlertag—August 13, 1940—dawned under a dull overcast, and the early-morning attack planned by Luftflotte 2 was called off. But the cancellation order came too late to reach the crews of Oberst Fink's KG 2, who flew on without fighter escort and bombed the Coastal Command airfield at Eastchurch. At the same time, heavily escorted Stukas and bombers from Luftflotte 3 came in over the southern coast to attack RAF ground installations, but their aim was frustrated by poor visibility and strong fighter defenses. Goering then halted operations pending his further order at two in the afternoon.

The simultaneous attacks by the two *Luftflotten* on the areas east and south of London were intended to stretch and, hopefully, to snap the British aerial defense line—"to see if we [the RAF] could fight over Kent and Essex only at the expense of our resistance over Sussex and Hampshire."[86] The afternoon weather permitted a resumption of operations, and between four and five o'clock there was heavy fighting both east of London and over the south coast near Southampton and Portland. Another Coastal Command airfield, Detling, was badly hit, but no important damage was inflicted on Fighter Command's fields or other installations. The radar stations were left untouched.

In keeping with the concentration of attack on the RAF, that night the Luftwaffe went in search of aircraft factories. A bomber group, Kampfgruppe 100, with crews specially trained for night operations succeeded in landing eleven bombs on a Nuffield factory producing Spitfires at Castle Bromwich. Successful as it was, this raid was something of a freak, for night bombing remained on both sides a game of blindman's buff.

All in all, the Luftwaffe had little to show for its efforts on *Adlertag*.[87] It flew 1,485 sorties—double the number flown by Fighter Command—but its bombers had accomplished little, and the toll in the air now began to reflect the odds against the attacker. During the heavy fighting on August 8, 11, and 12 the Luftwaffe had lost a hundred

---

* On Aug. 11 Goering had informed Hitler that he would give the *Adlertag* order as soon as three days of good weather were in prospect. The Fuehrer, who had been impatient since the end of July, approved this decision.

planes to the RAF's seventy-four—a ratio of about four to three. But on August 13 the Luftwaffe lost forty-five aircraft to the RAF's thirteen. Even the three-to-one ratio does not fully state the difference, for six of the British pilots were saved and returned to duty.

The Luftwaffe's higher proportionate losses were primarily due to the fact that on *Adlertag*, for the first time, its bombers were committed en masse. Fighter Command concentrated its efforts against the vulnerable bombers, and the "sitting ducks" were not only far more numerous than on prior occasions but also, as a necessary consequence, less heavily escorted per capita by fighters.

But these unimpressive consequences were unknown at OKL headquarters, where rosy reports from the field commands and poor intelligence continued to foster false optimism. By the Germans' count, 134 British planes had been destroyed for 34 of their own, and OKL declared itself "satisfied" with this result.[88] On August 14 Generalmajor Stapf came to Halder with a report from OKL on the "results of air operations" on the four days of heavy combat—August 8, 11, 12, and 13:[89]

Primary objective: Reducing enemy fighter strength in Southern England. Results very good. Ratio of own to enemy losses, 1:3.* We have lost 3% of our first-class bombers and fighters, the enemy 15%.

Fighters: Ratio of losses 1:5 in our favor; in terms of first-line aircraft, 4% and 30%. We have no difficulties in making good our losses. British will probably not be able to replace them.

Ground organization: Eight major air bases have been virtually destroyed . . .

Continuation of assault depends on weather conditions, which do not look too good for the immediate future. . . .

Next targets: Essential production plants. Naval bases and units are for the time being classed as targets of opportunity.

Most of this report was a pipe dream. No important Fighter Command air base had suffered damage of any consequence, and those hit were put back on an operational basis in a matter of hours. The estimate of British losses was hopelessly exaggerated, and British aircraft production by this time was substantially higher than the German.

The poor results might have been the consequence of bad weather or bad luck. So, too, it is easier to be wise after the fact than in the clutch. But on the tactical level *Adlertag* must be marked down as a botched job. Why were the bombers not concentrated on a few major

* In fact the Luftwaffe on those 4 days lost 145 planes to the RAF's 87.

Fighter Command airfields, instead of Coastal Command and forward "emergency" fields like Lympne? Why were the invaluable radar stations ignored? Meteorological uncertainties precipitated confusing orders and counterorders; early in the morning KG 2's bombers came unescorted, and at noon a *Gruppe* of Messerschmitt 110s from Luftflotte 3 took off prematurely and came over Portland, with neither bombs to drop nor bombers to escort, and lost five aircraft on their pointless sortie.

Adlertag had come, but the eagle did not swoop to the kill; rather, he fell off the perch.

CHAPTER FIVE

Course and Consequence

ANOTHER BIG ATTACK, ordered by Goering for August 14, had to be canceled on the evening of the thirteenth because of bad weather forecasts. During the morning of the fourteenth the Luftwaffe was grounded, and nothing very large was undertaken that afternoon. Uneasiness over the heavy Stuka losses was reflected in the appearance of some ten Messerschmitt 110s carrying bombs, which they dropped on Manston airfield, destroying some hangars. Otherwise, Luftflotte 2 contented itself with shooting down barrage balloons and sinking the Varne lightship. Luftflotte 3, using the weather as cover, sent its bombers over southern and western England, flying unescorted in small formations (*Ketten* and *Rotten*). Eight RAF stations were attacked, but the damage was not serious. All in all the Luftwaffe flew fewer than five hundred sorties on the fourteenth, at a cost of ten aircraft; the RAF lost eight.[1]

Adlerangriff

But the next day, Thursday, August 15, the Battle reached its peak. The Luftwaffe flew 1,786 sorties—more than on any other single day—and for the first and only time all three *Luftflotten* were committed in simultaneous daytime attacks. Total losses (109 aircraft) were likewise the highest for any one day's fighting, as the Germans lost seventy-five and the British thirty-four planes.* Though not so

---

* The British lost more planes (39) only on Aug. 31, while the Luftwaffe never subsequently suffered more than the 71 losses of Aug. 18 and the 60 of Sept. 15. The British loss figures include only fighters, since their bombers, training planes and other types were not considered to have been involved in the Battle of Britain.

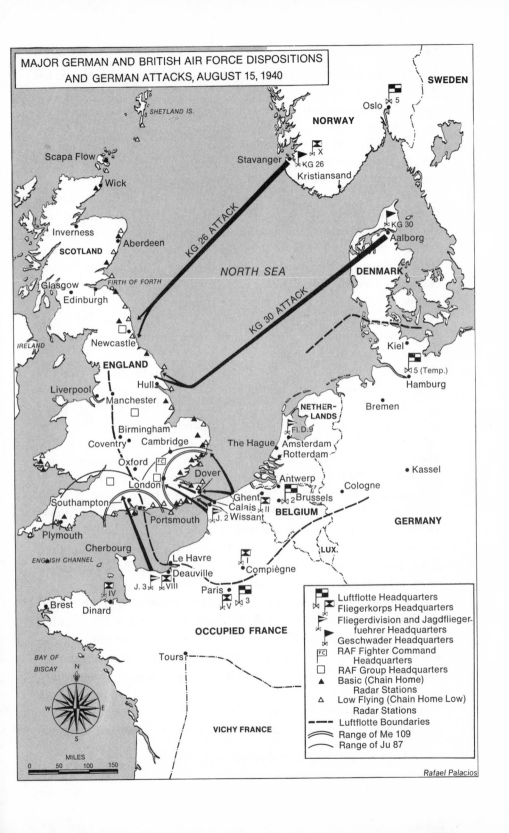

MAJOR GERMAN AND BRITISH AIR FORCE DISPOSITIONS AND GERMAN ATTACKS, AUGUST 15, 1940

SWEDEN

SHETLAND IS.

NORWAY

Oslo ⚑ 5

Scapa Flow

Wick

Stavanger ▶ X
☒ KG 26

Kristiansand

Inverness

SCOTLAND

Aberdeen

☒ KG 30

Aalborg

DENMARK

NORTH SEA

Glasgow

FIRTH OF FORTH

Edinburgh

IRELAND

Newcastle

KG 26 ATTACK

KG 30 ATTACK

Kiel

⚑ 5 (Temp.)

ENGLAND

Hull

Hamburg

Liverpool

Manchester

NETHER-
LANDS

Bremen

Birmingham

Fl.D.9

Coventry   Cambridge

The Hague   Amsterdam
Rotterdam

Oxford

FC

Dover

Kassel

London

Antwerp

Cologne

Southampton

Ghent
Calais ☒ II
Wissant

☒ 2 Brussels

BELGIUM

Portsmouth

J. 2

GERMANY

Plymouth

LUX.

Cherbourg

ENGLISH CHANNEL

Le Havre

⚑ I

Deauville

Compiègne

J. 3 ☒ VIII

Brest

Paris

Dinard

☒ IV

☒ V   ⚑ 3

OCCUPIED FRANCE

*BAY OF
BISCAY*

N

Tours

W   E

S

VICHY FRANCE

MILES
0   50   100   150

⚑ (Luftflotte HQ)	Luftflotte Headquarters
☒ (Fliegerkorps)	Fliegerkorps Headquarters
▶	Fliegerdivision and Jagdflieger-fuehrer Headquarters
⊢ (Geschwader)	Geschwader Headquarters
FC	RAF Fighter Command Headquarters
□	RAF Group Headquarters
▲	Basic (Chain Home) Radar Stations
△	Low Flying (Chain Home Low) Radar Stations
– – –	Luftflotte Boundaries
)))	Range of Me 109
)	Range of Ju 87

Rafael Palacios

labeled, this day, much more than August 13, deserved to be called *Adlertag*.

The attacks were carried out under orders issued by Goering on the night of August 13,* calling for co-ordinated attacks by Luftflotten 2 and 3 on the RAF ground installations, under heavy fighter escort.[2] On the evening of the fourteenth, Goering gave further orders for the commitment of Luftflotte 5 in the afternoon of the fifteenth.[3]

Most of the action on this crucial day occurred in the afternoon, though one heavy attack on the coastal airfields at Lympne and Hawkinge was carried out late in the morning by forty-odd fighter-escorted Stukas of Luftflotte 2. A few minutes after noon, the radar stations along the Northumbrian coast detected a sizable group of aircraft about one hundred miles east of the Firth of Forth, heading southwest. They were two *Gruppen* of Heinkel-111 bombers of KG 26, escorted by a single *Gruppe* of Messerschmitt 110s of ZG 76—something over one hundred aircraft in all, from Luftflotte 5's main Norwegian air base at Stavanger.

With such good warning, No. 13 Group (the northernmost group of Fighter Command, with headquarters at Newcastle-on-Tyne) was able to patrol five squadrons; two of these hit the Germans offshore and put the attacking force in disarray. The Heinkels reached the coast, but were unable to bomb accurately or even to penetrate to their intended targets, which included the fighter airfield at Usworth and two bomber fields farther south. Some houses in the coastal town of Sunderland were destroyed, but there was no other damage. Not one British aircraft was shot down, while the Germans lost at least fifteen. The Messerschmitt 110s proved useless as escorts; they had been flown without rear gunners to save fuel (Stavanger is about three hundred miles from Newcastle), and were no match for Spitfires and Hurricanes even under more favorable circumstances.

Half an hour later, Generaloberst Stumpff's forces made their second effort. It was launched from Aalborg in northern Jutland, even farther than Stavanger from the British coast, and was first detected by radar about half an hour after midday, over the North Sea and heading for the coast of Yorkshire. The attacking group comprised about fifty Junkers 88s—the Luftwaffe's newest and fastest bomber—from KG 30. Relying on speed and surprise, the Germans came in over Scarborough without fighter escort, and attacked the Bomber Command airdrome

---

* Bad weather prevented their execution on the fourteenth.

at Driffield. Damage was heavy and ten Whitley bombers were destroyed on the ground. Eight of the Junkers were shot down by fighters from No. 12 Group, so that, in all, Luftflotte 5 lost twenty-three aircraft out of about 160 committed.

Now it was No. 11 Group's turn, as for the first time the Luftwaffe succeeded in staging a series of "rolling" mass attacks. Early in the afternoon Luftflotte 2 sent some forty escorted Stukas over Essex and Suffolk and a hundred escorted bombers over Kent. The fighter airfields at Martlesham, Eastchurch and Hawkinge were hit, as well as two aircraft factories near Rochester. Late in the afternoon, well over two hundred aircraft (including forty-seven Stukas) from Luftflotte 3 came in over the south coast and attacked Portland and Fighter Command's field at Middle Wallop. Bomb damage was light, but action in the air was intense, as the RAF brought down twenty-five of the attackers while losing sixteen of its own planes. Shortly after six o'clock Luftflotte 2 struck again with sixty or more aircraft, many of which penetrated to the outskirts of London. The fighter fields at West Malling and Croydon were badly hit, as well as two aircraft factories near Croydon.

So ended the biggest and costliest day of the Battle of Britain.[4] Both sides thought they had accomplished far more than the facts warranted. The RAF claimed the certain destruction of 182 German aircraft—more than twice their actual toll. The Luftwaffe's claims were much wilder, even "within the family." At the OKW Operations Staff situation report the following morning, Major von Falkenstein reported[5] that "108 enemy planes were downed" (treble and more the true count), while acknowledging the loss of only fifty-five German machines.* Nevertheless, Falkenstein characterized the results of the attack as "not too favorable," and attributed the Luftwaffe's heavy bomber losses to weather conditions which hampered the fighter escort.

On August 16 the Luftwaffe pressed the attack with virtually undiminished force. Although Luftflotte 5 did not then or ever again join in the daytime raids, the Luftwaffe's sorties totaled over 1,700. Of these only some four hundred were bombers, and the high ratio of fighters to bombers no doubt reflected OKL's increasing concern over the bomber losses during the past few days. Cloudy weather restricted aerial combat, and the losses on both sides dropped, while remaining

---

* Quite possibly the losses of Luftflotte 5 (23 planes) had not yet been fully reported to Falkenstein from the Luftflotte combat headquarters, which moved from Oslo to Hamburg on Aug. 15 and returned to Oslo on Aug. 16.[6]

in much the same ratio as on the previous day.* Fourteen British planes were destroyed or badly damaged on the ground at the Tangmere fighter base, which was successfully attacked by Luftflotte 3's Stukas. Two Junkers 88s scored heavily in bombing the hangars at the Brize Norton flight-training school, housing no fewer than forty-six Oxford trainers, all of which were destroyed.[7] Other airfields were raided with less conspicuous success, and the Ventnor radar station on the Isle of Wight was again attacked and damaged.

On August 17 there was a lull.† Sunday, August 18, however, was a significant and unusual day, for the losses were nearly as heavy as on August 15, although the Luftwaffe flew only 750 sorties. Luftflotte 2 staged both morning and afternoon attacks, while Luftflotte 3 confined itself to a single midday raid, which was both effective and exceedingly costly. A large group of Stukas lost their fighter escort and suffered heavy losses over Portsmouth.[8] But some got through to the No. 11 Group sector airfield at Kenley and gave it a severe mauling, in the course of which half a dozen Hurricanes were destroyed on the ground. Another contingent put out of action the radar station at Poling, in west Sussex, but the other attacks on RAF installations accomplished little. The German losses were astonishingly high— seventy-one planes, or nearly ten per cent of the entire committed force.‡

Five days of poor weather ensued, during which the Luftwaffe carried out no operations in strength and losses on both sides were negligible. At night the futile sparring continued, as the German bombers rarely hit their targets, while the RAF night fighters and antiaircraft defenses were unable to bring down a single enemy plane.

Thus August 18 may be said to mark the end of the first phase of *Adlerangriff*, and indeed it was so regarded on both sides, where stock-taking and tactical planning were the order of the day. In England, No. 11 Group was bearing the brunt of the Battle, and on August 19 its commander, Air Vice-Marshal Park, issued new instructions based on the lessons of the preceding week. More than before, the RAF fighters were to engage the German bombers and avoid unnecessary

---

* The Luftwaffe lost 45 and the RAF 21 aircraft, not including the Oxford trainers at Brize Norton, which did not count as fighters.

† The Luftwaffe liaison officer at OKW gave bad weather as the reason for the inactivity on Aug. 17, although in fact the weather over the Channel was good. Only 77 German planes came over England; apparently the Luftwaffe was resting after two days at full stretch.

‡ The British lost 27 fighters, but the Germans claimed to have destroyed 138.

combat with the dangerous single-engined Messerschmitts. The group's seven sector stations, which exercised direct control of the fighters in the air, were to be protected by heavy patrols whenever a serious threat developed.[9]

On the other side, Goering had started to overhaul the Luftwaffe's tactics on August 15, when, on this peak day of the Battle, he summoned the *Luftflotten* commanders to Karinhall. The heavy losses of Stukas were very worrisome; the chief of staff of Fliegerkorps VIII (Oberstleutnant Hans Seidemann), which had lost 30 Stukas on August 18, regarded that date as the "black day" of the Battle. For their better protection, Goering now ordered that each attacking Stuka *Gruppe* should be escorted by three fighter *Gruppen*. Another symptom of acute concern was his insistence that no air crew sent against England should comprise more than one officer.

Goering also criticized the commanders for wasting their strength on secondary targets, and singled out for caustic comment the August 14 attack on the Varne lightship off Dover. The need for concentration of all possible force against the RAF was re-emphasized; Kampfgruppe 100 (specially trained night bomber units) was to go for the aircraft factories, and rolling mills were selected as a "bottleneck target" (*Engpassziel*).[10]

Most of this made perfectly good sense, but at the same meeting Goering also declared that it was questionable whether further attacks on radar stations would serve any purpose, since none had been put out of action. In fact the Isle of Wight station had been knocked out, but in any event Goering's observation betrayed a gross underestimate of the importance of the radar chain, and their subsequent immunity* was a godsend to the hard-pressed British.

On a more general basis, OKL's estimate of the Luftwaffe's accomplishments was wildly optimistic. As of August 16 it was estimated that 770 British fighters had been destroyed (out of 900 available on July 1), and that 300 new planes had been brought up. On this basis, OKL concluded that the British still had about 430 fighters, of which 300 were fully operational.[11] In fact British production had, so far, exceeded the losses, and Fighter Command was feeling the pinch in pilots rather than planes.

On August 19 the Luftwaffe leaders again forgathered at Karinhall. "We have reached the decisive period of the air war against England,"

---

* As already noted, single stations were badly hit on August 16 and 18, but there were no attacks thereafter.

Goering announced, and once more he stressed that the Luftwaffe's "first aim" was "the destruction of the enemy's fighters." Operational errors must be speedily detected and corrected, for "only thus can we avoid unnecessary losses in the future." The RAF fighters had been avoiding combat with the Messerschmitt 109s, and to counter this the Luftwaffe would "force them into battle by directing bomber attacks against targets within range of our fighters." A long tactical discussion ensued, during which the operations of fighters, Stukas, and level-flight bombers were separately reviewed, and direct contact and consultation between the fighter- and bomber-unit commanders was recommended.[12]

On August 20, Generalfeldmarschall Erhard Milch began a six-day visit to the units of Luftflotte 2. Throughout most of the war Milch functioned with great ability at RLM as, essentially, the Luftwaffe's rear commander, in charge of production, supply, administration, and the other supporting functions. But he had a taste for the headier wine of operational command, which he had indulged during the first few days of the Norwegian campaign by taking command of the newborn Luftflotte 5. This was the only time that he assumed a field command, but he was, after all, second only to Goering in the Luftwaffe hierarchy, and in this capacity he submitted a lengthy report on his observations at the front, replete with comments on many of the unit commanders as well as tactical and logistical suggestions.

Fink at KG 2, Galland at JG 26, and Luetzow at JG 3 were among those who won high praise. At JG 54, on the other hand, the *Geschwaderkommodore,* Major Mettig, impressed Milch as "not a fighter pilot type," and one of the *Gruppenkommandeure,* Hauptmann Ultsch, as "zealous but not outstanding." These assessments either caused or coincided with changes which were shortly made; Mettig was relieved by Major Hannes Trautloft on August 25, and Ultsch was replaced early in September.

Luftflotte 2's bombproof combat headquarters at Cap Blanc-Nez struck Milch as an "ideal" place for battle leadership, as did the joint headquarters of Jafues 1 and 2 nearby at Wissant. Von Doering was not on hand, and Osterkamp was in sole command of the headquarters; Milch remarked that Osterkamp's long experience ensured the high caliber of his performance. The pilots were having trouble distinguishing friend from foe in the heat of combat, and to aid them Osterkamp wanted to paint part of the Messerschmitt's propellers white.

As for the bombers, Goering's recent order that the combat crews should not include more than an officer each was unduly hampering the unit commanders, who, when they flew, needed another officer to take charge of the aircraft so that the commander could direct the formation. Troop morale was good, but not as high in the bomber as in the fighter units—hardly a surprising situation, inasmuch as the bomber crews were taking the heavy casualties.[13]

On August 24 the weather improved, and the Battle was resumed at full throttle. In accordance with the decisions taken at Karinhall, the day attacks were now concentrated on the RAF fields in the south-eastern corner of England that lay within range of the Messerschmitt 109s. Except for a lull on August 27 and lessened activity on the twenty-fifth and the twenty-ninth, there were heavy and determined raids on these fields every day from August 24 through September 6, and this period may be rightly (as it is generally) regarded as the second and crucial phase of the Battle.

The Battle of Biggin Hill

Important changes in the leadership and deployment of the German forces accompanied the shift in tactics. On August 20 Generaloberst Keller was transferred from Fliegerkorps IV to Luftflotte 1 on the quiet eastern front, and was replaced by Generalleutnant Kurt Pflugbeil, another bomber specialist, but eight years younger than Keller.*

Youth was the keynote of changes at lower levels of command, the purpose of which was to move up some of the young veterans of the Luftwaffe's birth and of the Condor Legion.[14] As *Gruppenkommandeure* and *Staffelkapitaene*, they were the rising front-line commanders of the Battle and were making great names for themselves —Werner Moelders, Adolf Galland, Helmut Wick, Wilhelm Balthasar, and Walter Oesau, to name the most famous.

At the beginning of the Battle, the next-higher level of commanders —the *Geschwaderkommodore*—were older officers, some of whom, like Osterkamp, had even seen service in the First World War. Now Oster-

---

* Pflugbeil had flown in the First World War and served as a regular officer of infantry in the Weimar years, during which he received clandestine air training in Russia and Italy. In the Luftwaffe he had commanded the bomber training school and been inspector of bombers, and in 1940 he was commanding Luftgau Belgium–Northern France. He was replaced in this last capacity by General der Flieger Wilhelm Wimmer, who had been acting commander-in-chief of Luftflotte 1, the command of which was now assumed by Keller.

kamp was replaced as *Kommodore* of JG 51 by Moelders, and was promoted to *Jagdfliegerfuehrer,* first sharing the task with and eventually replacing the older incumbent, von Doering.* Galland, who had been a *Gruppenkommandeur* in both JG 27 and JG 26 (Schlageter), took over as *Kommodore* of the latter on August 22.† Wick, slightly junior to Moelders and Galland,‡ was made *Kommodore* of JG 2 (Richthofen) early in October.[17]

Aircraft as well as men were reshuffled. The Stukas that had suffered so severely during its early days were now virtually withdrawn from the Battle, and on August 29 Richthofen's Fliegerkorps VIII, comprising the greater part of the dive-bomber force, was transferred from Luftflotte 3 to Luftflotte 2 and moved to the Pas de Calais, awaiting possibly more congenial employment in the event of an invasion of England.

Since Luftflotte 2, in the Pas de Calais and the Low Countries, was closer to the target area than Luftflotte 3, Kesselring's units increasingly bore the main burden of the day fighting, and by day the Battle took the form of a duel between Luftflotte 2 and Park's No. 11 Group. Simultaneously the Luftwaffe stepped up its night bombing operations, with a series of raids on Birmingham and Liverpool in which Luftflotte 3 often took the lead.

---

* The precise dates of these shifts cannot be established. Moelders was appointed to succeed Osterkamp on July 22, but was wounded on July 28 during his first sortie as the new *Geschwaderkommodore,* and Osterkamp had to remain at JG 51 for some 4 weeks of Moelders' hospitalization. Meanwhile the Pas de Calais was filling up with newly-transferred fighter units, and it was decided that a single *Jafue* in Luftflotte 2 would be over-burdened. Osterkamp was designated Jagdfliegerfuehrer 1, and worked with von Doering. At some time late in 1940 von Doering went to the RLM as inspector of fighters, and Osterkamp remained as the sole *Jagdfliegerfuehrer* of the *Luftflotte,* with the old designation of Jagdfliegerfuehrer 2, while 1 disappeared.[15] Von Doering was born in 1889, Osterkamp in 1892; the latter was a naval aviator in World War I whose 32 victories put him 26th on the list. In World War II Osterkamp had 6 more victories, and shared with Oberstleutnant Friedrich Vollbracht, Kommodore of ZG 2, the distinction of achieving combat victories in both wars.

† The command history of JG 26 may be taken as illustrative of the "youth movement" in the Luftwaffe.[16] From its establishment in 1938 and until Dec. 9, 1939, it was led by Generalmajor Eduard Ritter von Schleich, born in 1888, eleventh-ranking ace of the First World War and a civilian aviator to 1935. When Schleich left to take over the fighter training school in Vienna, he was succeeded by Major Hans Hugo Witt, born in 1900, a regular-Army officer transferred to the Luftwaffe. After the fall of France, Witt was promoted and assigned as operations officer to Jagdfliegerfuehrer 2 (von Doering). His replacement was Major Gotthardt Handrick, born in 1908, pentathlon winner at the 1936 Olympiade and a Condor Legion veteran. When Galland (who had been transferred to JG 26 as a *Gruppenkommandeur* in June) replaced him, Handrick was transferred to service in Rumania.

‡ Galland was born in 1912, Moelders in 1913, and Wick in 1915. Wick, 25 in 1940, was the youngest *Major* in the Wehrmacht.

As the Battle recommenced on the twenty-fourth, new tactics were soon observable on both sides. Despite the discontinuance of attacks on the British radar chain, the Germans were well aware of its importance, and now they screened their intentions by more or less constant patrolling over the Straits and feint attacks, to wear out and scatter Fighter Command's forces. The British, in order to protect their fields, sought to evade contact with the 109s and engage the bombers as far out as possible. As a countermeasure the Luftwaffe greatly increased the proportion of fighters to bombers, but this step necessarily reduced the weight of the bomber effort.

Nevertheless, the Luftwaffe's new methods paid immediate dividends, both in greatly increased damage to No. 11 Group's fields and in a higher ratio of British to German losses. The action on August 24 typified most of what was to follow. Shortly after midday, units of Luftflotte 2 hit Manston airfield and knocked it out of action; the squadron based there had to be withdrawn, along with most of the ground staff. A few hours later Kesselring's flyers were back in force, and damaged the field at North Weald seriously and that at Hornchurch slightly. Then Luftflotte 3 came over in what proved to be one of its last big daylight raids and wreaked havoc at Portsmouth, killing over a hundred persons. Throughout the day the Luftwaffe flew slightly more than a thousand sorties, and the score was twenty-two Fighter Command losses to thirty-eight for the Luftwaffe. Among the former were four Defiants, and a few days later this ill-starred type was withdrawn from the Battle and relegated to night fighting.[18]

From the twenty-fifth to the twenty-ninth the pace slackened somewhat, as the Luftwaffe's sorties dropped to an average of seven hundred per day. Fighter Command succeeded in blocking a number of attacks on the fields, but at Warmwell, Debden, and Eastchurch the raiders did serious damage. During these five days Fighter Command lost seventy-seven aircraft, the Luftwaffe 117.

On the last two days of August the attack on the RAF airfields reached its climax, with 1,345 Luftwaffe sorties on the thirtieth and 1,450 on the thirty-first. Primary targets were No. 11 Group's vital sector stations at Biggin Hill and Kenley, just south of London. Despite Park's most determined efforts to protect his fields, Biggin Hill was badly hit in both the morning and the afternoon of the thirtieth, and Kenley was also hurt, as well as the Coastal Command station at Detling. German bombers also reached the town of Luton, and seriously damaged the Vauxhall aircraft factory. On the thirty-first Debden was heavily attacked, and that afternoon the bombers again reached Biggin Hill.

Thus No. 11 Group's ground crews and sector staffs, including the WAAFs, joined the pilots in the front line of the Battle. At Biggin Hill the operations building, aircraft repair shops and NAAFI were knocked out, hangars destroyed, and telephone communications severed. There was much heroism and no demoralization, but the station was so beaten up that two of its three squadrons had to be moved elsewhere.

Attacks on Fighter Command's airfields continued during the first five days of September, during which the Luftwaffe put up an average of better than seven hundred sorties per day. On September 1 Biggin Hill was hit twice; the operations room was demolished and four Spitfires were destroyed on the ground. The field had been raided six times in three days, and, apart from material damage, the staff had suffered seventy casualties. The fields at Hornchurch, North Weald, West Malling, Eastchurch, Detling and Debden were also attacked during this period, with varying success. On September 4 a dozen Junkers 88s got through to the Vickers factory near Weybridge and inflicted very heavy damage and casualties. The output of Wellington bombers dropped from ninety a week to four, and full production was not restored for many months.[19]

On September 1, while preparing to move his army-group headquarters from France to Poland, Generalfeldmarschall von Bock encountered his Commander-in-Chief, von Brauchitsch, at La Baule. Finding Brauchitsch uncommunicative about the "big picture," Bock ventured the observation that during the last few days, for the first time, the Luftwaffe had made some real headway (*wirklich "ziehen"*).[20]

Whatever the basis of Bock's impression, he was close to the truth—closer, indeed, than some of those at OKL who should have known better. The Luftwaffe's blows were striking home and Fighter Command was being painfully hurt, but it was only the beginning of what might have been a much greater success for the Luftwaffe.

During the two weeks from August 24 to September 6 Fighter Command had lost some 290 planes, while the Luftwaffe lost about 380 aircraft of all types. But of these latter only about half were fighters, so that the British losses in fighters were far heavier than those of the Germans. During the second of these two weeks the situation was even worse for Fighter Command, which lost 161 aircraft in air battles alone, compared to 189 German fighters and bombers shot down.

Fighter Command's loss of 39 aircraft on August 31 was the heaviest it sustained in any one day's fighting. While British factories were turning out better than 125 new fighters each week (double the rate of German fighter production), Fighter Command's losses were now outstripping new production, and the aircraft reserve was dwindling.

But although the trend was dangerous, Britain's fighter-aircraft situation was not critical. On September 6 there were 127 Spitfires and Hurricanes in the ready reserve, and another 160 nearly finished. It was not so much in planes as in pilots that Fighter Command was running short.

When the Battle began, Fighter Command was about 200 pilots short of its establishment of 1,588, and fewer than 1,000 were fully trained for combat. During August 260 pilots were turned out by the training units, while 148 were lost and 156 wounded. But during the August 24–September 6 fortnight 103 pilots were killed or missing and 128 wounded, constituting a weekly wastage of over ten per cent of Fighter Command's combat strength. Actually the situation was worse than the bare figures indicate, for the experienced pilots were terribly battle-weary and few of the new men were really battle-worthy.[21]

If to these heavy losses be added the damage to the airfields in the London area and the growing threat to the aircraft factories, it may be seen that Fighter Command, while still basically intact and fighting well, was badly strained and facing grave problems. But as early as September 4 there were indications that OKL's power of concentration was faltering again, as part of its strength was diverted to factory towns. On September 6 the oil installations at Thameshaven were heavily bombed.

These excursions were premonitory of the Luftwaffe's fateful shift of tactics on September 7, which ushered in the third phase of the Battle of Britain, when London became the prime target.

The Battle of London

The reasons for this drastic alteration have been much debated. During the Battle of France, the German high command had been able to observe its progress in geographic terms, by kilometers advanced and cities captured. The Battle of Britain afforded no such ready or sufficiently accurate gauge. Therefore, to understand its course, it is vitally important to know how the Battle *appeared* to the antagonists at the time. Early September was the time of decision for Sea Lion, and the answer hung on the Luftwaffe's success or failure over southeastern England. How did the Germans see things during the first week of September?

On August 30 Generalmajor Stapf dropped in at OKH headquarters to give Halder a progress report on the Battle,[22] covering the eighteen days from August 8 (the first day of heavy fighting) through August 26. According to Stapf, the RAF during that period had lost 791 fighter aircraft, or fifty per cent of its fighter strength of 1,515.* German losses Stapf set at 169 fighters out of 1,464 (twelve per cent) and 184 bombers out of 1,800 (ten per cent).

Making full allowance for the difficulties of accurately assessing the British losses, these were horrendous misestimates.† Furthermore, the Germans had lost nearly 500 fighters and bombers, rather than the 350-odd acknowledged by Stapf. It is true that on both sides the claims were inflated, but it is difficult to explain Stapf's understatement of the German's own losses on any basis other than deliberate conceal-ment by OKL.

Stapf's report was distorted even more fundamentally. He told Halder (with substantial accuracy) that German aircraft production was about 900 a month, but set British (including American!) produc-tion at less than 650 planes of all types monthly. This gross under-estimate,‡ coupled with the overestimate of the British losses, resulted in a completely false picture of Fighter Command's situation and pros-pects late in August.

Was OKL feeding the Army soothing syrup? If so, they were feeding it to OKW as well. On September 3 Major von Falkenstein gave the OKW Operations Staff a comprehensive report on the results of the Battle from August 5 to September 1:[23]

Losses since 8 August: RAF, 1,115 fighters and bombers; Luftwaffe, 252 fighters and 215 bombers. . . . Eighteen [British] airdromes destroyed and twenty-six damaged. Ten per cent of the ground organization, offering facilities for fighter-plane repairs, has been destroyed. No serious damage

---

* Stapf divided this figure into 915 "first-class" and 600 "second-class" aircraft. The basis of the classification does not appear, and the 791-loss figure was not divided in his report. Stapf also reported that the British had lost 80 bombers, constituting about 5 per cent of the bomber strength, which he set at 1,100 of the first and 600 of the second class.

† Actually, Fighter Command had lost 261 aircraft during that period.

‡ As already noted, British production was about 500 fighters and 1,000 bombers and other types per month.

has so far been inflicted on British bombers. . . . Of the British planes reported shot down by us, a great number can probably be quickly repaired. According to Luftwaffe estimates the British had on 1 July more than 900 and a reserve of 250 fighter planes; on 1 September 600 fighter planes, of which 420 were ready for commitment, and a reserve of 100 in the factories. . . . The British aviation industry had an output in July of 300 bombers and 300 fighter planes. . . .

Conclusion: The British fighter defense is severely crippled. In case the German attacks on British fighter planes are continued in September, and if the weather is favorable, the British fighter defense is likely to be so weakened that air attacks on British production centers and port installations can be increased, with the result that British supplies will suffer seriously. Whether England will then continue to fight is an open question.

The only accurate assessment in this entire report was that the British bomber force had not been seriously damaged. Falkenstein's figures on British losses and the British rate of production were as wild as Stapf's, and his report likewise embodied an understatement of German losses.* As for the crucial estimate of British fighter strength on September 1, in fact Fighter Command had about 750 (rather than Falkenstein's 420) planes available for operations, and a reserve nearly double the "100 in the factories" allowed by Falkenstein. Small wonder, therefore, that his general conclusions exuded a glow of optimism that bore little relation to the actualities.

Given these rosy reports, and the considerable success which was in fact being achieved, why were the Luftwaffe's tactics altered? "Never change a winning game" is a good rule for sports and war alike. The decision to shift the *Schwerpunkt* of the Luftwaffe's attack from the airfields to London was made on August 31 and was put into execution on September 7. The reasons for the decision, as revealed by the attendant circumstances, were both strategic and tactical.

In terms of air tactics, the basic reason for a change was that although the Luftwaffe was beginning to get the upper hand, its progress toward the big goal, "air superiority," was not rapid enough. If Sea Lion was to be attempted, it would have to be during September, for thereafter the weather would be too uncertain. On August 16 an OKW directive had been circulated fixing September 15 as the target date for Sea Lion. The timetable of preparations specified September 1 as the day to begin the movement of tugs, Rhine barges, and other ele-

---

* From Aug. 8 to Aug. 31 inclusive the Luftwaffe lost 653 planes, as compared to 467 reported by Falkenstein. Losses publicly admitted in the German communiqués were even lower.

ments of the invasion fleet down the North Sea coast to the embarkation ports on the Channel coast.

But by the end of August, despite the enormous losses which were thought to have been inflicted on the RAF, it was plain enough that the Luftwaffe had not yet attained a sufficient superiority over the crucial areas to warrant launching the invasion. Hitler himself was well aware of this; in conversation with Galeazzo Ciano on August 29[24] he blamed the Luftwaffe's failure on "the persistent bad weather," and expressed the opinion that "if the weather is more favorable in future . . . two weeks are sufficient to gain that mastery of the air over Britain which is indispensable in order to neutralize British naval superiority and carry out the landing."

But the weather might not improve and, even if it did, this estimate left no margin of safety for an invasion on September 15. Could not something be done to accelerate a decision in the air?

The Luftwaffe's main obstacle had been the short range of its Messerschmitt 109s, which restricted the effective scope of daytime operations to the southeast corner of England. But within that narrow battlefield lay most of London. Thus far the great city had been spared while the Luftwaffe concentrated its forces on the RAF airfields and other targets. The reasons for this restraint, however, were not exclusively military; London was forbidden as a target by Hitler's direct orders. Whether the Fuehrer thought that attacking the capital would stiffen his enemies' will to resist, or wanted to reserve this assault as a final trump, or both, is not clear. Whatever his reasons, the prohibition was reiterated as late as August 24 in an OKW order that stated:[25] "Attacks against the London area and terror attacks are reserved for the Fuehrer's decision."

London's immunity was by no means universally popular in the Luftwaffe; Fliegerkorps II had recommended such attacks as the tactical basis of the *Adlerangriff*.[26] Dissatisfaction was especially keen at the combat level, where the fighter pilots were increasingly irked by the evasive tactics of their opponents, who shunned combat and went for the bombers whenever possible, and where bomber and fighter pilots alike were exasperated by Fighter Command's constant reappearance in strength, despite the Luftwaffe communiqués announcing its progressive annihilation.[27] In his postwar memoirs Galland, one of the leading German aces of the Battle, writes:[28]

We therefore had to get used to the fact that our offensive could only be directed against a small and extraordinarily well-defended sector of the

British Isles. But this sector included the capital, the heart of the British Empire, London. The seven-million-people city on the Thames was of exceptional military importance as the brain and nerve center of the British High Command, as a port, and as a center for armament and distribution. The fact that London was within the range of day bombing attacks with fighter cover . . . must be regarded as one of the positive sides of our offensive.

We fighter pilots, discouraged by a task which was beyond our strength, were looking forward impatiently and excitedly to the start of the bomber attacks. We believed that only then would the English fighters leave their dens and be forced to give us open battle.

We may pass for the moment the question of whether Galland's tactical analysis was right. Right or wrong, his views were academic as long as the Fuehrer ruled London out of bounds. But during the last week of August a curious sequence of events persuaded Hitler to lift the ban.

As already remarked, from the beginning of the Battle's "second phase" the Luftwaffe had stepped up its night bombing operations. On the night of August 24 about 170 German bombers were over England. Some of them were directed to the oil installations at Rochester and Thameshaven, east of London, but through navigational errors they overshot their targets and dropped their bombs over central London; fires were started and other damage was caused in a number of London boroughs, including East Ham and Bethnal Green.[29]

Meanwhile Air Marshal Sir Charles Portal's Bomber Command had been pecking away at the Germans, putting a nightly average of sixty to seventy bombers over Germany and the invasion coast. Daytime sorties were only a quarter as numerous, and were carried out only when the cloud cover was heavy enough to enable the Blenheims to hide from the German fighters. These few sallies, directed against the Luftwaffe's airdromes along and behind the Channel coast, were largely ineffective.

Bomber Command's night operations, like those of the Luftwaffe, were comparatively safe but highly inaccurate.* Barges and other naval targets in the potential invasion ports were the top-priority targets, but during July and August the concentrations were insufficient to justify much effort. Nearly three quarters (by weight) of the

---

* A notable exception to Bomber Command's rather discouraging record of performance during July and August was the attack on the Dortmund–Ems canal, carried out by 5 Hampden bombers on the night of Aug. 12–13, which blocked the canal for at least 10 days and measurably delayed the movement of barges and other vessels from the Rhineland to the invasion ports. See *infra*, pp. 256–57.

British bombs dropped during July and August were intended to hit aircraft factories, oil installations, and railroad marshaling yards, but 1,450 tons of poorly aimed bombs had little effect on the German war potential.[30]

For obvious operational reasons (bomb loads and navigational problems) the British Air Staff and Bomber Command preferred to attack the targets in the Ruhr and elsewhere in western Germany that were closest to England. Berlin lay over five hundred miles east of Bomber Command's nearest fields. But as British casualties from Luftwaffe raids mounted, Churchill and the War Cabinet called for retaliation. The accidental bombing of central London on the night of August 24 brought a prompt demand for a reprisal attack on Berlin, which was carried out the very next night by a force of eighty-one bombers,[31] and Bomber Command's aircraft were again over Berlin on the nights of August 28, 30, and 31, and thereafter on numerous occasions.

Operating at such a distance, the twin-engined Wellingtons and Hampdens could not carry much bomb load. They were not directed to the heart of Berlin, and were given specific industrial targets, mostly on the city's outskirts. But on the night of August 28 bombs that fell near the Goerlitzer railroad station killed ten persons, and the raid on the night of the thirtieth over Siemensstadt caused some temporary loss of production at the Siemens electrical works.[32]

Compared to what Berlin suffered a few years later, these raids in the late summer and fall of 1940 were the merest pinpricks, and they were unimpressive enough compared to what was shortly to hit London. But the people of London were expecting to be bombed; the Berliners were not. The Flak was noisy, the shelters were unfamiliar, and the psychological effect was considerable. William L. Shirer, an eyewitness, reported:[33] "The Berliners are stunned. They did not think it could ever happen. . . . Goering assured them it couldn't. The Berliners . . . believed him. Their disillusionment today therefore is all the greater. You have to see their faces to measure it. . . . For the first time the war has been brought home to them."

The Berlin raids were likewise unwelcome to Adolf Hitler. Since August 17 he had been at the Berghof enjoying an Alpine summer and redrawing the map of central Europe. On August 28 Ciano arrived to participate with Ribbentrop in arbitrating the boundary dispute between Rumania and Hungary, whose representatives arrived in Vienna on August 29. On August 30 the second Vienna award was promulgated, but Hitler was already back in Berlin.

For the news of the raids had struck a very jarring note among those assembled to abide the Fuehrer's dispensation. Abruptly he forsook his mountain retreat and sped back to Berlin.[34] On the afternoon of August 30 Jodl informed Warlimont that Hitler had given permission for reprisal attacks with strong forces against London.[35] Thus the long-standing ban was lifted, and that night Hitler had opportunity for personal observation of the third RAF attack in the Berlin area.

The permission was granted just at the time of mounting pressure inside the Luftwaffe for a change in tactics. Goering himself had little use for Sea Lion, but the target date was approaching, and the first OKL orders on the subject had been distributed on August 27.[36] Hitler was well aware that the Luftwaffe had not yet attained a sufficient air superiority to justify an invasion (as he told Jodl on August 30),[37] and Goering and his staff concluded that attacks on London might expedite the air victory.

On August 31 an OKL order set the wheels in motion for the big change in tactics,[38] and Goering summoned the commanders to meet him at The Hague on September 3. There appears[39] to have been considerable divergency of views between Kesselring, the optimist, and Sperrle, the pessimist, as well as disagreement about targets. However, Hitler had not yet given permission for "terror" attacks on residential areas, and the conferees decided to concentrate on the London docks.

Hitler himself took charge of the propaganda aspects, with the two-fold purpose of pinning on the British the blame for the coming onslaught and satisfying the German public's appetite for revenge. On the afternoon of September 4 he made a surprise appearance and speech in the Berlin Sportpalast at the opening of the winter relief (*Winterhilfe*) campaign. The audience was shrewdly chosen, for it consisted largely of women nurses and social workers who would be most likely to observe the air raids and their results, and whose approval of Hitler's threats was nothing short of hysterical.[40]

The Fuehrer first accused the RAF of cowardice for not venturing over Germany by day, and then of brutality for the indiscriminate bombing of residential areas. Then:[41]

"I have waited three months without responding, with the thought that they might stop this mischief. Herr Churchill saw in this a sign of weakness. You will understand that we are now answering, night for night, and in growing strength. And if the British Air Force drops 2,000 or 3,000 or 4,000 kilograms of bombs, then we will drop 150,000, 180,000, 230,000, 300,000, 400,000 and more kilograms. When they declare that they will attack our cities in great strength, then we will eradicate [*ausradieren*] their cities. We will put a stop to the work of these night pirates, so help us God! The hour will come when one of us will break, and it will not be National Socialist Germany!"

The sequence of events touched off by the Luftwaffe's accidental bombing of London on August 24 has led some to conclude that the Luftwaffe's shift to a tactic of concentration on London was purely retaliatory.[42] It is true that the RAF's Berlin raids provoked Hitler into lifting the ban on London as a target, and but for them the concentration on London might have been delayed; but reprisal was only one of several motives. Galland and others[43] believed that the London raids would aid in bringing Fighter Command to decisive battle in the air. In addition, there was hope that heavy attacks on the port might disorganize and soften the British resistance. As it was put in the Naval War Diary:[44] "The purpose of the High Command is the total destruction of the vital harbor, dock, industrial, and supply installations of London by the continuous employment of the Luftwaffe, as a means of hastening the end of the war [*Kriegsentscheidung*]."

Governed by this mixture of motives, late in the afternoon of Saturday, September 7, the Luftwaffe launched the first of its daylight* attacks on the London area. The Reichsmarschall's personal train was brought to the Pas de Calais, and Goering, Kesselring, Loerzer and other generals and staff officers took station at Cap Gris-Nez to watch the Battle's progress.

At about four o'clock in the afternoon British radar picked up the German planes assembling over the Channel coast; within an hour some three hundred bombers and twice as many fighters were converging on London. They came in two great waves—"Valhallas," as the Germans called their big formations of bombers and escorting fighters[46] —one of which flew straight up the estuary, while the other took a more southerly approach over Sussex and Kent. Woolwich, Thameshaven, Tilbury and West Ham suffered severely under a rain of high explosive bombs and incendiaries. Great fires were started which were still burning when darkness fell and served as a beacon for 250 more bombers that came over London during the night. Apart from the heavy material damage, about a thousand Londoners were killed—a heavier civilian toll than had been taken by the Rotterdam raid four months earlier.[47]

---

* On the night of Sept. 5–6 some 70 aircraft had been sent to bomb the London docks, in what the Germans regarded as the "first" attack on London.[45]

At Fighter Command, Park was still chiefly concerned to protect his sector stations, and he had not anticipated the concentration on the London docks. As a result, comparatively few of the German bombers were engaged before they had reached their targets and dropped their bombs, and most of the heavy fighting took place as the Luftwaffe formations were homeward bound. On this occasion the German fighter cover was effective, and their bomber losses light. In the day's fighting, forty-one German aircraft (mostly fighters) and twenty-eight British fighters were lost.[48]

All in all, it was a successful day for the Luftwaffe, and no one saw any reason to drop or radically alter the new tactics.* A report by the Luftwaffe liaison officer at naval headquarters stated:[49] "The further conduct of the attack on London is expected to involve day operations by Luftflotte 2 with very heavy fighter escort, and night operations by Luftflotte 3, with the object of destroying the city's harbor installations, supplies, and power sources."

Fluctuating weather and the need to rest the crews prevented the Luftwaffe from maintaining a full scale of effort against London on a daily basis. During the week following the big attack of September 7 there were four days of light activity (September 8, 10, 12, and 13). On September 9, 11, and 14 there were heavy daylight attacks on London, though not quite so many aircraft were committed as on the seventh. On the nights of September 8, 9, and 11 some two hundred bombers were sent over London, and during the other nights fifty to 180.

Of the three large daylight raids, the one on September 11 was least successful. Some two hundred bombers from Luftflotte 2 and seventy from Luftflotte 3 approached London late in the afternoon, but Fighter Command had anticipated their course and timing, and many of the bombers jettisoned their loads and turned back. Damage to the dock area was light, and twenty-eight German aircraft were shot down, while Fighter Command lost nineteen planes.

On the eleventh the Luftwaffe attacked in about the same strength. Luftflotte 3's bombers went for Southampton and badly damaged the nearby Supermarine (Spitfire) factory; Luftflotte 2's much larger force penetrated to the London dock area, but the damage was not extensive. In the air, however, the Luftwaffe had much the better of it. This was the only major day engagement in which Fighter Command's losses

* Goering's optimism was no doubt reinforced by the OKL's claim to have destroyed 93 British aircraft in the day's fighting—more than treble the true count.

were larger than the Luftwaffe's, as twenty-nine of its aircraft were shot down for twenty-four German planes destroyed. September 14 was another bad day in the air for the British, as Fighter Command's loss of fourteen planes just matched their toll of German aircraft. On this occasion OKL held back most of its bombers in preparation for a big attack the following day, but large flights of fighters succeeded in luring Fighter Command into action.[50]

It is apparent, therefore, that the Luftwaffe's change of tactics did not much relieve the strain on Fighter Command *in the air*. Indeed, the results bore out Galland's expectation that attacking London would bring up the British fighters and lead to large-scale engagements. In these, considering that the Germans committed bombers as well as fighters, the Luftwaffe more than held its own. From September 7 to September 14 the British lost ninety-four fighters, the Germans 135 bombers and fighters.* Even more serious for the British was the loss of fifty fighter pilots killed and several more incapacitated by wounds.

It was *on the ground* that Fighter Command stood to gain as the German bombers concentrated over the London docks and ignored the British airfields, their erstwhile targets. By early September five forward fields and six of the seven sector stations in No. 11 Group had been damaged and the conduct of operations seriously hampered. Park himself declared that a few more days of attack on his sector stations might have put the defenses "in a perilous state." Of course, he could have moved his squadrons back to fields beyond the reach of the German fighters, but this would have exposed London and the southeastern counties to a virtually unchecked rain of bombs, and would have left Fighter Command much less advantageously deployed in the event of an invasion.

Relaxation of the pressure on the RAF's ground organization might have been justified by commensurate advantages to the Germans. But the bomb damage in the London area was of no strategic significance. Despite the explosions and the fires, the casualties and the rubble, civilian morale did not crack. Rail communications were often interrupted, but repairs were prompt, and the damage to transport and communications was never so extensive as to hamper reinforcement of the beaches, had Sea Lion come to pass. Warehouses and docks suf-

---

* British and German losses were both considerably lighter than during the preceding weeks, because of the exceedingly light activity on Sept. 8, 10, 12, and 13, for which bad weather was chiefly responsible.

fered, but no critical shortages were caused. Neither as preparation for an invasion nor as absolute air war à la Douhet were the London attacks soundly conceived or even marginally successful.

Repulse: September 15, 1940

But that was not the way things looked on September 14 to Hermann Goering and the OKL staff. Their crews had seen the great fires burning in London for many hours after the raids of September 7. The bad weather thereafter had been a nuisance, but the RAF seemed to be weakening. Its resistance to the attacks on September 11 and 14 had appeared somewhat desultory, and the Luftwaffe had fared well on the score sheet. Perhaps a few more days of good weather and heavy raids would really knock the "Lords" out of the air.

Furthermore, the Germans were getting encouraging reports about the effect of the London raids. Right after the first big attack on September 7 the Japanese military attaché in London sent Tokyo a report —given to or intercepted by the Germans—on the "good effect of the German air attacks." Two days later the German military attaché in Washington, General Friedrich von Boetticher (a chronic source of highly colored, overoptimistic "gen"), told Berlin: "The morale of the British population is strongly affected. Signs of great weariness. Optimism has disappeared. Effect in the heart of London resembles an earthquake. Great damage done to public utility services (gas, electricity, water)."[51]

Flushed with favorable reports alike from his crews and from friendly foreign observers in the target area, Goering thought he had every reason to press home the attack on London. On September 13 he came to Berlin to attend Hitler's luncheon reception for officers (including five from the Luftwaffe) recently appointed to the rank of *Generaloberst*. Either on this or some closely previous occasion, Goering gave Hitler a rosy account of the Luftwaffe's recent achievements and prospects. The Fuehrer glowed and told his luncheon guests that "in the present favorable situation he would not think of taking such a great risk as to land in England."[52]

However, the season had reached the point where it was just about now or never for Sea Lion. The autumn was but a week away, and October would bring storms in the Channel and more clouds in the sky. In Libya, Graziani had just begun his measly little offensive into

Egypt, which Mussolini had promised to bring off when Hitler was ready to pounce on England. Sea Lion required ten days of mine sweeping, mine laying, loading, and other preparations, so if it was to be undertaken during September Hitler had to give the order by about the middle of the month.

And so, despite his cavalier dismissal of Sea Lion at lunch on September 13, on the next day Hitler sat down with a smaller and more purposeful group to canvass the prospects. Raeder, Brauchitsch, and Halder were there, and Jeschonnek standing in for Goering.[53] The Fuehrer led off by observing that Germany's interest lay in a speedy end to the war, that a successful landing in England would be most likely to accomplish this, and (a bouquet for Raeder that must have frightened that prudent monarch of the sea) that "the Navy has attained all targets set for it in preparation for the Channel crossing." As for the Luftwaffe:

"Accomplishments of the Air Force are beyond praise. Four or five days of good weather, and a decisive result will be achieved. . . . We have a good chance to force Britain to her knees. Effects to date are enormous, but total victory must wait for these four or five days of clear weather. . . .

"Enemy fighter forces have not yet been totally eliminated. Our own air victory reports fail to give an entirely reliable picture.* In any event, the enemy has suffered severe losses.

"Seen as a whole, however, and nothwithstanding all our successes, *the prerequisites for 'Seeloewe' have not yet been completely realized. . . .*

"Attacks to date have had enormous effect, though perhaps chiefly upon nerves. . . . Even though victory in the air might not be achieved before another ten or twelve days, Britain might yet be seized by mass hysteria. . . ."

Raeder then chimed in, agreeing with Hitler and proposing a postponement of *Seeloewe* until early October. Furthermore: "If Luftwaffe has achieved complete victory by that time, we might not even need to undertake the invasion."

Strategically speaking, the discussants were in a never-never land for fair. On the one hand, the Luftwaffe had failed to destroy the RAF, and thus the prime prerequisite of invasion was lacking. On the other hand, the Luftwaffe was wreaking such havoc (echoes of von Boetticher) that the English might soon succumb to "mass hysteria," and it was so close to victory that an invasion might be quite unnecessary!

* According to the OKW communiqués,[54] from Aug. 9 to Sept. 12 the Germans had destroyed 1,800 British aircraft, nearly all presumably fighters. Since this was about double Fighter Command's effective strength including new production, it had become apparent to OKL that totals based on the crews' reports were wildly inflated.

Since all this made little sense, it was impossible to come to any rational conclusion about Sea Lion. Accordingly, Hitler merely postponed the time for decision three days, to September 17. "The decisive factor," he reiterated, "is the relentless prosecution of our air effort."

Jeschonnek thought he saw an opening: "Physical destruction exceeds our expectations. But there has as yet been no mass panic, because residential sections have not been attacked and destroyed so far. Wants free hand in attacking residential areas."

In fact residential areas galore had been hit, but it is true that they had not been targeted. In any event, and despite Raeder's enthusiastic approval of the suggestion,[55] the Fuehrer was not yet ready for *Terrorangriffe*. He appeared to agree with Jeschonnek, but really held him off:

"All right, but attacks on strategic targets must have first priority, because they destroy war potential which cannot be replaced. As long as .there is still a strategic target left we must concentrate on it: railroad stations, targets in outlying areas, gas and water works. Bombing calculated to create mass panic must be left to the last (possibility of retaliation against German cities). The horrible threat of bombing population concentrations must be our last trump."

And so, for all the talk, the only result of the meeting was an OKW order postponing until September 17 the decision date for Sea Lion, and directing the Luftwaffe to keep it up:[56]

The air attacks against London are to be continued and the target area is to be expanded against military and other vital installations (e.g., railway stations).

Terror attacks against purely residential areas are reserved for use as an ultimate means of pressure, and are therefore not to be employed at present.

Sunday, September 15, dawned a bit misty but with the promise of fair weather over the Channel and southeastern England. By eleven in the morning the British radar plots showed a big buildup of enemy aircraft over the Pas-de-Calais, and it was clear that a major attack was imminent. In fact OKL was about to shoot the works, with over two hundred bombers from Luftflotte 2 under heavy escort committed over London in two great waves, and about seventy more bombers from Luftflotte 3 dispatched on a diversionary attack over Portland.

Suspecting that the good weather presaged heavy fighting, Winston Churchill chose this morning for a visit to the headquarters of No. 11 Group at Uxbridge. At about eleven o'clock he and Mrs. Churchill joined Air Vice-Marshal Park in the gallery of the operations room. "I don't know whether anything will happen today," said Park. "At present all is quiet." At about the same time, No. 504 Squadron (Hurricanes) at Northolt had a visit from two American generals and a rear admiral, who had dropped in to observe "life at a fighter squadron."[57]

Whether from carelessness, overconfidence, or a desire to get the show under way without delay, the Germans neglected to carry out the usual diversionary flights and feints that they had been employing to cover the direction of the main thrust. This was a principal cause of the Luftwaffe's undoing that day, for it enabled Park to commit his squadrons in good time and at the right places, and meet the oncoming "Valhallas" well to the east of London. Ten squadrons operating in wings of two each, and two more single squadrons, harried the Germans all the way in from Canterbury.

Now Park committed six more squadrons of his own, and called on Air Vice-Marshal Leigh-Mallory's No. 12 Group for support.* Leigh-Mallory and his officers, including the famous legless Douglas Bader, commanding No. 242 Squadron of Hurricanes, favored the commitment of their forces by large wings of three or more squadrons;† the assemblage of so large a formation took time, and Park had complained that No. 12 Group was never there when needed. But on this occasion a wing of five squadrons led by Bader—some twenty-four Spitfires and thirty-six Hurricanes—hit the Germans just as they reached London. The bomber formation broke up, and few of the crews were able to make their drops with any accuracy. Their loads were scattered all over London and, while a few good hits were scored, the damage was nothing like as severe as it had been on September 7. Four more fighter squadrons pursued the Germans as they streamed back toward France.

Early that afternoon the second and larger wave came in over Dover. Again the British anticipated well; in all, thirty squadrons went up in

---

* At about this point Churchill asked Park, "What other reserves have we?" And Park replied, "There are none." So complete a commitment did, to be sure, involve the risk that a large number of fighters would have to come down simultaneously to refuel, with scanty protection against fresh attacks. The incident has often been cited to show how close the RAF was to defeat, but in fact there had been comparable situations before. On this occasion Fighter Command had some 250 planes in the air, and most of them were actually engaging the Germans. That is just what they should have been doing, and why the day ended so favorably for the British.

† In RAF slang a "Balbo," after the Italian politician and aviator Italo Balbo, who led mass flights of Italian aircraft.

defense, and most of them succeeded in engaging. While the fighting over London was at its height, a *Geschwader* (KG 55) of Heinkel 111s from Luftflotte 3 came over Portsmouth unescorted. The bombers reached the target undisturbed, but their aim was inaccurate and the damage slight. Late in the afternoon a group of Messerschmitt 110s bombarded the Supermarine factory near Southampton, but failed to hit the plant.

So ended the day's fighting, and that evening Churchill was told (as was then publicly announced) that 183 German planes had been shot down. This time the British figures were as badly inflated as were the Germans' customarily; the actual count was about one third of the claim.* But the British had lost only twenty-six aircraft, and it was plain enough that the days' laurels were theirs by a wide margin.

OKL itself was well aware that things had gone very badly. At OKW, Falkenstein reported[57] "large air battles and great losses for the German formations due to lack of fighter protection." At naval head-quarters, the OKL liaison officer reported that over London large flights of enemy fighters (no doubt Bader's wing) had been en-countered, and that the British fighters had attacked sharply and followed the bombers on the return flight all the way to the middle of the Channel. The day's operations, involving over three hundred bomber and a thousand fighter sorties, had been "unusually disadvan-tageous," and the heavy losses had been chiefly incurred while the bombers were homeward bound, in small groups and without fighter escort.[59]

Unspoken but implicit in these gloomy appraisals was the death of Sea Lion. Fighter Command's victory over London was not the only cause of its demise; for the past several nights Bomber Command had been hitting the Channel ports where the invasion "fleet" was assem-bling, and had been taking a mounting toll of prahms, tugs, and stores. Sea Lion was pinched to death; the invasion could not be launched because Fighter Command was unconquered, and the invasion forces could not be safely held at the ready because Bomber Command was chewing up their transport and supplies.

And so on the evening of September 17 the SKL war diary recorded the Fuehrer's decision that Sea Lion be indefinitely postponed.[60] The stated grounds were that the enemy air force was "by no means de-

---

* The official British postwar claim is sometimes given as 60 and sometimes 56; the German records indicate a loss of 52 aircraft, but only 43 were acknowledged in the German communiqué.

feated"; rather, it was showing increasing activity in attacking the Channel harbors and breaking up the invasion assemblage.

Apparently because of the initial (and exaggerated) claim that over 180 German war planes had been destroyed,[61] September 15 has since been celebrated as "Battle of Britain Day." In fact Fighter Command's victory bag was considerably larger on both August 15 and August 18, and from the tactical standpoint the fighting on August 15 was the most significant, for it showed the worthlessness of the Messerschmitt 110 as an escort, the unacceptable hazards of unescorted bomber attacks even in northern England, the serious deficiencies of the Stuka, and Fighter Command's ability to withstand a mass attack by all three *Luftflotten.*

But if August 15 was tactically crucial, September 15 was strategically decisive. As the German crews turned in their reports and OKL took count of the missing, all hope of a speedy defeat of the RAF was dissipated. The British will and ability to resist would not crumble, and to launch an invasion under these circumstances would be madness. The war would not end in 1940, and the Germans would have to seek new avenues to victory. The Battle of Britain was not quite finished, but what remained was of little import compared to what had transpired during the five weeks from August 11 to September 15, which well deserves memorializing as the day when the Germans realized that their strongest efforts had been repulsed.

From Battle to Blitz

After the first London raid on September 7, Goering's headquarters train ("Robinson") remained near the Channel coast, and on September 15 it arrived at Boulogne.[62] On the next day, the Reichsmarschall summoned the *Luftflotte* and *Fliegerkorps* commanders for a general conference (*Besprechung*), to take stock of the situation and review their tactics.[63] As usual, the meeting began with a Goering monologue:

"The weather situation requires a change in our assault tactics. Up to now we have been seeking to bring the enemy to battle in the air. But the bad weather has given them time to reorganize.

"From the reports of our crews, we get the following picture of the enemy situation—

"All available fighter and anti-aircraft defense has been assembled in the London area. Proof of this is that Luftflotte 3, making two small attacks, found only weak fighter defenses in the area west of London.* . . .

"In line with this estimate of the enemy, it follows that we should keep at him with all our means, as with four to five more days of heavy losses he ought to be finished off . . .

"With co-ordinated attacks all over England, there would be many places where no fighters would be encountered. For the enemy is under the absolute necessity of combating the attacks on London. If unexpectedly he should fail to do this, so much the better for us, as then with stronger forces we can destroy his capital.

"Accordingly, these will be the new tactics:

(a) Large-scale attacks only in the best weather, but then repeated assaults with, at times, three to four hundred bombers.

(b) During the present changeable weather, attacks in small units (a full *Gruppe*) under the strongest possible escort of one- and two-engined fighters. Thus the bombers will serve both as a decoy [*Lockvogel*]† and as a means of destroying important targets in London. . . . The fighters must give the bombers close escort.

(c) When the weather is unsuitable for formation flying, harassing raids by single aircraft.

(d) Continuing attacks in waves may be resumed when the enemy is again strained by heavy losses. Such attacks are very exhausting for our own fighters. . . ."

There were more overtones of fatigue and pessimism in the discussion that followed. Generalmajor von Doering, the *Jafue* 2, who on August 29 had claimed "unquestionable fighter superiority,"[64] reported that his fighters had been surprised the previous day by a new British tactic of close-formation assault in strength—obviously Bader's wing had made a deep impression. "All well and good," replied Goering, whistling in the dark. "It bunches the enemy fighters for our attack on them." Losses among the experienced fighter pilots were getting serious, and caution was enjoined; the pilots should model themselves on Moelders and Galland.‡ It was agreed that the construction of winter quarters should be commenced—a prudent decision, but hardly in tune with Goering's prediction of victory in four or five days.

And Sea Lion? Goering had never taken much stock in that project, and now he declared roundly that it should not be allowed to inter-

---

* Presumably Goering was referring to KG 55's Portland raid of Sept. 15 and another Luftflotte 3 operation against Southampton on Sept. 11.

† I.e., to lure the British fighters into the air.

‡ At that time, Moelders and Galland were respectively the No. 1 and No. 2 German fighter "aces."

fere with the Luftwaffe's planned operations.* Nevertheless, air defense of the invasion harbors was a very "urgent" matter.

In conclusion, Goering laid down for Kesselring and Sperrle their respective assignments. In good weather Luftflotte 2 would carry out the "decoy" attacks over London, to wear down and disunite the enemy fighters, while Luftflotte 3 might attack Southampton and Bristol. In bad weather, both should carry out harassing attacks. At night, both should attack London with maximum strength, and Luftflotte 3 might also hit Liverpool. Special crews from both *Luftflotten* would attack thirty aircraft industrial targets, to be designated by the OKL intelligence staff (Schmid). Fliegerdivision 9 was to continue mining the Thames and to experiment with land mines in London. Luftflotte 2 was also to destroy the British coastal batteries, in preparation for Sea Lion.†

Bad weather had prevented any important operations on the day of the conference (September 16). The next day was not much better, but on September 18 some seventy bombers were sent over under heavy escort. Once again Bader's "Balbo" of three squadrons hit the bombers near London; during the day's fighting nineteen German and twelve British planes were shot down.

The previous evening Sea Lion had been indefinitely postponed. Why, then, was the Battle continued?

One reason was that, although Hitler had abandoned any serious thoughts of invasion, he did not wish the British to know this. Rather, he wanted to maintain the threat of a landing and thus keep the enemy under pressure. An obvious relaxation of the air offensive would not have been in keeping with that design.

But this was not the governing factor in the thinking, if such it may be called, at OKL. As we have seen, the *Adlerangriff* was planned long before *Seeloewe* was even a gleam in the eye. Goering had never taken the invasion plan seriously, so its official abandonment neither surprised nor interested him very much. His hope throughout had been to bring England to terms by the Luftwaffe's independent impact on morale and economy. Only five days earlier he had told Hitler that a few days of good flying weather would do the trick. The events of September 15 had badly shaken this prediction, but Goering could not afford to throw in the sponge and lose countenance. Nor, indeed, did

* *"Seeloewe darf die Operationen der Luftwaffe weder Stoeren noch belasten."*
† The conference took place the day before Sea Lion was indefinitely postponed.

he need to, for if the RAF was still obstinately battle-worthy, so, too, the Luftwaffe was by no means beaten.

An accurate reflection of the face OKL was putting on at this time is furnished by the account of a meeting between Generalmajor Walter Warlimont of OKW and Kesselring's chief of staff, Generalleutnant Wilhelm Speidel.[65] On September 18 Warlimont began a four-day tour of Holland, Belgium, and northern France, to study at first hand the state of preparations for Sea Lion* and the prospects of winning the air war. During his journey Warlimont visited the combat head-quarters of Luftflotte 2 at Calais, and upon returning to OKW he reported (on September 23) to Keitel and Jodl that airfields in the coastal region were well laid out and camouflaged, and that both Kesselring and Speidel blamed the bad weather for the repeated post-ponement of heavy attacks. Likewise the tactical co-operation of fighters and bombers still presented difficulties.

As for the course of the Battle up to that time, Speidel declared that during its opening phase the Luftwaffe had successfully beaten down the British fighter defenses. However, Luftflotte 2's request for permission to attack London had first been refused; only after great pressure had permission finally been granted. Then there was only one day of good weather, so that the attack could not be carried out as planned. This had given the English a breathing spell, during which reinforcements of planes and personnel had been called up, so that the enemy fighter defenses were strengthened. Then the inexperienced pilots went after the German bombers recklessly and often resorted to ramming, while the better flyers engaged the Messerschmitts.

For these reasons it had become necessary to renew the attack against the British fighters, so that now the Luftwaffe was simultane-ously committing large formations of fighters and bombers, the latter especially at night. The Luftwaffe crews were experienced and superior to the British, and were fully confident that they would bring the Battle to a successful conclusion.

Speidel estimated the British fighter strength at about three hundred, with a monthly increment of 250 new planes.† As for the bombers, there was a sharp division of opinion. The former German air attaché in London, Generalleutnant Rudolf Wenninger, who was specially

---

* Sea Lion was indefinitely postponed on the eve of Warlimont's departure, but, whether or not he knew this at the time, his trip was not canceled.

† In fact Fighter Command had 715 aircraft available for operations on Sept. 21, and monthly production of new Hurricanes and Spitfires alone was well over 400 during September.

attached to the staff of Luftflotte 2, thought that the British had about eight hundred bombers and that they were being held in reserve for the anticipated high point of the air war at the time of a German landing in England. But Kesselring doubted that they had such strong forces available.*

Speidel's assessment of the Luftwaffe's prospects was both benighted and disingenuous. Perhaps his gross underestimation of Fighter Command's strength was sincere, and the product of Beppo Schmid's slipshod intelligence. But Speidel must have been cognizant of the difficulties rehearsed and the decisions reached at the Boulogne conference on September 16. The Luftwaffe simply could not sustain constant large-scale daytime bomber sorties; Fighter Command's defense was too fierce, and the strain and the losses suffered by the German crews too great. Already the main emphasis of the bomber offensive was shifting toward night operations, and the commitment of bombers by day was dwindling rapidly. By the time of Warlimont's visit there was no apparent means by which the Germans could bring the Battle to a victorious conclusion.

Nevertheless it was far from finished, though bad weather in combination with fatigue and caution held down the scale of daytime activity for nearly a week after September 18. But on September 25 the Germans sent over some 275 bombers, and a force of about sixty from Luftflotte 3 got through to Bristol and hit the Filton aircraft works, which were then producing Blenheim bombers and the new Beaufighter. Their aim was good; production was curtailed for many weeks, and there were more than 250 casualties.

On the next day the Luftwaffe delivered another sharp blow. Twenty-six bombers with a double escort of fighters came over Southampton and unloaded seventy tons of bombs on the Supermarine aircraft factory at Woolston. Three completed Spitfires were destroyed and others damaged; a far more serious consequence was the complete stoppage of production. Fortunately, Spitfire production was in the process of transfer and dispersal, but October production was down slightly from September and was more than eighty below what had been planned.[66]

Sustained and well-executed attacks of this sort earlier in the Battle would have sorely crippled Fighter Command. By the end of Sep-

---

* On this occasion the habitually optimistic Kesselring was right, for Wenninger's estimate was high. Bomber Command's operational strength at that time was not much over 500 aircraft, many of which were obsolete.

tember, with shortening days and worsening weather, it was too late for the Luftwaffe to score decisively. Furthermore, the war in the air was turning against the Germans. During the nine days of September 7 through 15 they had knocked down 120 British fighters for a loss of 195 of their own planes. In eleven days from the sixteenth through the twenty-sixth, Fighter Command lost only 53 planes to 118 for the Luftwaffe.[67]

Both sides were tiring, but the unfavorable ratio of more than two to one boded ill for the Germans. To the other services, the victorious "front" was still maintained. On September 26 Generalmajor Stapf reported to OKH[68] that the enemy had only "about three hundred fighters available, including two hundred older types" (presumably Hurricanes).

Perhaps emboldened by the successful attacks on the twenty-fifth and the twenty-sixth, on September 27 Luftflotte 2 sent three waves of bombers toward London, and Luftflotte 3 struck again at Bristol. It was a disastrous day for the Luftwaffe, for the British defense was strong and only a few of the bombers reached their targets. Some fifty German planes failed to return (many of them fell into the Channel), while Fighter Command suffered twenty-eight losses.

About a week earlier Hermann Goering, indulging his prerogatives as Reich Chief Forester, had forsaken the Battle for the pleasures of the Reichsjaegerhof at Rominten in East Prussia. Here he received Germany's leading fighter ace, Major Werner Moelders, who on September 21 had shot down his fortieth British plane and been invested with the Knight's Cross of the Iron Cross with Oak Leaves.*

While Goering and Moelders were hunting the stag on the Rominterheide, the latter's closest rival, Major Adolf Galland, made his fortieth kill, over the Thames estuary on September 24.† Galland was promptly whisked off to Berlin for his Oak Leaves investiture, and was received by Hitler at the Reich Chancellery. The Fuehrer did not much like Goering's fly-boys, especially Galland, whom he thought to look Jewish. On this occasion, however, Hitler concealed his distaste; he listened patiently to Galland's praise of the British adversaries and his strictures on the vainglorious tone of German propaganda broadcasts about

---

* The Oak Leaves (*Eichenlaub*) was the highest decoration for heroism then being awarded. Moelders was the second recipient; the first was the "Hero of Narvik," Generalleutnant Eduard Dietl, who had been so honored at the Kroll Opera House celebration on July 19, 1940.

† In view of the gross inflation of the Luftwaffe's victory claims, the individual records of the German aces are suspect.

the Battle. Far from disagreeing, Hitler placated Galland with a long disquisition on the virtues of the Anglo-Saxon race and the tragic consequence of the strife between Germans and English, which he had tried so hard to avoid.

Galland flew on to Rominten, on Goering's command invitation to join him at the Reichsjaegerhof. His account continues:[69]

The Reichsjaegerhof was a log house made of tree trunks, with a thatched roof jutting out far over the eaves. Goering came out of the house to meet me wearing a green suede hunting jacket over a silk blouse with long puffed sleeves, high hunting boots, and in his belt a hunting knife in the shape of an old Germanic sword. He was in the best humor. . . .

After congratulating me he said that he had a special treat in store for me. He gave me permission to hunt one of the royal stags, which were usually reserved for him. It was a so-called "Reichsjaegermeister" stag. He knew them all and each one had a name; he watched over them and was loath to part with one of them. . . . That night no mention was made of the war in general or the Battle of Britain in particular."

The next morning (September 27) Galland shot his stag—"a really royal beast, the stag of a lifetime." But the idyllic mood was rudely shattered that afternoon by the reports of the day's fighting over England: "They were devastating. During a raid on London exceptionally high losses had been sustained. Goering was shattered. He simply could not explain how the increasingly painful loss of bombers came about." Galland gave him scant comfort:

I assured him that in spite of the heavy losses we were inflicting on the enemy fighters, no decisive decrease in their number or fighting efficiency was noticeable. . . . Even if the German figures of enemy aircraft destroyed were perhaps overestimated, the fact that their fighter strength obviously did not diminish could only be accounted for in this way: England, by a great concentration of energy, was making up her losses . . .

To the tired German crews and their baffled commanders, Fighter Command must indeed have seemed like the fabled Hydra. If one totaled the figures in the Luftwaffe daily communiqués, some two thousand British fighters had by now been destroyed—more than there were supposed to have been (or were) in all—yet the RAF was still operating with undiminished vigor. Galland put his finger on the reasons for the seeming miracle: British plane wastage was far lower and production far higher than the German intelligence staff estimated, and now events were exposing the error so plainly that it had to be acknowledged.

Fighter Command had survived the Luftwaffe's best efforts to destroy it; Goering and his staff were at their wits' end, and now their own losses were mounting. There was just enough momentum for a last lunge. On September 30 the Luftwaffe put up 173 bombers and flew over a thousand fighter sorties. Luftflotte 2 sent two waves of bombers toward London, one in the morning and the other at noon. About thirty bombers made target, but their losses were heavy and the damage was light. In the afternoon Luftflotte 3 sent forty Heinkels under heavy escort to bomb the Westland aircraft factory at Yeovil. They got through, but clouds obscured the target, and the bombs fell several miles away, at Sherborne.

This was the last day of massed bomber attacks. Again the Germans were badly smashed, losing forty-eight machines while shooting down only twenty British fighters. After a not unpromising start, the daytime attacks on London had failed. The damage to the great city had fallen far short of the Germans' expectations, and during the twenty-four days from the seventh through the thirtieth of September the Luftwaffe had lost 433 planes to 242 for Fighter Command.

The Battle itself did not end abruptly, but during October the nature of the day fighting was radically changed. Since August the Germans had been experimenting with bomb-carrying fighters. At first only the two-engined Messerschmitt 110s and 210s were used,* but later the 109s were also pressed into service as "Jabos." London was attacked with fighter-bombers for the first time on September 20.[70]

In October, the regular bombers (*Kampfflieger*) were virtually retired from the day fighting, and the main burden of the bombing was taken over by the Jabos. Approximately a third of the fighters (some 250) were converted to serve as fighter-bombers. The Messerschmitt 109s carried a single 500-pound bomb, and the 110s carried two of them and four 100-pounders as well. The fighter pilots hated their new role, both because they were virtually helpless when attacked and because it was obvious that they could accomplish nothing more than pinpricks. As Galland put it, the fighter-bomber as a strategic weapon was "a stopgap and a scapegoat," and the reaction among the pilots was exceedingly bitter.[71]

Indeed, the entire Jabo tactic was little more than face saving. Sea

* The first fighter-bomber ("Jabo") operations were carried out by an experimental group (Erprobungsgruppe 210) attached to Fliegerkorps V. The use of fighter-bombers had been planned by OKL even before the beginning of the Battle, and the attacks on the British radar stations early in the Battle were carried out by these aircraft.[72]

Lion had been indefinitely postponed on September 17, and on October 10 it was finally abandoned and the Army and Navy units were released for other employment. The prospect of invasion and the hope of destroying Fighter Command had both gone up in smoke, and it was ridiculous to pin any strategic hopes on fighter-bombers. From the German standpoint, the Battle no longer had a *raison d'être*.

Nevertheless, it sputtered on its futile course throughout October. For better protection against radar and fighters alike, the German formations came in at twenty thousand feet or more, and the losses on both sides fell precipitously. Occasionally a few Junkers 88s (the fastest and most maneuverable bombers) were mixed in with the Jabos, and on October 29 the Stukas made a belated reappearance over Portsmouth. Late in October a few Italian bomber and fighter units commenced operations from bases in Belgium, but they attempted only two daytime attacks (October 29 and November 11) against coastal targets, and accomplished virtually nothing.[73]

For all the pointlessness of the autumn day fighting, the strain on Fighter Command was considerable. The pilots were dead tired, and the high-altitude attacks were difficult to intercept. Occasionally the air combat reached considerable proportions; on October 7 the British lost seventeen aircraft and the Germans twenty-one; on the twenty-fifth the comparable figures were ten and twenty, and on the twenty-ninth seven and nineteen. During the entire month of October the Germans lost 325 planes to about 150 for Fighter Command.

In November and December the day fighting petered out. The Stukas were used fairly often against Channel convoys, and the fighter-bombers made "tip-and-run" raids along the coast. The last big dog-fight developed near the Isle of Wight on November 28, and was signalized by the shooting down and death[74] of the youthful German ace, Major Helmut Wick, the *Kommodore* of JG 2, the Richthofen Geschwader.[*]

In terms of the air raids as a whole, the Battle had long since dwindled to a mere sideshow. After the middle of September the main weight of the German attack was shifted to night bombing and so, as the Battle faded, the Blitz bloomed.

The Luftwaffe, to be sure, had started night attacks against the

---

[*] Moelders, Galland and Wick were the only German pilots awarded the Eichenlaub during the Battle of Britain. Dietl had won his after Narvik, and three submarine commanders (Prien, Kretschmer, and Schepke) also won this decoration in 1940. Wick was succeeded as *Kommodore* of JG 2 by another famous ace, Wilhelm Balthasar.

British homeland on June 5, nearly a month before daytime operations were begun. Until late August, however, the night raids were scattered, and rarely involved more than sixty or seventy bombers. On August 24 the scale of night operations was stepped up. From then until September 6, Luftwaffe bombers flew an average of 190 sorties each night, and Luftflotte 3 several times concentrated over 150 bombers in raids on Liverpool and Birkenhead. Few bombs hit their intended targets, and only a handful of bombers were shot down; night bombing and night fighter operations were still in a primitive state.[75]

Up to this point, the night raids were not, properly speaking, part of the Battle of Britain, for they had very little relation to the Germans' strategic purpose of destroying Fighter Command. On September 7, however, day and night operations were both geared to the new tactics of concentration on London. From then until the middle of November the Luftwaffe put a nightly average of 163 bombers over London.*

For two or three weeks beginning September 7, the night operations might legitimately be regarded as part of the Battle of Britain. Of course, Fighter Command could not be encountered in the air at night, but part of the new tactical theory was that a sustained attack on London would bring the British fighters into the air to defend the city, and if Fighter Command could do little to halt the night bombers, that might make them all the more anxious to protect the city by day. So, too, the Germans hoped that paralysis of transportation and communications around the London area, together with adverse effects on civilian morale, might crack the will to resist, and perhaps lay the basis for a Sea Lion operation against a disorganized and dispirited defense.

But these results were not achieved, Sea Lion was abandoned, and after September 30 the scale of the day fighting was sharply reduced. The night Blitz, however, continued undiminished. During the month of October the Luftwaffe dropped nearly six times more bombs by night than by day,[76] and thereafter the day bombing degenerated into sporadic small raids which lasted into the winter and then ceased entirely.

With the shift to night raids, the German bomber losses dropped precipitously. Night fighters and antiaircraft were generally ineffective,

---

* Since the average includes a dozen or so nights when the weather or some other factor prevented sizable operations, the average for nights of full operation was considerably higher. Also, the Luftwaffe continued its night harassing attacks over the rest of England.

and the weather became a far more dangerous enemy than the British. During September 165 German bombers were destroyed by enemy action and sixty-five were lost on operations but not by enemy action. In October, when the bombers were used chiefly at night, the comparable figures were sixty-four and seventy-eight, reflecting the increasing hazards of navigation and crash landings.[77]

Since the Germans were unable either to destroy Fighter Command or by any other means to lay a sound basis for invasion, other reasons must have governed their decision to continue the Blitz. These do not appear to have been articulated at the time, but they are readily inferrable.

In part, the reasons were political and psychological. In the Sportpalast on September 4, Hitler had vowed to favor the British with a hundred times the weight of explosives that Bomber Command was dropping on the Fatherland. Abandonment or marked curtailment of the air offensive against England would have damaged the prestige of the Luftwaffe and, indeed, of the Reich itself. From Goering's standpoint especially, such a confession of failure would have been unthinkable.

But there were operational reasons as well. The day raids entailed heavy losses. Though painful, these might have been tolerated if they had caused commensurate damage. But it soon became apparent that nothing significant could be accomplished with the puny payloads of fighter-bombers, and the pilots were griping savagely about the bloody futility of the desperate makeshift.

The night bombers, on the other hand, had little to fear from the British defenses. As long as they remained above the effective ceiling of the antiaircraft guns and were able to surmount the navigational hazards, the bomber crews could pretty well count on a safe return.

Furthermore, the night attacks were now doing heavy damage. Aim at specific targets was poor, but it improved with experience and the development of navigational aids. Scruples about residential areas were cast off, and the concentration of one or two hundred bombers over London and other large urban areas ensured results which, if strategically indecisive, were visible and sensational.

The first big night raid on September 7 set the London dock area ablaze and left over 300 dead and 1,300 seriously injured civilians. For ten weeks thereafter, with only occasional respites due to bad weather, London was subjected to a remorseless nightly pounding that left great scars in every borough. The docks and the railway stations and yards suffered especially badly. On October 15 the Luftwaffe achieved the biggest concentration over London, when 410 bombers dropped 538 tons of high-explosive bombs and 177 incendiary canisters. Today, of course, these figures look puny, but this was a sufficient load to shut off nearly all rail travel in and out of London, cut the tubes at many points, cause floods from broken water mains, start 900 fires (many very extensive), kill 400 civilians, seriously injure 900, and render many hundreds of others homeless.[78]

Until the middle of November London remained the main target of the night raiders.* Then, with the great attack on Coventry on the night of November 14,† the Luftwaffe abruptly changed both its tactics and its strategy. Thereafter Birmingham, Southampton, Bristol, Liverpool, Sheffield, Manchester, Glasgow, Hull, and Portsmouth joined London as the chosen targets of 200-bomber raids. Exclusive concentration on London had not had the hoped-for shattering moral effect, and the dispersion of effort to other cities manifested a shift toward a sustained "blockade" strategy, to be implemented by attacking ports and industrial centers.

The aerial part of the strategy of attrition lasted until the middle of May 1941, after which a large part of the bomber force was withdrawn to the east, in preparation for the invasion of Russia. The naval phase lasted much longer and did not reach its peak until the winter of 1941–42. But the Blitz and the war at sea were no part of the Battle of Britain, launched by the Luftwaffe in the summer of 1940 for the purpose of bringing the British to terms before the end of the year. That effort had been repulsed by the end of September, and by the time Coventry was set ablaze the Battle was long since over.

At what point did the Germans become aware that the *Adlerangriff* had been repulsed, and that the Battle, from their standpoint, was a strategic failure? Hitler probably saw the handwriting on the wall by the middle of September, when he ordered that Sea Lion be indefinitely postponed. Goering, no doubt, found it difficult to acknowledge failure even to himself, and probably until the end of September, when he had to abandon the heavy daytime attacks, he clung to the hope that his Luftwaffe could lay Britain low.

---

* From Sept. 7 through Nov. 13, 1940, the Luftwaffe flew 11,117 bomber sorties over London and dropped 13,651 tons of high-explosive bombs and 12,586 incendiary canisters.

† The Luftwaffe put 450 bombers over Coventry (40 more than in the London raid of Oct. 15) and dropped about 500 tons of high-explosive bombs and 900 incendiary canisters.

At lower levels, the illusion of success died hard. As late as October 3, Major von Falkenstein reported to OKW that from July 1 to September 30 Fighter Command had been reduced from 1,250 to 500 aircraft and fighter pilots* and that "the figure of 500 fighter planes and 500 pilots is still very high." Not until November 14 (the day before the successful night attack on Coventry) could Falkenstein bring himself to acknowledge to his staff colleagues at OKW:[79] "In the main, air warfare against England can be carried out only by night. During the day only if skies are cloudy. It seems, therefore, that the reduction of the British fighter planes has proved a failure."

Elsewhere the estimates were only a bit more accurate. On October 7, Generalmajor Hoffmann von Waldau, the operations officer (Ia) of OKL, visited OKH headquarters at Fontainebleau and discussed the air situation with Halder.[81] "OKL had underestimated British fighter strength by about 100 per cent," Waldau confessed. "On the other hand, bomber strength is much smaller than estimated. British air strength is now estimated at 300–400 modern and 150–200 obsolescent fighters and about 400 bombers." If the acknowledgment of past error was long overdue, the current estimate was still on the low side.†

As for the Luftwaffe's own situation, Waldau told Halder that since the beginning of the Battle bomber strength had dropped from 1,100 to 800 and fighter strength from 950 to 600 aircraft.‡ On this basis, Waldau presented an estimate of the Luftwaffe's future capabilities which was both gloomy and prescient: "Our air strength by next spring will at best have regained the level held at the beginning of the air war against England. We would need four times that strength to force Britain to surrender. Two-front war cannot be sustained."

The nub of the matter could hardly have been put more succinctly. Britain could not be defeated without an enormous increase in the size and production rate of the Luftwaffe, and no steps were being taken to bring this about. Therefore there was no foreseeable prospect of renewing the Battle on more favorable terms, and if the Soviet Union were invaded (a project known to both Halder and Waldau), the Luftwaffe's forces would be divided and hopelessly inadequate.

* As of Sept. 28, 1940, Fighter Command had 732 aircraft and 1,581 pilots (many with limited combat experience) available for operations. As of June 29, the comparable figures were 587 planes and 1,200 pilots.[80]

† On Sept. 26, 1940, Bomber Command had 569 aircraft available for operations.[82]

‡ The comparable figures reported to OKW by Falkenstein on Oct. 12 were higher:[83] 898 bombers (1,015 on Aug. 10) and 730 fighters (933 on Aug. 10). Probably Waldau's figures were based on a stricter standard of immediate serviceability.

Retrospect

It is apparent from the foregoing account that the German air attack against Britain, which began on a large scale in July of 1940 and continued well into the spring of 1941, had diverse and often confused strategic aims. In assaying the historical significance of the Battle of Britain, therefore, it is essential to isolate that part of the air attack which is rightly so called.

Although the limits cannot be drawn with utter precision, the Battle proper was that part of the air attack by which the Luftwaffe sought to establish decisive superiority over Fighter Command, and to wreak such havoc on the ground as would render the British helpless to resist invasion, or induce them to sue for peace, during the autumn of 1940. In terms of time, the crucial period of the Battle comprised the seven weeks from August 12 to September 30.

The Germans did not achieve their aim, and thus the Battle resulted in a repulse of their offensive effort. It remains to summarize, in retrospect, the reasons why they failed, and to scrutinize the tactical and strategic consequences of the Battle and its outcome.

In substantial part, the causes of the Luftwaffe's failure were built in long before the Battle began. The lack of four-engined heavy bombers, the vulnerability of the Stukas and the Messerschmitt 110s, the short range of the Messerschmitt 109s which limited their escort potential to the southeastern corner of England—these defects were both grave and, at the time, irremediable. But were they inevitably fatal to the Luftwaffe's prospects? Might they have been compensated for by tactics other than those employed?

The early days of the Battle exposed the weaknesses of the Stukas and the Messerschmitt 110s, and the inability of the German bombers to attack by day without escort in the face of British fighter opposition. Thereafter the German offensive mainly consisted of mass sallies by the level-flight bombers heavily escorted by Messerschmitt 109s, necessarily limited to the "hot corner" of England that lay within the German fighters operational range.

But even the 109s were unable to give the bombers effective cover or sufficiently deplete Fighter Command's resources. Try as they did, the German fighter pilots could not prevent the Spitfires and the Hurricanes from getting through the screen and breaking up the bomber formations. Then the vulnerable bombers were obliged to scatter and flee, often jettisoning the bomb loads well short of their targets. This greatly diminished the damage on the ground, while at the same time the bombers were suffering losses which, to be sure, could be borne over a few weeks, but were intolerable over the long pull in relation to the unimpressive consequences of the bombings and the low rate of German aircraft production.

The nub of the difficulty was that the Messerschmitt 109 was basically an interceptor, suited more to defense than to offense. In combat it was fully equal to the Spitfire and superior to the Hurricane. But, with a ninety-minute operational endurance, it could not stay over England long enough to press home a series of attacks, especially when saddled with escort responsibilities for which it was ill-adapted. Consequently, and although the Germans shot down many British fighters, they were unable to inflict decisive injury on Fighter Command, which prudently ordered its pilots to eschew unrewarding combat with the Messerschmitts and concentrate on the bombers.

In addition, the entire tactical concept of close fighter cover for massed bomber formations proved illusory. On both sides the fighters had fixed armament firing forward and aimed by maneuvering the aircraft. Their attack was best carried out by getting on the opponent's tail, and this put a high premium on altitude, speed, and surprise. The German fighters could not achieve these conditions by hovering around the slower, low-flying bombers; to catch the British fighters, the Germans had to come in high and fast on a "free hunt" (*freie Jagd*). If the Luftwaffe had been strong enough to drive the British fighters from the sky, the bombers would then have had clear sailing. But the opposing fighter forces were pretty evenly balanced, and under these conditions there seemed to be no way to prevent the British fighters from disrupting and decimating the bomber formations.

The hard-pressed bomber pilots cried for the illusory comfort of close, visible escort, and Goering railed at the fighter commanders for their failure to fend off the enemy.[84] New formations were tried, but none proved satisfactory. Osterkamp, von Doering, Junck, and their younger colleagues struggled with the problem, but to no avail.

The old days of sustained dogfighting were over; as Alexander McKee has put it,[85] fighter combat had turned into a game of "ambush." On both sides, the successful fighter pilots taught their juniors the same lesson. "The first rule of all air combat is to see the opponent first," declared Galland,[86] while Pilot Officer J. E. Johnson, training for combat at Coltishall, was admonished by Squadron Leader Billy Burton to "look around all the time" because:[87] "Your life depends on spotting the 109s before they bounce you."

Tied to the course of the bombers, the German fighters had far less chance either to bounce their opponents or to avoid being bounced themselves. If a German found a British fighter on his tail, he would ordinarily dive and use the 109's superior speed to draw away. If the other way around, the British pilot would put his more maneuverable plane into a tight turn that the Messerschmitt could not follow, and use clouds or sun glare to lose his antagonist. In either event, the German was likely to end up miles from the bomber formation he had been escorting, and running so low on fuel that he had to turn back toward his base in France.

Thus the very nature of air combat between the evenly matched fighter forces precluded effective defense of the bombers. As General-leutnant Herbert Rieckhoff vividly described the German dilemma:[88]

There was no true defense in an air battle between fighters. The only effective defense was your own attack.

If one had the lesser speed, then one could not choose the time and place for the attack, which would then be forced upon one by the opponent . . . and all that then remains is to flee. . . .

In order to protect a bomber group, the fighters had to fly in such a manner that they were able to see the entire group and be in a position to intercept and turn back an English fighter attack. That is why the escort had to remain relatively close to the bombers and approximate their speed. . . . Thus they found themselves at a disadvantage in each encounter with the attackers, who came from a greater height and with higher speed.

Since the Messerschmitts were unable to protect the bombers against attack, was there any possibility of evading the British fighters? Obviously Fighter Command's ability to disperse and destroy the attacking bombers depended on finding and engaging them, preferably before they had reached their objectives. If the British had been dependent upon patrols and visual observation to detect the enemy's approach, their situation would have indeed been desperate. The Heinkels and the Dorniers were fairly and the Junkers 88s unusually fast for those times, and but for the radar screen they might have approached the coast undetected at a variety of points, with a very good chance of getting in and out of the British skies without being heavily engaged. This would have greatly broadened the area of attack, dispersed the defenses, and left the Messerschmitts more opportunity to engage in the *freie Jagd* that was most likely to erode the resistance of the Spit-fires and the Hurricanes.

Destruction or neutralization of the British radar chain, therefore, should have been one of the Luftwaffe's prime tactical objectives, especially as the Messerschmitts' escort shortcomings became increasingly apparent. This might have been accomplished by destroying the radar stations, by escaping their coverage through low-level approaches, or by jamming or other radio countermeasures. As we have seen, the Germans were aware of the vital importance of the radar screen. Nonetheless their efforts to counteract its menace were desultory and halfhearted, and strikingly reveal the shortcomings of the Luftwaffe's staff and intelligence work.

The prewar erection of the radar masts along the British east coast had not gone unobserved in Germany, where radar research was also in progress. Generalmajor Wolfgang Martini, chief of the Luftwaffe signals branch, suspected the towers' true purpose and, anxious to establish the wave length and the operational capacities of the British radar chain, persuaded Goering and Milch to fit out the old airship *Graf Zeppelin* as a flying radio-monitoring station.[89]

Late in May 1939 the airship, with Martini himself on board, made a night flight up the eastern coast of England. She was promptly spotted by the surprised radar observers, but her own receivers failed to pick up the radar transmissions. Months were spent modifying the receivers and the aerials, and early in August the *Graf Zeppelin* made two more flights along the radar chain. Again the reconnaissance was fruitless.

Shortly after the war began, both the *Graf Zeppelin* and her sister ship were destroyed by fire. The Germans continued developmental work on their own radar, but made no further efforts early in the war to penetrate the mysteries of the British system or to develop jamming techniques.

The vital radar screen operated unhampered throughout the first month of the Battle of Britain. In the meantime the Germans had been installing jamming transmitters along the Channel coast, and in September these began to cause the British radar operators considerable difficulty.[90] But it was too little and too late. British radar observation was not seriously impaired, and within a few weeks the crucial period of the Battle was over.

Below a flight level of five hundred feet, however, the radar screen was comparatively ineffective, and throughout the Battle the British were apprehensive of the consequences should the Luftwaffe resort to low-level attacks. In fact a few such attempts were made. On August 18 Generalmajor Stephan Froehlich's KG 76, attacking Biggin Hill and Kenley (both sector stations just south of London), sent over the bulk of its planes at normal altitude, but two *Staffeln* (one at each target) came in a few feet above the Channel waters and the fields of Sussex. Biggin Hill was not badly hit, but at Kenley the damage was serious and eight aircraft, including four Hurricanes, were destroyed on the ground.[91]

As a controlled experiment in low-level attack, these raids left much to be desired. Even if the Germans could have accurately assessed the damage, they could not have determined how much of it was attributable to the two low-flying *Staffeln*. Furthermore, the concurrent approach of the bombers at customary altitude may have detracted from the surprise factor, for at both fields the defenders were alerted.* At all events, the ground-level *Staffeln* suffered severely. The ground defenses brought down four of the eighteen Dorniers and damaged five others so severely that two had to ditch in the Channel and three others made forced landings in France.

Probably as a result of these losses, Goering's staff rendered a negative verdict on the experiment, to the general effect that low-level attacks were "possible only under conditions of absolute surprise, otherwise very costly [*verlustreich*]."[92] But it seems apparent that these tactics were never sufficiently tested, and whether they could have been successfully developed remains conjectural.†

Physical destruction of the radar stations was the third and most direct approach to the problem. As we have seen,[93] they were ticketed as a prime target at the very outset of the *Adlerangriff*, but Goering promptly concluded that they were an unrewarding objective, and after August 18 the stations were left undisturbed. This decision was not based on a reasoned or informed evaluation, and in retrospect it appears indefensible. Yet Goering was not alone in his misjudgment.

* The German plan was that the high-flying bombers would strike first, on the theory that the dust, smoke, and damage would affect the quantity and accuracy of the antiaircraft fire, to which the low-flying planes would be very vulnerable. At Biggin Hill the timing failed, so that in fact the low-flying *Staffeln* arrived some twenty minutes before their high-flying comrades.

† The British radar screen was also unsatisfactory when the attackers approached at altitudes above 20,000 feet. Late in the Battle the German fighter-bombers came in at such heights, forcing Fighter Command to put up high-flying spotter patrols. However, the Luftwaffe was unable to use the very high-level approach for massed bomber attacks.

The radar masts were difficult to hit, and for all the Germans knew the transmitting, receiving, and plotting equipment might have been underground, beyond the reach of bombs. They made no real effort to find out, and never realized that they had succeeded in knocking out the Ventnor station by means of delayed-action bombs.

It is of interest in post-mortem that the Germans never attempted to destroy the stations by commando or airborne raids. Of course, these would have been uncertain and costly operations. But the stakes were very high, and a single successful penetration might have yielded information of great value for subsequent bombing attacks. However this might have been, the idea was never seriously entertained.

Jamming, evasion, destruction—the story is the same in each instance. The Germans perceived the importance of the radar screen and made initial efforts to surmount the difficulty. But there was no follow-through and no systematic staff analysis of the problem as a whole. Thus the radar story is a dismal echo of the faulty conception and slip-shod planning on which the *Adlerangriff* itself was based. Handicapped as the Luftwaffe was by its built-up limitations, its leaders failed again and again to make the most of what they had.

But it may well be that these technical obstacles were not the only reason why the Germans gave up on the radar stations so easily, for it appears that the Luftwaffe leaders were not all of one mind with respect to the desirability of their destruction. For one, Oberst Paul Deichmann, then chief of staff of Fliegerkorps II, thought that, since the object of the *Adlerangriff* was to destroy Fighter Command, it was better that the British *should* be warned of an approaching attack, so that their fighters would come up and offer combat in which they could be destroyed in the air.[94]

Although Deichmann's views did not initially prevail, the failure and early abandonment of the attacks on the radar stations in fact brought about the situation which he had deemed preferable. The course of events lent small support to his analysis, for it was the radar screen which made unescorted bomber attacks suicidal, forced the Germans to confine their operations within the narrow range of the Messerschmitt 109s, and enabled the British to concentrate their fighter forces in southeast England and engage the attacking forces before they reached their targets.

But apart from the merits of the matter, Deichmann's views betray an underlying confusion in the Luftwaffe high command about the basic tactical concept of the *Adlerangriff*. Where was the intended battlefield? If on the ground, the German bombers were the sword and the Messerschmitts merely a shield. If in the air, the Messerschmitts were the sword and the bombers merely the bait to draw the British fighters within reach of its swing.

One trouble with the second concept was that if the hook was lightly baited the fish would not rise, while if it was sufficiently baited the bait's value would equal or exceed that of the fish. If its offensive power was to be preserved—whether to blockade Britain or support the Army if invasion was attempted—the Luftwaffe could not tolerate the losses in bombers that Fighter Command was able to inflict, given the shortcomings of the Messerschmitts as escort.

Hermann Goering impaled his ample backside first on one and then on the other horn of the dilemma. During the first part of the Battle —especially in the last week of August—the main battlefield was on the ground, at Fighter Command's airfields. Then, as we have seen, the attack was shifted to London, on the dual theory that Fighter Command could be drawn up to its destruction in the sky, while economy and morale were being destroyed on the ground. These foggy and fluctuating tactics led the Luftwaffe into a cul-de-sac, from which it could have escaped only by destroying or otherwise rendering ineffective the radar chain, and thus enlarging the battlefield beyond the dimensions that Fighter Command could cover.

Hitler himself made no effort even to understand the Battle, much less (saving the semipolitical question of bombing London) to guide its course. Goering, vain as a peacock, would hardly have enjoyed the Fuehrer's direct involvement in Luftwaffe planning, and in any event Hitler seemed totally uninterested, and even antipathetic toward the German flyers. Ruminating on the matter at Nuremberg,[95] Goering opined that Hitler's lack of comprehension of aerial warfare stemmed from his inability "to think in the third dimension." Hoping to educate his Fuehrer, Goering had left him in the company of his ace fighter people, only to find that they had made a very bad impression— especially Galland, whose nasal configuration caused Hitler to label him a *"Halb-jude"* despite Goering's wounded expostulations.

So Goering was allowed to run the Battle of Britain as his own private war, without stimulus or criticism from OKW or from the Army or the Navy. No outside corrective influences were brought to bear; Goering had always wanted all the credit, and now no one wanted to share the blame for a failure. When it became plain that air superiority was beyond the Luftwaffe's reach, Hitler does not seem to have been greatly surprised or even disappointed, and one may indulge the suspicion that the Fuehrer was secretly relieved that he had thus been spared the necessity of a close and agonizing decision whether or not to launch Sea Lion. As Commander-in-Chief, Goering bore immediate and direct responsibility for the Luftwaffe's setback, but it was Adolf Hitler, the Supreme Commander, who left everything to Goering, and nothing that Hitler did in connection with the Battle of Britain reflects anything but discredit on his leadership.

How great, then, were the dimensions of the Battle in the context of the war as a whole? Tactical and strategic consequences must be sharply distinguished, for the latter were profound and enduring, while the former were evanescent and, in a strictly military sense, of little significance.

In the air the German losses consistently exceeded those of the British, primarily because the Germans were committing bombers as well as fighters, and because German planes disabled over Britain were lost, whereas British aircraft in the same plight could often land in reparable condition. But the British fighter losses exceeded those of the Germans, partly because of the Hurricane's combat inferiority to the Messerschmitt 109, and partly because the British fighters concentrated on the German bombers and, when so engaged, were more vulnerable to a "bounce" from the Messerschmitts.

Thus during the crucial months of August and September Fighter Command suffered* 832 fighters destroyed and 532 damaged, compared to 668 and 436 respectively (including both 109s and 110s) for the Germans.[96] But over 500 German bombers, 67 Stukas, and 139 other aircraft were also destroyed, so that during those two months the Germans lost nearly 1,400 aircraft of all types from all causes.†

In an immediate way, the British losses were of course more serious, for if Fighter Command had been overwhelmed Britain would have been laid open to invasion or, at least, to a murderous battering by unhampered bombers. On the other hand, the British were in no position to follow up whatever advantage they might then have gained

---

* The figures reported in the several sources vary considerably and often are not strictly comparable for reasons which may or may not be sufficiently stated in the tables—e.g., whether the totals include only losses due to enemy action, or all operational losses, or losses on the ground, or training and ferrying losses. Likewise, the classification of an aircraft as "destroyed" or "damaged" involves imprecise criteria.

† British losses in bombers and other aircraft types (aside from fighters) during this period were not heavy.

over the Luftwaffe, so that, whatever the outcome of the Battle, the Germans would not have confronted imminent peril.

As we have seen,[97] early in September Fighter Command's aircraft losses gave real cause for concern, for during the four weeks from August 11 to September 7 the total wastage of Spitfires and Hurricanes exceeded new production by some four hundred aircraft, and the reserve was running low.[98] But the adverse trend did not continue; for the entire two months, fighter production slightly exceeded gross wastage, and at the end of the Battle Fighter Command was stronger in aircraft than it had been at the beginning.[99]

For the British, the fighter-pilot casualties were far more critical. During August and September they lost 307 pilots, and 308 were wounded or otherwise injured—nearly a quarter of Fighter Command's strength.[100] Declining losses after mid-September and a gradual pickup in the rate of training saved the situation. German personnel losses were much higher, for they included bomber crews and reflected the imprisonment of all who were obliged to crash-land or hit the silk over England.[101] During August and September JG 26, for example, lost fifteen pilots killed and seventeen made prisoner, or about a third of its flying strength.[102] On both sides the losses of experienced pilots caused a deterioration in operational efficiency, but the effects were not of lasting consequence.

Because the rate of German aircraft production remained virtually static, it took the Luftwaffe far longer than Fighter Command to recoup the losses sustained in the Battle. Galland estimates[103] that the bombers lost about one third and the fighters nearly one quarter of their strength, and his figures are not far from those reported to Halder by Waldau early in October.[104] So, too, events bore out Waldau's prediction that the Luftwaffe would regain its former strength by the spring of 1941.[105]

The significant factor in the Luftwaffe's situation was not the losses it had sustained but the Germans' failure to expand the production base. In the Battle of Britain the Luftwaffe was injured painfully but not mortally,* and there is little reason to quarrel with Galland's overall judgment that[106] "it is . . . wrong to speak either of annihilation or

---

* In fact the Luftwaffe's total losses were higher during the two months of the Battle of France (May and June) than during the two crucial months (August and September) of the Battle of Britain. Fewer fighters were lost during the Battle of France (367 as compared to 668), but the bomber losses were slightly higher (521 to 508), and the Stuka (122 to 67), reconnaissance (166 to 46), and transport (213 to 11) losses very much higher.

of a decisive defeat of the German Luftwaffe in this battle. Those who express the point of view that the back of our air force was broken and that it was never again in a position to recover from this blow misunderstand the real situation."

Despite radar and the vigor of Fighter Command's reaction to the approach of German bombers, many reached and dropped their bombs on or reasonably near their targets. There were thousands of civilian casualties,[107] and many more thousands of people lost their homes. Cultural monuments were destroyed, and damage to the harbors and to public utilities was extensive. During the first month of the Battle the more exposed airfields, such as Manston, were rendered virtually unusable, and the continued habitability of the vital sector stations at Biggin Hill and Kenley was seriously threatened. Especially during the latter part of the Battle, several of the raids on aircraft factories were skillfully executed and highly successful.

In human and material terms these results were far from negligible, even though the bomb tonnage now seems trifling. But in the hard scale of military success or failure, it was of no great significance. Britain's lifelines to the world outside were not cut, her defenses against invasion were not appreciably weakened, and her morale was stiffened. Despite all the courage, skill, and determination with which the German bomber crews carried out their tasks, they accomplished nothing of real importance to the shaping of the war's course.

It is, indeed, the extraordinary disparity between the tactical and the strategic consequences that gives the Battle of Britain its epic quality. The forces engaged were small compared to those in other decisive battles of modern time, and neither side decisively weakened the other. Yet the stalemate in the air and the resultant abandonment of Sea Lion were, as Admiral Ansel has put it,[108] "the pivotal event of the war and one in history." A parallel to the First Battle of the Marne has often been remarked,[109] not without justification, for in both cases the threat of a speedy German victory was averted by a repulse of strategic dimensions.

Thus, for the British in 1940, as for the French in 1914, a successful defensive battle was not only an immediate and dire necessity, but also a *sine qua non* of ultimate victory. After the Battle of the Marne, however, the French still stood toe to toe with an enormously powerful adversary who could renew the assault on the same ground, and they faced the prospect of a long and bloody struggle at close quarters. In the fall of 1940, thanks to the Channel and the seasons, the end of the

Battle gave the hard-pressed British the much-needed benefits of a partial disengagement. Despite the continuing Blitz and the sharpening strife on the Atlantic, there was little possibility of a major assault until the following spring, and the British knew that by then—with ground forces greatly strengthened and aircraft production far outstripping the Germans'—they would be in much better case to meet it. In this respect the Battle of Britain was more decisive than the Battle of the Marne, and its consequences were more lasting.

For the Germans, the Luftwaffe's repulse marked the failure of the strategy adopted in July. It was not a mere matter of letting the winter pass and renewing the Battle in the spring. The great opportunity presented by Britain's critical weakness after Dunkirk had passed. Hitler realized full well that if Britain could not be successfully assaulted in September it was highly unlikely that the prospects would be as good, let alone better, the following spring, and he had said as much at the Berghof conference on July 31.[110] Accordingly, he now faced the necessity of reviewing and reshaping his basic strategy for the conduct of the war, which plainly was going to last for another year and probably a good deal longer.

And what of the Luftwaffe itself, and the Battle's significance for the continuing war in the air? As we have seen, there is no basis for the widespread impression that the German air arm was irreparably weakened. The Battle's meaning in terms of air power is not to be found in its outcome, but, rather, in its aftermath. The Luftwaffe leaders failed to learn, or at least to profit by, the lessons which the Battle should have taught them.

For the *Adlerangriff* had painfully exposed the Luftwaffe's limitations. Its bombers were too light and its fighters too short-winded for strategic employment. Much of its equipment, especially the Stukas and the Messerschmitt 110s, was of only limited utility against a first-class opponent. German radar and ground control were developing too slowly. The reserve was far too thin and the rate of aircraft production too low for sustained operations. High-level staff work was erratic and often amateurish. Beset by all these difficulties, Goering's forces faced determined and skilled antagonists whose power was growing by leaps and bounds and who would soon be able to take the offensive.

Therefore it was not enough to repair the damage that the Luftwaffe had suffered during the Battle. The art of war develops fastest when it is being practiced, and if the Luftwaffe was to be the master and not the victim of coming events, and outmatch its adversaries, radical measures were called for to broaden its production base, refine its technology, and increase its striking power.

These needs were seen but not heeded. As early as February 1939, Oberstleutnant Herman Plocher, then a branch chief in the RLM, had criticized the so-called "horizontal" plan of putting nearly all the strength into front-line units instead of maintaining a sizable reserve. Plocher's advocacy of a "vertical" organization with reserves for sustained fighting fell on the deaf ears of Jeschonnek, who had just been made Chief of Staff.[111] After the fall of France, Raeder was told[112] that the Luftwaffe would be "nearly doubled by the end of 1940." After the Battle of Britain even Goering seems to have had flashes of awareness, and it is reported[113] that early in 1941 he told Hitler that "the only way of arriving at a negotiated peace with England" was "to reorganize the Luftwaffe and give it time to recover."

But Hitler talked Goering down on the basis that Russia would be conquered in a few months, and that thereafter the Luftwaffe could be rested and expanded.[114] Goering played along and, whatever his inward thoughts, was soon peddling the same line to Moelders and Galland.[115] Those junior officers, who saw the handwriting on the wall, could make no headway with their remonstrances.

And so nothing was done, either before or after the invasion of Russia, to put matters right. The production base was not expanded; the four-engined bomber was not developed; the higher leadership continued to live in a haze of false optimism and dilettantism. Already committed in the west from the North Cape to the Pyrenees, within a few months the Luftwaffe found itself engaged in North Africa, the Balkans, and the entire length of the Mediterranean. Then came the attack on the Soviet Union, and the Luftwaffe was called on for tactical support all along the enormous front from Finland to the Black Sea. It was never given the breathing spell that the Fuehrer had promised Goering; instead it was stretched to the breaking point over a vast geographical expanse. After 1943, Milch and Albert Speer performed miracles in building a defensive fighter force against the Allied bombing attacks, and during the last year of the war the experiments with jet aircraft and rockets bore fruit. But the fighter force was overborne; the new weapons came too late.

Thus the Luftwaffe never regained the *relative* striking power (relative, that is, to its adversaries) which it enjoyed in 1940. The Battle of Britain was a turning point for the Luftwaffe and marked the beginning of a downward trend which, in an abstract sense, might have been averted, but which was inevitable under the leadership of Hitler and Goering. As Richard Suchenwirth has written in a perceptive essay:[116]

> In a very real sense, the Battle of Britain was the handwriting on the wall. And neither Goering, Jeschonnek, nor Udet had been able to decipher it. If they had understood its significance, there would still have been time to correct the defects and to launch a new and more forceful attack against the West. For conflict with the West was inevitable. . . . It was to take a lot more writing on the wall, however, before the Luftwaffe top-level leaders learned to read even a part of it. By the time that point had been reached, of course, it was already too late.

And so, while Britain survived her moment of greatest peril, the Luftwaffe passed its peak. The German strategy had failed and a new one had to be evolved in the fall of 1940. The decisions then made laid the basis for Germany's ultimate defeat, and it is therefore not too much to say that the second half of 1940 was the crucial period of the Second World War.[117]

A battle with such immediate and far-reaching consequences must be regarded as one of the decisive battles of history. Likewise it was one of the least bloody, and it was also unusual in that both sides came to the fray somewhat inexperienced in the use of their weapons and were obliged to perfect their tactics in the course of combat.

The Armada had its Drake and Trafalgar its Nelson; in the Battle of Britain no commander won comparable renown. On the German side there was no basis for acclaim, for the leadership of Kesselring and Sperrle and the *Fliegerkorps* commanders was energetic but uninspired, and Goering—posturing in medieval hunting costume at the Reichsjaegerhof while his flyers were being shot down by the hundreds —cut a preposterous and repulsive figure.

Surely, though, fame might have dealt more generously with the men who led the "so few." Park's tactics of engaging the enemy as soon as possible, without first massing his fighters in large formations, fell under increasingly sharp criticism from the commander of the adjacent No. 12 Group, Air Vice-Marshal Trafford Leigh-Mallory. The Air Staff was won over to his conceptions, and in November Leigh-Mallory replaced Park at No. 11 Group and Park was transferred to training duties. At about the same time Dowding was sent on a mission to the United States, and Air Marshal Sholto Douglas took over at Fighter Command. Both Dowding and Park were subsequently promoted and honored,* but neither these laurels nor their inestimable services have won for them enduring fame in the annals of warfare. Glamour has clung longer to the names of the leading fighter pilots on both sides: Douglas Bader, "Sailor" Malan, and Stanford Tuck; Moelders, Galland, Wick, Balthasar, and Oesau.

But perhaps the verdict of time, unkind as it may be to Dowding and Park, is a just one. The Battle of Britain was not won by the brilliance of a field commander. It was a triumph of professional competence in the higher ranks of the Royal Air Force and the civil service, and of gallantry on the part of a few thousand young men inspired by the desperate plight of their country and the personal example of one of the greatest war leaders of all time.

Winston Churchill sang the Battle of Britain even as it was being fought. As the pages of history turn and the details of the Battle fade, it is his name that will symbolize all the heroes of Britain's finest hour.

---

* Both became air chief marshals and were awarded the Grand Cross of the Bath; Dowding became the first Baron Dowding of Bentley Priory.

Interlude

The "Invasions" of 1900-1914

S AKI WAS NOT the only man of his time who wrote of a German invasion of England. On the contrary, from the turn of the century to the beginning of the First World War, the European literary market was fairly glutted with articles, books, and plays based on the idea of an invasion of Britain from the Continent.[1] In some of these works the invasion plans and methods were conceived with considerable care and imagination, and interestingly reflect the problems with which the Wehrmacht grappled in 1940.

During the first few years after 1900, the French were often cast in the invading role—a theme apparently nourished by fears aroused by the Fashoda crisis of 1898 and the abortive project for a tunnel under the Straits of Dover. In *La Guerre Fatale: France-Angleterre,* a widely read book published in 1900, the author[2] envisaged a landing by chasseurs at Deal, a spot which Halder's staff found promising for their Sea Lion plans forty years later.

But the diplomatic winds were shifting, and with the birth of the Anglo-French entente in 1903 and the growth of German naval power colored by the Kaiser's bombastic rhetoric, Germany soon replaced France as the object of invasion fears. Henry James, wintering on the Sussex coast at Rye, voiced his apprehensions in a letter written in 1910:[3]

I myself, frankly, have lost the desire to live in a situation (by which I mean a world) in which I can be invaded from so many sides at once. I go in fear, I sit exposed, and when the German Emperor carries the next war (hideous thought) into this country, my chimney-pots, visible to a certain distance out at sea, may be his very first objective.

German writers contributed to the growing tension. Eisenbart's *Die Abrechnung mit England* ("The Reckoning with England"), published in 1900, in which the war opened with German cruiser raids on British merchantmen, was perhaps the first notable German example of this sort of writing. But the book which really established the idea of a German invasion as a major theme of British literature—and perhaps the most successful of all from an artistic standpoint—was Erskine Childers' *The Riddle of the Sands*, published in 1903.[4]

Childers' novel did not involve an actual invasion, but, rather, the intelligence operations by which the British discovered the German plans. The assembly and embarkation area for the German troops was to be the Frisian coast, shielded by the East Frisian Islands. The invasion fleet was to consist of large lighters towed by tugs, not unlike the barges and tugs that would have carried the Sea Lion forces. In Childers' account the transport ships would be collected and loaded in the numerous streams of the Frisian littoral. The High Seas Fleet would then make a sally into the North Sea to draw off the British battle fleet, while the invasion fleet would make the 240-mile passage to the east coast of England, and land either in Lincolnshire on the north shore of the Wash or in Essex between Foulness and Brightlingsea.

If Childers wrote chiefly to entertain, the purpose of William Le Queux, author of *The Invasion of 1910*,[5] was to persuade as well. Published in 1906, Le Queux's book attacked Britain's so-called "blue water" strategists, who held that the Royal Navy sufficiently protected her shores and pooh-poohed the need of large ground forces. Field Marshal Earl Roberts, hero of the Boer War, contributed an introductory letter and used the book in support of the campaign he was then waging, in the House of Lords and the press, for increased armaments and a nationwide organization of civilian rifle clubs. This contentious work ran serially in the *Daily Mail*, sold over a million copies, and was translated into twenty-seven languages.

Of all the books in this genre, *The Invasion of 1910* was the most detailed and calculated with respect to the German plan of attack.[*]

---

[*] In the preface to his book, Le Queux declared that his conception of the invasion "was submitted to a number of the highest authorities on strategy, whose names, however, I am not permitted to divulge," and implied that Lord Roberts was one of the "authorities." A commentator on the book[6] has ventured the rather

Recognizing the superiority of the Royal Navy, in Le Queux's account the Germans resorted to surprise and special operations in order to establish temporary control of the North Sea and land the invasion army. The first troops were landed, with no declaration of war, on Saturday, September 1, 1910. A number of British warships were bottled up at the dockyards in Chatham by sinking German merchantmen in the channel of the Medway. Part of the North Sea Fleet was destroyed at anchorage in the Firth of Forth by a surprise destroyer attack, and the rest was engaged and sunk or put out of action off Berwick by the German High Seas Fleet. Thus, until the main battle units of the British Navy could be brought from the Atlantic and the Mediterranean, the Germans could land with impunity on the eastern shores of England.

And land they did—south of the Wash at Sheringham and Lowestoft in Norfolk and Maldon in Essex, north of the Wash in the mouth of the Humber at Hull and Goole—from ships that had departed (as in Childers' version) from the ports of East Friesland. Within three weeks most of England between London and Manchester was in German hands, as well as London itself north of the Thames, as six German army corps under von Kronhelm* swept back the ill-trained, ill-equipped, and outnumbered British territorials.

At the end of six weeks, however, Kronhelm was defeated by circumstances the possibility of which gave pause to Brauchitsch and Halder when they were planning Sea Lion. The British fleet, when once assembled, swept the Germans out of the North Sea and cut off the invasion army in England. Deprived of supplies, and harassed by a *levée en masse* organized under civilian command as a "League of Defenders," Kronhelm capitulated on October 12, 1910. But strategically it was no victory for the British, as Germany had meanwhile annexed Denmark and Holland, and Kaiser Wilhelm II rejected with contempt the British demands for indemnification. A peace treaty was signed in January 1911, but England was left "internally so weakened that only the most resolute reforms" could restore her former greatness.

No one could outdo Le Queux for literal detail, and his successors

---

cynical suggestion that Le Queux was obliged to modify his original conception to meet the requirements of Lord Harmsworth of the *Daily Mail,* who wished the invasion to take place in areas where the sales of his newspaper would be advantaged.

* Le Queux was less than sufficiently familiar with German military organization; von Kronhelm's initial proclamation at Beccles was issued by him as commander of the 3rd Army, but signed by him as commander of the 9th Corps. Elsewhere he is described as commanding the "Imperial German Army in England," and sometimes as a general, sometimes as a field marshal.

turned to more dramatic and fanciful facets of the invasion theme. George du Maurier's son Guy, an officer of the Royal Fusiliers, wrote a play about an invasion of Essex which held the London stage for eighteen months.[7] A German writer envisaged an airborne army of 500,000, victorious after landing in southern England;[8] Englishmen wrote books called *When England Slept* and *The Swoop of the Vulture*. P. G. Wodehouse satirized this last item in *The Swoop! or, How Clarence Saved England*, which began with imaginary headlines on the day of invasion: "FRY NOT OUT, 104. SURREY 147 FOR 8. A GERMAN ARMY LANDED IN ESSEX THIS AFTERNOON. LANCASHIRE HANDICAP: SPRING CHICKEN 1, SALOME 2, YIP-I-ADEE 3. SEVEN RAN."

In the last years before the outbreak of war, the war theme attracted higher talent. Writing in 1913, Saki was interested not so much in the invasion itself as in the social consequences of a German occupation.[9] In 1914, Sir Arthur Conan Doyle, in a short story called "Danger," forecast the horrors of unrestricted submarine warfare, the same year H. G. Wells wrote of "atomic bombs" in *The World Set Free*.

And thus, ironically enough, it was the war itself that put an end to literary speculation about German invasions of Britain. The involvement of France and Russia eliminated any serious possibility of such an operation in the war's early stages, and by 1915 there were upwards of two million men in British uniform.

In the between-war years, public fears and literary fancies were focused principally on aerial bombardment, and even at the outbreak of the Second World War no one in England gave much thought to the perils of invasion from the sea. In *The Defence of Britain*, published in 1939 on the eve of war, Liddell Hart raised the question whether Britain could be invaded, and concluded that "the development of air-power has greatly diminished the possibilities of sea-borne invasion" and that "England herself, in consequence, is at least more secure than ever before against invasion in the familiar sense."[10] In October of 1939, somewhat troubled by the dispersion of the Fleet caused by the *Graf Spee*'s depredations in the South Atlantic, Winston Churchill (then First Lord of the Admiralty) alerted the First Sea Lord to the possibility of a German landing "say at Harwich, or at Webburn Hook, where there is deep water close in shore." But this was written out of abundance of caution, and Churchill coupled his warning with the qualification that he did not think such a thing "likely," and a disclaimer of intention "to raise those invasion scares" which he recalled from 1914.[11]

PART III

Sea Lion

CHAPTER SIX

Invasion Plans

"**A**s ENGLAND, in spite of the hopelessness of her military position, has so far shown herself unwilling to come to any compromise, I have therefore decided to begin to prepare for and, if necessary, to carry out an invasion of England." So began Hitler's Directive No. 16 for the Conduct of the War, issued on July 16, 1940.[1] During the ensuing nine weeks the preparations were not only begun but virtually completed, and by mid-September a makeshift armada of barges, tugs, and other small craft lay in the Channel harbors, ready to embark the assault troops and follow the course of Julius Caesar and William the Conqueror.

The invasion fleet never put out from shore, but the story of Sea Lion lives on as a gripping historical might-have-been and, more importantly, as a complex and controversial study in grand strategy. The decision whether or not to attempt the invasion lay in the mind and the will of Adolf Hitler alone, and the true nature of his aim and expectation is still the subject of lively debate.

Historians of projects that never materialize are understandably reluctant to minimize their original likelihood. Thus Ronald Wheatley calls[2] Sea Lion "a serious and important element in Hitler's strategy" and concludes[3] that "there can be no doubt that Hitler seriously meant to invade Great Britain if this was possible." Karl Klee, author of the most detailed study, decries[4] the idea that Sea Lion was a mere deceptive device (*Taeuschungsmassnahme*), and describes it as a seriously prepared military undertaking which might have been carried out if the necessary conditions had been achieved. Peter Fleming goes much further, declaring[5] that "no respectable evidence, indeed no evidence at

199

all, supports the view that Hitler never really meant to carry out the invasion, for which elaborate and costly preparations were made . . ."

In important respects the burden of these writings is valid. The preparations for Sea Lion were indeed "serious" and "elaborate and costly," and in the formal and articulated aspect of German strategy —that is to say, in the directives and what was said openly at staff conferences—the projected invasion was, as Wheatley says, "a serious and important element." The overt criteria were "possibility" and "necessity." *If* the Luftwaffe achieved conditions under which the invasion could be launched without undue risk of failure, and *if* despite these circumstances Britain still refused to seek peace, *then* the invasion was to be carried out, as the *coup de grâce* to finish off a mortally wounded adversary.

Nevertheless, the problem is not so simple as these formulations suggest. How strongly determined was Hitler to bring about the conditions which would have made invasion "possible"? What standards of "possibility" and "necessity" did he apply, or would he have applied had the Luftwaffe come closer to victory in the air?

Contrary to Fleming's categorical denial, there is abundant evidence indicating that Hitler did not seriously attempt to make an invasion possible, and that this attitude—perhaps best described as one of ambivalence—was known in important quarters of the Wehrmacht. For example, on September 5, while the invasion fleet was assembling, it was reported at an OKW staff conference[6] that Goering "is not interested in the preparations for Operation *Seeloewe* as he does not believe the operation will ever take place."* Likewise, Generalfeldmarschall Gerd von Rundstedt, commander of the army group to which the principal assault units were subordinated, regarded Sea Lion as "nothing more than a political bluff" which was not to be taken seriously.[8] His views, based on a private conversation with Hitler about July 19, were fully shared by the army group staff, including the chief, General Georg von Sodenstern.[9] There were other high-ranking and well-informed skeptics,[10] and in at least one instance this derisive attitude filtered down to the troops.[11]

With both the air Commander-in-Chief and the field commander of the ground troops that were to be landed convinced that Hitler would not undertake the venture, it is plain that the question of Sea Lion's reality is more complicated than the conclusions of Wheatley, Klee, and

* Goering's disbelief in the reality of Sea Lion is confirmed by other records and recollections.[7]

Fleming would suggest. Yet the preparations were made, and the project was treated with the utmost seriousness by the Army General Staff, the Naval War Staff, and numerous subordinate commanders and staffs.

The issue does not arise from lack of evidence, but, rather, from conflict in its abundance. Intent is a subjective thing, and Hitler was not a man of disciplined and steady purpose. His inward conception of Sea Lion must be deduced not only from what he said and did about that project, but also from what he did not do about it and what he said about other matters that simultaneously occupied his attention, as well as the strategic background from which the project emerged.

Precursor Plans

Military studies of hypothetical operations, especially if made when the issue is academic or remote, tend to be cautious and to stress the difficulties and obstacles to success. To this general rule the early German staff studies of an invasion of England are no exception. They were made in November and December of 1939* while the Allied armies still lay in full strength along the French frontier, and at a time when the prospect of such a problem's actual emergence seemed both distant and highly unlikely.

Furthermore, these early plans were based on a much more confined geographical situation than the Germans enjoyed at the time of Sea Lion, when the entire Channel coast was in their hands. In the winter of 1939–40, it was expected that *Fall Gelb* would result in occupation of the Low Countries, but not necessarily of the French coast. Accordingly, the 1939 plans envisaged embarkation from Baltic and North Sea ports, and landing on the east coast of England north of the Thames. The tactical foundations of these plans, therefore, are so different from those of Sea Lion that their detailed examination would serve little purpose. Other features, however, are not without interest.

The first naval invasion study was initiated by Raeder himself, at a staff meeting on November 15, 1939.[13] Ten days earlier he had dis-

---

* As mentioned *supra*, p. 107, Schmid's air-war study of July 1939 concluded that Britain could not be defeated by aerial attack alone, and that an invasion would be necessary.[12] He did not develop the thought, and his reference to invasion is interesting today primarily because a year later Goering acted on the opposite basis—to wit, that the Luftwaffe alone could achieve victory and that an invasion would therefore not be undertaken.

cussed the matter with the commander of Naval Group Command West, Admiral Alfred Saalwaechter, and Raeder's mind appears to have turned in this direction while ruminating on the projected Norwegian operation and the possible consequences of occupying the Low Countries. At all events, a memorandum was then drawn up in the Operations Section of SKL; Raeder initialed it on November 29 and forwarded it to OKW, where it was received without much interest.[14]

The first few pages of this study embodied conceptions which were to recur again and again in the Navy's papers on the invasion. Before troops could safely be landed on the English coast, British naval forces would have to be eliminated or "completely sealed off from the proposed landing area," and the RAF must be completely destroyed. The magnitude of these preconceptions obviously staggered the author himself,* who then observed that "the achievement of these . . . conditions will in all probability result simultaneously in the complete collapse of her will to resist; thus a landing, followed by occupation, will scarcely be necessary." Invasion, impossible or unnecessary! It is fascinating to find this theme, so characteristic of the Navy's attitude throughout, at the very top of the file.

As for the embarkation area, the Channel coast was thought to be too exposed to enemy counteraction, and therefore the German North Sea ports were favored, despite the longer sea voyage. Landing areas would have to be selected so as to meet the Army's need for rapid deployment, but should be confined to the east coast of England between the Thames and the Tyne. With a rather dour concession that a landing in Britain "appears to be a possible expedient for forcing the enemy to sue for peace," the memorandum concluded.

At about the same time a like inquiry was in process at OKH, under circumstances that remain a bit mysterious. The document was signed by the O. Qu. I of the General Staff, General Karl-Heinrich von Stuelpnagel, and stated that the study had been undertaken on orders from the Commander-in-Chief, von Brauchitsch. But the undertaking is not mentioned in Halder's diary, and what moved Brauchitsch in this direction is not now known.

The Army plan (called *Nordwest*) was based on the assumption that Holland and Belgium would be in German hands and that the invasion force would be embarked in Dutch and Belgian ports. The main land-

---

* The document was prepared by a junior officer, Kapitaenleutnant(?) Hansjuergen Reinicke, under the supervision of the chief of the Operations Section of SKL, Konteradmiral Kurt Fricke.

ings were to be made in East Anglia, with a diversionary attack north of the Humber. Sixteen or seventeen divisions would be required, including two airborne, four armored, and two motorized divisions. The initial assault would establish a bridgehead at Yarmouth and Lowestoft; a second wave, comprising panzer troops, would advance westward in order to cut London's communications to the north; a third and larger wave, including both panzer and motorized units, was then to capture London.

The Army plan did not deal with such problems as transport, air cover, and landing operations. On such matters OKH solicited the views of OKM and OKL. How long would it take to mount the assault? What were the possibilities of supplying the landed forces by air? For these and many other questions Stuelpnagel's subordinate Major Helmuth Stieff was named as "co-ordinator."

The Luftwaffe's reply, dispatched on December 30, was brief and brisk. The proposed airborne landings would, it was predicted, "run into the strongest point of the enemy air defense"; therefore the operation could be carried out only "under conditions of absolute air superiority and even then only if surprise is ensured." Air attacks on the convoys "would suffice to make transport almost impossible." Therefore: "In conclusion, a combined operation with a landing in England as its object must be rejected. It could only be the last act of a war against England which had already taken a victorious course, as otherwise the conditions required for success . . . do not exist."

Again, a verdict of impossible or unnecessary, in which OKM joined in its comments transmitted to OKH on January 4. Given the disparity between the opposing navies, it would be impossible to hold off the British Home Fleet, even with the Luftwaffe's assistance. If despite the risk the landing was to be attempted, the diversionary attack north of the Humber must in any event be abandoned, for this would stretch the Navy's already inadequate resources to the breaking point. As for the time element: "The time in which to prepare the transport ships is proposed as about three months . . . , but this estimate presupposes that at least one year previously certain measures have been taken in the dockyards . . ."

Altogether a gloomy clutch of papers, notably similar in tone to the Luftwaffe papers of 1938 and 1939 discounting the prospects of aerial warfare against Britain. So in the winter of 1939–40 the three service staffs briefly turned their attention to the idea of invading England and decided that it would not work. There is no evidence that Hitler knew anything of these studies, but it is virtually certain that he would have agreed with their conclusions had they been brought to his attention.

The Decision to Prepare

The rapid success of the western offensive foreshadowed the fall of France, and Guderian's breakthrough to Abbeville on May 20 made it apparent that the entire Channel coast would soon be in German hands. As Raeder had foreseen, under such circumstances the question of invading Britain (if she refused to make peace) was bound to arise. The very next day he was at the Fuehrer's headquarters, where, after reviewing general naval matters in the presence of Hitler, Jodl, and a naval aide, he discussed privately with Hitler "details concerning the invasion of England, which the Naval Staff had been working on since November."[15]

Writing nearly twenty years later,[16] Raeder declared that he raised the matter with Hitler not at all to urge that an invasion be undertaken, but, rather, to forestall "irresponsible" suggestions leading to "impossible demands." If it was gilding the lily a bit to tell Hitler that the Navy had been working on the subject "since November" when in fact it had lain dormant since early January, still the cautionary teachings of the winter were not forgotten, for Raeder also recalls[17] admonishing the Fuehrer that "an essential preliminary for the success of any landing operation was the Luftwaffe's absolute command of the air over the English Channel," which must be "so complete that apart from command of the air it must be in a position, if not completely to prevent any intervention on the part of the British naval forces, then at least to make such intervention costly."

There is no record of the Fuehrer's reaction to Raeder's *démarche*.* But he said nothing that ruled out further study of the question, for after Raeder's return to his headquarters work was resumed in SKL, and by May 27 Fricke had produced a new memorandum, entitled "Studie England."[18] It assumed that the entire Channel coast would be available, and compared the relative advantages of launching the assault along the North Sea coast from the Scheldt in Holland to

---

* Long after the war Raeder's aide, Korvettenkapitaen Kurt Freiwald, told Admiral Ansel (Ansel, *Hitler Confronts England*, pp. 35-39) that Hitler was noncommittal and "almost indifferent," since he expected the English to "come around."

Denmark and landing on the eastern shore of England between the Thames and the Tyne (as in the Navy's 1939 plan), as against using a more southerly route from the Continent between Cherbourg and the Dutch island of Texel to the southeastern part of England between Weymouth Bay in Dorset and Yarmouth in East Anglia. On both sides the proposed areas overlapped, and none of them closely resembled those ultimately selected.

The northern route was much longer, but the launching harbors were better protected, and the east coast of England was thought to be preferable for landing operations. Nevertheless Fricke plumped for the southern route, on the ground that the crossing itself would be easier to protect against the Royal Navy. Beyond this Fricke stipulated the usual conditions, including virtual elimination of the Royal Air Force, and cautioned that "long preparations" would be required to assemble the shipping and lay the mine screens.

Meanwhile the Navy was taking over the Channel harbors evacuated by the Allies, and was preparing for their utilization as bases. Admiral Karlgeorg Schuster was given the over-all naval command in France and Belgium,* and early in June he was directed to make a survey of shipping in the newly occupied areas. Simultaneously the Naval Ordnance Office was examining the use of heavy coastal artillery to close the Straits of Dover, the Intelligence Section was preparing a detailed study of the south and southeastern shores of England, and the Operations Section was studying the problem of laying and clearing mine fields in the Channel.

All this, however, was internal to the Navy; outside SKL the possibility of invasion was barely contemplated, and then only to be rejected. Early in June Milch raised the matter with his chief,[19] but neither then nor later had Goering any use for the project. The OKW directive for the conduct of the war issued on June 14 made no mention of invasion, outlined a blockade strategy for future warfare against Britain, and described the Army's mission as already "fulfilled."[20] The naval liaison officer at OKH, Kapitaen zur See Otto Loycke, reported to OKM on June 21 that the Army General Staff was "not concerning itself with the question of England" and regarded invasion as "impossible."[21] As for Hitler himself, on June 17 Warlimont of OKW told Fricke:[22] "Regarding a landing in England . . . the Fuehrer has not spoken of any such plan up to now, as he is fully aware of the extra-

---

* Initially designated "Kommandierender Admiral West," which was changed in mid-June to "Kommandierender Admiral Frankreich."

ordinary difficulties of such an undertaking. Therefore up to now OKW
has done no preliminary work or made any preparations."

Hitler's awareness of the difficulties presumably was gained from
his conversation with Raeder on May 21. Nonetheless the idea did not
completely leave his mind, for he discussed invasion with Mussolini at
Munich on June 18,[23] though what was said we do not know. Two
days later, however, things started to take a more definite turn when
Raeder came for another conference with Hitler, this time in the
presence of Keitel, Jodl, and the Fuehrer's naval aide, von Puttkamer.[24]

For this occasion Raeder was armed with a long agenda of matters
seemingly far more urgent than the question of invading England—
submarine construction, a dispute with Goering, Norway, and blockade
operations—as well as visionary projects such as the occupation of
Dakar (which he favored) and Iceland (which he thought fantastic
and impossible). Only after several other subjects had been discussed
did the naval chief present his "report on the preparations for an
invasion of England," based on the studies that had been going forward
at SKL. From these Raeder had learned that no suitable landing craft
were on hand, and that no more than forty-five seaworthy barges could
be made available within a fortnight.[25]

This deficiency figured prominently in his report to Hitler. Two
specific proposals from non-naval sources* for novel types of landing
craft were discussed, and then Raeder requested that "the Navy alone
should make and carry out decisions with regard to the construction
of special craft." Hitler agreed and told Keitel to issue instructions to
this effect.

Beyond this, Raeder discussed possible landing areas, the use
of mines, and the available shipping, and reiterated the familiar
warning that "air supremacy is necessary for an invasion." He closed
with an observation that suggested the need for staff work in other
quarters: "The Army must check the composition of the divisions required for this purpose [invasion] and all superfluous material must
be left behind."

Once again the written record gives no indication of Hitler's reaction
to the report. His naval aide later recalled it as essentially negative,

---

* One of them, emanating from Generalmajor Adolf von Schell (a transportation
specialist on the OKH staff), was for light, fast craft powered by aircraft engines.
The other was the brainchild of one Gottfried Feder, an early Nazi and a high
official of the Ministry of Economics. Feder envisioned an enormous and amphibious concrete tank, capable of carrying upwards of 200 men and of crawling out of
the water and onto the shore. Neither project came to anything.

because of the high risk of failure and the heavy casualties that would undoubtedly be sustained.[26] Nevertheless, the Fuehrer must have given his entourage some indication that the matter was not dead, for on June 25 (the day he finally departed his headquarters at Brûly-de-Pesche) the Luftwaffe officer attached to the OKW Operations Staff, Major von Falkenstein, sent a letter[27] to the operations officer at OKL, Oberst Otto Hoffmann von Waldau, which opened with the somewhat enigmatic observation, "Within the next few days the Fuehrer should be presented with the basis for a Channel crossing."

In earnest of fulfilling this need, real or supposed, Falkenstein attached a brief memorandum entitled "Luftwaffe Basis for a Landing in England." It set forth little more than the prerequisite of air superiority, the necessary delay incident to regrouping and deploying the air units, and the possibility of using the paratroops of Fliegerdivision 7. Despite the sketchy nature of this work, Falkenstein declared that it ought to be shown to Jeschonnek, the Chief of the Luftwaffe General Staff. Apparently this was done, but without effect, for Hoffmann von Waldau noted on the document that Jeschonnek "declines to take a stand, since the Fuehrer has *not* considered a Channel crossing." The Luftwaffe staff thus at the outset struck an attitude of indifference toward the invasion which it maintained throughout.

Despite Jeschonnek's cool rebuff, Falkenstein was by no means the only one at OKW who had concluded that the Fuehrer would soon be considering strategic alternatives among which an invasion was bound to be numbered. Jodl had sensed the same need, and the result was the now famous memorandum of June 30 in which Jodl discussed the various ways in which the war against England might be continued.[28] Therein an invasion was listed as the third of three ways (the others being siege and air terror attacks) by which England could be directly attacked. Jodl gave "top priority" to defeating the RAF and thus paralyzing Britain's will to resist. As for an invasion:

A landing in England can only be contemplated after Germany has gained control of the air.

A landing in England, therefore, should not have as its objective the military defeat of England, which is an objective that the Luftwaffe and Navy can achieve, but rather to give the *coup de grâce* [*Todesstoss*], if necessary, to a country whose war economy is already paralyzed and whose air force is no longer capable of action.

This situation will not occur before the end of August or the beginning of September.

We must count on the opposition of about twenty English divisions, so at least thirty German divisions must be used.

An invasion must nonetheless be prepared in all details as a last resort [ultima ratio].

An operational plan and the necessary preparations for it will be presented separately.

Much of this passage closely resembles the Fuehrer's own expressions on later occasions, and it may thus be assumed to reflect his own thoughts with fair accuracy. Foremost is the concept that invasion was not a promising road to the defeat of a previously unvanquished foe, but only a step that might be necessary as a finishing off—hence the often-to-be-repeated idea that if the necessary preconditions for invasion were once achieved the invasion itself might be quite unnecessary.

However, since invasion *might* be necessary, it must be planned, and perhaps prepared. That was the immediate thrust of Jodl's memorandum, and Hitler agreed.[29] Accordingly, on July 2 an OKW directive[30] entitled "The War against England" was issued over Keitel's signature, informing the OKW staff and the service chiefs* that the Fuehrer and Supreme Commander had decided:

(1) That a landing in England is possible, providing that air superiority can be attained and certain other necessary conditions fulfilled. The date of commencement is still undecided. All preparations to be begun immediately. . . .

(4) All preparations must be undertaken on the basis that the invasion is still only a plan, and has not yet been decided upon. Knowledge of preparations must be restricted to those immediately concerned.

Despite the references therein to "preparations," this was an order to plan rather than actually to prepare. The second paragraph of the directive required the three service commands to submit estimates and proposals: from the Army, estimates of the strength of the British ground forces; from the Navy, a survey of sea routes and landing places for an invasion force of twenty-five to forty divisions; from the Luftwaffe, a prediction on the attaining of air superiority and proposals for the use of airborne troops. By the third paragraph, all these services were enjoined to "co-operate in evolving a plan for the transport of the maximum number of troops with the minimum of shipping and aircraft space."

* Only 5 copies were made, which clearly shows that this was purely a planning rather than an operational directive.

Sharp differences among the three services in their reaction to this planning order were immediately apparent. The Luftwaffe as good as ignored it, and Goering and his staff continued for the next two months to maintain a virtual boycott of the invasion planning conferences. The Navy was, of course, well prepared to furnish the information called for by the Keitel directive. Now that invasion was being openly discussed, however, Raeder took a very sour view of its chances of success, and the memoranda henceforth issuing from SKL were increasingly calculated to put a chill on the project.

It was, in fact, the Army that now emerged as the strongest promoter of an invasion. This was not altogether surprising. The Navy lacked the necessary resources, and most of its warships had been sunk or disabled in the Norwegian venture. The Luftwaffe's losses in the Battle of France had been substantial, and Goering was tired of playing second fiddle to the Army. In contrast, the Army had come through the campaign virtually unscathed, and now the troops, flushed with victory, lay in great strength along the Channel coast, within eyeshot of Germany's lone surviving and grievously stricken enemy. As the days passed after the French collapse and the British gave no sign of yielding, it was only natural that pro-invasion thinking should spread.

Thus, the negative attitude in OKH circles reported by Loycke to SKL on June 21 did not accurately reflect the trend. Indeed, at that very time two junior officers of the Operations Section at OKH had just been put to work preparing an invasion plan.* Halder himself was beginning to contemplate the problem; on June 23 the assistant chief of the OKH Operations Section, Oberstleutnant Adolf Heusinger, visited the headquarters of Bock's Army Group B at Versailles and reported[31] that Halder thought it "not impossible that we will be forced to land in England." The invasion idea promptly spread among Bock's staff, and shortly Halder was confronted with objections from that quarter to the OKH regrouping order, which then gave Army Group B no part of the Channel coast and thus appeared to exclude it from the coming operations against England.[32]

At the end of June Halder went to Berlin for a weekend at home, and had the meetings with Weizsaecker, Schniewind, and Emil Leeb

---

* These were Hauptmann Alfred Philippi and Hauptmann Wilhelm Willemer. According to their postwar account to Admiral Ansel (*Hitler Confronts England*, pp. 105-06), their plan called for "a modest crossing in the Dover Narrows by three divisions, aimed for a landing between Ramsgate and Hastings," which was to be carried out as "a super river-crossing" and establish a bridgehead which could then be used as a base for the conquest of England.

which have already been mentioned.[33] The conference with Schniewind on July 1 will now repay closer examination, for it went too smoothly and thereby sowed the seeds of continuing misunderstanding between the two services.

The prerequisite of air superiority was initially reiterated, and Halder was thus led to the usual hopeful corollary that in that event "perhaps we can dispense with land warfare." Schniewind stressed the necessity of smooth seas for the passage, and pointed out that after the middle of October fog would likely be encountered. The Continental coast from Le Havre to Ostend was mentioned as the "line of departure for invasion," and it was noted that except for the cliffs at Dover, Dungeness, and Beachy Head the English shore had a "firm bottom" and was "suitable for assault." The two chiefs of staff then discussed troops and shipping, and Halder recorded:

(d) A large number of small steamers could be assembled . . . 100,000 men in one wave. Only small coastal craft suitable.

(e) Artillery cover for second half of stretch across water and on beaches must be furnished by Luftwaffe.

(f) Underwater threats can be neutralized by net barrages. Surface threats can be minimized by mines and submarines supplementing land-based artillery and planes.

All this sounded promising to Halder. Whether by accident or by design, Schniewind apparently made no effort to impress upon his opposite number the extraordinary difficulties the Navy would face in assembling the necessary shipping, making safe passage for the assault troops, and maintaining supply to a bridgehead. Quite possibly he did not grasp the seriousness of Halder's purpose, and was being hospitable and discursive.[34]

Whatever the explanation of this failure of communication, Halder returned to his headquarters (newly established at Fontainebleau) with a very imperfect awareness of the Navy's limitations and basically pessimistic attitude. Halder himself was full of drive and enthusiasm for the project, and he lost no time in turning OKH into a beehive of invasion activity, looking toward the Army's report to Hitler in response to the OKW order of July 2, and toward August 15 as a possible target date for the invasion.

The proximate consequences of the order of July 2 and of these initial conferences have already been described.[35] When Ciano visited Berlin on July 7 and 8 he found Hitler still uncertain about "what form the attack against England will develop" and Keitel exceedingly cautious about the likelihood of invasion, which would be "an extremely difficult operation." Then Hitler went off to the Berghof, where on July 11 he listened to Raeder's very negative report and agreed with the Navy chief that invasion should be regarded only as a "last resort."

Thus ostensibly the invasion was relegated to the foot of the list of possibilities. Nevertheless, Hitler had by no means abandoned the idea, for the previous day Keitel, on Hitler's instructions, had put out an order entitled "Artillery Protection for Transports to Britain," and calling for the installation of heavy batteries at the Dover Straits;[36] the Fuehrer had a passion for big guns and constantly overestimated their efficacy. More important, Jodl was hard at work on a first OKW study of invasion tactics (entitled *Loewe*), which was completed on July 12.[37] Then, on July 13, Brauchitsch and Halder arrived at the Berghof with a sanguine report and detailed plans. These Hitler approved without much discussion, and he told the Army chiefs that an appropriate OKW order was being issued.

The order itself was forthcoming on July 16 in the form of Hitler's Directive No. 16, entitled "Preparations for an Invasion of England," a project to which was given the cover name *Seeloewe*.[38] It was largely derived from Jodl's memorandum of July 12, and it embodied not a decision to invade but a decision to prepare for an invasion, to be carried out only "if necessary."

Despite its tentative character, however, the directive embodied a major operational decision. It is one thing to write paper plans for an amphibious assault; it is quite another to prepare for it. Implementation of the order to prepare would require extensive troop redisposition and training, a massive concentration of shipping, tremendous expense and economic dislocation, and the hazard of psychological defeat if the operation was not carried out. All this Hitler now undertook almost casually, despite Raeder's warnings and his own earlier misgivings and lack of interest. Why?

It must be remembered that Hitler had for some time listened to Goering's assurances that the Luftwaffe would be able to knock the RAF out of the air, reduce Britain to a virtually defenseless condition, and, very possibly, bring her to the point of capitulation. Now he was also treated to an optimistic analysis by the Army leaders, who regarded invasion as quite practicable if Goering made good on half of his boasts.

True, Hitler was skeptical that Goering could achieve such decisive results, and it appears that he was more aware of the Navy's limitations than were Brauchitsch and Halder. But there was always the chance that Goering might really bring it off, and that the Army's estimate of invasion possibilities might be sound. If so, the fruits would be a speedy victor's peace or, at least, conquest of the British homeland.

Then, too, Hitler still nourished hopes that increased pressure on the British would bring them to their senses. The threat of invasion would, he believed, be strong pressure, but not unless the threat looked real. The Continental coast lay open to British aerial reconnaissance. If no shipping was assembled, if no reports of amphibious training exercises filtered across to England, verbal threats of an invasion would be empty wind.

These were the strategic considerations which supported the decision to prepare for an invasion, embodied in the directive of July 16. But because of his own skepticism Hitler drew back from any committal of his own prestige or energies. That is why he did little more than read memoranda from Jodl and listen to reports from the service chiefs, in sharp contrast to his furious activity prior to the Battle of France, when he had prodded and needled and dominated the planning. That is why he let Goering run his own private war in the air and ignore Sea Lion, and why he never showed himself on the Channel coast, either to the air crews that were so heavily engaged over England or to the troops that were preparing for the seaborne assault. And that is why, except for a few puerile manifestations of his passion for heavy guns, Hitler never did anything himself to bring about the conditions which would make invasion possible.

The Problem of Command

Goering received the Sea Lion directive of July 16 with indifference, and his staff, preoccupied with preparations for the *Adlerangriff*, did next to nothing to implement it. At OKH the order was welcomed (though not in all details), and the Army's invasion activities rapidly swung into high gear.

But at SKL the reaction was one of dismay. Raeder's primary purpose in raising the matter with Hitler had been to emphasize the difficulties and the Navy's limited resources, and to head off impractical proposals from other quarters. Now, despite these precautions, OKM was confronted with a directive which saddled the Navy with missions and responsibilities far beyond its capabilities.

Even more worrisome was the Army's sudden wave of invasion enthusiasm. Raeder, Schniewind, and Fricke had supposed that their Army opposites would be alive to the dangers and would reinforce the Navy's cautioning influence on the Fuehrer. The Army had nevertheless reversed its field in a most alarming fashion. Upon receipt of the invasion directive, the SKL diarist sadly recorded:[39]

It appears that OKH, which a short time ago strongly opposed such an operation, has now put aside all its doubts and regards the operation as entirely practicable, undoubtedly lacking knowledge, or at least full information, of the difficulties in regard to sea transport and its protection and the exceptional danger to the whole army taking part in the operation. SKL is, on the contrary, convinced that, if the enemy takes the proper course, the success of the operation would be doubtful.

The planning for Sea Lion was plagued from start to finish by the differing viewpoints which this entry reflects.

These interservice difficulties sharply expose an initial and basic problem in the planning and conduct of the invasion: who was to be in command? On this matter the provisions of Hitler's directive (lifted almost verbatim from Jodl's memorandum of July 12) were brief and simple—perhaps too simple:

The Commanders-in-Chief of the respective branches of the Wehrmacht will lead their forces, under my orders. The Army, Navy and Air Force General Staffs should be within an area of no more than 50 kilometers from my Headquarters (Ziegenberg) by August 1st. I suggest that the Army and Navy General Staffs establish their headquarters at Giessen.

Thus no single service or field headquarters was established in command over the operation. The Fuehrer himself would exercise direct command, and the stipulations governing the service headquarters' locations appeared* to presage a close degree of control. Furthermore, there would be no way of settling interservice disputes other than by recourse to Hitler, who alone could make decisions binding on the entire Wehrmacht.

The directive of July 16 has been sharply criticized by the historians of Sea Lion,[40] chiefly for its failure to set up a single headquarters under a commander with full authority over the preparation and conduct of the invasion. Indeed, Admiral Ansel describes this "faulty

---

* These provisions with respect to location of the headquarters were never put into effect, and none of them was moved.

command structure" as constituting the "gravest weakness" in the entire plan, because:

> There was only Hitler from whom the soul of a plan could issue; he had appointed no accountable professional clothed with authority or responsibility for getting *Sea Lion* ready and going. As a result, instead of a natural flourishing growth under an interested sponsor, as problems were surmounted, each one uncovered condemned *Sea Lion* further to an unremitting three-cornered wrangle.

Assuredly the Sea Lion directive was pregnant with such consequences. So, too, Admiral Ansel's critique is likely to seem natural and valid to those mainly mindful of General Eisenhower's supreme command of the Allied invasion forces in Normandy. Yet it is questionable that Hitler's failure to designate a single commander for Sea Lion was really as remarkable or significant a lapse as Ansel suggests. No such commander had been appointed for the Battle of France, in which cooperation between the Army and the Luftwaffe was excellent even though Brauchitsch and Goering reported independently and directly to Hitler. True, Hitler's famous and ill-advised "stop-order" before Dunkirk[41] was in part the product of Goering's jealousy of the Army, but there is no reason to think that Hitler would have acted otherwise if the command structure below him had been unified.

Of course, Sea Lion and the campaign in France are not comparable, inasmuch as the latter was primarily an Army show, with the Luftwaffe in a supporting role and the Navy barely involved. As an amphibious operation, Sea Lion more closely resembled the invasion of Norway (*Weseruebung*), and a reminiscent glance at the command structure of that undertaking may be enlightening,[42] for in that instance Hitler commenced by doing just what Ansel says he should have done for Sea Lion.

Thus the initial Hitler directive for *Weseruebung*, issued on March 1,[43] vested in Army General von Falkenhorst the "leadership" (*Fuehrung*) of the entire operation, subject to Hitler's own direct orders. Luftwaffe units detailed for *Weseruebung* were to be under Falkenhorst's tactical command, while other air and naval units were to be employed "in agreement with" Falkenhorst. But these provisions enraged Goering, and only four days later a new OKW directive specified that all Navy and Luftwaffe units would remain under their own respective commanders-in-chief. This left the command of mixed assault forces in a state of chaos, and on March 14 Hitler had to issue a "clarifying" directive,[44] under which transport operations would be under the senior naval or air force officer as the case might be, while all land operations would be under the Army.

Thus the idea of unified command had but a brief glimmer of life, and died over a month before the invasion of Norway was launched. Apart from the directives, Falkenhorst had neither the rank nor the prestige to settle major interservice disagreements, all of which were dealt with at OKW, usually by Hitler in consultation with Jodl and the service commanders-in-chief. So it would have worked out with Sea Lion.*

Within the Wehrmacht the relations among the three services were not such that an over-all Sea Lion commander from any one of them would have been willingly accepted by the others. Nor was it Hitler's way; throughout the war he much preferred to keep the levers of inter-service command in his own hands.

Admiral Ansel is quite right in pointing out the grave defects in such a system of personal command by the Chief of State. Nevertheless, these drawbacks did not prevent the initiation and vigorous execution of the western campaigns in the spring of 1940, and there is no reason to believe that they would have blocked Sea Lion had the Fuehrer continued to put his own shoulder to the wheel. The basic trouble with Sea Lion was not the command structure within the Wehrmacht, but the lack of foresight, initiative, and will at the highest levels.

The Invasion Plan: First Edition

Sea Lion was dependent on the Navy for transport across the water, and on the Luftwaffe for protection against the RAF and for a variety of supporting missions. The plan ought therefore to be framed in accordance with the available resources of those two services. Nevertheless, defeat of the British ground forces and occupation of the island were the Army's responsibility, and in that basic sense the plan of attack had to be an Army plan.

The first Army plan was developed at OKH headquarters at Fontainebleau during a period of two weeks beginning on July 3.† Halder

---

* In his memorandum of July 12, 1940, Jodl himself noted the parallel between the command structure for *Weseruebung* and the one he was recommending for Sea Lion.

† OKH headquarters was moved to Fontainebleau on July 2, the same day that the initial OKW order, calling upon the three services for preliminary invasion plans, was issued.

himself, fresh from his overly encouraging conference with Admiral
Schniewind, took charge of the staff work, utilizing a planning group
headed by the chief of the Operations Section, Oberst Hans von
Greiffenberg.* Other OKH staff specialists (artillery, tanks, engineers,
and intelligence) were heavily involved, and much of the "donkey
work" was done by Major Pistorius, a junior officer in the operations
section.[45]

The outlines of the Army plan emerged very rapidly. On July 3
Halder, in conference with Greiffenberg and Oberst Walter Buhle
(chief of the OKH section for Army organization), designated the 250-
mile stretch of coast between Cherbourg and Ostend for launching
the assault. Precise landing points were left for subsequent selection,
but the chosen embarkation area postulated landings on the southern
coast of England, from the mouth of the Thames to Cornwall. A first
wave of six divisions, reinforced with four armored battalions, was
envisaged. August was to be the month (since in October fog would
present new difficulties), and the whole operation was to be regarded
as a "large-scale river crossing" (*grossen Flussueberganges*).[46]

Two days later Halder surveyed the project with Brauchitsch, who
had just returned from a visit to Berlin. August 15 was now selected
as the target date. The bulk of the armor would be embarked in the
area around Calais, but there would be "another echelon later from
Cherbourg." Time was pressing, and it was agreed that "practical
work" should be commenced without delay, including selection of the
corps and divisions that would carry out the assault.[47]

During the next ten days these general plans were particularized and
put in form for the OKH report to Hitler, as required by the OKW
directive of July 2. On July 11 Brauchitsch approved the draft presented to him by Halder, calling for an assault wave of thirteen divisions.[48] Following the Fuehrer's approval of the plan on July 13, Halder
and Greiffenberg set about drafting the necessary OKH orders to the
field.

The first and most important of these, addressed to Rundstedt's
Heeresgruppe A and Bock's Heeresgruppe B, was issued on July 17.[49]
The invasion was to be carried out by three "attack groups" (*Angriffs-
gruppen*), one each centered on Calais, Le Havre, and Cherbourg. The

* Ordinarily this responsibility would have been undertaken by the O.Qu. I,
but this office was in a state of interregnum. Generalleutnant Friedrich Mieth, who
had been acting O.Qu. I during the western campaign, was assigned in June to
the Armistice Commission, and his successor, Generalleutnant Friedrich Paulus, did
not take over the office until early September.

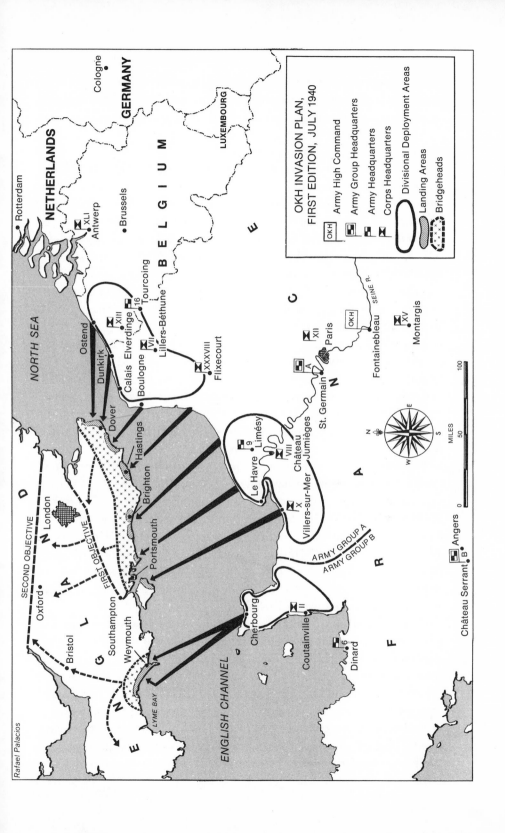

Rafael Palacios

OKH INVASION PLAN,
FIRST EDITION, JULY 1940

Army High Command — OKH
Army Group Headquarters
Army Headquarters
Corps Headquarters
Divisional Deployment Areas
Landing Areas
Bridgeheads

NETHERLANDS

GERMANY

Cologne
Rotterdam
Antwerp
XLI
Brussels

BELGIUM

LUXEMBOURG

NORTH SEA

Ostend
Dunkirk
Calais
Elverdinge
Boulogne
Tourcoing
16
XIII
VII
Lillers-Béthune
XXXVIII
Flixecourt

Dover
Hastings
Brighton
Portsmouth

SECOND OBJECTIVE
FIRST OBJECTIVE
London
Oxford
Bristol
Southampton
Weymouth

ENGLAND

Le Havre
9
VIII
Château
Jumièges
Limésy
Villers-sur-Mer
X
St. Germain

SEINE R.

Paris
XII
A
Fontainebleau
OKH
XV
Montargis

C

E

N

A

R

F

ARMY GROUP A
ARMY GROUP B

Cherbourg
II
Coutainville
6
Dinard

LYME BAY

ENGLISH CHANNEL

Château Serrant
B
Angers

N

E

S

W

MILES

0   50   100

Calais group was to cross the Straits and land at various points from Ramsgate to Hastings, the Le Havre group would go ashore between Brighton and Portsmouth, and the Cherbourg group would land well beyond the Isle of Wight, on the shores of Lyme Bay just west of Weymouth.

The Calais group, under Generaloberst Ernst Busch's 16th Army, was the largest of the three, with an assault wave of six infantry divisions to be followed by three mechanized and four more infantry divisions. The dirty work of establishing the beachhead was to be handled by three corps of two infantry divisions each—Vietinghoff's XIIIth, Manstein's XXXVIIIth, and Schobert's VIIth—embarking respectively at Ostend, Calais, and Boulogne. If these assault units were successful, Reinhardt's XLIst Corps, with two panzer divisions and one of motorized infantry, would be landed to provide the Sunday punch by striking directly toward London.

Generaloberst Adolf Strauss of the 9th Army was to command the Le Havre group, which would also utilize Dieppe and Caen as embarkation ports. The assault wave of four divisions under Heitz's VIIIth and Christian Hansen's Xth Corps would be followed by a second wave of two infantry divisions and Hoth's XVth Corps of three mechanized divisions, which were to drive northward toward Aldershot and cut off London from the west.

The 16th and 9th Armies were both to be under Rundstedt's army group. The Cherbourg group, however, was to be under Bock's army group, and would be directly commanded by Generalfeldmarschall Walther von Reichenau of the 6th Army. The assault wave comprised three infantry divisions under Brockdorff-Ahlefeldt's IInd Corps. Kleist's mechanized XXIInd Corps and three more infantry divisions constituted the balance of this group, the function of which was to draw off British forces from the main invasion area and cut off Cornwall by advancing toward Bristol.

All this added up to thirty-one divisions in the assault force, and in addition there were to be eight infantry divisions in the OKH reserve. The total of thirty-nine divisions included eight panzer, three motorized, and two mountain divisions, and would have comprised a force of over half a million men, with many thousands of horses and hundreds of tanks. Truly a gigantic invasion force, to be landed on a coastal stretch over 225 miles long; small wonder that the Navy quailed before the prospect of providing it with safe passage, and sadly concluded that OKH had strayed far from the sober realities.

When the OKW directive of July 16 was received at Halder's office, the Chief of the General Staff complacently recorded[50] that it contained "the essential points of my recommendations made at the Berghof on July 13." And so it did, at least in principle,* for the OKW directive adopted the Army's target time ("middle of August"), and, while it did not specify the number of divisions to be committed, it directed that the operation cover "a broad front extending approximately from Ramsgate to a point west of the Isle of Wight." But Halder's satisfaction was destined to be short-lived.

The over-all invasion plan, as described in the OKW directive, called upon the Navy to "provide" and, with the assistance of the Luftwaffe, to "safeguard" the invasion fleet. The Luftwaffe was also to "prevent all enemy air attacks" and support the Army's landing and its advance inland.

In broad outline this plan was well enough, but the sweeping language of the OKW directive, as well as the geographical scope of the operation it envisaged, threw SKL into a state of great alarm. On July 9, SKL had set up a planning staff (Sonderstab Nordwest) and had asked OKH and OKL to transmit their Sea Lion plans, including especially a listing of the troops and equipment, so that sea transport might be fitted to needs.[51] The Army plan for the force of thirty-nine divisions in three groups had shown how grandiose were the soldiers' ideas, and on July 17, in conference with Brauchitsch, Raeder had stressed the hazards of the crossing and indicated that the August 15 target date was out of the question.[52]

Now the Fuehrer too seemed, in the Navy's eyes, to have gone out of his mind. On July 15 Raeder had summoned his staff and exhorted them to concentrate their energies on Sea Lion, despite the obvious difficulties of the operation.[53] But now this OKW directive! It was just too much, and on July 19 SKL transmitted a long memorandum to OKW,[54] attacking the whole basis of the plan as extravagant: "The task allotted to the Navy for 'Sea Lion' is out of all proportion to the Navy's strength and bears no relation to the tasks that are set for the Army and the Luftwaffe." The first point was valid enough, but the airmen, had they given it much heed, might have felt equally put upon by a directive that required the Luftwaffe not only to "eliminate"

---

* The OKW directive, contrary to the OKH plan, called for the designation of a single army group to lead the invasion forces. This point was not insisted upon, and when the landing front was subsequently narrowed it became academic, as Bock's army group and Reichenau's 6th Army then dropped out of the picture.

the RAF, but also to engage all enemy vessels approaching the embarkation and landing points, and to "destroy coastal defenses covering the landing points, break the initial resistance of the enemy land forces, and annihilate the reserves behind the front."

Having listened to the Navy and the Army separately at the Berghof before issuing the OKW directive, Hitler now summoned all three services to conference in Berlin on July 21. For once the Luftwaffe was represented, though Goering did not deign to come and sent Jeschonnek as his stand-in. True to Luftwaffe form, Jeschonnek took no position on the feasibility of Sea Lion, and merely asked for a "free hand" to let loose the *Adlerangriff*.[55]

Otherwise, the records of this conference are rather full on what was said, but not altogether clear on who was talking.[56] Whether from the mouth of Hitler or Raeder, the Army's "river-crossing" concept (echoed in Jodl's memorandum of July 12) took a severe beating; so did the OKW directive's description of a "surprise crossing." On both counts the criticism was sound. The notion that an invasion fleet could be assembled in the Channel ports under the eyes of the RAF, and still achieve "surprise" on the English beaches, was nothing short of lunacy. So, too, river crossings can be covered by artillery* and ordinarily have little to fear from the enemy's high-seas fleet.

The conference did not get very far into the specifics of the problem. Brauchitsch continued to talk optimistically ("not fully aware of the difficulties," in Raeder's jaundiced view), but Hitler described the Channel crossing as "very hazardous" and declared that the invasion was "to be undertaken only if no other means is left to come to terms with Britain." About the only thing that came clear was that the Navy could not meet the August 15 date. Raeder was unable to fix another time without further study, and it was arranged that he would report later that week.

The lugubrious SKL memorandum of July 19 had remarked that the "exceptional difficulties" inherent in the operation could not "be assessed individually until a detailed examination of the transport problem has been made." Naval staff work now was concentrated on this matter, utilizing the Army and Luftwaffe replies to SKL's earlier

---

* Hitler continued to lay great store by the heavy batteries being installed opposite Dover. On July 13 the chief of naval ordnance recommended that the Fuehrer be promptly advised that these batteries could give no substantial support to the invasion. Nevertheless, the OKW directive of July 16 called for "the largest possible number of heavy guns" in order "to safeguard the crossing and to cover both flanks against enemy interference from the sea."

(July 9) request for a statement of their transport needs. The Army declared that some 90,000 fully equipped men (in twenty-six regimental combat groups from thirteen divisions), 4,500 horses, and 650 tanks would have to be landed in the first wave, divided among the three attack groups on the landing front from Ramsgate to Lyme Bay. The Luftwaffe wanted the first wave also to include fifty-two anti-aircraft batteries. For the second wave, the Army specified a load of 160,000 men, with equipment to match and over 50,000 horses.[57]

In the Navy's eyes, the sea transport problem now assumed frightening dimensions. Since the landings would have to be made on open beaches (the English ports being too well-defended), only small craft were suitable, and most of these would have to be extensively converted for beach unloading. Shipping space in such quantity could be procured only by scouring the rivers and coasts of Germany and the occupied countries for barges, tugs, trawlers, motorboats, and small steamers. The dislocation of the German economy would be serious, if not disastrous. A host of other problems sprang to mind. How long would it take to unload the first wave on the hostile shores? What would the "turn-around" time be, and how soon could the second wave be brought in? In what volume could the flow of supplies be maintained, once the troops were ashore?

Pondering these problems, Raeder conferred again with Hitler on July 25, in the presence of Keitel, Jodl, and Dr. Fritz Todt, the Minister of Armaments. The naval commander-in-chief assured Hitler that "every effort" was being made to complete preparations by the end of August, but that the prospects were highly uncertain. He would "try to give a clear picture by the middle of next week," and Hitler promptly scheduled another conference to receive and consider Raeder's report.[58]

Before it was held, however, the Navy took dead aim at the Army's invasion plan, with memoranda categorically declaring that the Army's requirements could not be met. The first of these arrived at OKH on the evening of July 28; Halder, in a great state of disgust, recorded its burden and apparent implications:[59]

In the evening we receive a memorandum from SKL which upsets all draft plans for the Channel crossing. Apart from asserting that loading for the jump-off would be impossible on open beaches and would have to be done only in designated ports, it states that Navy needs ten days to put the first echelon [*erste Staffel*] across. If that is true, all previous Navy statements were so much rubbish and we can throw away the whole plan of invasion.

It had taken the Army nearly a month to realize that the Navy was talking a different language. Such were the fruits of misguided companionability at the Schniewind-Halder conference of July 1, and the ensuing lack of communication at the top levels of the two services. The Navy's *démarche* was the death knell of the Army's first plan, and initiated a period of interservice acrimony that lasted through most of August.

Broad or Narrow Landing Front

The day after this rude awakening, Halder brooded on the new situation with Brauchitsch and Greiffenberg. It was agreed that the Army could "not carry through . . . the operation on the basis of the resources offered by Navy." The stipulation of ten days to land the first *Staffel* was "unacceptable." Greiffenberg was then sent off to Berlin to see if he could make some headway with the Navy.[60]

Meanwhile the Army liaison officer at OKM, Oberst Hermann von Witzleben, was in conference with Raeder and his staff, putting forth the Army's "minimum requirement" of a thirteen-division first wave, to be landed in two or three days on the broad front Ramsgate–Lyme Bay.[61] SKL, on the other hand, had just completed a memorandum for Raeder's use in reporting to Hitler, the plain purpose of which was to kill Sea Lion entirely.[62]

Initialed by Schniewind and Fricke, this document concluded that the invasion fleet could not be protected against the Royal Navy; that preparations could not be completed until the middle of September, and the weather thereafter would greatly endanger the flow of supplies; that the Navy could not meet the Army's requirements of broad front and rapid landings; that for these reasons SKL had to advise against undertaking Sea Lion in 1940. Further consideration might be given to the project in the spring of 1941. Schniewind, however, added a note expressing his opinion that "the probability of carrying out the operation at all" appeared "extremely doubtful." In conference at SKL on July 30 Raeder approved the memorandum, and stated his belief that, if Sea Lion were to be carried out despite the Navy's views, the two western landings should be dropped and the operation restricted to the crossing at the Straits of Dover.[63]

Thus when Greiffenberg returned to OKH on July 30 he had nothing encouraging to report—only the Navy's negative attitude, a long list of particular dangers and difficulties, and information that the Luftwaffe was doing nothing about landing operations. That evening Brauchitsch and Halder met to review the "over-all situation created by the Navy's position," and concluded that "the Navy, in all probability, will not provide us this fall with the means for a successful invasion of Britain." Postponement of the operation until the following spring did not seem promising, and the two Army leaders proceeded to survey alternative strategies for the further prosecution of the war.[64] As they flew off to the Berghof early the following morning, matters seemed to have reached a virtual impasse.

But if the contending parties expected the conference of July 31 to precipitate a showdown and a final decision from the Fuehrer, they were to be disappointed. There was no intellectual confrontation, only a physical meeting. Raeder made his report in line with the SKL memorandum, and recommended postponement of the operation until the following spring. Hitler questioned the advantages of delay and directed that the preparations continue, with target date September 15, but put off deciding whether or not to launch the invasion, pending the results of the *Adlerangriff.** Raeder questioned the wisdom of the proposed landing in Lyme Bay, and recommended confining the assault to a single area in the Straits of Dover. Brauchitsch and Halder listened and, so far as the records of the conference disclose,[65] said absolutely nothing!

And the Fuehrer? Raeder's memorandum of the conference is silent on his reaction, if any, to the narrow-front recommendation, and he reported to SKL the next day that Hitler had made no decision on the issue.[66] Halder's notes indicate that Hitler decided, *in Raeder's presence,*† that the Army should prepare to carry out the invasion by September 15 on a wide front [*breite Basis*].

Whatever Hitler did or did not say at the meeting with Raeder, however, the Army's views prevailed. The OKW record of the conference[67] is somewhat equivocal, for Hitler's decision for the broad front was qualified by his observation that, if necessary, the front could be narrowed in the course of the operation! But the new OKW direc-

---

* No representative of the Luftwaffe was present.
† Raeder left the meeting after the decision to proceed with the Sea Lion preparations, and before the discussion of an attack against Russia.

tive on Sea Lion, issued over Keitel's signature on August 1, was categorical:[68]

(1) Preparations for "Sea Lion" are to be continued and completed . . . by September 15.
(2) Eight or fourteen days after the launching of the air offensive against Britain . . . the Fuehrer will decide whether the invasion will take place this year or not; his decision will depend largely on the outcome of the air offensive. . . .
(4) In spite of the Navy's warning that they can only guarantee the defense of a narrow strip of coast (as far west as Eastbourne), preparations are to be continued for the attack on a broad basis as originally planned. . . .°

What are we to make of this extraordinary method of handling a basic tactical issue, and of the contradictory records? Why did Brauchitsch and Halder sit silent when Raeder proposed so drastic and, to them, unwelcome a change in the invasion plan? One cannot avoid the impression that Raeder was given a "snow job"; that the Army leaders had been tipped off that Hitler would decide in their favor, and preferred not to have the issue debated openly.

Hitler, presumably, was not much interested in the tactical problems, however basic, of an operation which would never come to pass or would be undertaken only against an enemy already beaten by the Luftwaffe into a virtually defenseless condition. His primary aim was to keep the preparations going, and a man-to-man decision for or against Raeder's narrow-front proposal would have caused either the Army or the Navy unbearable loss of face and might have upset the apple cart. Furthermore, the invasion preparations would be readily observable by the British, and if they stretched all along the coast from Ostend to Cherbourg this would increase both the pressure and the uncertainty where the blow might fall.

If Raeder heard nothing contrary to his recommendations at the conference, he might regard, or at least treat, the broad-front OKW directive as the product of misunderstanding, and continue the preparations while renewing his plea for the narrow front. Or perhaps Raeder was given a secret hint that the broad-front directive was a temporary expedient, subject to change. Such double-dealing would certainly have been a poor basis for planning a combined operation,

---

° The fifth and final paragraph postponed the removal of the three service headquarters to the Giessen area "until immediately prior to the commencement of the operation." Since that time never came, these moves were never made.

but was by no means out of character for a Fuehrer who had other ends in mind.

At all events, when Raeder returned to OKM he issued instructions that further preparations should be based on the single landing area in the Straits of Dover, and on August 2 he sent letters to both OKH and OKL stating that the transports for Sea Lion would move from the coastal area Ostend–Étaples to landing beaches between the North Foreland and Eastbourne. These letters were received by their addressees before the arrival of the OKW broad-front directive, which, though dated August 1, did not reach its destination for several days.[69]

On August 2 Brauchitsch, Halder, and Raeder were all at Sylt to watch a demonstration of beach assault craft and techniques. They conferred at length on tactical invasion questions, but—whether from mutual unawareness or calculated reticence—the front-width issue was not mentioned.[70] Halder went on to view more weapons tests in northern Germany, and did not return to his office at OKH until the morning of August 4. There he was greeted by Oberst Adolf Heusinger (Greiffenberg's chief assistant) with news of the Navy's narrow-front letter, which, as Halder saw it,[71] "completely misconstrues outcome of Berghof conference and orders preparation of crossing only at narrowest point at Dover." He at once telephoned Jodl, who assured him that the Navy had "completely misinterpreted" the decision, and that the OKW's broad-front directive was "under way."

Thus apprised that the dispute was now in the open, the OKW began to lay the basis for conciliation and compromise. On August 5 Jodl undertook[72] to explain Raeder's misunderstanding on the ground that Hitler had made his broad-front decision after the *Grossadmiral's* departure.[*] Furthermore, the Fuehrer had not, after all, decided that the invasion would be *carried out* on the broad front—only that *preparations* should continue on that basis. To this Raeder (in conference with Keitel) agreed, pending further review of the matter between the two service staffs.

Brauchitsch and Raeder had in fact discussed the problem at a meeting in Berlin that same day. They were unable to resolve the issue, and agreed only to remit it to their respective chiefs of staff,[73] an idea to which Halder, fuming at Fontainebleau, did not take kindly

---

[*] This explanation is possible, but does not square with Halder's chronologically entered notes of the July 31 conference, which summarize Raeder's comments about submarine warfare after the recording of the broad-front decision.

—"What would be the good of it, since we have no common basis for discussion?"[74]

Halder continued to seethe on August 6, when Oberst von Witzleben arrived with the latest Navy information on transport capacity, which showed "that Navy insists on landing to be made on narrowest frontage. Plans of this sort are not debatable, because success of landing operation cannot be assured in so narrow a frontage." Furthermore, the Luftwaffe had not started the big air offensive, and now the Navy was saying that this delay was jeopardizing the September 15 target date. It was all simply disgusting, and in his diary Halder ladled out liberal portions of blame for everyone except, of course, the Army:[75]

We have here the paradoxical situation where the Navy is full of misgivings, the Air Force is very reluctant to tackle a mission which at the outset is exclusively its own—and OKW, which for once has a real combined-forces operation [*Wehrmachtsfuehrungsaufgabe*] to direct, just plays dead. The only driving force in the whole situation comes from us. But alone we can't swing it.

Such was the atmosphere at Fontainebleau when Schniewind and Fricke arrived the following evening (August 7). Halder did not receive them in his office, but, rather, on his special train, which promptly pulled out and headed for Normandy, where Halder was to watch some demonstrations of newly devised craft for the beach assault. Whether or not so calculated, the *mise en scène* was much to Halder's purpose—autoptic evidence that the Army, at least, was serious about this invasion business.

Halder at once announced that the single landing between Dover and Beachy Head was out of the question;[76] for reasons of a "land-tactical nature" the flanks would have to be protected, and for this purpose there must be landings to the west, preferably at both Lyme Bay and Brighton, but certainly at the latter, and to the north, between Deal and Ramsgate. But the admirals boggled at these proposals on the usual ground: the broad sea passage could not be protected and the landings on the western beaches would take too long. Halder stressed the possibility of surprise, but the admirals were sure that there would be no surprise. They then declared that sea transport resources were so limited that the broad-front invasion could take forty-two days, a period which Halder characterized as "utterly prohibitive."

The conferees made absolutely no headway; their views were "diametrically opposed," and they parted company in agreement only that "the issue must therefore be settled at a higher level." Halder is said[77] to have labeled the Navy's proposal "sheer suicide" and declared that he might as well put the assault troops "straight through a sausage machine."

So it was up to OKW, which meant Hitler himself. The Army representative on the OKW Operations Staff, Oberstleutnant Bernhard von Lossberg, had already started to probe the interservice dispute by sending his assistant, Hauptmann Fett, to Fontainebleau. On August 3 Fett had conferred with Heusinger, and on his return reported other facets of the problem.[78] On the broad-front basis, the Navy had estimated that it would take fourteen days (and more if the weather or the British Navy interfered) to put ashore the twenty-two divisions of the assault wave (thirteen divisions) and the mechanized troops (nine divisions). There was also disagreement between the Army, which wanted the paratroopers to help in establishing the bridgeheads, and the Luftwaffe, which proposed their use as a mobile reserve after the bridgeheads had been won. This argument tied in with the Army-Navy dispute about Lyme Bay, for Brauchitsch had come up with the idea (soon abandoned) of using airborne troops to capture a port on Lyme Bay so that the seaborne troops could then land in a harbor instead of on open beaches.[79]

On August 9, at OKW, Generalmajor Walter Warlimont (Jodl's immediate subordinate and chief of the Plans Section of the Operations Staff) told his staff that it would be necessary to develop a basis for Hitler's decision on the interservice wrangle. They were soon to be "assisted" in this undertaking by a new position paper from OKH, dated August 10 and presented at OKW by Oberst von Witzleben on August 12. The single landing between Folkestone and Beachy Head was once again categorically rejected, but there were hints of compromise on other points. The Lyme Bay landing, said the Army, must be retained *if possible*—that was as good as conceded! The landing at Deal to guard the northern flank was necessary and must be made "early"—well, at least it did not have to be simultaneous with the main landing. *But* on the simultaneous Brighton landing west of the main force the Army remained adamant; this was a *sine qua non*, as was also a schedule of not more than four days to land the ten divisions of the first wave (the three for Lyme Bay having fallen out) between Ramsgate and Brighton.[80]

In conference with Warlimont and his staff Witzleben explained the theory of the Army's position.[81] The trouble with the single-front land-ing—especially if the landing schedule were to be as slow as the Navy predicted—was that it would enable the British, favored by high land commanding the beaches and by marshy terrain that was bad for tanks, to build a strong defensive perimeter that would be impossible to breach. The Brighton landing would prevent this and open things up so that the German armor might break through.

Warlimont (or one of his associates*) now proposed a further com-promise, which might meet the Army's needs at Brighton. This was to land a battle group, partly by air and partly from about five hundred motorboats, each carrying six to twenty men and light weapons. Witz-leben remarked only that, from the Army's standpoint, at least four reinforced regimental combat groups would be required. Lossberg set to work on a written projection of the new idea (learning in the process that the motorboats could not carry more than six thousand men, and that therefore the airborne contingent would have to be larger) and presented the proposal to Jodl.[82]

Meanwhile Raeder had been mustering his forces for another hoped-for showdown with Hitler. Once more SKL furnished him with a memorandum; this time the strategy would be to acknowledge that the Army's demands were abundantly justified *from their standpoint,* but were simply beyond the Navy's capacity to fulfill.[83] It was a good negative gambit because, if accepted, it spelled the end of the invasion.

Sea Lion, indeed, seemed to be on its last flippers. Hitler returned to Berlin from the Berghof at noon on August 13, ostensibly to be present for *Adlertag,* and late that afternoon, flanked by Keitel, Jodl, and von Puttkamer, he was closeted with Raeder and Schniewind. The naval chief requested a prompt decision on the landing-front issue, and made his planned comments on the OKM memorandum of August 10: the Army's attitude was understandable, but the Navy could not cope; therefore, invasion should be regarded as an *ultima ratio,* to be used only if there was no other way of bringing England to treat for peace. Hitler expressed complete agreement, and added that if a landing attempt were to fail, the British would gain considerable prestige; therefore it would be better to wait and see the results of the *Adleran-griff.* He would make a decision after talking to Brauchitsch on the morrow.[84]

Meanwhile the Warlimont compromise plan was burgeoning at lower

---

* Participating with Warlimont in this conference were the Army and Navy representatives in his planning section, Lossberg and Fregattenkapitaen Wolf Junge.

levels. As reported to Jodl that evening, a fleet of five hundred motor-boats (each carrying ten men and equipment) would land two regi-mental groups (of about 2,100 men each) in Brighton Bay, and about five thousand parachute troops would simultaneously be dropped on the southern Downs to hold off the British and protect the seaborne landing. In addition to dropping the paratroopers, the Luftwaffe would launch an all-out attack on London, so that refugees from the city would block the roads and demoralize the surrounding populace.[85]

Jodl himself, whether elevated by the Fuehrer's return to Berlin or stimulated by the interservice impasse, had been wafted into a more rarefied strategic atmosphere, and was hard at work on an "estimate" or "appreciation" (*Beurteilung*) of "the situation presented by the viewpoints of the Army and Navy on a landing in England."* Only part of this highly revealing study was directly concerned with Sea Lion, for the burden of Jodl's song was that there was no need to attempt an invasion in the face of inordinate risks, since there were "other ways to bring England to her knees"—for example, by air and sea blockade, and by the capture of Egypt and Gibraltar.[87]

As for Sea Lion, if attempted it must under no circumstances fail, for the political would far exceed the military consequences. If failure was to be avoided, Jodl thought, the Army was right in requiring a landing front from Folkestone to Brighton, and a landing schedule that would put a first wave of ten divisions ashore in the first four days and at least three more divisions in the next four days. If the Navy could not do this, then to attempt a landing would be "a desperate act for a desperate situation," whereas in fact Germany was under no neces-sity of taking such risks.

A deft and flexible man was Jodl. His study certainly *appeared* to support the Army's position. But the following morning, when Fricke of SKL came to OKW and found Keitel blind to the difficulties of the broad front, Jodl was so sympathetic to the naval position that Fricke reported him as being "of the opinion that only a landing on a narrow front would have any real prospect of success."[88] Plainly, Jodl was playing his Fuehrer's game of lip service to both the soldiers and the sailors, without making any real effort to resolve the difficulty in operational terms.

* The memorandum is dated Aug. 13, 1940, and Keitel read it the same day.[86] Presumably Hitler read the document or was apprised of it on either the 13th or the 14th; his comments on the 14th appear to reflect the contents of Jodl's paper.

Later that day Hitler received the seven Army *Generalfeldmar-schaelle* at the Reich Chancellery, to bestow on them the batons that were the symbol of their exalted rank. Raeder too was there, and, for once, so was Goering. At the ensuing repast of celebration, Hitler treated his guests to a short *tour d'horizon*. Jodl's memorandum had been helpful: [89]

The Fuehrer stated that he does not intend to carry out the operation if the risk is too great, as he considers that the aim of defeating England is not *exclusively* dependent on invasion, but can also be achieved by other means. Whatever final decision may be taken, the Fuehrer wishes that in any case the threat of invasion be maintained.

Such a speech was hardly calculated to strike fire into the hearts of his listeners, who included the top commanders of the invasion troops, Rundstedt and Bock.[90] After the speech, Raeder buttonholed Goering and poured out his misgivings about the Army and the broad front. Raeder found the Reichsmarschall uncommonly pleasant and in full agreement[91]—which is hardly surprising, since Goering continued to discount Sea Lion and probably regarded the whole argument as academic.

Everything seemed to be going the Navy's way, and now Raeder's subordinates moved in again, hoping to kill off the unlucky project for good and all. Schniewind waded in with a memorandum sharply attacking the Army's proposal to use airborne troops to bolster the western landings:[92] "airborne troops can influence neither the weather nor the sea; they cannot prevent the destruction . . . of the few harbors, nor hold off the enemy fleet or even a small part of it." The likelihood that even the main landing in the Straits would succeed was so small that there was no justification for thinking about Brighton, much less Lyme Bay. Fricke, for his part, again sought out Jodl, this time with the suggestion that Sea Lion be continued only as a threat or, at most, on a narrow-front basis, with Brighton as well as Lyme Bay abandoned. The harassed Jodl indicated no disagreement with these ideas.[93]

But once again the Navy's efforts to force the issue to a conclusion failed, as Hitler slithered out from between the conflicting pressures. The Fuehrer had talked to Brauchitsch during the baton ceremonies, and later that day he gave instructions to Keitel and Jodl[94] which furnished the basis for a new OKW directive, issued on August 16.[95] Preparations for launching the invasion on September 15 were to be continued, and shipping was to be assembled all along the coast from

Ostend to Le Havre, in order to avoid concentration and conceal the intended area of attack.

On the disputed questions, however, the directive "decided" virtually nothing. The Lyme Bay landing, to be sure, was dropped, since the Army had virtually conceded this point. But Brighton? The preparations should not "exclude the possibility of an attack on a narrow front," but must also "leave open the possibility of a single landing in the Brighton area." Were the airborne troops to be used in the first wave or as reinforcements? Suggestions on this problem were "invited" from both the Army and the Luftwaffe. Would there be an invasion at all? "Final orders will not be given until the situation is clear."

On that ultimate question Hitler's uncertainty was hardly surprising, for the *Adlerangriff* was just beginning, and until some reliable signs of success were apparent Sea Lion remained hypothetical. Preparations were to continue, but the new outlines of the operation were murky indeed. The Army's July plan, obviously, would have to be scrapped, and a new one developed within the limits of the Navy's capacities.

The Invasion Plan: Second Edition

To this task the Army now turned, with determination if not enthusiasm. On August 16 Brauchitsch and Halder went to the coast to inspect the embarkation ports and observe landing maneuvers; when the latter returned to OKH headquarters at Fontainebleau on the eighteenth, he found the OKW directive of August 16 and took it with reasonably good grace. Brauchitsch got back on the twentieth and proposed that the Cherbourg invasion force be kept together and in readiness despite OKW's veto of the Lyme Bay landing. But Halder convinced his Commander-in-Chief that this would be a futile gesture "because we won't have the necessary landing-craft lift." Later that day Brauchitsch and Halder conferred with Greiffenberg, outlining "points still to be clarified with Air Force and Navy in Berlin."[96]

In fact much remained to be settled, for the Navy, having succeeded in killing off the Lyme Bay landing, now set out to do a hatchet job on Brighton. Exploiting the equivocal language of the OKW directive, SKL on August 20 sent an order to the main naval headquarters in the west (Marinegruppenkommando West in Paris, under Generaladmiral Alfred Saalwaechter), the tenor of which was that there would be *no* invasion by the direct route from Le Havre to Brighton except

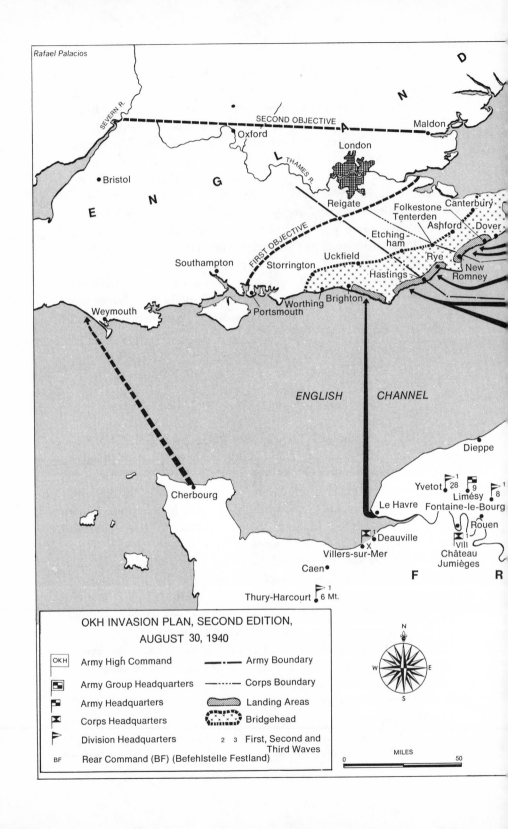

Rafael Palacios

SECOND OBJECTIVE

SEVERN R.

Maldon

Oxford

London

THAMES R.

Bristol

E N G L A N D

Reigate

Folkestone
Canterbury
Tenterden
Ashford
Dover

Etching-
ham

FIRST OBJECTIVE

Southampton

Storrington

Uckfield

Rye

New
Romney

Weymouth

Worthing
Portsmouth

Hastings

Brighton

ENGLISH   CHANNEL

Dieppe

Yvetot
28
1
9
1
Limésy
8

Cherbourg

Le Havre
Fontaine-le-Bourg

Rouen

1
Deauville

1
VIII

Château
Jumièges

Villers-sur-Mer
X

Caen

F

R

Thury-Harcourt
1
6 Mt.

OKH INVASION PLAN, SECOND EDITION,
AUGUST 30, 1940

OKH	Army High Command	—·—·—	Army Boundary
	Army Group Headquarters	—···—···—	Corps Boundary
	Army Headquarters		Landing Areas
	Corps Headquarters		Bridgehead
	Division Headquarters	2 3	First, Second and Third Waves
BF	Rear Command (BF) (Befehlstelle Festland)		

N
W   E
S

MILES
0   50

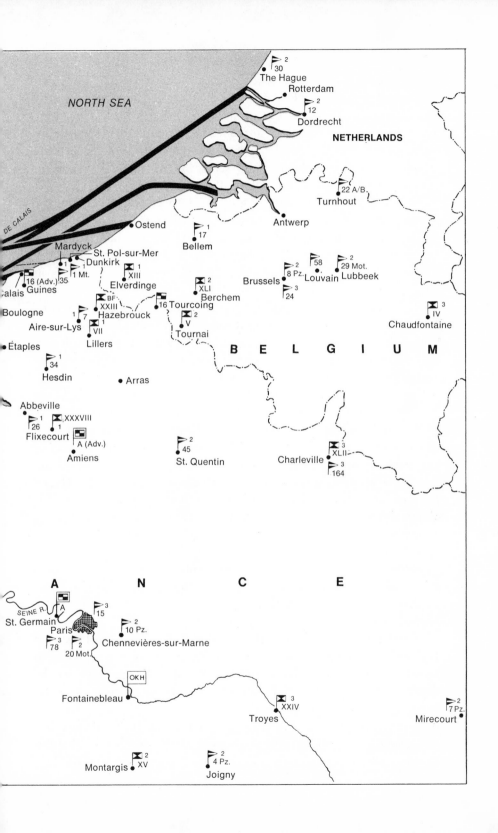

NORTH SEA

NETHERLANDS

⚑ 2
• 30
The Hague
Rotterdam
⚑ 2
• 12
Dordrecht

22 A/B.
Turnhout

DE CALAIS

• Ostend

Antwerp

⚑ 1
• 17
Bellem

Mardyck
St. Pol-sur-Mer
⚑ 1
1 Mt.
Dunkirk
XIII
Elverdinge

⚑ 2
8 Pz.
58
⚑ 2
29 Mot.
Brussels
Louvain
Lubbeek

⚑ 2
XLI
Berchem

⚑ 3
24

16 (Adv.)
35
Calais
Guines

Boulogne

Aire-sur-Lys
1 7
BF
XXIII
Hazebrouck
1
VII
Lillers

16 Tourcoing
⚑ 2
V
Tournai

XIV
• IV
Chaudfontaine

B E L G I U M

Étaples

⚑ 1
• 34
Hesdin

• Arras

Abbeville
⚑ 1
• 26
Flixecourt
XXXVIII
1
A (Adv.)

Amiens

⚑ 2
• 45
St. Quentin

XLII
⚑ 3
164
Charleville

A   N   C   E

SEINE R.
A
15
⚑ 3
St. Germain
Paris
⚑ 2
10 Pz.
⚑ 3
78
⚑ 2
20 Mot.
Chennevières-sur-Marne

OKH

Fontainebleau

XXIV
Troyes

⚑ 2
7 Pz.
Mirecourt

XV
Montargis
⚑ 2
4 Pz.
Joigny

under especially favorable circumstances. Otherwise the Le Havre contingent would run along the French coast to Boulogne and cross the Channel on the left wing of the main invasion fleet. The Navy's purpose, plainly enough, was to reduce the Brighton operation—in the Army's eyes a vital part of the invasion plan—to a contingent basis which would enable the Navy to scrap the whole thing unless the "circumstances" were to the sailors' liking.[97]

Accordingly, when Greiffenberg of OKH (accompanied by the two liaison officers, Witzleben and Loycke) turned up at SKL on August 22 to "clarify" outstanding questions, the result was another in the long succession of impasses. The Brighton "compromise" put forward at OKW on August 9 had envisaged a fleet of five hundred motorboats to make the single direct run from Le Havre to Brighton; Fricke now offered two hundred motorboats and one hundred motorized coastal sailboats, plus twenty-five small steamships. Greiffenberg countered with a demand for seventy-five steamships. Fricke threw up his hands, and the conference broke up with the usual agreement to disagree and leave the responsibility of decision to OKW.[98]

The frustrated Greiffenberg made a beeline to OKW and sought out Warlimont. There were four well-trained invasion divisions at Le Havre, and the shipping offered by the Navy was utterly insufficient to carry them across the Channel. The Navy's suggestion that part of this force be moved north and shipped from Dutch harbors was unfeasible. The Army needed at least seventy steamships at Le Havre, but the Navy insisted that so large a force could not be risked, as the shipping losses might well be so heavy as to endanger the flow of supplies and reinforcements to the main beachhead.[99] Thus unburdened, Greiffenberg took his departure for Fontainebleau, where he reported to Halder late in the afternoon of August 23. What he had to say about the Navy's proposals was so unwelcome that the Chief of Staff glumly concluded that "on such a basis an invasion has no chance of success this year."[100]

After Greiffenberg's departure from Berlin, Warlimont had resumed his role as the great compromiser. Military plans are not supposed to be sliced like so much cheese, but Warlimont had a keen eye for the middle of the road. The Navy had offered twenty-five steamers at Le Havre; the Army wanted seventy or seventy-five; the midpoint was fifty, and perhaps the Navy could be talked into it. If this amount was still insufficient to lift the four divisions at Le Havre, then let the fifty steamers and the motorboats take the assault wave, and send the four divisions' rear echelons north for embarkation at other ports. The group sailing direct from Le Havre would be called the "green movement" and the main force embarking from Boulogne–Rotterdam the "blue movement."

So armed, Warlimont at once got in touch with SKL and wooed the admirals with the argument that, since Hitler had made it clear that Sea Lion would not even be attempted unless the prospects were highly favorable, the Navy could afford to risk fifty ships at Le Havre. In the course of discussion a further refinement was worked out. Only twenty-five of the steamers would follow the motorboats in the "green movement" direct to Brighton. The other twenty-five would sail to Boulogne and go across with the "blue movement." If all went well they would continue westward along the English coast to Brighton; otherwise they would discharge their loads somewhere east of Beachy Head.

It was all getting terribly complicated, but Warlimont was persuasive, and on the morning of August 23 Raeder agreed to the compromise "solution." The Army, however, remained obdurate. On the morning of August 24 Warlimont, by telephone, described the new plans to Greiffenberg (Halder was again away on an inspection trip), without success. Brauchitsch himself, said Greiffenberg, would go to the Berghof on August 26 and clear up the matter in personal conference with the Fuehrer.[101]

But Brauchitsch's intervention, rarely decisive with Hitler, was in any event too late. Keitel and Jodl had both approved Warlimont's handiwork, the Navy was in the bag, and no doubt everyone at OKW was heartily sick of the interminable wrangle.* On August 25, Warlimont was able to tell Fricke that the Fuehrer would reach a decision in line with the August 22 plan.

And so it worked out on August 26.[102] The Army would have to adapt itself to the Navy's capacities, said Hitler, and that meant (as Brauchitsch informed Halder following the former's return from the Berghof) "restriction of Le Havre to jump-off of a small first wave of the Brighton group," with the rest to go from Boulogne.[103] On August 27, Hitler's decision was embodied in an OKW directive signed by Keitel.[104]

---

* Hitler had been at the Berghof since August 17, Keitel and Jodl joined him there on the 21st, and Warlimont's staff was moved to nearby Salzburg on the 23rd. Distance and pleasant surroundings no doubt dulled OKW's interest in the details of Sea Lion.

Thus OKW sawed the baby in half, giving to the Army a landing force which it thought inadequate, and saddling the Navy with a transport responsibility which it thought excessively dangerous. Grumbling, Halder resigned himself to the outcome, observing:[105] "The best thing for us to do is to develop our preparations on this basis, despite its many great drawbacks."

There still remained the problem, to be worked out with the Luftwaffe, of how best to use the airborne troops. These comprised three parachute regiments grouped under the command of the Luftwaffe's Fliegerdivision 7, and the Army's 22nd Infantry Division, which had been trained for air landing operations and effectively used in conjunction with the paratroops in Holland.[106]

It is a sharp commentary on the Luftwaffe's lack of interest in Sea Lion that until the last week of August no consideration had been given to this matter. On August 20 Halder had noted the need for a "comprehensive discussion" with the Air Force,[107] and the next day, when Greiffenberg set off on his mission to "clarify" matters with the Navy, he was also under instructions to visit Goering's headquarters. In conference with his opposite number, Generalmajor Hoffmann von Waldau, Greiffenberg proposed that the airborne troops be divided and used at the extremes of the right and left wings, with the main force to be used at Brighton to participate in the thrust to the north, and a smaller group north of Dover to guard the right flank of the whole operation.[108] Upon his return to Fontainebleau Greiffenberg reported in this sense to Halder, and indicated that the three paratroop regiments and one regiment of glider-borne troops would be committed.[109]

Neither at OKW nor at OKH did Greiffenberg report any disagreement with the Army's proposals on the Luftwaffe's part. In fact the matter was far from settled, and for the next three weeks it remained in a state of hopeless confusion. Partly this was due to a sudden state of alarm about the security of the Rumanian oil supply;* late in August it appeared that it might be necessary to send one of the three regiments of paratroopers to guard the Ploesti oil fields. Early in September this crisis eased,[110] but uncertainty over the airborne plans for Sea Lion continued.

The principal issue was that the Luftwaffe, taking a leaf out of the

---

* The Germans were worried about the possibility of hostilities between Rumania and Hungary, which would have threatened the supply of oil from the Ploesti oil fields, and might have led to Russian or British intervention in Rumania.

Navy's book, was reluctant to commit its paratroopers at Brighton and wanted to confine their use to the Folkestone area, just across the Straits. The matter was resolved in an astoundingly haphazard way; no one seemed to know what anyone else was doing or deciding. On September 4 it was reported at an OKW situation conference[111] that the Luftwaffe had not yet "submitted suggestions for the employment of parachute forces." On September 10 Halder, recording the discussion at a conference at Rundstedt's headquarters,[112] noted that the Army wanted airborne support not only at Dover and Brighton, but at Beachy Head as well. Two days later an OKW staff officer returned from Fontainebleau with information that[113] "the Army has agreed that parachute forces will be dropped at Dover only." But on September 14 Rundstedt's Army Group A issued its operational order for the execution of Sea Lion, in which the subordinate army headquarters were informed that one parachute regiment would be dropped on the right wing at Dover and the two others at Brighton and Beachy Head,[114] and on September 17 (the day that Sea Lion was indefinitely postponed by Hitler's order) Halder and Greiffenberg were still discussing the issue as if it remained unsettled.[115]

Actually, there was division of opinion within both services. In the Luftwaffe, Kesselring (to whose Luftflotte 2 Fliegerdivision 7 was subordinated) favored a bold distribution of the airborne troops,* and raised no objections to the Army's plan. On the Army side, Generaloberst Ernst Busch, as commander-in-chief of the 16th Army, was naturally pleased with the prospect of having the entire airborne force committed in support of his right wing, even though OKH might think it better to use the greater part in support of the 9th Army's left wing at Brighton.

Busch went so far as to request formally that the entire Fliegerdivision 7 be used in the Dover–Folkestone area. He was turned down on September 11 by Halder[116] and on the next day by Kesselring.[117] On September 17, however, when the acting† commander of the

---

* In his postwar memoirs, Kesselring wrote (*A Soldier's Record*, p. 70): "The most arresting fact about Sea Lion is that the lessons of the German airborne landings in Holland were completely ignored and it was proposed to do without the support of parachutists." This error must be due to faulty memory, but it reflects Kesselring's (and Student's) optimism about the possibilities of invasion and his disagreement with the cautious or indifferent attitudes of some of his colleagues.

† The commander, General Kurt Student, was still convalescing from his wound sustained during the occupation of Rotterdam.[118] He appears to have submitted some ideas about the conduct of the invasion, but did not resume his command until the fall of 1940, after the project had been abandoned.

Fliegerdivision, Generalmajor Richard Putzier, came to a conference at 16th Army headquarters, Busch had better luck, for Putzier announced that Goering had decided to use the entire unit (comprising three parachute regiments and one regiment of glider troops) on the 16th Army's right wing.* When this news was telephoned to OKH, Busch's staff was informed that Brauchitsch did not regard the decision as binding, but that matters would probably work out as Putzier had indicated.[119]

It was, of course, quite inexcusable that such basic matters had not been determined weeks earlier. It is hard to escape the conclusion that if Hitler had been seriously trying to bring off Sea Lion such delays would not have been tolerated. At any rate, that very night he ordered the operation indefinitely postponed. The next day (September 18) Luftflotte 2 finally got around to issuing an order governing the employment of Fliegerdivision 7,[120] specifying that it was to occupy the high ground north and northwest of Folkestone in order to assist the forward movement of Busch's right wing and stave off British attacks from the direction of Canterbury, and then join with the seaborne troops in an attack to capture Dover. But by then the whole matter was rapidly becoming academic.

Thus, in the wake of the Army's protracted negotiations with a reluctant and fearful Navy, and in the course of belated, half-baked conversations with a preoccupied and indifferent Luftwaffe, the outlines of the final invasion plan emerged. The entire plan was not embodied in any single OKW document or order; its elements and details must be assembled from the several orders issued by the three service commands—notably the OKH order of August 30,[121] the OKM orders of August 20 and 30,[122] and the Luftwaffe Commander-in-Chief's order of September 5[123]—and by the principal field commands assigned to Sea Lion, including Rundstedt's army group (Heeresgruppe A) and Busch's 16th Army, Kesselring's Luftflotte 2, and Admiral Guenther Luetjens' headquarters at Trouville,† which was to have direct tactical command of the invasion fleet.

---

* However, Putzier refused to put the airborne troops down where Busch wanted them, north and northwest of Dover, where they would have protected Busch's right flank. Kesselring (said Putzier) thought this too risky, and insisted on making the drop west of Folkestone, nearer to the beaches where the seaborne troops of the right wing were to land.

† Luetjens was the Commander-in-Chief of the Fleet (Flottenchef), but for Sea Lion he wore another hat as Seebefehlshaber West, and his headquarters at Trouville was called Seebefehlsstelle West.

In consequence of abandoning the Lyme Bay landing, the Army's command structure for the invasion was greatly simplified. Bock's army group (Heeresgruppe B) dropped out of the picture completely,* and so, for all practical purposes, did Reichenau's 6th Army and the IInd Corps headquarters,† which was to have commanded the three divisions ticketed for the Lyme Bay landing.‡

Accordingly, field command of all the Army forces devolved upon Rundstedt's Heeresgruppe A, with headquarters at St.-Germain-en-Laye, near Paris. These forces were to make four landings on the southeastern English coast, at landing areas designated B, C, D, and E.§ Areas B and C were contiguous, and reached from Hythe, just west of Folkestone, to Cliff's End, east of Hastings. Landing Area D extended east of Beachy Head from Eastbourne to Bexhill, and Area E lay to the west, from Brighton to Worthing.

The main thrust of the assault (*Schwerpunkt,* in German military parlance) was across the Straits at Areas B and C, and was to be undertaken by Busch's 16th Army. At Area B, between Folkestone and Dungeness, the XIIIth Corps, commanded by General Heinrich von Vietinghoff, would make the initial assault with two infantry divisions—the 17th (Generalleutnant Herbert Loch), on the right, and the 35th (Generalleutnant Hans Reinhard), on the left. At Area C, east of Dungeness, Generaloberst Eugen Ritter von Schobert of the VIIth Corps would go in with Generalleutnant Eccard Freiherr von Gablenz's 7th Infantry Division, on the beaches opposite Rye, and General Ludwig Kubler's 1st Mountain Division, on the heights east

* On Aug. 31 Bock was informed that his headquarters was to be moved east, and on Sept. 3 OKH ordered a general regrouping as part of the buildup in the east preparatory to the invasion of Russia, already secretly projected for the following year. Bock's headquarters was moved to Posen, and the 4th and 12th Armies' headquarters were also moved to Poland, along with several corps headquarters and a number of divisions. In France, Leeb's Heeresgruppe C assumed command of the units previously under B.

† The OKH order of Aug. 30 provided that Heeresgruppe B (replaced by C after Sept. 11) would not participate in the initial phase of Sea Lion but, if the naval situation should develop favorably, might later embark from Cherbourg and land in Lyme Bay, advance toward Bristol, and occupy Devon and Cornwall. In this event, command was to be exercised through the 6th Army and the IInd Corps, using the 6th and 256th Infantry Divisions.[124]

‡ Of the three infantry divisions, one (the 12th) was moved at the end of August to Holland, for use as one of the second-wave divisions of the 16th Army. The other two (the 31st and 32nd) were sent to the east early in September. The corps and divisions that had been allocated to the second and third waves of the Lyme Bay landing were released for other employment.[125]

§ Landing Area A was to have been in the Ramsgate–Deal area. As already described (*supra,* p. 227), this landing was abandoned at the Navy's insistence.

of Hastings. The troops of all the assault divisions were divided into two echelons (*Staffeln*), of which the first would make the initial attack with light weapons and the second would follow in immediately with heavier weapons and equipment.

The landings at Areas D and E were to be conducted by General-oberst Adolf Strauss's 9th Army. The Bexhill–Eastbourne landing was to be handled by General Erich von Manstein's XXXVIIIth Corps, comprising the 34th Infantry Division (Generalmajor Werner Sanne), at Bexhill, and the 26th (Generalleutnant Sigismund von Foerster), to the west at Pevensey, the landing place of William the Conqueror.

At Landing Area E the situation was more complicated, owing to the odd Warlimont compromise that had been used to end the long Navy-Army controversy over the Brighton landing. The first echelon of three divisions, embarking from Le Havre in the "green movement," was under the VIIIth Corps, commanded by General Walter Heitz, while the second echelon, which was to load at Boulogne and sail in the "blue movement," was subordinated to General Christian Hansen's Xth Corps.[126] In the landing area,* Generalmajor Ferdinand Schoerner's 6th Mountain Division was on the right, nearest to Beachy Head, Generalleutnant Rudolf Koch-Erpach's 8th Infantry in the center, and Generalmajor Johann Sinnhuber's 28th Infantry on the extreme left wing of the entire landing force.†

The hope was that these nine divisions of the first wave would be able to establish a bridgehead twelve to twenty miles deep and hold it against British counterattack for the week or ten days until the second wave could be loaded and landed. Since the *Schwerpunkt* lay with Busch, the greater part of the second wave was to come in on the right. The 16th Army's reinforcements from the second wave comprised General Georg-Hans Reinhardt's mechanized XLIst Corps, with two armored divisions and a division plus two independent regiments

---

* Presumably, after the troops of both echelons had been landed they would have been divided between the two corps on a divisional basis.

† Under the original OKH plan (July), the first wave of the 9th Army, all of which was to sail from Le Havre, comprised the 8th and 28th Divisions, under the VIIIth Corps, and the 6th Mountain and 30th Infantry Divisions, under the Xth Corps. When it was decided to reduce the scale of the Le Havre embarkation, the 30th Infantry was sent to Holland,[127] where, together with the 12th Infantry—simultaneously moved from the Cherbourg area—it was subordinated to the Vth Corps in the 16th Army's second wave. The necessity of embarking the second echelon of the 9th Army's first wave in Boulogne no doubt explains the simultaneous shift of the XXXVIIIth Corps's subordination from the 16th Army (July plan) to the 9th Army (final plan).

of motorized infantry,* and General Richard Ruoff's Vth Corps of two infantry divisions.† Strauss's 9th Army would get Generaloberst Hermann Hoth's mechanized XVth Corps, with two armored divisions and one of motorized infantry.‡

Thus strengthened to a force (including the three airborne regiments) of about nineteen divisions, the invasion force would strike west and northwest with the main weight on the right, the 16th Army pivoting on the 9th§ and aiming for the area just south of London, with the line Gravesend–Guildford–Portsmouth as the immediate objective of the attack, which, if successful, would put the Germans into occupation of Surrey, Sussex, and Kent. Thereafter the third wave (two corps with four infantry divisions for the 16th, one corps of two infantry divisions for the 9th), the 6th Army troops at Cherbourg, and OKH's general reserve forces would be brought over as opportunity and necessity dictated, to complete the conquest of Britain.

The Luftwaffe, unlike the Army, designated no single field headquarters (comparable to Rundstedt's army group) for the conduct of Sea Lion. The two top combat commands in the west, Luftflotten 2 and 3, were assigned to support the 16th and 9th Armies respectively. Kesselring's Luftflotte 2 had the dominant role, corresponding to that of the 16th Army. It was expected that the Stukas, recently withdrawn from the Battle of Britain because of the heavy losses they were sustaining, would be the most effective aircraft to serve as "airborne artillery" in support of the landings, by dive-bombing the British coastal batteries and other defensive shore emplacements. Accordingly, the bulk of the Stuka formations, grouped under the command of General Wolfram Freiherr von Richthofen in Fliegerkorps VIII, were allocated to support Busch's first wave at Landing Areas B and C. Comparable support for Strauss's landings at Areas C and D was to be provided by Generaloberst Ulrich Grauert's Fliegerkorps I, using level-flight bombers and the few Stukas left in Luftflotte 3.‖

---

* These were the 8th and 10th Panzer Divisions, the 29th Motorized Infantry Division, the motorized SS Regiment Leibstandarte Adolf Hitler, and the motorized-infantry Regiment Grossdeutschland, an elite regiment from which Hitler's military bodyguard was drawn.

† These were the 12th and 30th Infantry Divisions, transferred respectively from Cherbourg and Le Havre.

‡ These were the 4th and 7th Panzer Divisions and the 20th Motorized Infantry Division.

§ *Cf.* Halder's description:[128] "Ninth Army's role is that of a hinge on which attack of Sixteenth Army swings in a northwestern direction."

‖ During the early part of the Battle of Britain, Fliegerkorps VIII was part of Luftflotte 3, operating against southern England from the Normandy peninsula.

To hinder the flow of British forces toward the beachhead, other bombers from Fliegerkorps II (of Luftflotte 2) and Fliegerkorps IV and V (of Luftflotte 3) would attack bridges and other transport targets north and west of London. Following the disagreements and decisions already described, the Luftwaffe leaders decided to commit all of the airborne troops near Folkestone, to assist the right wing of the 16th Army.

The entire plan depended, of course, on getting the ground forces— or enough of them—safely across the Channel, and here the burden of responsibility fell primarily on the Navy and secondarily on the Luftwaffe. To protect the invasion lanes it was envisaged that the Navy, assisted by the mine-laying aircraft of Fliegerdivision 9 (under Luftflotte 2), would sweep up British mines and would lay German mine barriers eastward from the North Foreland, across the Channel from Beachy Head toward Dieppe, and east of the Isle of Wight. Fifteen submarines and the main force of destroyers (of which there were ten) and torpedo boats (about twenty-four) were to be stationed outside the western mine barrier, and six submarines and all the motor torpedo boats north of the eastern barrier.[130] Bombers from Luftflotten 2 and 3 would attack British warships, in the North Sea and west of the invasion lanes respectively.

The Naval War Staff (SKL)in Berlin retained over-all command of the naval operations. From SKL the chain of command ran to Marinegruppenkommando West, under Generaladmiral Saalwaechter, in Paris, and then to the Seebefehlshaber West, Admiral Luetjens, at Trouville. The former was to control the operations of the warships,* while the latter had the key task of the whole undertaking—tactical command of the invasion transport fleet.†

Luetjens divided his force into four main "transport fleets" (*Transportflotten*) designated B, C, D, and E, corresponding to the landing areas for which each of them was earmarked. The leaders (*Transportflottenfuehrer*) of these four groups were the "seagoing admirals" of

---

At the end of August it was shifted to Luftflotte 2, and at about the same time Fliegerkorps I was transferred from Luftflotte 2 to Luftflotte 3.[129]

* The submarines were under the direct command of the Befehlshaber der Unterseeboote, Vizeadmiral Karl Doenitz, the destroyers under Kapitaen zur See Erich Bey (Fuehrer der Zerstoerer) and the torpedo boats under Kapitaen zur See Hans Butow (Fuehrer der Torpedoboote).

† Also directly subordinate to Marinegruppenkommando West was Admiral Karlgeorg Schuster, the Commanding Admiral for France (Kommandierender Admiral Frankreich), to whom were in turn subordinated the coastal and harbor commandants and other inland naval commands.

the seaborne invasion, though in fact only one of them held flag rank.

Vizeadmiral Herrmann Fischel, in command of Fleet B, had a particularly difficult and crucial task, for he was to assemble off Calais four groups of ships from Dunkirk, Ostend, and Rotterdam carrying the troops and equipment of the XIIIth Corps, and lead the assemblage across the Straits to Landing Area B. Kapitaen zur See Gustav Kleikamp's Fleet C was to set out from Calais with ships that had been loaded both there and in Antwerp, and take the VIIth Corps across to Area C. Fleet D, commanded by Kapitaen zur See Werner Lindenau, was to lead a huge fleet of tugs and barges, loaded with General von Manstein's XXXVIIIth Corps, from Boulogne to Area D. At Le Havre, Kapitaen zur See Ernst Scheurlen had the most complicated and well-nigh desperate assignment, for his Fleet E was to cross in three groups and by two routes. The thirty motorboats and motorized sailing ships carrying part of the first echelon of the Le Havre forces (under the VIIIth Corps) would cut directly across the Channel to Brighton, while the rest of these forces were on fifty freighters, of which twenty-five would sail up the coast to Boulogne and make the crossing with Fleet D and twenty-five would go by the direct route or via Boulogne, according to the naval prospects.*

The invasion armada comprised ships of three basic types. Leading were small naval craft—mine sweepers, patrol boats, motor launches, and special craft carrying artillery to provide covering fire for the operation. The initial landing would be made from these ships by picked troops in assault boats (*Sturmboote*) and pneumatic rafts (*Flossaecken*).†

Immediately behind came the main body of the assault troops—the first *Staffel*—in prahms (*Praehme*), the converted river barges which were, *faute de mieux*, the standard beaching craft for the operation. None of them was powered sufficiently for the Channel crossing, and more than half were not powered at all. Consequently, all were to be towed across the Channel by tugs (*Schlepper*). Each tug would take two prahms in line; the combination was called a *Schleppzug*, and a group of these a *Schleppverband*. Approaching the beaches, the prahms would cut loose from the tug and run up on the beach under their

---

* Both of these groups of freighters were under the command of Kapitaen zur See Ulrich Brocksien. The unity of command over vessels which, according to the plan, might be widely separated strongly suggests that the Navy intended to send all the freighters by way of Boulogne.

† These first men ashore were called the *Vorausabteilung*. There were to be about 2,000 at each of the four landing areas.

own power or pushed by accompanying motorboats. The bows had been converted to open and allow troops, horses, and vehicles to go over a ramp to the beach.

About two hours behind the first *Staffel* came the second *Staffel*[*] in steamers, each towing two prahms. A group of steamers was called a *Geleitzug*. At the beaches, the freighters would, of course, have to lie offshore; their passengers and cargoes were to be taken ashore by the prahms and whatever other beachable boats might be available.

The invasion fleet was slow and unwieldy. It was also, by the standards of those times, very large. Von Fischel's fleet for Beach B, for example, comprised two *Schleppverbaende* of 100 tugs and 200 prahms from Dunkirk and Ostend with the first *Staffel* of the VIIth Corps, and two *Geleitzuege* of 65 steamers and 130 prahms with the corps's second *Staffel* (and the rest of the first) from Ostend and Rotterdam, as well as 30 motorboats and the naval craft for the *Vorausabteilung*. In the four fleets there were, in all, some 165 steamers, 400 tugs, 1,100 prahms, and 250 motorboats.

Diminished as it was by the altered plan, the first wave (*Treffen*) of the invasion force still comprised nine divisions—including the Luftwaffe ground personnel, the paratroops, and special units, perhaps 300,000 men and 50,000 horses.[†] If they had been able to gain a foothold and the Navy had succeeded in bringing over the second and third waves, there would have been some 700,000 men and 125,000 horses in southeastern England,[‡] with heavy weapons, airfield crews, and hundreds of tanks and vehicles.

None of the German Navy's handful of large warships, it will be noted, was to be used in the close waters of the Channel. Instead, the warships were to be employed, together with troops and aircraft in Norway, for a deception operation, under the cover name *Herbstreise* ("Autumn Journey").[131] This was, in essence, a feint against the eastern coast of Britain, intended to draw off British forces to the north, away from the invasion area.

Finally, there were elaborate and drastic plans for the administration of the occupied areas. Military economic staffs were established

---

[*] The units allocated to the first *Staffel* crossed without troops and equipment unnecessary for the assault; these were brought over in steamers along with the second *Staffel*.

[†] A report by the 16th Army to Heeresgruppe A dated Sept. 20 showed 110,000 men and 24,500 horses in the 4 divisions of the first wave. The first wave of the 9th Army comprised 5 divisions.

[‡] The 16th Army return showed 112,000 men in the second wave and 106,000 in the third. The second and third waves of the 9th Army were about half as large.

for the sequestering of goods of the most diverse nature. All able-bodied males between seventeen and forty-five were to be interned and transferred to the Continent. The Gestapo drew up an immediate arrest list of over two thousand names of politicians, writers, and others, ranging from Winston Churchill to Virginia Woolf. Much of the literature (including prohibitory placards for public posting) makes amusing reading in the comfort of long retrospect, but it would have been a pretty sinister business if Sea Lion had ever gained a foothold in Britain.[132]

CHAPTER SEVEN

Deployment and Dispersion of the Invasion Force

INVASION PLANS, no matter how carefully considered, would have no value for operational and little for psychological purposes unless troops and staffs were deployed and trained for their execution. The tasks of the Luftwaffe were onerous and probably beyond its capacities, but they were not unfamiliar in character, and their discharge would have required no significant shifting of the units deployed along the Channel coast for the Battle of Britain.

The Army and the Navy—especially the Army—stood in very different case. For all its tradition of professionalism, the Army General Staff had next to no experience with amphibious operations. The Norwegian venture (prepared and controlled not by OKH but by OKW) was not much of a guide, because there it had been possible, owing to the enemy's weakness, to run the ships right into the main ports and unload the troops at the piers. For Sea Lion the soldiers would have to go in over open beaches—quite another story. During the First World War the German Navy had landed a division on the beaches of Oesel, a Russian-held island (now called Sarema) at the mouth of the Gulf of Riga. This little venture in the sheltered Baltic against weak opposition left no deposit of amphibious tradition in the German high command, and it may fairly be said that both Army and Navy came fresh and green to the problem in 1940.

The amphibious problem, needless to say, had many facets, but the core of the task was to master the technique of, and to procure and assemble the shipping and equipment necessary for, transporting the invasion force across the Channel *and landing it over open and strongly defended beaches.* The Chief of the Army General Staff perceived this at the outset, and *preparation* for the invasion began with Halder's conferences with Admiral Schniewind and General Emil Leeb (the chief of Army Ordnance) in Berlin on July 1.

Halder's notes of these meetings[1] plainly reflected his preoccupation with the beach problem. What kind of available craft could both negotiate the Channel and run on and off the beaches? Armor had played the key role both in Poland and in the Battle of France; how could tanks be put on the beaches with the assault troops? General Leeb opined that about 120 tanks could be made ready for underwater use (*Unterwasserfahrt*). Halder at once concluded that it was "necessary to set up special experimental teams soon in order to get tank, engineer, and naval experts together for practical tests on a broad basis."

Preparations

With this thought in the forefront of his mind, Halder returned to Fontainebleau and set to work. Within forty-eight hours he had selected the man to head up the Army's "experimental team"—General der Panzertruppen Georg-Hans Reinhardt, a fifty-three-year-old product of the General Staff who had led the XLIst Corps (armored) with great success during the Battle of France. On July 6 Reinhardt came to Fontainebleau for briefing on his assignment. He was to have a headquarters in Berlin and carry out the tests at Putlos, an Army test station on Kiel Bay, and at the North Frisian island of Sylt, in the North Sea off the coast of northern Schleswig. Submersible tanks, transport craft, smoke, assault boats—all the problems of transport and beach assault were to be Reinhardt's province. His task had diplomatic as well as technical aspects, for his first assignment was to "establish teamwork" with the Navy, the interested technical branches of the Army (tank and engineer specialists in particular),* and the civilian Organisation Todt.[2]

Reinhardt was not one to let the grass grow. Back in Berlin and utilizing the staff of his XLIst Corps as a nucleus, he rapidly put together an *ad hoc* staff designated Versuchsstab (Experimental Staff) R.[3] On July 10 he was at SKL, enlisting the Navy's co-operation in the

---

* The OKH staff specialist on tanks was Oberst (soon to be Generalmajor) Wilhelm Ritter von Thoma, who later won fame and was taken prisoner by the British in Africa. The engineer specialist was General Alfred Jacob.

tests to be held at Sylt,[4] and on July 14 he submitted his first report, warning that the submersible tanks might not prove out and stressing the need for shallow-draft craft that could unload troops and equipment directly onto the beaches.[5]

Meanwhile Halder and his staff had been selecting the units for assignment to Sea Lion and preparing the Army plan for submission to Hitler. The day after Hitler gave his verbal approval, Halder called a conference of all the interested OKH staff sections, to parcel out their assignments in preparing for the operation.[6] On the morning of July 17 (following receipt of the previous day's OKW directive on Sea Lion), preparations were officially begun with the issuance of the first OKH order to the Army field headquarters,[7] listing the army group, army and corps headquarters and the divisions for the first two invasion waves (*Treffen*) and establishing a transport schedule which would bring the first-wave divisions to their training areas on the Channel coast during the last few days of July and the first few of August. That afternoon the plan was explained to the army-group and army operations officers in conferences at both Fontainebleau and St.-Germain (Rundstedt's headquarters).[8]

On July 19, while Brauchitsch and Halder were in Berlin for the triumphal Reichstag session, Reinhardt came in to report his further progress and problems. In consultation with the Navy he had come to a decision on, if not a fully satisfactory solution of, the landing-craft problem. The only craft available in large numbers that looked to be both seaworthy for the Channel and beachable were the long river barges, widely used on the Rhine and other West European waterways, which the invasion staffs called *Praehme*—prahms.* There were some two thousand of these scattered along the inland rivers and canals, but they would all need conversion for use as landing craft, especially so that the bow could be opened to unload over ramps to the beaches. Reinhardt told his superiors that the conversion would be handled at eleven different shipyards, nine of which were in Holland and Belgium, and that Army engineers ought to be made available to expedite the process.[10]

Apart from prahm conversion, the conferees saw the two main unsolved problems as the unloading of heavy vehicles and the delivery of

---

* Variously spelled in English as "praam," "pram," "praham," and "prahm." According to General Halder,[9] the German Navy distinguished between the river barges of Germany (*Praehme*), France (*Penichen*), and the Low Countries (*Campine*).

seaborne covering fire during the landing operations. On these and comparable matters Reinhardt was to work in close co-operation with the OKH transportation and engineer specialists, Gercke and Jacob, and as equipment and technique were perfected he was to prepare instructional pamphlets for distribution to the troops.

Obviously the engineers would play a vital part in the unloading phase of the landing operation. Thirty-five engineer battalions might be collected from the Army divisions in Germany and those then scheduled for deactivation. Training centers for the engineers, each capable of handling a battalion, had already been set up at Sylt, Emden, and Husum (a small harbor town in Schleswig, on the North Sea). The amphibious tank tests and training were to be concentrated at Putlos, and the prahm unloading at Sylt, where a meeting of commanders would be held at the end of the month to take stock of the results.

A few days later General Jacob went to Emden to view an engineer troop exercise; on July 26 he was back in Fontainebleau, reporting to Halder and Loycke.[11] His principal conclusion was that the first assault troops should use only self-propelled craft, unless it should prove possible to get some of the powerless barges ashore by lashing them alongside cutters. Otherwise, the powerless barges should be used only for the later waves, after a beachhead had been established. Jacob estimated that the self-propelled and cutter-lashed barges might total about a thousand; as a practical matter, this meant that about half of the landing fleet would be available for the first wave.

Beyond this, the engineers had concluded that there were far too many horses in the planned assault wave; automotive transportation should be substituted as far as possible. Rafts could be constructed from bridging materials, floated on bulletproof gasoline tanks, and used as a platform for seaborne Flak at the beaches. Assault boats and pneumatic rafts should be available in large quantities to expedite the landing.

To expand and disseminate this new learning, it was agreed that the engineer troop commanders should be the first pupils at Reinhardt's schools. Meanwhile "rafts and other craft for use in the crossing will be sent to the jump-off beaches, and training courses will be organized . . . so that the troops can start to practice embarkation and landing as soon as they arrive."

Engineers along the North Sea, tank men on Kiel Bay at Putlos.

Late in July picked small units from the armored divisions* were sent there to test and get practical experience with amphibious, or, more correctly, submersible tanks. Reinhardt's early misgivings about these "U-Panzer" ("U" for *unterwasser*) were largely overcome as the tests progressed, and in a report on July 30 he went so far as to recommend that the Luftwaffe avoid bombing the shallow waters along the landing beaches, so as to leave the bottoms smooth for the submersible tanks.[13]

On August 2 Raeder, Brauchitsch, Halder, and their staffs for-gathered at Sylt.[14] Considering that Reinhardt had been at work less than a month, he had much to show them. The submersible tanks made a good impression. The machine-gun mountings on the prahms looked efficient, and the causeways and bridges for traversing flats and shal-lows were satisfactory. On the key problem of unloading the prahms over ramps, however, Halder was critical of the high angle of descent (*da zu hochkantig*) and labeled the design "unsatisfactory."

After the demonstrations there was a general conference on landing tactics. The time would be dawn on a day when dawn would come about two hours after high tide, so that the landing craft would settle firmly as the tide went out, and would surely refloat at the next high tide. The "main difficulty" disclosed by the demonstrations was how to maintain covering fire from the landing craft as they approached the shore, and still be ready for quick disembarkation. There would be special training courses at Emden for commanders, and for armored and engineer troops as well as infantry.

All this, of course, depended upon the Navy's success in com-mandeering and converting the necessary shipping, and in clearing away wreckage and otherwise preparing the embarkation ports. The Army had been plunging ahead, full of enthusiasm and blessed with abundant manpower. The Navy had neither, and until the latter part of July naval preparations lagged. SKL did not really get down to business until July 14,[15] and then a general reorganization of the naval command structure in France and the Low Countries had to be effected before much practical work could be begun. Generaladmiral Saalwaechter moved his headquarters (Marinegruppenkommando West) from Wilhelmshaven to Paris, and took over-all command of

---

* Thus the 2nd Panzer Regiment (of the 1st Panzer Division), stationed near Orléans, sent to Putlos 2 companies of picked troops under a battalion commander, Major Hyazinth Graf Strachwitz von Gross-Zauche und Camminety, a 47-year-old reserve officer who later became a divisional commander and one of the most decorated Army officers.[12]

naval operations in the west,* including Sea Lion. From Saalwaechter the new chain of naval shore command ran through the Commanding Admiral for France, Admiral Schuster, also located in Paris, and the commander for the Channel coast, Vizeadmiral Friedrich-Wilhelm Fleischer, at Boulogne, to the harbor commandants at Calais, Boulogne, Dunkirk, and the other Channel ports, who had the unenviable task of cleaning up the harbors. Also subordinate to Schuster were special naval headquarters (*Kriegsmarinedienststellen*) in the invasion ports, whose commanders were to be responsible for fitting out the shipping, allocating it among the Army "customers," and supervising the loading.

Apart from ships, the Navy was woefully short of men. At the SKL conference on July 23[16] it was estimated that 24,000 men would be needed to man the invasion fleet—16,000 for the prahms alone, the rest for the steamers and the motorboats and other small craft. Where were they all to come from, unless the inland waterways were scoured for every last river boatman that could be found? Even on administrative matters the Navy was simply overwhelmed, especially when the Army began to appear in strength along the Channel coast, full of energy and demands.

For all these difficulties, by the end of July things were on the move. The new headquarters were in process of establishment, and the collection and conversion of shipping was well under way. The Army needled, but it also helped to alleviate the manpower shortage by putting Army engineers to work in the harbors, and in other ways. While SKL and OKH wrangled about broad and narrow fronts, at the operational level the co-operation was much smoother.

Meanwhile by train, by truck, and on foot the troops ticketed for the invasion had been moving toward their positions along the coast. Some of the corps and divisional staffs learned of their new mission even before the first OKH order was issued,† while others remained in the dark almost until they reached the beaches. As the redeployment progressed, the higher field headquarters were holding staff conferences and issuing their first orders on troop organization and training

* Until late July, Saalwaechter had been at Wilhelmshaven and Generaladmiral Rolf Carls (Marinegruppenkommando Ost) at Kiel. When Saalwaechter went to Paris, Carls moved to Wilhelmshaven, and the name of his command was changed to Marinegruppenkommando Nord.

† Somehow the XVth Corps (Generaloberst Hoth), comprising the mechanized troops that were to be used in the 9th Army's bridgehead, was unusually well and soon informed, for it was holding staff conferences on Sea Lion with subordinate units as early as July 13.[17] Most of the lower headquarters apparently learned of the new mission shortly after July 21.

for the invasion.[18] By the end of the month these preliminary steps had been largely completed.

Thus July was a month of tactical planning, testing of amphibious techniques and equipment, redeployment of troops, and first steps toward the collection and conversion of shipping. August was to be the month of intensive training for the invasion troops and staffs.

The focus of action now shifted to the lower echelons of command. At OKH, Brauchitsch and Halder had Russia, Africa, and other problems to consider, and with respect to Sea Lion the front-width issue with the Navy took much of their attention. For the time being there was not much more to be done at OKH regarding the actual preparations, so both the Commander-in-Chief and his Chief of Staff frequently took off for the Channel coast to observe the training activities at first hand.

At the highest field headquarters—the army groups and the naval group command—Sea Lion was not especially lively. Partly this was a matter of geography, for Rundstedt at St.-Germain and Saalwaechter at Paris were nearly as far from the operational scene as was OKH at Fontainebleau. Their headquarters (and the same was true of Bock's*) tended to become mere routing offices for orders and reports passing between OKH or SKL and the headquarters on the coast. Rundstedt's Heeresgruppe A, with the operations of two armies to co-ordinate, could have taken a much larger part in Sea Lion than it did. However, as has already been noted,[19] neither Rundstedt nor his staff had taken the invasion plan very seriously.† If they had, probably they would have established a forward command post of the army group on the coast, but, although one was projected in the event that the invasion was actually undertaken,[21] it was never established.

In consequence of this rather casual attitude at St.-Germain,‡ the

---

* The role of Bock's Army Group B in the initial assault was superfluous. The Lyme Bay landing involved only 3 first-wave divisions under one army (the 6th) and one corps (the IInd), and there was really no need for the interposition of an army group headquarters between the 6th Army and OKH.

† Rundstedt visited the 9th Army (at Dieppe) on July 31, and the 16th Army (at Ostend, Dunkirk, Gravelines, and Le Havre) from Aug. 3 to Aug. 6. He does not seem to have observed any of the amphibious demonstrations in August and September.[20]

‡ It should not be thought that Heeresgruppe A was totally neglectful of its responsibilities. Conferences were held, orders issued, and the necessary paperwork was properly handled. But there was no initiative from St.-Germain, and the army group's war diary reflects the lack of leadership. Entries dealing with Sea Lion are rather sparse and perfunctory; throughout the summer of 1940 a frequent entry for the day is *"Keine besondere Ereignisse"* (no special developments).

army headquarters became the main centers for the planning and guidance of training for Sea Lion, and it is in the war diaries of the armies and their subordinate corps and divisions that the best available accounts of the Army's training activities are to be found. The fortunes of war have governed the survival or disappearance of these; likewise, some diarists slighted their work or were by nature laconic, while others entered full and sometimes rather excited accounts of the day's doings. For example, very few records of Strauss's 9th Army for this period have come to light, and there are other serious gaps.* Fortunately, however, many records of Busch's 16th Army and its subordinate formations are available for study.

The 16th Army composed the main striking force, and Busch and his staff, headed by Generalleutnant Walter Model as chief of staff and Oberstleutnant Hans Boeckh-Behrens as Ia, were highly competent officers who tackled the invasion project with energy and determination. Thus the 16th-Army headquarters at Turcoing (in France north of Lille and just south of the Belgian border) became the main center of direction for the Army's invasion preparations, and their nature and progress can be gathered from its records,† together with those of the VIIth, XIIIth, and XXXVIIIth Corps and several of the divisions, especially the 7th, 17th and 35th Infantry Divisions.[22]

Well-trained and battle-hardened units were selected for Sea Lion, but none of them had had amphibious experience. What did these troops need to learn? The essence of the problem was how to carry a defended beach by assault, but this involved numerous subsidiary techniques, of which the following were probably the most important:

1. Selecting the essential equipment for the assault, and loading troops and equipment on the prahms and other craft in a way that would permit speedy and efficient unloading at the beaches.

2. Maintaining covering fire from ships to shore as the assault troops approached the beaches.

3. Disembarking on the beaches under fire, and getting troops and equipment across the sand and mud flats to firm ground.

4. Developing a flexible command system that could survive the confusion and mixing of units that would inevitably accompany a strongly resisted landing.

* The Heeresgruppe B diaries for 1940 are missing after July 14, and very little is available from the IInd, VIIIth, XVth, and XLIst Corps.

† The ensuing text is based upon the records listed in note 22, unless otherwise specified.

5. Organizing the beachheads so that reinforcements could be rapidly sorted out and distributed, casualties evacuated, and a tactical basis laid for their expansion into bases for offensive operations.*

For the most part, troops and officers alike were full of energy and enthusiasm, and were determined to find ways and means to lick the toughest of these difficult and unfamiliar problems. Here and there, to be sure, there was pessimism or even scorn for the undertaking. The Bavarians of the 1st Mountain Division did not take kindly to the sea and had a low opinion of the prahms, which they regarded as neither seaworthy nor satisfactory for an assault. The loading and unloading exercises were ridiculed as "*Wasserpantomimen*" that put everyone in a foul mood, and one of the divisional commanders has recorded his impression[24] that "no one seriously believed in the success of so dilettantish a project." But such attitudes were the exception; more typical were those expressed by the diarist of Manstein's XXXVIIIth Corps, commencing training near Boulogne at the end of July:

The 16th Army under Generaloberst Busch is now selected for the attack against the English island. Since Caesar and William the Conqueror no foreign power has succeeded in setting foot on English soil. Even the attempts of Napoleon failed.

To the XXXVIIIth Corps has fallen the task of being in the front line of the attack. For the German Army, this is an entirely new kind of warfare; nothing can be based on the experience of earlier campaigns. Extensive preparations, reorganization, and intensive training are necessary. Tests of all sorts are in process, so as to exploit all possibilities for the success of this plan . . .

And on the first day of August:

Preparations for the task are immediately commenced. Exercises are carried out on land and sea. Everything is new, everything must first be contrived and tested. Every unit must strive to advance the work with its own ideas. The inventive spirit is absolutely necessary to solve the many problems. It is the inspiration and the wish of all the troops to sweep all difficulties out of the way, and put England to rout.

---

* *Cf.* the list of training problems in the divisional history of the 31st Infantry Division, in the Cherbourg–Lyme Bay group:[23] "Maneuvering on the water with fishing boats and pneumatic rafts; landing under heavy fire; shooting from sea to land with all weapons, including light field howitzers; antiaircraft defense on ships and rafts; rescue operations; carrying coastal bluffs and cliffs; loading equipment on wagons and bicycles; waterproof packing of ammunition, radio equipment, and rations; readying of life jackets and emergency construction materials."

When the invasion divisions reached their destinations, the three armies standing along the Channel coast—the 6th, 9th, and 16th—divided their forces by corps and divisions into "occupation groups" (*Besetzungsgruppen*) and "operations groups" (*Operationsgruppen*).[25] The former took over the responsibilities for internal security and administration and for coastal defense; the operations groups, comprising the units assigned to the first wave (*Treffen*) of Sea Lion, were thus left free to concentrate on training.

The first-wave divisions were promptly divided into two *Staffeln*, the first *Staffel* of each division comprising two regimental combat groups for the assault, and the second comprising the division's third regiment and most of the transport and other equipment. The first *Staffel* in turn was divided into three groups, the first consisting of the initial assault squads in small, fast "storm boats," the second following in company strength in large self-propelled landing craft, and the third comprising the regimental staff and the main body in battalion strength, loaded in the towed prahms.

All of the assault divisions were now beefed up with special units, not part of the usual complement of a division, assigned to them by OKH (*Heerestruppen*). These generally included antiaircraft, combat engineer, smoke and antitank battalions, bridging units, and supplementary artillery.

Reinhardt's experimental schools in Schleswig could accommodate only a few engineer and tank units. Many of the troop commanders of the assault divisions and a few special units were sent to Emden for special training. But the bulk of the instruction had to be given on the Channel coast, and for this purpose the 16th Army on July 31 directed the establishment of a training center at Le Touquet, to which each division was to send a small group of officers and men.[*] The course was to last from the fifth to the fifteenth of August, and the "graduates" would then return to their units as qualified instructors.

And so, during the first week of August, the entire Channel coast from Ostend to Cherbourg came alive with German soldiery engaging in the various forms of amphibious training. Here some were maneuvering in small boats and rafts; there others were practicing firing rifles, machine guns, or light artillery from "rocking platforms" specially constructed to simulate the motion of small craft lying off the coast. Still others were scouting out suitable areas for landing practice;

---

[*] The 17th Division sent 7 officers and 50 men, and the 35th Division 5 officers and 30 men, pursuant to the orders from their respective corps.

at the promontory of Cap Gris-Nez troops of the 1st Mountain Division were practicing maritime cliff-scaling. And at all levels, from company to army, staff officers were meeting to assimilate the results and think up better ways of surmounting the difficulties.

As soon as the troops got down to business, a chorus of complaint rose from one headquarters after another. *Where were the prahms and other craft necessary for practicing loading and unloading?* Back in the middle of July, General Reinhardt had complained that his tests had had to be postponed because the Navy had been slow about delivering his promised boats.[26] Now every unit on the coast was feeling the same pinch. Small motorboats and rafts were all right for the very first assault troops, and many German soldiers had learned to use these for river and canal crossings; but the bulk of the invasion troops would be going ashore, if at all, by prahm, and there was much to be learned about loading, handling, and the use of ramps to get on the beaches.

Near the northern end of the invasion area, the 35th Infantry Division was especially exercised. Its regiment training at Nieuport (the 109th) was facing "grave difficulties" because the boats in the harbor were not seaworthy. The division was scoured for men with some experience as inland-waterway sailors (*Binnenschiffer*); only two were found, and the Navy could give no help. On August 6 the divisional staff was lamenting that not one ship had yet been supplied, and that the corps had warned that none could be expected for another three days at least. Farther south it was the same story. As late as August 22 the Xth Corps noted that for lack of shipping the troops were still using makeshift training devices, and the next day the 8th Infantry Division bewailed the loss of the only steamer previously available, which had hit a mine at cost of the ship and nineteen dead trainees, while the 17th Division, training at Breskens in Holland, criticized the training limitations imposed by mine warnings, the narrow field of practice fire, the lack of blank cartridges, and the non-appearance of shipping promised them by the 16th Army.

For the time being there was little that the Navy could do about it, since the great mass of prahms were still being collected and moved to Duisburg, Mannheim, or the Dutch ports for conversion. The acute shipping shortage naturally stimulated interest in the possibility of devising new types of craft that could be speedily constructed and distributed. The day after the assemblage of high brass at Sylt to view Reinhardt's accomplishments (August 2), Halder had paid a visit to the Luftwaffe experimental station on the Rangsdorfersee, where Oberst Fritz Siebel, an aircraft manufacturer seconded to the

Luftwaffe by Goering, was developing "ferries" (*Faehren*) from bridge pontoons trussed together and propelled by air screws.[27] The demonstration was unimpressive; the craft was slow and Halder thought it unseaworthy.[*]

Four days later Halder was off to Carteret, on the coast southwest of Cherbourg, where an Army engineer officer, Oberst Strobl, was making rafts out of bridging equipment floated on empty gasoline drums and barrels.[29] These were more successful, and Strobl had mounted 88-millimeter antiaircraft guns and light (20- and 37-millimeter) artillery on them, in order to provide covering fire for the beach assault. They were to be called "Herbert ferries," after the type of bridging equipment used. In the final invasion plan some forty Siebel and Herbert ferries were allocated to the invasion forces, primarily for antiaircraft protection at the beaches.

This was all very well, but it accomplished nothing in mitigation of the landing-craft problem. Faced with so crucial a shortage, the troops roamed the coastal areas and the rivers and canals, hoping to find a bit of what the Navy could not yet provide. Some units were luckier or better scroungers than others. On August 4 the 17th Infantry proudly recorded the discovery of three prahms and a fishing boat in Breskens, "the nucleus of our training fleet." A few divisional engineers were at once sent off to the shipyards at Rotterdam to see how the Navy was converting the prahms for Sea Lion, so that the division could do the work itself. But such good fortune was unusual, as most of the coastal vessels had fled to Britain during the Battle of France.[30]

Another big difficulty was the state of the northern Channel ports, with their facilities smashed and harbors cluttered with sunken ships. The same was true of the inland waterways; early in August the 35th Infantry staff thought it would take a month to clean up the destroyed bridges and sunken boats in the canals between Ypres and the coast. The harassed and undermanned Navy simply could not do everything at once. On August 16 Halder made a trip down the shore from Ostend, visiting Dunkirk, Calais, Boulogne, and Dieppe, and gloomily recorded:[31]

Practically nothing has been done in the harbors. Most of the waterfront installations are intact, but the approaches are in many cases badly blocked. Sunken vessels are obstructing the harbor basins.

Navy experts say that entering and leaving the harbors offer no difficulties.

[*] Later on, utilizing water screws, Siebel developed the highly useful "Siebel ferries" extensively used by the Germans in the Mediterranean and other close waters.[28]

As to loading, they believe it could be done from the quais only with cranes, and many of these have either been destroyed or put out of commission by the fleeing British.

There is no evidence of any repair work going on. So I instruct the engineers to build some floating loading platforms for loading the barges in the harbors, so that at least these vessels could be loaded without cranes.

On August 17 the 16th Army's first training course at Le Touquet concluded with elaborate demonstration exercises. Brauchitsch and Halder were there,[32] with commanders and staff officers from all the major units.* The day began with a staff conference on the utilization of shipping; this was followed by a demonstration of beach assault craft, which Halder thought well of. Then there was practice fire from the rocking platforms, in which, Halder thought, rate of fire was sacrificed to illusory hopes of accuracy. "More area firing," he counseled.

After this the visitors were driven to Boulogne and they all put out to sea, protected by mine sweepers, heading back to Le Touquet, some fifteen miles to the south, where a landing in regimental strength was staged. Halder strongly objected to the use of firecrackers on the beach to simulate covering fire from the sea: "The demonstration disregards our actual problem and is therefore unsatisfactory." He also observed, with what must have been a landlubber's interest, that the "invasion fleet" made much slower progress toward Le Touquet than on the return trip to Boulogne, because of the set of the current.

When the higher staffs returned to their headquarters from Le Touquet, they found waiting for them the OKW directive of August 16, eliminating the Lyme Bay landing. The three divisions training for this operation on the Normandy peninsula had been left pretty much on their own.† On August 2 Bock visited Reichenau's headquarters at Dinard for a Sea Lion conference, but the army-group commander then went off for three weeks on other business.[34] Brauchitsch came to Normandy on August 19, but by then the Lyme Bay landing had already been "scrubbed" by OKW, though no word of this had as yet reached the troops.

Stationed as they were much the farthest from the Rhine and the Dutch shipyards, the Normandy divisions' prospects of getting any

---

* Neither Rundstedt nor his chief of staff turned up; Heeresgruppe A was represented by its Ia, Oberst Guenther Blumentritt.

† Few records of the IInd Corps or of the 31st and 32nd Divisions have come to light; most of the available information about the Normandy training for Sea Lion is derived from the diaries and other records of the 6th Army and the 12th Infantry Division.[33]

prahms or steamers for training were correspondingly remote. However, the regional naval command sent them some fishing boats, and the training was pressed with great vigor. The harbor at Cherbourg was not much damaged, and the 6th Army also expected to use smaller ports in Normandy and Brittany (St.-Vaast, Barfleur, Granville, St.-Malo) and in the Channel Islands (St. Peter Port and St. Helier) to embark the troops. Since there was steep ground behind the Portland Bill, where the 12th Infantry was to land, techniques for capturing cliffs and bluffs were stressed, and Brauchitsch was shown such an exercise at Carteret when he visited the area on August 19. Apparently he was sufficiently impressed with the troops' progress to leave them training despite the OKW directive of August 16, and on his return to Fontainebleau he told Halder[35] that the Cherbourg group ought to be "kept in readiness."

On August 24 Halder and Bock appeared on the scene and watched landing exercises of the 31st Division, at St.-Malo and Cancale.[36] But the next day Halder sent word that the instructional courses at the IInd Corps would have to be canceled for lack of shipping and other naval resources.[37] On August 28 the 12th Infantry Division was ordered to prepare for transfer to Rotterdam, and soon thereafter the other two assault divisions (the 31st and 32nd) and Bock's army-group headquarters were sent off to the east, and the Cherbourg group was eliminated from the assault plan.

Meanwhile, from Le Havre to Holland the exercises grew more rigorous as the troops accustomed themselves to the sea and its vagaries. The 9th Army seems to have been a bit slower than the 16th in getting started; the 8th Division, for example, did not get its engineers on the coast to search out suitable training places until August 12, and landing exercises (considerably hampered by sunken ships and the mine hazard in Dieppe harbor) did not begin until August 16. To the southwest, the Xth Corps allocated Honfleur, Deauville, Trouville, and Dives to the 30th Infantry, and the coast north of Caen to the 6th Mountain Division. On August 18 (the day after the 16th-Army demonstration at Le Touquet) Brauchitsch watched landing exercises of the 30th Infantry and 6th Mountain Divisions at Trouville and Merville.

Everywhere it soon became apparent that the landing would present a special problem of command in that the regular units would inevitably be broken up, mixed, and scattered as they hit the beach.[38] Many boats would be sunk, and the survivors would go ashore in rescue craft; many others would be beached far from their intended destinations. It was obvious that each prahmload should be, so far as possible, self-sustaining until matters could be sorted out on the beach. Equally it was plain that a very flexible command system would have to prevail during the early stages of the landing, so that troops that found themselves thrown together could, regardless of the mixture and the regular order of battle, form themselves into effective combat units under temporary *ad hoc* command.*

The Emden training school was extended into September, and a second round of instruction at Le Touquet began August 23. By August 19, the 7th Division was far enough advanced to practice operations from a bridgehead established at Gravelines. By now corps and divisional staff officers were interchanging visits to watch each other's exercises and profit by the exchange of experience under diverse conditions. As general landing techniques were mastered, the staffs were able to turn their attention to the operations to ensue; on August 25, for example, the 16th Army was reviewing a memorandum from the XIIIth Corps on how to capture Dover, which, lying "in a valley between chalk cliffs 150 meters high," should be taken "from the flanks and rear" by a northerly group landed on Sandwich Bay and a southerly group (which should include mountain troops) landed near Folkestone.

Reinhardt, meanwhile, was steadily producing useful pamphlets on technical problems. On August 9 he issued one on "getting across beaches and sand dunes with vehicles of all kinds," advising the invasion forces that wheeled vehicles could make it only over corduroy roads (good for sand but not mud) or plank roads (good for both); that tanks Marks III and IV could make it on their own, but Marks I and II only if the beaches were flat; that tractors could make it, but only with great care. Two weeks later came another tract on the proper utilization of shipping space.[39]

On August 20 Halder told Brauchitsch that Reinhardt's special staff should be disbanded. His XLIst Corps was to go across with the 16th Army's second wave and provide the main punch for the drive on London; on September 1 the corps staff was moved from Berlin to Antwerp.[40] The armored divisions, which were to go ashore on the beachheads won by the first wave, were given loading and unloading exercises, beginning about the middle of August. Small parties were

---

* Reporting to OKH on Sept. 4, Heeresgruppe A characterized this problem as "very difficult" and proposed to land special staffs with the first *Staffel* for the sole purpose of straightening out the mixed units.

taken to the coast for special instruction, but much of the training was done inland, on rivers such as the Marne and the Seine.[41]

The first wave was, however, to include the amphibious tanks developed at Putlos. By August 22 there were already 210 "U-Panzers" available.[42] These were the standard German medium tanks (Marks III and IV, weighing about twenty-three tons and armed with 3.5-, 5-, or 7.5-centimeter cannon), waterproofed and equipped with a buoyed air intake. Specially converted prahms would anchor off the beachhead and discharge these tanks down a ramp into the water (not over twenty-five feet deep); the tanks would then travel on the bottom and emerge on the beach.[*] The final OKH order for Sea Lion, issued August 30, called for some 250 U-tanks organized in four independent battalions, one each to ship from Ostend, Dunkirk, Calais, and Boulogne; of these, two were subordinated to the XIIIth Corps and one each to the VIIth and XXXVIIIth Corps.[43]

By mid-August the Navy, overwhelmed at first by the scale of all this Army bustle, was beginning to get its tasks sorted out. The new organizations and headquarters for Sea Lion in France and the Low Countries were established during the first two weeks, and the collection of prahms and freighters proceeded throughout Germany and the occupied areas. By the fifteenth over 1,700 prahms had been collected, but of these only an eighth had been converted and fitted for dispatch to the mounting ports.[44]

Ten days later, however, things were in better case. On August 24 SKL gave the crucial order[†] for assemblage of the invasion fleet along the Channel, to begin on the first of September.[45] The 16th Army reported the arrival of the first prahms at Ghent on August 27, and noted that the passage from Rotterdam to Calais would take about nine days, and to the Somme three more;[47] this indicated that it would be mid-September before the bulk of the shipping could be got into

---

[*] The Army also used the light (9.5-ton) Mark II tank for conversion as a floating tank (*Schwimmpanzer*). On Aug. 18 Putlos had 52 of them, but it is not clear that they were thought fit for use in Sea Lion. A single battalion of flame-throwing tanks was assigned to the 16th Army, to be taken over in the second *Staffel* of the first wave.

[†] Although collection and conversion of shipping was the Navy's main task during August, of course it had other problems galore, including especially repair and preparation of the invasion-port facilities. On Aug. 21 German naval intelligence suffered a severe blow when the Royal Navy changed its major codes, some of which the Germans had been reading. During the third week of August, SKL was considering using the old battleships *Schlesien* and *Schleswig-Holstein* as monitors to augment the covering fire for the landing, but by Aug. 22 this idea was abandoned as impracticable.[46]

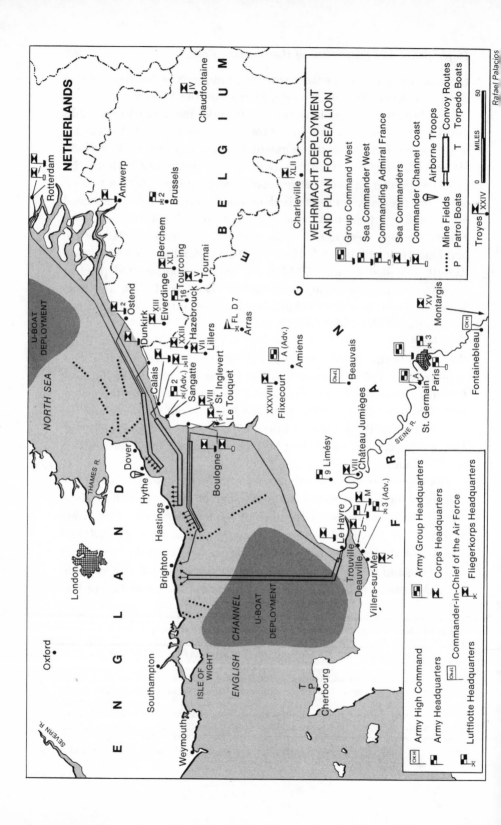

Rafael Palacios

WEHRMACHT DEPLOYMENT
AND PLAN FOR SEA LION

| Group Command West |
| Sea Commander West |
| Commanding Admiral France |
| Sea Commanders |
| Commander Channel Coast |

····· Mine Fields   ⚓ Airborne Troops
P Patrol Boats   ⇕ Convoy Routes   T Torpedo Boats

0   MILES   50

NETHERLANDS

Rotterdam
Antwerp

BELGIUM

Brussels
Berchem
Elverdinge
Tourcoing
Tournai
Hazebrouck
Lillers
Ostend
Dunkirk
Calais
Sangatte
St. Inglevert
Le Touquet
Boulogne

Chaudfontaine
Charleville
Troyes
Montargis

Arras
Amiens
Flixecourt
Beauvais

Château Jumièges
Limésy
Le Havre
Trouville
Deauville
Villers-sur-Mer

St. Germain
Paris
Fontainebleau

FRANCE

SEINE R.

NORTH SEA

U-BOAT
DEPLOYMENT

ENGLAND

Oxford
London
Southampton
Isle of Wight
Weymouth
Cherbourg
Brighton
Hastings
Hythe
Dover

THAMES R.
SEVERN R.

ENGLISH CHANNEL

U-BOAT
DEPLOYMENT

| Army High Command | Army Group Headquarters |
| Army Headquarters | Corps Headquarters |
| Commander-in-Chief of the Air Force |
| Luftflotte Headquarters | Fliegerkorps Headquarters |

place for the invasion. Since tides, moon, and weather had dictated the week of September 20 for the landing, timely completion of the assemblage was touch and go.

By the end of the month, when the shipping movement to the ports was begun, SKL was able to report the readiness of 168 steamers (over 700,000 BRT), 1,900 prahms, 221 tugs and an equal number of steam fishing trawlers that could be used as tugs, and some 1,600 motorboats.[48] It was still not enough, but it began then to appear that the Navy would probably be able to satisfy the minimum requirements for shipping space soon after the middle of September. Whether enough of the fleet would survive the Channel passage was, of course, quite another question.

With the shipping finally in prospect and troop training well advanced, the Army now began its final redispositions and preparations for the great day. Until September 1, Sea Lion might have been discounted as a gigantic exercise, for nothing had been staked except time and money. When the tugs and prahms began to creep down the coast and clutter the Channel harbors, however, the affair took on a much more serious aspect. The concentration of craft was bound to attract the attention of the Royal Air Force, and the German internal economy lay partly paralyzed for lack of inland water transportation. The summer was waning, and time was running short; decisions must be made.

For nearly three weeks the *Adlerangriff* had been on full tilt, and now the Luftwaffe was gathering itself for the big attack on London. All summer the German radio had been blaring "We Sail against England." At the VIIth Corps headquarters in Lillers, Generaloberst von Schobert (a strong supporter of Hitler) received a Bavarian Nazi bureaucrat, Hans Danser, who brought with him a new march, "England zerkrache,"* which the corps adopted as a sort of theme song. If there were to be an invasion, in many quarters there would be no lack of confidence.

Climax

During the first few days of September, as the prahms and tugs and other elements of the invasion fleet emerged from the German rivers

---

* Idiomatic; roughly translatable as "England, Burst!"

and the Dutch harbors and crept southward along the coast,* the
Luftwaffe gathered itself for the big attacks on London that were to
usher in the Blitz. Autumn, and the certain prospect of worsening
weather that would both hamper the flyers and render the risks of
invasion prohibitive, lay but a few weeks ahead. Time was running
short, and the simultaneous assault on London and assemblage of the
invasion shipping embodied what the German leaders knew must be
a last effort—in 1940, at least—to bludgeon or frighten the British into
submission. The direct attack against the British homeland was building up to its climax.

On September 3 OKW issued a time-schedule directive fixing
September 20 as the earliest possible date for departure of the invasion
fleet, and the twenty-first as the earliest date for "D Day," the day of
the landing.[49] Initial orders would be given ten days in advance, on
"D minus 11"—September 11—and final orders on "D minus 3," subject
to cancellation up to twenty-four hours before the scheduled landing
time.

When this directive reached SKL, Raeder was on the Channel coast
inspecting the harbors and invasion preparations at Boulogne, Calais,
and Dunkirk. He returned to Berlin on the fourth, and the next day
he surveyed the whole situation with his staff in preparation for a conference with Hitler on the sixth, in which the only other participants
were Keitel, Jodl, and the Fuehrer's naval adjutant, von Puttkamer.
On this occasion the conversation ranged very widely, as it often did
when Hitler and Raeder were closeted without the chilling presence
of the Army leaders. That the Fuehrer and his naval chief should have
spent so much time on non-invasion matters, including such remote
and secondary questions as the future treatment of Sweden and Finland, is a strong indication that the participants did not really expect
that Sea Lion would ever be mounted.

But if there was any understanding to such effect it was a tacit one.
Raeder reported that mine-sweeping activities in the Channel had
started, and that flank mine barrages north of the Straits had been laid.
Mine sweeping had been much hampered by the weather and "the
situation in air warfare"—an observation which Raeder hastened to
qualify (perhaps with tongue in cheek) by disavowing any criticism

---

* On Sept. 1 the SKL war diary recorded the beginning of "assemblage on a
large scale" of the shipping for Sea Lion, with movements from the Elbe, the
Weser, and the Frisian Islands harbor of Borkum. The larger and more seaworthy
craft sailed on the sea close inshore, while many of the prahms and small craft were
moved to the coast by rivers and canals.

of the Luftwaffe. Fresh from his trip to the Channel and equipped with charts and memoranda, Raeder briefed the Fuehrer on the harbors, supplies, the allocation of shipping, and the progress of its assemblage. In conclusion, Rae der announced, the deadline established by the OKW order could be met "if air supremacy is increasingly established." In that event, Sea Lion could be carried out "if attended by favorable circumstances."

At the troop level, meanwhile, the nature of the preparatory activities was undergoing a marked change. The 12th and 30th Infantry Divisions, now allocated to the 16th Army's second wave (*Treffen*), moved north to the Rotterdam area. Also moving north were the second echelons (*Staffeln*) of the 16th Army's first wave, which were to be shipped out of Rotterdam and Antwerp on steamers and, it was hoped, would arrive at the landing beaches just behind the first echelon. With most of the steamers now on hand at these ports, the troops were started on an intensive series of embarkation and loading exercises.

At Ostend, Dunkirk, Calais, Boulogne, and Le Havre* the harbors were rapidly filling with the tugs, prahms, and other small craft that would embark the first echelon. Now for the first time it was possible to practice loading and beaching with larger troop units. The final decisions were made on the allocation of shipping to each of the ports, and then the corps and divisional staffs, in consultation with the naval commands, parceled out the craft at each port among the units to be embarked. Each division established a special loading staff (*Verlade-stab*) to specify the troops and equipment of the first echelon, and the order and manner in which they would be embarked.

This was a highly complicated process, unfamiliar to the staffs, and involved a good deal of trial and error. The 17th Infantry Division's war-diary entries from the fifth to the eleventh of September reflect the natural exasperation of a front-line command confronted with a series of changing orders from the corps. On the fifth the division's initial loading plans were altered at a conference with the XIIIth Corps chief of staff, at the conclusion of which it was laid down that the division's assault group (*Vorausabteilung*) would embark at Ostend and Dunkirk and the main body of the first *Staffel* at Ostend. Three days later at another corps conference the assault group was shifted to Dunkirk and Calais and the main force to Ostend and Dunkirk. Critical

---

* Le Havre was also receiving the 50 steamers and 300 motorboats allocated for the "green movement" to the Brighton beaches.

of the new order and annoyed to have wasted so much time and energy, the divisional staff did not have long to wait for more troubles. On September 10 there was yet another meeting at the corps headquarters, attended this time by naval officers whose views in part ran contrary to those of the army (16th) and corps staffs. In the end the *Vorausabteilung* was shifted back to Ostend and Dunkirk, and the main group was divided, with two thirds to be embarked at Ostend and one third at Dunkirk. In the course of all this the total amount of shipping allocated to the division was cut by one third.[50]

In contrast to all this activity along the coast, at Fontainebleau Sea Lion was not so much in evidence during the first ten days of September. After OKH issued its basic invasion directive on August 30, Brauchitsch and Halder turned their attention to other things— Rumania, Finland, North Africa, the build-up of forces in the east, the situation in France, and Army personnel and organizational problems. To be sure, Sea Lion was not wholly forgotten; at several conferences Halder concerned himself with air reconnaissance, amphibious tanks, and the division of smoke-screen responsibilities between the Army and the Navy. But his diary entries for those days reflect no sense of urgency about the invasion, and not until September 10 did it again occupy the bulk of his time and attention.[51]

On the afternoon of that day, Brauchitsch and Halder set out on a two-day train trip to survey the plans and preparations at the armygroup and army headquarters.[52] At St.-Germain (headquarters of Heeresgruppe A) they found Rundstedt away on leave! During the staff conference, two serious flaws in the plan came to light.

The first grew out of the distribution of loading ports between the two armies. The 9th Army was limited to Boulogne and a single loading of lightly armed assault units at Le Havre; the 16th Army had five large ports from Rotterdam to Calais. Projection of the probable consequences indicated that the 16th would get its entire first wave (*Treffen*) across in three days, while this might take the 9th Army as much as two weeks. If so, the whole landing front would be out of balance, and the left wing gravely jeopardized.

The second problem related to the division of command functions between England and the mainland. Halder noted:

The ideas on command functions of the armies [9th and 16th Army headquarters] and those of the staffs left on the mainland [*Heimatstaebe*] are all in a muddle. It is erroneous to suppose that the higher operational staffs in their entirety should go across right at the start, and concern themselves no further with the follow-up, or leave its leadership to deputies. Rather, it is one of the chief tasks of the top command to cope wtih unforeseen difficulties during the crossing, and this requires that they remain on the mainland. The commanders themselves may and should go across, but their staffs must stay behind to make these adjustments.

After the conference at army group, Brauchitsch and Halder sat down with the naval chiefs, Saalwaechter, Luetjens, and Fischel, to review the measures taken to safeguard the invasion fleet. Then the special train started off toward Rouen, and the following morning they were at Strauss's 9th-Army headquarters. Here the impressions formed the previous day at St.-Germain were strengthened. The allocation of troops and equipment between the first and second *Staffeln* had been too "mechanical," and the follow-up staff organization needed tightening. Shipping schedules indicated that only the forward assault elements (*Vorausabteilungen*), with six to seven thousand men and no guns heavier than 37-millimeter, would cross from Le Havre, while the main body of the first *Staffel* and the heavier artillery would go by way of Boulogne. Again Halder foresaw grave danger for the left wing. At St.-Germain, Brauchitsch had suggested speeding the 9th Army's crossing by loading the second *Staffel* of the three VIIIth–Xth Corps divisions at Calais, behind the first *Staffel* of the VIIth Corps. The conference at the 9th Army now convinced Halder that something would have to be done to give Strauss's forces access to Calais.

Brauchitsch and Halder then flew to the 16th Army's headquarters near Roubaix. Here there were fewer problems, and the discussion chiefly concerned the use of amphibious tanks, smoke screens, the role of the airborne troops, and support of the XIIIth Corps's landing by Richthofen's Stukas.

After dinner, Brauchitsch went on to the Channel coast and Halder returned to Fontainebleau. The following day—the twelfth—Brauchitsch visited Manstein's XXXVIIIth Corps and watched landing exercises, while Halder reviewed the results of his trip with his staff (which had been augmented a few days earlier by the arrival of Generalleutnant Friedrich Paulus,* the new Q.Qu. I) and, later that day, with Generaloberst Busch. That evening Halder and Busch flew to Berlin, where a Fuehrer luncheon reception for all the recently promoted *Generaloberstent* had been scheduled for September 13. After the meal Hitler conferred with Halder and the two invasion-army

---

* Paulus had been chief of staff of Reichenau's 6th Army. He was replaced in that capacity by Oberst Ferdinand Heim.

† Present were 14 Army and 5 Luftwaffe *Generalobersten*, Generaladmiral (equivalent naval rank) Rolf Carls, Goering, Brauchitsch, Keitel, Jodl, a few other military of lesser rank, and Martin Bormann.

commanders, Strauss and Busch, who made a report on invasion preparations. Halder noted[53] that "no special difficulties" arose, but Hitler
made it clear that he was not then of a mind to attempt an invasion.[54]

The following day Raeder, Brauchitsch, Halder, and Jeschonnek
(representing Goering) were closeted with Hitler for what was to have
been the decisive conference on Sea Lion. The Navy had been pushing
the invasion shipping toward the invasion ports as hard as it could,
but the movement had been hampered by weather and mines, and
Raeder had been advised by his staff that the assemblage would not
be completed by September 14.[55] Since ten days' warning was regarded
as necessary, and the period of good invasion weather (as well as lunar
and tidal conditions) would end September 27, the time margin was
wearing thin. Nevertheless, the discussion proceeded on the basis that
the Navy could meet a target date of September 27. The hope of
achieving sufficient air superiority by that time appeared remote, but
Hitler decided to keep alive the possibility of attempting invasion between the twenty-fourth and the twenty-seventh, so he postponed
decision until the seventeenth and ordered that all preparations be
continued.[56]

While all this was going on in Berlin, the army-group and army staffs
had been endeavoring to eliminate, or at least mitigate, the shortcomings noted by Brauchitsch and Halder on the tenth and eleventh of
September. Halder, upon his return to Fontainebleau on the fifteenth,
had a visit from Rundstedt's chief of staff, General Georg von Sodenstern, who reported that the shipping plans had been readjusted so that
the 9th Army could use Calais beginning on the third day (S plus 2)
after Sea Lion was begun, and that "a sufficient number" of steamers
would be available.[57]

To meet the command problem for the "follow-up," the 16th Army
established two special staffs. One, called Landungsstab E ("Landing
Staff England"), would establish command posts at Dover and Hastings, and would have a flying squad of "landing officers" to supervise
the unloading and distribution of supplies.[58] The other was to be
called Befehlstelle Festland ("Command Post Mainland"), and was
to consist of a special staff attached to the XXIIIrd Corps at Bruges.
This command would start functioning on the third day of the invasion; it would carry out the orders transmitted from England by the
16th Army, establish subposts to control shipping and supplies from
the Channel ports, handle the wounded and the prisoners evacuated

from the bridgehead, and be responsible for launching the second and third waves (*Treffen*).[59]

By the middle of September, basic orders for the invasion had been issued by most of the field commands. The OKH directive had gone out on August 30; Heeresgruppe A issued a provisional order on the fifth and a final order (signed by Busch, deputizing for the absent Rundstedt) on the fourteenth of September, the same day that Admiral Luetjens, as Seebefehlshaber West, put out his operational orders for the invasion fleet. The 16th Army's provisional order was issued on the ninth, and supplemental directives went out on the fourteenth and the nineteenth. At the lower levels, corps and divisional orders poured out from the third to the twenty-first of the month.

Throughout August and early September the Luftwaffe had been basically indifferent to the invasion preparations. Now, as the final orders were drawn and S-*Tag* (if it were ever to come at all) loomed, the Army field headquarters made desperate, if belated, efforts to lay the groundwork for effective air support. Commitment of the airborne troops was settled by the visits of Kesselring and Putzier to the 16th-Army headquarters on September 12 and 17.[60] But for establishing beachheads the Stukas of Richthofen's Fliegerkorps VIII were of first importance.

The dive bombers had taken a bad beating during the early part of the Battle of Britain. Late in August they had been withdrawn from the fray and moved north to the Pas-de-Calais, behind the 16th Army. By September 9, air liaison officers from Fliegerkorps VIII were arriving at the headquarters of the first-wave divisions.[61] Air-ground staff consultations at the corps level had got under way several days earlier,[62] and on September 13 the 16th Army was able to put out an order informing its corps that the strongest support, two *Geschwader*, would be given to the XIIIth Corps at Dover, Folkestone, and Sandgate, and that a *Staffel* would attempt to destroy the British batteries presumed to be situated near Dungeness. One and two-thirds *Gruppen* would assist the VIIth Corps, and another *Gruppe* would be held in reserve.[63]

All this was hastily improvised and pretty slapdash. A few days later Richthofen was complaining that he did not have enough aircraft to cover the 16th Army's entire front, and suggesting that perhaps its first wave should be reduced to one corps[64]—a narrow-front concept even more extreme than the Navy's of the previous month.

The 17th Infantry Division, on the extreme right, would be crossing in the area of the big German railroad batteries, so there was need to co-ordinate their fire with the Stuka attacks. On September 17 it was finally worked out that before the dive bombers were committed the railway guns would concentrate on the British batteries at Sandgate, and that after the air attack they would strike first at Folkestone and then at the Dover batteries. The following day, ignorant that Hitler had just postponed Sea Lion "indefinitely," the division finally worked out the composition of the mixed task force—U-tanks, bicycle troops, a machine-gun battalion, Flak and paratroops from the 7th Fliegerdivision—that would make the strike for Dover soon after landing.[65]

There simply had not been enough time, thanks largely to the Luftwaffe's coming late to the planning table, to work out all such matters. Had the invasion been launched, much improvisation would have been necessary. Capacity to make the attempt depended in the last analysis on timely arrival and distribution of the shipping, and from about September 10 great importance attached to the reports on the number of craft in transit and actually available at the invasion ports, and how far that quantity fell short of what would be necessary.

The shipping "establishment" for the first wave of Sea Lion called for some 165 steamers, 390 tugs, and 1,130 prahms, to be distributed among the seven jump-off ports—Rotterdam, Antwerp, Ostend, Dunkirk, Calais, Boulogne, and Le Havre—according to the specific needs of each. But considerable losses were anticipated, especially among the craft that would be beached (prahms and motorboats). For reserves and to ensure space for the later waves, nearly two thousand prahms were collected and converted.

By September 11 the SKL calculated that about sixty per cent of the invasion craft were on hand in their designated ports, and that the assemblage would be completed in time for execution on September 21, should the signal be given.[66] Bad weather and enemy action (mines and air attacks) delayed the process during the next ten days, and the planned schedule was not fully met. Indeed, the SKL reports of September 11 were probably inflated, for on September 17 the Commanding Admiral for France reported only 734 prahms and 86 tugs (less than sixty-five and twenty-five per cent respectively of the first-wave needs) in place in their proper ports.[67]

In fact, the shipping allocations were never fully met. Enough prahms were converted and on hand, but their distribution was still incomplete when, on September 17, Hitler gave the order to postpone Sea Lion, and there still were shortages, especially at Boulogne, when the assemblage reached its peak—about September 21. Tugs were the main problem; they had been in short supply from the very beginning, and by September 19 there still were only 110 in the invasion ports (less than one third of the first-wave requirements) and another 186 en route.[68]

The result of all these circumstances was a considerable imbalance in the shipping situation. The 164 steamers were to be used only at Rotterdam, Antwerp, Ostend, and Le Havre. They were all on hand, the three northern ports were on the main route for prahm distribution, and Le Havre had enough barges available from the Seine.[69] The shipping plans called for only twenty-five tugs at Le Havre and none at the northern ports, so these four harbors were in pretty good shape. Dunkirk and Calais were well stocked with prahms but short on tugs.* Boulogne remained short of both; British aerial reconnaissance on September 17 counted only 150 prahms[71] (330 were needed for the first wave), and by September 21 the port was still thirty per cent below its quota of prahms[72] and must have been very low on tugs.

Of course, if the invasion had been launched on September 26 or 27 (the end of the period of favorable moon and tide), there would have been four or five days left to bring up more tugs. With good luck and skillful improvisation, it might have been just possible to find shipping space and provide motive power to embark and transport the first wave.

However that might have been, in fact the Germans were never readier to attempt the invasion than they were on the twentieth of September. The basic orders had been distributed, the shipping assemblage was nearing completion, and the bulk of the assault troops were ready and willing. At VIIth Corps headquarters, Generaloberst von Schobert received his subordinate commanders at lunch, with a "*Sieg heil!*" to the Fuehrer and another rendition of "England zer-krache."[73] But already, whether or not Schobert himself knew it, Sea Lion was as good as dead.

Abandonment and Aftermath

The question of why Hitler did not give the order to launch Sea Lion is easily answered: conditions were never created under which he could regard the attempt as sufficiently promising of success. But if

---

* At Calais, the VIIth Corps reported on Sept. 18 that its two assault divisions (7th Infantry and 1st Mountain Divisions) lacked only three prahms. On Sept. 20 the Corps reported 180 prahms and 23 tugs on hand; the allocation to Calais for the first wave was 200 prahms and 100 tugs.[70]

it be asked when and why Hitler decided that the prospects of success were so remote that the project should be abandoned, the answer is somewhat more complicated.

The timing of the invasion, had it been attempted, was closely tied to lunar and meteorological factors, and the Army and the Navy had conflicting interests. The Army wished to land just before dawn—traditionally the sailor's most dangerous hour, as daybreak may suddenly disclose the proximity of hostile vessels undetected in the dark. Furthermore, the Navy feared that the slow, unwieldy, and closely packed invasion fleet would confront insuperable navigational difficulties if the crossing were to be attempted in total darkness. Some moonlight was therefore essential. Finally, it would be highly desirable to land soon *after* high tide, so that the beaching craft would sit tight on the sands and would surely refloat on the next high tide.

The Navy could not be ready before September 15, and the first period thereafter offering the proper combination of tide, moon, and time was from September 19 to September 26 or 27. The meteorologists reported a history of bad Channel weather in mid-September, but improving toward the end of the month. Ten days were necessary after the invasion order had issued, to assemble and load the force. All this meant that the time for decision would fall between September 10 and September 17, probably between the fourteenth and the seventeenth. If that period passed unused, the next favorable time would be October 8, and this would call for a decision on or about September 28.[74]

For these reasons, the OKW directive of September 3 had specified September 11 as the earliest date on which the Sea Lion order might be given.[75] On September 10, however, Hitler decided not to make any decision on the next day, chiefly because the results of the "intensified air war" (the mass daytime attacks on London had begun only three days earlier) could not yet be ascertained. Furthermore, the twenty-fourth would probably be a better day for the landing, and accordingly he would come to a decision on the fourteenth.

When Jodl informed Warlimont of this postponement, the latter produced a draft of an OKW order to put Sea Lion into execution, which he and his staff had prepared in co-operation with the three service commands. This document, no copy of which has come to light, never moved any higher; the OKW war diary records only that, because of the postponement, the draft was to remain in Jodl's keeping.[76]

On September 13, when the *Generalobersten* came to Berlin on the Fuehrer's invitation to lunch, Hermann Goering put in one of his rare appearances for interservice conversation and conviviality. Very likely he gave a glowing account of the progress of the air war; certainly something cast a rosy glow over the occasion, for Hitler "took a very optimistic view and said that in the present favorable situation he would not think of taking such a great risk as to land in England."[77] Jodl, who was present, thought this comment indicated that Hitler was ready to drop Sea Lion entirely, and he was surprised when the morrow—the scheduled day of decision—brought only another postponement.[78]

This last decision not to decide took place on the afternoon of September 14, with Raeder, Brauchitsch, Halder, Jeschonnek, and the top OKW staff in conference with the Fuehrer, who did most of the talking.[79] "A successful landing followed by occupation would end the war in short order," he declared, and this would be good because Germany had already "obtained all that could be of any practical value to us," the international political situation might suddenly change, and therefore "a long war is undesirable for us."

There followed encomiums for the Luftwaffe ("accomplishments are beyond all praise") and the Navy ("has attained all targets set for it in preparation for the Channel crossing"). "The Navy be praised!" sighed Halder into his diary,* and indeed these bouquets for the other services must have smelled sour to the Army chiefs. The Navy's poverty of resources had forced a dangerous constriction of the invasion front and postponement of *der Tag* to the end of the summer. The Luftwaffe had ignored Sea Lion until September, and had so far failed to establish the necessary conditions. Now the Army's extensive preparatory efforts were about to go down the drain without a word of thanks.

Largely due to the hindrance of bad weather, according to Hitler, the British fighter forces had not yet been eliminated, and therefore "the prerequisites for Sea Lion have not yet been completely realized." But four or five days of good weather might do the trick, and the British should not be relieved of the pressure of threatened invasion:

Attacks to date have had enormous effects, though perhaps chiefly upon nerves. Part of that psychological effect is the fear of invasion. The anticipation of its imminence must not be removed. Even though victory in the air

---

* "*Lob der Marine!*" in the original.

should not be achieved for another ten or twelve days, Britain might yet be seized by mass hysteria. If within the coming ten or twelve days we achieve mastery of the air over a certain area, we could by a landing operation compel the enemy to come out with his destroyers against our landing fleet. We could then inflict such losses that the enemy would no longer be able to protect the convoys.

This last idea of using the invasion force as a bait to lure British destroyers to their doom was nothing short of military insanity. If the invasion were successful and Britain occupied, there would be no more convoys; if unsuccessful, by Hitler's own reckoning the consequences for the Germans, in terms of prestige and otherwise, would be so disastrous that the possibility was not to be contemplated. In any event the Luftwaffe was not well equipped to effect a sea blockade, and at that time there were only forty-eight submarines, and rarely more than eight or ten simultaneously on operations.[80] But no one challenged the Fuehrer's notion, and he went on to say, rightly enough, that cancellation of Sea Lion could hardly be kept secret. Therefore, he concluded, it must not be ordered "now."

Raeder indicated agreement, and suggested that the September target dates be dropped and October 8 (the next favorable day by tide and moon) be "kept in view." But Hitler would not go so far, and specified September 17 as the next day for decision, so as to make possible a landing on the twenty-seventh. If that did not work out, then October 8 would be the next target day.

At this point Brauchitsch spoke up, offering to "unfreeze" the time schedule by accepting a daytime landing under cover of smoke.* But no one else took up the idea, and the conference turned to other subjects. That evening OKW put out a directive[81] postponing the operation and fixing September 17 as the next decision day. In the meantime, all preparations were to be continued. To a puzzled Warlimont, Jodl explained that of course this did *not* mean invasion without first achieving air superiority, and that the primary consideration was to keep the British under pressure.[82]

By September 17 things were not better but worse. At SKL it was remarked that the RAF, far from being defeated, was showing in-

---

* To his naval colleagues Raeder opined that "this sudden change in the Army's initial stubborn demand [for a pre-dawn landing] can be traced to the fact that the front-line generals, like the Navy, are opposed to a night crossing." Perhaps, but it is also possible that Brauchitsch, tired of the cat-and-mouse game with which he had been victimized, wanted to force a decision one way or another as soon as possible.

creased activity. The weather had not improved, and the forecasts were not encouraging. For these reasons, Hitler decided to postpone Sea Lion "indefinitely" (*auf unbestimmte Zeit*). An order to this effect went out from OKW that evening.[83] Thus matters swung full circle very rapidly; on the thirteenth Hitler shrugged off Sea Lion as unnecessary because things were going so well, and on the seventeenth he postponed it indefinitely because things were not going well at all.

The instructions from OKW specified that the state of readiness for invasion was to be maintained, and that the Fuehrer wished to keep open the possibility of a landing in October should the air warfare and the weather prospects develop favorably. But the failure to fix another decision day and the explicitly indefinite postponement bespoke Sea Lion's death knell. What had moved Hitler to do on the seventeenth what he had been unwilling to do on the fourteenth?

There is no contemporary record, but persuasive reasons are not difficult to infer. Even if the Luftwaffe had scored impressive gains, the weather factor would still have been crucial, and from this standpoint October was dangerously late in the season, for fog was to be expected by the middle of the month and the worsening fall weather would hamper both air operations and seaborne supplies and reinforcements to the bridgehead.

Likewise, the Luftwaffe's excuses for its failure to achieve air dominance were fast wearing thin. At the Fuehrer's conference on September 14 (as on previous occasions) the weather was blamed, and indeed it had been bad. On September 15 it improved; the Luftwaffe launched a mass day attack on London and lost over fifty aircraft—one of its worst defeats during the Battle of Britain. After this, the great expectations voiced for the advent of good weather, and Hitler's talk of "mass hysteria" gripping the British, sounded pretty hollow. The prospects of *Luftherrschaft* flickered and dimmed.

Furthermore, assemblage of the invasion fleet in the Channel ports had at last given Bomber Command opportunity to play a part that—unlike the pinprick Berlin raids—was more than psychologically effective. On September 4, light bombers (Blenheims) began these attacks,* and two days later the XXXVIIIth Corps diarist noted that the shipping concentrations at Boulogne had been observed by the RAF, and that nightly air raids were in progress.[84] That night the medium

---

* There had been a raid near Dunkirk on Aug. 24, prior to the concentration of invasion shipping, that caused casualties to XIIIth Corps troops, remarked in the diaries of the 17th and 35th Infantry Divisions.

bombers were used over the Channel, and there were sharp raids on Ostend during the nights of September 7 and 11.[85] The VIIth Corps recorded its "worry," while SKL described the raids as "unacceptable" and demanded better Flak protection from the Luftwaffe.[86] By September 13, SKL recorded the loss, through enemy action against the harbors, of three steamers, three tugs, and fifteen prahms.[87]

These losses were merely annoying, but much worse was to come, as the ship concentration in the harbors increased and Bomber Command increased the scale and tempo of its attacks. On the nights of September 14, 15, and 16 there were raids all along the coast, with considerable losses at Le Havre, Calais, Dunkirk, and especially at Antwerp, where a large ammunition dump was hit. The echoes of these raids reverberated in the reports from the Army and Navy units near these ports,[88] and had been heard in Berlin[89] just before Sea Lion was postponed "indefinitely."

Finally, there was the appearance of things. First Hitler had said he would decide about Sea Lion shortly after *Adlertag,* and then it had been postponed to September, with "decision days" successively on the eleventh, the fourteenth, and the seventeenth. If another such day were specified, there would have to be still another order of postponement, which might look ridiculous, or the order to begin Sea Lion, which appeared highly improbable. Much better, then, to put off the matter "indefinitely," so that Sea Lion, if not undertaken, could be allowed to die quietly.

But the invasion's demise was marked by more than the order of postponement without term. On the very night the order was issued Bomber Command brought off its most successful attack on the Channel harbors. Damage was especially heavy at Dunkirk, where at least fifteen prahms were sunk and over fifty others were damaged (the reports varied somewhat), and a large ammunition dump—the 35th Division's entire supply—was blown up. Calais also suffered badly, losing a tug and seven prahms.[90]

The next day, September 18, the reports of these raids caused something approaching consternation at SKL.[91] Shipping movements to the invasion ports were halted, and plans were laid to disperse the craft already there so that they would not offer so inviting and concentrated a target for bombs. Fricke got in touch with Jodl to describe the situation and the hazards, and on September 19 OKW issued a Fuehrer directive which in effect ratified the steps already taken by SKL.[92] Despite the shipping dispersal, this order called for maintenance of the ten-day alert period, but as a practical matter, and as SKL had made clear to OKW, the Navy was working on the basis that fifteen days would have to be allowed to reassemble the ships and mount the invasion.

In his postwar memoirs Sir Arthur Harris (in 1940 deputy chief of the Air Staff and later commander-in-chief of Bomber Command) declared:[93] "It was definitely Bomber Command's wholesale destruction of the invasion barges in the Channel ports that convinced the Germans of the futility of attempting to cross the Channel . . ." The record hardly supports so sweeping a judgment. Destruction of the prahms and other invasion craft was not "wholesale."* Even if Bomber Command had never struck the Channel ports it is highly unlikely that Hitler would have given the "go" signal, in view of the Luftwaffe's failure to knock out Fighter Command.

Nevertheless, Bomber Command's operations were proof positive that the British still had an air force that could not only defend but also strike; and if it could sink prahms in the Channel ports, no doubt it could do the same in the Channel itself or at the invasion beachheads. Furthermore, it was made plain that further losses would be sustained if the invasion fleet remained concentrated in the exposed harbors. It is very likely, therefore, that these raids contributed to the decision for "indefinite" postponement, and it is beyond question that they caused the dispersal of invasion shipping which began on September 20, and which made reinstitution of the invasion alert a lengthier process and a far more unlikely prospect than theretofore.

And so, beginning September 20, many of the ships and prahms were taken to smaller harbors, or to nearby canals and river mouths. The immediate objective was achieved, in that losses were much reduced, though Bomber Command had another successful night over Calais and Ostend on September 22.[95] But the dispersal could not be hidden from British aerial reconnaissance, and it soon became apparent that the threat of invasion was easing.[96]

Indeed, the Germans could not long hide the truth from themselves, though for another week or more they did their best. It had throughout been Hitler's principal purpose to use the menace of invasion as additional "pressure" on the British, and this aim he did not abandon on

---

* As of Sept. 21, SKL calculated that 21 steamers and 214 prahms were "lost or damaged"—in each case about 12.5 per cent of the available craft. Only 4 tugs had been sunk.[94] These losses were serious, but not large enough to prevent loading the first wave, though of course the shipping reserve was depleted.

September 17. Apart from the shipping dispersal, everything possible was done to perpetuate the plausibility of Sea Lion. The troops continued to train, and the staffs to confer. On September 21 Halder went to the Pas de Calais for a map exercise, "a very careful and thorough study on staging, embarkation, and crossing to Britain," at XIIIth Corps headquarters, and a beachhead exercise of the 7th Infantry Division. Three days later he attended map maneuvers at 9th Army headquarters and inspected Le Havre, where he found plentiful signs of Bomber Command's recent activities, and on September 25 he was at St.-Germain for similar studies conducted by the staff of Heeresgruppe A. Upon his return to Fontainebleau, Halder reviewed with Brauchitsch the results of his trips. But on September 28 he recorded sourly that the "chronic state of indecision" about Sea Lion was "intolerable," and thereafter the subject practically vanished from his diary.[97]

Hitler's "indefinite"-postponement order was not passed on to the field headquarters. Through the balance of September and the first few days of October, troop exercises and staff activities at the corps and lower levels continued virtually unabated. But the shipping dispersal and the worsening autumn weather told their own story, and soon there were other signs. For example, on September 29 the chief of staff of the XXXVIIth Corps, Oberst Arthur Hauffe, was transferred to a new post as chief of staff of the German military mission to Rumania. Such a move would have been most unlikely had Sea Lion been at all imminent, and the corps staff rightly drew the inference that it was not. Invasion enthusiasm at this headquarters died hard; three days later, landing exercises were staged for the 9th Army commander, Strauss, and on October 3 the corps's diarist was bemoaning the probability that all the amphibious training would go for nothing, and vowing that if invasion should again become likely "the XXXVIIIth Corps will not be found unprepared."[98]

While the troops continued their exercises, at the high-command level strong pressures were building up to relax the state of alert for Sea Lion, and indeed to cancel it entirely. On September 26 Raeder conferred at length with Hitler "under four eyes." In the course of a rambling, extravagant dialogue of global scope, Raeder observed that the Navy would not be able to maintain readiness for Sea Lion after the middle of October, since the disorganization of the Navy's normal structure was interfering with the submarine training program and the manning of the new battleships. Accordingly, he requested a final decision by October 15.[99]

So far as appears from the record, Hitler greeted the request with silence. But the pretense that Sea Lion was still alive could no longer be maintained. The Tripartite Pact (Germany-Italy-Japan) was signed the very next day; Ciano was in Berlin for the ceremony, and he conferred twice with the Fuehrer. A week earlier, in Rome, Ribbentrop had boasted to Mussolini that a period of good weather would lead to invasion "on a vast scale" and that a single German division could knock out the British ground forces.[100] But on September 28 Ciano gathered from Hitler that there would be no landing and no speedy defeat of Britain, and found the Fuehrer revealing a preoccupation with the possibility of a long war.[101]

At the end of September, OKH dispatched a memorandum to OKW strongly urging abandonment of the ten-day alert for Sea Lion,[102] which was still formally in effect. The expansion and winter training of the Army was being hindered, said OKH, because the crack divisions ticketed for Sea Lion should soon be required to give up a third of their troops to furnish trained cadres for the newly constituted divisions. Furthermore, there were special troop units temporarily attached to Sea Lion that should be with the divisions recently moved to the east—a not-too-subtle reference to the buildup for the next year's projected invasion of Russia. If it was desired to maintain through the winter the possibility of Sea Lion as *coup de grâce* for a broken England, OKH suggested a three-week alert period. If only "pressure" was the object, then there should be rearrangements designed to preserve the appearance of an invasion threat while enabling the winter training and reorganization to proceed. A decision by mid-October at the latest was requested.

Jodl and Warlimont, who well knew that the ten-day-alert period no longer had any practical significance,[103] reviewed the Army's proposals on October 2.[104] On Warlimont's recommendation, Jodl authorized lengthening the stipulated warning to fifteen days, and set mid-October as the time for decision on the degree of preparedness that would be required during the winter.

OKH was so informed by telephone that evening. Heeresgruppe A had not waited for permission from on high and had already authorized the fifteen-day alert. On October 4 OKH, apparently without further consultation with OKW, fixed a twenty-day period.[105] Brauchitsch then took off for the coast to put the field commands out of their misery of uncertainty. At Rotterdam on October 5 and at Antwerp the next day, the Commander-in-Chief watched loading exercises and then, to an assemblage of corps and divisional commanders and staff officers, expressed his thanks for all their labors of preparation: "The army had reached the highest degree of readiness, but the bad weather had prevented the Luftwaffe from vanquishing the enemy." The winter was to be devoted to intensive training.[106]

The Fuehrer had meanwhile gone to meet the Duce at the Brenner Pass—where there was talk of the air war but no suggestion that an invasion was in prospect—and thence to the Obersalzberg. He returned to Berlin October 9, to find Jodl armed with an order putting an end to the state of readiness for Sea Lion.[107] It was high time; the Army's reorganization was already begun, the German transportation system was badly strained for lack of inland-waterway bottoms, and in Norway General von Falkenhorst was clamoring for more shipping to supply the occupation forces. On October 12 the order was issued over Keitel's signature:[108]

(1) The Fuehrer has decided that from now on until Spring, preparations for "Sea Lion" shall be continued solely for the purpose of maintaining political and military pressure on England.

Should the invasion be reconsidered in the Spring or early Summer of 1941, orders for renewal of operational readiness will be issued later. Meanwhile military conditions for a later invasion are to be improved.

(2) All measures taken to reduce operational readiness must conform to the following principles—

(a) The British must continue to believe that we are preparing an attack on a broad front.

(b) But at the same time our war economy must be relieved of some of the heavy strain placed upon it by our invasion preparations.

(3) In particular, as regards—

(a) The Army, the formations allocated for "Sea Lion" can now be released for other duties or employment on other fronts. We must, however, avoid any noticeable reduction in the forces in coastal areas.

(b) The Navy must take all measures to release personnel and shipping, particularly tugs and fishing craft, for other tasks. Movements of shipping in connection with dispersal must be carried out unobtrusively and spread over a considerable period of time.

The way was now cleared for OKH to complete the general regrouping which had been begun early in September,[109] and to establish the new headquarters and divisions called for by the Army's program of expansion. On October 15, for example, von Schobert was designated to command a newly-to-be-created 11th Army; the irrepressible general sent a goodbye message to his VIIth Corps troops ending with the familiar but now unintentionally wistful "England zerkrache," staged a great parade tattoo (*Zapfenstreich*) in Lillers, and on the seventeenth was off to his new post.[110] Ten days later Leeb's Heeresgruppe C left France for Dresden, and at the end of the month OKH itself departed Fontainebleau and returned to its old field headquarters at Zossen near Berlin, leaving Rundstedt, newly entitled Commander-in-Chief West (OB West), in command of the troops in France and the Low Countries.

In an effort, largely futile, to keep the British in fear of invasion, loading exercises and other amphibious maneuvers were continued through the remainder of 1940 and even into 1941. The Navy undertook to design "ideal" landing craft suitable for mass production.[111] The Luftwaffe, now that the project was academic, put on a great show of invasion activity, no doubt to cover its own earlier indifference and failure to establish the aerial prerequisites. On September 19, for example, Luftflotte 2 dispatched to Heeresgruppe A a liaison officer, Major Rauch, who, although he soon learned that Sea Lion had been indefinitely postponed even before his arrival, stayed at St.-Germain until November 1.[112] Interservice jealousies flared even over Sea Lion's corpse; on November 11 Luftflotte 2 sent a stiff note to the 16th Army rejecting the idea that the Befehlstelle Festland[113] would be an interservice headquarters and insisting that all air units remain under Luftwaffe command.[114]

For a time, Sea Lion appeared to be in a state of hibernation, with its resurrection in the spring of 1941 a real possibility. Early in November Hitler was still discussing the prospect with Brauchitsch and Halder, and his Directive No. 18 of November 12, though largely concerned with other matters, spoke of the need for "improved conditions" in the event that a spring invasion might prove "possible or necessary."[115] But as the Wehrmacht's center of gravity moved eastward and Hitler's resolve to invade the Soviet Union hardened, Sea Lion passed into the realm of might-have-beens. This was by no means to the liking of all his advisers; Halder, for example, continued to regard Sea Lion as "the surest way to hit England," and as late as November 25 he recorded his pleasure that Hitler was again "taking an interest" in the operation.[116]

Early in December, however, Hitler's strategic intentions crystallized, and on the fifth he told Brauchitsch and Halder that Sea Lion could be left out of their considerations.[117] Occasionally thereafter his mind turned back to the western strategy, and in January he discussed with Goering and Student the possibility of occupying Ireland by airborne operations.[118] But the time for Barbarossa was approaching, and therefore Sea Lion was transmuted into a deceptive device, to conceal the meaning of the buildup in the east.[119] In April 1941, OKH issued ostensibly genuine orders for an August invasion of England under the cover name "Shark" (*Haifisch,* replacing *Seeloewe*), with an adjunct operation from Norway named "Harpoon" (*Harpune,* replacing *Herbstreise*). Both were spurious, and they were "called off" soon after the invasion of Russia.[120]

The course of events in that country, and the expansion of the war into a global conflict at the end of 1941, finally eliminated Sea Lion as a practical problem of German strategy. Still, it was not until February 1942 that Raeder finally proposed the cancellation of all commitments of personnel and material for Sea Lion, which, at that date, were still "considerable." The Fuehrer gave his consent,[121] and on March 2 an OKW directive was circulated which stipulated a full year's warning if the project were revived.[122] And that was the end of Sea Lion.

Critique and Consequences

On September 10, three days after the Luftwaffe had begun its mass attack on London, it was recorded in the SKL war diary that:[123]

> The planned preparations for Sea Lion call now for the Luftwaffe to concentrate less on London and more on Portsmouth, Dover, and the fleet. . . . However, the Naval Staff do not propose now to approach the Luftwaffe or the Fuehrer with such requests, since the Fuehrer regards the great attack on London as possibly decisive of the war, and as systematic and prolonged bombing of London might bring the enemy to a frame of mind that would make Sea Lion quite unnecessary.*

From a wealth of ready examples, this entry reflects most clearly the extraordinary weakness of Germany's military leadership at the time of her greatest apparent strength. It is plain enough that the Luftwaffe had no real interest in establishing the conditions which would improve the prospects of invasion, and that the Navy was far from

---

* Two days later the SKL diary again contained an observation about air warfare which was "independent of the present necessities of the sea war" and was being conducted as an "absolute air war," with no effort to engage the British fleet.

eager to have those conditions brought about. Thus interservice preparations for the invasion finally sank to such a level of absurdity that the Navy hung back from bringing glaring tactical flaws to Hitler's attention, because those very flaws held off the contingency that Raeder and his staff most feared—an approximation of the conditions under which Sea Lion might actually be attempted. Given such negative attitudes at OKM and OKL, the Army's genuine zeal for the project was bound to be wasted.

It is perhaps unjust to lay much blame for this state of affairs on Raeder and his staff. Had the German Navy been twice its size at the beginning of the war, the nautical aspect of Sea Lion would still have been ominous enough. Norway had squandered the greater part of the Navy's combat strength. Raeder's pessimistic estimate of the prospects of a landing in the face of determined opposition was entirely sound, and he was enough of a politician to realize that his best chance of escape from the desperate dilemma lay in the fixing of prerequisites at so high a level that they could not be achieved or, if by some miracle they were, that there would then be little or no opposition to overcome.

The real assassins of Sea Lion were Hitler and Goering. The latter's hostility was conscious and, indeed, unconcealed. No doubt he hoped for the solo victory which had eluded him at Dunkirk, and in all probability he shared Raeder's judgment that as long as the British could fight back in the air and on the sea they could probably repel an invasion. But here the parallels end, for the Navy, despite the gloom at SKL, turned to the actual preparations with a will, and its accomplishments in improvising and assembling an invasion fleet in eight weeks were truly remarkable.

The Luftwaffe, in contrast, virtually ignored Sea Lion until September, by which time it was already too late to make the systematic and detailed preparations, in co-ordination with the other services, that the undertaking plainly required. True, the Luftwaffe was engaged in major combat with the British during July and August, while the Army and the Navy—except for the U-boats—were not. But Luftwaffe disregard of Sea Lion was not just a matter of preoccupation; on the contrary, the derogatory comments reliably attributed to Goering, as well as the "independent" manner in which the air war was conducted, show this indifference to have been a matter of deliberate policy.

The consequences of this neglect were plainly visible to Warlimont and Oberstleutnant Hellmuth Priess, another OKW staff officer, who on September 18 set out on a four-day tour of the principal invasion headquarters. Reporting back to Keitel and Jodl on September 23,[124] Warlimont declared that preparations for Sea Lion were not yet complete, and that this was "the result of making decisions too late on numerous unsettled questions among the three services." In part this had been due to the prolonged breadth-of-front dispute, but the Luftwaffe emerged as the principal culprit: "At Luftflotte 2, basic conferences on the employment of Fliegerkorps VIII, and on numerous other questions in connection with the 16th Army and with Fliegerdivision 7, had first been held on September 19,[125] two days before the earliest date originally set for the landing." The upshot had been highly unsatisfactory, according to Warlimont's account:

Fliegerkorps VIII can support only the two corps of the 16th Army, and indeed even there only in small measure, on account of the front's breadth of thirty kilometers. Neutralization of the flanks at Dover and Dungeness, as well as other tasks behind the front, would have to be handled by other units.

With respect to this matter, the commanding general of Fliegerkorps VIII [Richthofen] put forward the idea of landing only one corps at first, so that the Luftwaffe could give stronger support. The Chief of the Luftwaffe General Staff [Jeschonnek], who was present, joined in this proposal. But I [Warlimont] indicated that the strongest possible formations must be landed in the first wave, because of the enemy fleet and unpredictable sea conditions, and since the inevitable intervals between air strikes would require Army forces strong enough to stand alone. General Richthofen's proposal, therefore, was not discussed further.

This colloquy reveals the two air generals as lamentably ignorant of or remarkably indifferent to the Army's insistence on a strong first assault; one might almost conclude that neither had even heard of the long-drawn breadth-of-front debate and its painful resolution at the end of August. Jeschonnek had attended two Fuehrer conferences on Sea Lion, and Richthofen's Stukas had been out of the Battle of Britain for several weeks, so that he and his staff may have had some leisure to think about their mission in the event of an invasion. If Jeschonnek and Richthofen's ideas were so out of tune with the history and necessities of Sea Lion, it is unlikely that their colleagues in the Luftwaffe were closer to the realities. The fighter and level-flight-bomber leaders were still heavily committed over England, and as recently as September 16 they had been admonished by Goering not to allow Sea Lion to interfere with their own planned operations.[126]

The only man who could have straightened out the interservice mess, and mobilized the military leaders behind a unified program for the conquest of Britain, was Adolf Hitler. He made no attempt to do so, and this neglect, standing as it does in striking contrast to his energetic participation in the preparations for the Norwegian, French, and Russian campaigns, compels the conclusion that his failure was not due to indolence or lack of perception, but was, rather, a matter of deliberate choice.

Initially, as we have seen, his lack of aggressiveness was due to the euphoria of Compiègne and an ill-founded hope that the British, bereft of allies, would come to terms. But when these expectations were dashed, and Hitler decided to smite the British with Eagle and prepare for Sea Lion, why did he not then go all out and ensure a co-ordinated campaign and the fullest possible application of the Wehrmacht's power?

If he ever said why, apparently no record has survived. Nevertheless the course of the invasion preparations and discussions, together with other contemporaneous circumstances, make it possible to infer the reasons which he found persuasive. Hitler's conduct is logically explicable in the light of two politico-strategic concepts, one of which he explicitly stated and reiterated, while the other emerges clearly from the story of Sea Lion's short life.

To Raeder, to the *Generalobersten* assembled on September 13, and no doubt to Goering, Rundstedt, and others, Hitler said time and again that he did not wish Sea Lion to be undertaken if it would involve substantial risk of failure. It had to be virtually a sure thing; otherwise, in his view, the risk was neither necessary nor wise. The same theme crops up in Jodl's memoranda, which surely reflect Hitler's discussions with his OKW entourage.

The reason uniformly given for this conclusion was that failure of an attempted invasion would result in an intolerable loss of prestige. For this evaluation there were cogent reasons. Victory in France had made Hitler the focus of military and political power in Europe. He dispensed settlements and treaties in the Balkans. He confronted the problem of adjusting the rivalries of Italy, France, and Spain in the Mediterranean and Africa. He hoped to turn Japan to his uses in the global dimension of strategy. From Finland to Greece and to the Iberian Peninsula, no one could make a significant diplomatic or military move without reckoning with Hitler's reaction. To perpetuate his extraordinary sway over European affairs of state, Hitler rightly attached the utmost importance to his aura of invincibility. If the British (or for that matter anyone else) were to succeed in repulsing a major

German assault, that aura would be dissipated, and even if the material losses were tolerable the general consequences would be highly injurious, if not disastrous.

The other concept was that Hitler did not wish the issue of whether or not to attempt an invasion ever to be drawn too sharply, or in such a way that a negative decision would impair his personal prestige. Although it seems never to have been articulated, this second concept followed logically from the first. If there was to be no invasion unless success was virtually certain, there should never be a close question of its launching, for in the event of real doubt the decision must be negative. And if the psychological consequences of a repulse were to be avoided at all costs, then it was also important to avoid a situation where failure to attempt the invasion would be similarly injurious either to the Wehrmacht or to Hitler's newly acquired stature as a great *Feldherr*.

Given the German Navy's weakness and Britain's capacity for resistance *à l'outrance* against heavy odds, it was plain that Sea Lion, *no matter how well prepared,* would have faced substantial risk of failure unless England had first been really beaten flat by the Luftwaffe. If this had been accomplished, as Hitler and Raeder said to each other several times, the invasion might well be unnecessary; at most it would be a finishing-off operation against a disintegrating foe incapable of strong resistance. For the limited purpose Hitler had in mind, accordingly, he did not regard it as essential that the preparations be screwed up to the highest pitch. That is why he was indifferent to Goering's absence from the Sea Lion conferences, and why he allowed that worthy to run his own private war in the air, unco-ordinated with the land and sea preparations. Raeder was fully aware of this, and that is why SKL saw no point in complaining about the lack of relation between the London attacks and Sea Lion.

In fact, it is altogether probable that Hitler *did not want* Sea Lion to reach too high a plane of readiness and potential. It was all very well to decide in advance that invasion would be attempted only if its success was assured, but opinions might differ on the question whether or not that prospect was in view. If the Luftwaffe should achieve a large measure of but not full success in destroying Britain's defensive capacity, and if the Channel ports were swarming with troops led by eager and confident generals, the decision might be very difficult. And how much tighter it would be if the Fuehrer himself had been in the forefront of the plans and preparations, visible to the troops and staffs, and publicly committed to the success of the enterprise!

Hitler had no desire to march his men to the loading docks and then be obliged to march them away again. Much better to remain in Berlin or Berchtesgaden, and be able to blame the weather for the disappointing results of Eagle and the consequent abandonment of Sea Lion. Even "the greatest *Feldherr* of all time"* could afford to acknowledge that the elemental forces of nature were beyond his control.

In addition to all the foregoing, unquestionably Hitler's predilection for the idea of attacking Russia affected his strategic evaluation of Sea Lion. If the invasion were attempted unsuccessfully, the Wehrmacht's losses were not likely to be irreparable, but they might well be serious enough to jeopardize the prospect of a major campaign in the east the following summer. The same would be true if the invasion, even if successful, should encounter heavy opposition, for in that event there would be losses, and large numbers of troops would be committed in Britain beyond hope of speedy extrication.

Of course, Hitler wanted Sea Lion to *appear* to be strong, and to *be* strong enough to meet the riskless contingency which might develop if Goering made good his boasts. If Hitler spoke his mind with complete candor (assuming that he was candid even with himself) it was only to a few, including Goering and perhaps Rundstedt. Brauchitsch, Halder, and even Raeder were never really sure of Hitler's intentions. But his ambivalence could not be concealed, and there is good evidence that in the upper reaches of the officer corps it was widely believed or suspected that the Fuehrer was less than enthusiastic.[127]

Under these circumstances, it is probably idle to speculate on the question whether Sea Lion, if attempted, might have succeeded. Given the tempo of the planning and the temper of the leadership, the project was doomed. The preparations did not approach completion until late September; by then the *Adlerangriff* had failed. The season was too late, and it would then have been foolhardy in the extreme to launch the improvised and unwieldy invasion armada, the bulk of which would surely have been scattered and sunk by the Royal Navy before it reached the shores of England.†

Might Sea Lion, by dint of better plans and preparations and more

---

* Keitel's obsequy to Hitler upon receiving news of Pétain's request for an armistice.

† Admiral Ansel has written (*Hitler Confronts England*, pp. 305-16) a vivid and persuasive analysis of this hypothetical question.

determined leadership, have been undertaken in 1940 with reasonable prospect of success? Admiral Ansel declares[128] that "with correction of a few major misconceptions, the German armies could have invaded England." But he does not develop his thesis, beyond suggesting that by concentrating both their air and their naval efforts against the Royal Navy the Germans might have disputed local sea control in the Channel, and thereby "a major step toward rendering Sea Lion feasible would have been under way."

British naval power was indeed, as Admiral Ansel observes, the "ultimate bar to crossing." Nevertheless, it is difficult to see how the Luftwaffe could have done very much to eliminate or seriously weaken that bar. The Luftwaffe's fighter arm could provide cover for the bombers only over the southeastern corner of England. British warships could readily be held back from those waters and still remain close enough to intervene effectively in the event of invasion.* Unescorted bomber raids by day proved intolerably costly early in the Battle of Britain, and night bombing was far too inaccurate for this purpose.

Germany's naval weakness and lack of a truly strategic air force were defects which could not have been remedied in 1940. Any substantial case for the feasibility of invasion must be made (as Admiral Ansel's is not) within the limits imposed by these weaknesses. The most systematic attempt to build such a case has been made by Generalfeldmarschall von Manstein, who in the summer of 1940 was commanding the XXXVIIIth Corps and was thus deeply and directly involved in the Sea Lion preparations. His argument has two main branches.[130]

The first is that the invasion of Britain should have been envisaged as a possibility when the major offensive in the west was launched, and that preparations for such an invasion should have been begun while the campaign in France was still under way. The consequences would have been (1) that the armor would not have been held back from Dunkirk in 1940, and then the British Expeditionary Force would have been cut off and captured and England's capacity to resist invasion greatly diminished; and (2) that the invasion could have been attempted in August, with the assurance of another month of good weather, instead of in September.

This is all well enough, but of course it requires a complete rewrit-

---

* During the summer of 1940 the Royal Navy stationed 4 destroyer flotillas (36 ships) along the southeast coast. One of them was moved from Dover to Portsmouth after the heavy air attacks had begun.[129]

ing of the history of the six months preceding the actual conception of Sea Lion. If this were to be done, one might well also erase the Norwegian campaign and the naval losses thus incurred. Furthermore, Manstein's argument postulates a strategic vision which no one (including himself) revealed at the crucial time. The Luftwaffe had planned to attack England after the defeat of France, but it did so without pausing to consider carefully whether or not an independent air strike would be worth while. The Army planned to destroy the French Army without stopping first to think about what might have to be done thereafter. The Navy, to be sure, foresaw the strategic relevance of an invasion, but the admirals exploited their foresight largely in order to fend off a mission which they thought could not be successfully undertaken.

Manstein's second conclusion is much more challenging, for he thereby rejects the air-superiority prerequisite which everyone else treated as axiomatic: "The idea of gaining air supremacy over Britain by dint of an isolated aerial war commencing weeks in advance of the earliest possible invasion date was an *error of leadership.*" Whether or not he said anything like this at the time we do not know, but that does not detract from the hypothetical interest of his proposition.

Manstein rests this part of his case, however, not on the idea that the achievement of air superiority prior to invasion was undesirable (indeed, he explicitly acknowledges that it would have been advantageous) but on the basis that the Luftwaffe was not, and its leaders should have known that it was not, strong enough to achieve that goal in battle *over Britain,* where it was under serious operational disadvantages. Rather, he says, the air battle should have been joined over the Channel and the shore line, where the operational conditions would have been less unfavorable to the Germans, and should have been initiated "in immediate operational conjunction with the actual invasion."

In this analysis there is in retrospect much force. *If* the Germans' pre-*Adler* estimate of the comparative strength of Luftwaffe and Royal Air Force had been more accurate, and *if* Sea Lion had been conceived as the major operation for conquering Britain instead of as a mopping-up job after the Luftwaffe had done all the heavy work, then serious consideration might well have been given to Manstein's ideas.

But any such plan of action would necessarily have involved—as Manstein freely acknowledges—staking a great deal on an operation attended by a very substantial risk of failure. This Hitler was unwilling to do, for the reasons we have observed and inferred. The basic issue, therefore, is not the timing of the air attack, nor Dunkirk, nor any single operational factor. No matter how skillfully planned and diligently prepared, invasion was bound to be a risky undertaking, with great and perhaps decisively favorable consequences in the event of success, and serious but not immediately fatal consequences in the event of failure. Was Hitler's decision not to face the risk and seriously attempt the invasion strategically sound?

The answer must depend on the alternatives. Although he is far from explicit, Manstein leans toward the view that the hazards of a long war, though less immediate, were greater than those of Sea Lion:

If Hitler jibbed at fighting the Battle of Britain in the hour most favorable to himself, Germany must sooner or later land in an untenable situation. . . . In reality, because of his aversion to the risk of invading Britain, Hitler took on the far greater risk of a war on two fronts. At the same time, by taking so long over and finally discarding the invasion plan, he wasted a year which should have brought Germany the final decision. It was a delay Germany could never make good.

The last part of this indictment must be accounted valid. Hitler sometimes made erroneous decisions, but more often his shortcomings as a strategist were manifested in undue postponement of decisions, or in diminishing the potential impact of a decision by refusing wholly to abandon any of the alternatives.

The basic weakness of Germany's position was that she had become involved in a war of amphibious and potentially global dimensions with a Wehrmacht designed for Continental operations. Victory in the Battle of France was so rapid and complete that, for a moment, there was opportunity despite these limitations to cross the Channel and knock out Britain. It was a strategic error not to foresee and be prepared to embrace this opportunity, but, as already observed, the blame for this is not Hitler's alone, though he must bear primary responsibility for aggravating the consequences by his dilatoriness and false optimism after the defeat of France.

But the generals of the air and the ground, if not the admirals of the sea, were also somnolent, lackadaisical, or blind to the strategic imperatives. By the time everyone woke up, it was already too late to mount an invasion of Britain with reasonable prospect of success. Strategically, therefore, it is wrong to fault Hitler too severely for his lack of leadership in Sea Lion, for he and his advisers had already made mistakes that a belated outpouring of energy could not have cured.

Failure of *Adlerangriff* and the abandonment of Sea Lion marked also the failure of Hitler's summer strategy. The consequence was the re-emergence in September of the questions so much mooted in June. The various alternatives had to be re-examined, and thus the fall of 1940 brought a new period of planning and decision-making.

Conclusion

The Road to Nowhere

"**I**T IS BECOMING increasingly apparent," writes the German historian Karl Klee,[1] "that the whole complex of political and military events between the conclusion of the campaign in France and the opening of the campaign in Russia must be regarded as the actual turning point of the war. Due to the faulty appraisal of this situation by the highest German political authorities, the war from then on took a course leading to disaster for Germany." Following this assessment, Klee poses the question whether the Battle of Britain was intended to prepare the way for an invasion of England, or whether *Adler* and *Seeloewe* were two separate operations.

The very fact that this relation remains a matter of debate is a strong indication of how and why the war was taking a course disastrous for Germany. The apparent uncertainty does not arise from any lack of evidence, for the German military records have survived in abundance, and the course of strategic planning and decision can be followed in great detail. If these records leave the issue in doubt, accordingly, it is because the relation between the two undertakings was unresolved at the time the records were made.

Klee's continuing uncertainty, however, stems from his erroneous attribution of unity to the German military leadership. True it is that Adolf Hitler was the Supreme War Lord, with dictatorial powers of decision. But Hitler exercised his powers as Fuehrer much more erratically than is commonly supposed, and during the summer of 1940 the governance of the Wehrmacht was far from unitary. The relation between the Battle of Britain and Sea Lion is to be derived from the conceptions of those operations entertained by the men who planned and directed them, and at the time in question these men were not all of one mind.

The foregoing narrative, it is hoped, suggests how the principal German military figures would have answered Klee's question. For Brauchitsch and Halder, certainly, the air attack was primarily a measure preparatory for the invasion, for the Army leaders were solidly behind Sea Lion and saw it as the quickest road to a final victory. For Raeder and the SKL admirals, on the other hand, the Battle of Britain was no such thing; despite the effort and ingenuity they invested in Sea Lion, they thought it suicidal and earnestly hoped that it would never be attempted. From the Navy's standpoint, the Battle was the opening round in a sustained offensive by air and sea which, by destruction and blockade, would bring Britain to her knees without ever landing a German soldier on English soil.

Essentially that is also the way Goering viewed things, and it is remarkable that he and Raeder, constantly at odds personally, were on this matter in basic agreement strategically. Goering had as little use as Raeder for Sea Lion. Their differences, which were sharp, were primarily tactical: Goering disparaged the naval aspects of the struggle, refused to commit much of the Luftwaffe to joint air-sea operations, and hoped that his vaunted Eagle alone could carry the day. For him, therefore, the Battle was no preliminary; rather, it was the *Ding an sich.*

At OKW there was no unanimity. Warlimont and the "Indians" on the Operations Staff apparently held the Army's views and saw Eagle as a preparation for Sea Lion.[2] Keitel had few opinions of his own,[3] and Jodl, for all his technical competence, generally followed what he knew or believed were Hitler's views.

As for the Fuehrer, his was the greatest sin, for he permitted—nay, encouraged—both Eagle and Sea Lion without making them part of a considered strategy. At times he treated them as a primarily psychological offensive, the shock of which might bring the British to their senses and persuade them to yield to the inevitable before suffering utter defeat. At others, he hoped or pretended that Eagle alone might beat them into helplessness. On one occasion, as we have seen, he even advanced the preposterous notion of using the Sea Lion invasion fleet to lure the British Navy to destruction at the hands of the Luftwaffe.[4]

This instability of purpose was the consequence of Hitler's basic weaknesses as a strategist, of which two are especially evident during this period: his constant groping for the easy solution—an appetite which psychiatrists might ascribe to his *petit-bourgeois* nature and which no doubt was fortified by the cheap victories of the *Blumenkriege* and the first year of the war—and his inability sufficiently to perceive the relationships between specific operations, especially with respect to their aerial, naval, and economic dimensions. Thus he (and Goering) were chiefly responsible for the delay in mounting Eagle and Sea Lion, born of false hopes of peace, which gave the British their desperately needed breather from June to August. And thus Hitler allowed Eagle to be launched without carefully calculating either its chances of success or the consequences of its failure in relation to the other operations which he was contemplating.

What was lacking that accounts for such egregious failures in the strategic clutch? Looking back over the documents and discussions from which these decisions developed, their most striking and significant feature is the decline of the German General Staff in the initiation and evolution of strategic policy. The record of the German Supreme Command in the First World War has been widely and rightly criticized by historians; nevertheless, at the Imperial Headquarters Hindenburg and Ludendorff achieved at least the semblance and sometimes the actuality of general consultation and considered decision, and the leading General Staff officers were a frequent source of strategic ideas.[5]

After the First World War the position of Chief of the General Staff of the Army was sharply downgraded, but the "general-staff system" of training and selecting the Army's leaders continued to flourish. Many of the principal Luftwaffe commanders and staff officers were products of this system, and within the small Navy officer corps a like tradition of professional competence prevailed. Hitler had dealt severe blows to the Army's prestige and power in 1938, and the adverse results were observable in 1939. Nevertheless, Brauchitsch and Halder continued to put forward their strategic views throughout the winter of 1939–40, and during the successful campaign in the west. Field commanders such as Rundstedt, Leeb, Reichenau and Guderian, and staff officers such as Halder and Manstein, expressed themselves vigorously on questions of strategy and organization, often with considerable success.[6]

It might have been expected that the Army's remarkable victories in May and June of 1940 would have re-established the generals' public stature and influence in the conduct of the war. Brauchitsch and Halder had hoped for such a consequence, but Hitler's shrewd stage-management frustrated whatever ambitions they may have entertained,[7] and the summer of 1940 found them increasingly impotent in the realm of high policy. Outmaneuvered and outfaced by Hitler, they might at least have taken counsel with their senior colleagues in the field, to develop a strategy behind which the entire Army officer corps could have thrown its weight. But they seem to have made no such effort.

Neither did the field generals show any strategic initiative. At his comfortable headquarters in St.-Germain, Rundstedt and his staff relaxed, out of touch with the march of events.[8] The other two army-group commanders, Bock and Leeb, were likewise silent. Guderian, like Brauchitsch and Halder, favored a Mediterranean strategy, but he neither sought nor was asked to submit his views to OKW or OKH.[9] Manstein, who had contributed so brilliantly to the plan of attack in the west, grumbled to visitors to his headquarters that time was being wasted at the crucial moment,[10] but was preoccupied with the command of his own corps, which was part of the Sea Lion plan. There was no fresh source of energy and ideas; for all its tactical competence, the officer corps was strategically arid and almost indifferent.

Could not a bond of mutual discussion and planning have been established among the staffs of the three services? Hitler might be remote and dictatorial and Goering arrogant and unco-operative, but why could not Brauchitsch and Halder make common cause with Raeder and Schniewind, and with Luftwaffe commanders such as Kesselring and Sperrle, who were former Army officers? Perhaps some such approaches were made,[11] but if so they were too casual and occasional, or at too low a level, to be effective. For all their desirability under the unprecedented situation that confronted the Wehrmacht, such direct interservice relations were outside the orbit of traditional German military habit patterns, and the old mold withstood the pressure of the new circumstances.

Thus the strategic decisions made during the summer of 1940 were arrived at without benefit of interservice consultation and co-ordination, and without considering the relations between the several decisions, and the consequences that each had for the others. The available records do not indicate, for example, that the strategic relation between Eagle and the projected invasion of Russia was ever discussed. Yet the relation was obvious and important. The Luftwaffe had been designed primarily to support the Army, not for independent, long-range operations. If there was to be a land campaign on the far-flung eastern frontier, the Army would need the Luftwaffe as never before. Unless Eagle, or Eagle and Sea Lion jointly, were decisive, the Luftwaffe would almost certainly emerge from a prolonged and inconclusive struggle with the Royal Air Force in a depleted and battered condition. This would not be conducive to the speedy success in Russia which Hitler deemed vital; the general disregard of this factor is the more extraordinary in the light of Hitler's skepticism of the Luftwaffe's ability to knock out the British singlehanded,[12] and his obvious reluctance to venture on Sea Lion.

So, too, there was a direct relation between the decision to attack Russia in 1941 and the strategy constantly advocated by Raeder, and repeatedly approved by Hitler, of bringing Britain to terms by economic blockade, to be achieved primarily by aircraft and U-boats. Both Luftwaffe and Navy would require rapid enlargement and modification if such a result were to be achieved. How could this be done; how could the materials and the manpower possibly be obtained for an air-sea war in the Atlantic, if the Army and the Luftwaffe were chewing up great quantities of both, deep in Russia?

Such basic questions went unexplored, and so did the comparative merits of alternative strategies. Brauchitsch and Halder might tell each other that the Mediterranean was a more promising highway to victory than the road to Moscow, and Hitler and Raeder might chat about Dakar or the Canary Islands; however, Germany's resources could not support large-scale operations in both the Soviet Union and the Mediterranean or African areas, and if Britain could not be brought down by direct assault the choice was of crucial importance. Yet there seems to have been no occasion at which Hitler and the military leaders touched these matters in any systematic way, nor were any comparative staff studies made.

If the basic military questions were thus sloughed off, the economic and diplomatic aspects of the strategic situation were handled just as badly. As soon as it became apparent that Britain would not yield, and that the prospects of bringing her to terms in 1940 were at best uncertain, the German economy should at once have been geared to the prospect of a long war. The necessity of such steps was underlined when reliance upon a blockade of the enemy islands and an invasion of Russia in 1941 emerged as the major elements of the long-term strategy. However, there was no co-ordination of military and economic planning, and practically no contact between the military and civilian leaders except through Goering, who already had his hands full of

Luftwaffe problems, and who lacked the capacity for sustained concentration on economic matters. As a result there was no significant belt-tightening, there was no increase in the output of war materials, and the German economy in 1941 was no closer to a war footing than it had been in 1940.[13]

Equally damaging to the German cause was Hitler's failure to draw Italy into a co-ordinated plan for the conduct of the war. Meeting with Ciano on July 7, Hitler mentioned the need for "a unified concept as to the continuation of operations," to be achieved, if necessary, by another conference at the Brenner Pass. But a week later he was writing Mussolini, in a most cavalier vein, that it did not matter in the least where the blows against England might fall.[14]

Yet, if anything should have been clear in the summer of 1940, it was that Italy was not only a weak ally but also a dangerous one, in that her participation might well open new theaters of war, at times and places that might be highly disadvantageous to Germany. This being so, the closest possible alignment of Axis military and diplomatic policies was highly necessary. But neither Hitler nor Ribbentrop nor the German military emissaries in Italy took any real steps to achieve the "unified concept" of which Hitler had spoken to Ciano, and within a few months the Germans paid dearly for their neglect, when the Duce—greatly to the Fuehrer's surprise and chagrin—launched the inglorious and strategically stupid campaign in Greece.

Blunders and oversights which stem from such basic deficiencies of character and capacity among the leaders are bound to be repeated and even to multiply under the strain of adversity. The failure of Eagle and the abandonment of Sea Lion marked also the collapse of Hitler's summer strategy, and the necessity for a new assessment of the strategic alternatives. Once more the question was, *Was nun?* Once again Hitler exhibited his aversion for negative choice, and the generals their inability to formulate a strategy for his consideration.

The consequence was that the Wehrmacht soon became enmeshed in more undertakings and commitments than it could handle successfully. By the end of 1942 Germany had lost the strategic initiative, and soon thereafter she confronted insoluble problems and recurring crises. Small wonder, for the Army and the Luftwaffe were spread throughout Norway, Denmark, the Low Countries, France, Italy, the Balkans, Greece, Crete, and on the Mediterranean shores of Egypt and Libya, as well as along the thousands of miles of the Russian front.

Marked on a map, the conquests of the Wehrmacht were awesome, but the combination of decisions that led to them was military madness. He who cannot reject cannot select, and the downfall of the Third Reich was due, in no small measure, to Adolf Hitler's inability to realize that, in strategic terms, the road to everywhere is the road to nowhere.

Appendices, Charts, and Tables

GLOSSARY OF GERMAN MILITARY TERMS, COVER NAMES, AND ABBREVIATIONS

ABWEHR	Abw.	Intelligence dept. of OKW.
ADLERANGRIFF	—	Eagle Attack—cover name for the German air assault against Britain.
ADLERTAG	—	Eagle Day—cover name for the opening day of the *Adlerangriff*.
ARMEE	Arm.	An army (field formation; *cf.* HEER).
ARMEEKORPS	AK	Army corps.
ARMEEOBERKOMMANDO	AOK	An army headquarters.
AUFBAU OST	—	Eastern Construction—cover name for the deployment in preparation for Barbarossa.
AUSSER DIENST	a.D.	Out of service—retired.
BARBAROSSA	—	Cover name for attack on Soviet Union.
BEFEHLSHABER	Befh.	Commander.
CHEF DES GENERALSTABS DES HEERES	C.G.S.	Chief of the General Staff of the Army.
DIVISION	Div.	Division.
EISERNES KREUZ	E.K.	Iron Cross.
ERSATZHEER	Ersh.	Replacement and Training Army (home army).
FALL BLAU	—	Cover name for war with Britain.
FALL GELB	—	Cover name for attack on France and Low Countries, May 1940.

FALLSCHIRMTRUPPEN	F.S.Tr.	Parachute troops.
FLIEGERKORPS	Fl.K.	Air corps.
FLOTTENCHEF	—	Commander of the Fleet.
FLUGABWEHRKANONEN	Flak	Antiaircraft artillery.
GEBIRGSTRUPPEN	Geb.Tr.	Mountain troops.
GENERALKOMMANDO	GKdo.	Army corps headquarters.
GENERALQUARTIERMEISTER	Gen.Qu.	Principal staff officer for supply and administration at OKH and OKL.
GENERALSTAB DES HEERES	Gen.St. d.H.	General Staff of the Army.
GRUPPE	Gr.	Group; in Luftwaffe, about 30 aircraft in 3 *Staffeln*.
HEER	H.	The Army.
HEERESGRUPPE	H.Gr.	An army group.
HERBSTREISE	—	Autumn Journey—cover name for naval feint in North Atlantic to draw British naval forces from Sea Lion area.
HOEHERES KOMMANDO z.b.V.	Hoeh. Kdo.	Administrative or second-line headquarters at corps level.
JAGDBOMBER	Jabo	Fighter-bomber.
JAGDFLIEGERFUEHRER	Jafue	Highest field commander of fighter aircraft.
JAGDGESCHWADER	JG	Fighter squadron of 3 Gruppen.
JUNKERS 87	Ju 87	Junkers single-engine dive bomber (Stuka).
JUNKERS 88	Ju 88	Junkers twin-engine medium bomber.
KAMPFGESCHWADER	KG	Bomber squadron.
KETTE	—	Combat formation of 3 aircraft.
KOMMANDEUR	Kdr.	Commander (in the Army, of a division, regiment, or battalion).
KOMMANDIERENDER GENERAL	Kom. Gen.	Commanding general of a corps or its equivalent.
KRIEGSMARINE	M.	The Navy.
KRIEGSTAGEBUCH	KTB	War diary.
LUFTFLOTTE	Lfl.	Air fleet.
LUFTLANDETRUPPEN	L.L.Tr.	Air-landing (airborne) troops.
LUFTWAFFE	Lw.	The Air Force.

MARINEGRUPPENKOMMANDO	Mar.Gr. Kdo.	Highest naval sector head-quarters.
MESSERSCHMITT 109	Me 109	Messerschmitt single-engine fighter.
MESSERSCHMITT 110	Me 110	Messerschmitt twin-engine fighter.
MILITAERBEFEHLSHABER	Mil.Bef.	Military Commander in occupied territory, responsible to OKH.
OBERBEFEHLSHABER	Ob.	Commander-in-chief (of army groups, armies, air fleets, naval group commands, and a few other headquarters immediately under OKW, OKH, OKL, or OKM).
OBERBEFEHLSHABER DES HEERES	Ob.d.H.	Commander-in-Chief of the Army.
OBERBEFEHLSHABER DER KRIEGSMARINE	Ob.d.M.	Commander-in-Chief of the Navy.
OBERBEFEHLSHABER DER LUFTWAFFE	Ob.d.L.	Commander-in-Chief of the Air Force.
OBERKOMMANDO DES HEERES	OKH	High Command of the Army.
OBERKOMMANDO DER KRIEGSMARINE	OKM	High Command of the Navy.
OBERKOMMANDO DER LUFTWAFFE	OKL	High Command of the Air Force.
OBERKOMMANDO DER WEHRMACHT	OKW	High Command of the Armed Forces.
OBERQUARTIERMEISTER (I, IV, etc.)	O.Qu.	Principal OKH staff officer for operations (I), intelligence (IV), etc.
OBERSTER BEFEHLSHABER	Oberst. Bef.	Supreme Commander of the Armed Forces (Hitler).
PANZER	Pz.	Armor.
REICHSFUEHRER SS	RFSS	Leader of the SS (Himmler).
REICHSLUFTFAHRTMINISTERIUM	RLM	Air Ministry.
REICHSWEHR	Rw.	The armed forces from 1920 to 1935.
RITTERKREUZ	Ritt.	Knight's Cross of the Iron Cross.

SCHUTZSTAFFEL DER NSDAP	SS	Protection squads; Himmler's components of the Nazi Party.
SCHWERPUNKT	—	Point of main effort.
SEEKRIEGSLEITUNG	SKL	Naval War Staff.
SEELOEWE	—	Sea Lion—cover name for invasion of Britain.
STAFFEL	St.	Basic Luftwaffe formation of about 10 aircraft.
STURZKAMPFGESCHWADER	St.G	Dive-bomber squadron.
TANNENBURG	—	Hitler's headquarters in the Black Forest, June 28–July 6, 1940.
UNTERSEEBOOT	U-boot	Submarine.
WAFFEN-SS	W-SS	Armed and militarized components of the SS.
WAFFENSTILLSTAND	—	Armistice.
WEHRKREIS	Wkr.	German Army district, in peacetime equivalent to corps area.
WEHRMACHT	Wehrm.	The Armed Forces (from 1935).
WEHRMACHTBEFEHLSHABER	W.Bef.	Armed-forces commander in occupied territory, responsible to OKW.
WEHRMACHTFUEHRUNGSSTAB	WFst.	Operational staff of OKW.
WESERUEBUNG	W.	Cover name for invasion of Norway and Denmark.
WESTFELDZUG	—	Campaign in the west (France and Low Countries).
WOLFSSCHLUCHT	—	Hitler's headquarters at Brûly-de-Pesche, June 6–25, 1940.
ZEPPELIN	—	OKH headquarters at Zossen.
ZERSTOERER	Z.	A destroyer (naval).
ZERSTOERERGESCHWADER	ZG	Twin-engine fighter squadron.
ZUR BESONDERER VERWENDUNG	z.b.V.	For special employment.
ZUR VERFUEGUNG	z.V.	At disposal—retired officer available for duty.

APPENDIX B

DRAMATIS PERSONAE*

ALFIERI, DINO: Italian ambassador to Germany, 1940–43.

BADER, DOUGLAS R. S.: Famous British ace and leader of No. 242 Squadron in No. 12 Group of Fighter Command.

BOCK, FEDOR VON: *Generalfeldmarschall;* commander-in-chief of Army Group B.

BOETTICHER, FRIEDRICH VON: *General der Artillerie;* German military attaché in Washington.

BRAUCHITSCH, WALTHER VON: *Generalfeldmarschall;* Commander-in-Chief of the Army.

BUSCH, ERNST: *Generaloberst;* commander-in-chief of the 16th Army.

CHRISTIANSEN, FRIEDRICH: *General der Flieger;* Armed Forces Commander (*Wehrmachtbefehlshaber*) in the Netherlands.

CIANO, GALEAZZO: Italian Foreign Minister and son-in-law to Benito Mussolini.

DEICHMANN, PAUL: *Oberstleutnant;* chief of staff of Fliegerkorps II.

DOERING, KURT-BERTRAM VON: *Generalmajor;* Jagdfliegerfuehrer 2 (fighter-aircraft commander) in Luftflotte 2.

DOWDING, SIR HUGH C. T.: British Air Chief Marshal; commanding officer of Fighter Command.

ETZDORF, HASSO VON: German Foreign Office representative at OKH.

FALKENSTEIN, SIGISMUND FRH. VON: *Major;* chief of the Air Section of the OKW Operations Staff.

FELMY, HELMUTH: *General der Flieger;* commander-in-chief of Luftflotte (formerly Luftwaffengruppe) 2 in Braunschweig until his forced retirement in January 1940.

FINK, JOHANNES: *Oberst;* commander of KG 2, and Kanalkampffuehrer.

FISCHEL, HERMANN VON: *Vizeadmiral;* commander of Naval Station Ostend, and of Fleet B for Sea Lion.

* Omitted from this list are names of major historical figures who need no identification (e.g., Churchill, Hitler, Mussolini, Roosevelt, Stalin), and nonrecurring names sufficiently identified in the text.

305

FRICKE, KURT: *Konteradmiral;* chief of the Operations Section of the Naval War Staff.

FROMM, FRITZ: *Generaloberst;* commander-in-chief of the home army (Ersatzheer).

GALLAND, ADOLF: *Major;* group commander in and later commander of JG 26.

GERCKE, RUDOLF: *Generalleutnant;* chief of the Transportation Section of OKH.

GOERING, HERMANN: *Reichsmarschall;* Commander-in-Chief of the Luftwaffe and successor-designate to Hitler.

GRAUERT, ULRICH: *Generaloberst;* commander of Fliegerkorps I.

GREIFFENBERG, HANS VON: *Generalmajor;* chief of the Operations Section of the Army General Staff.

GREIM, ROBERT RITTER VON: *General der Flieger;* commander of Fliegerkorps V.

HALDER, FRANZ: *Generaloberst;* Chief of the Army General Staff.

HEUSINGER, ADOLF: *Oberst;* assistant and later (October 1940) successor to Greiffenberg in the Operations Section of the Army General Staff.

HOFFMANN VON WALDAU, OTTO: *Generalmajor;* chief of the Operations Section of the Luftwaffe General Staff.

JACOB, ALFRED: *General der Pioniere;* inspector of engineers and fortifications, OKH.

JESCHONNEK, HANS: *General der Flieger;* Chief of the Luftwaffe General Staff.

JODL, ALFRED: *General der Artillerie;* chief of the OKW Operations Staff (*Fuehrungsstab*).

JUNCK, WERNER: *Oberst;* Jagdfliegerfuehrer 3 (fighter-aircraft commander) in Luftflotte 3.

KEITEL, WILHELM: *Generalfeldmarschall;* Chief of OKW.

KELLER, ALFRED: *Generaloberst;* commander of Fliegerkorps IV and (later) commander-in-chief of Luftflotte 1.

KESSELRING, ALBERT: *Generalfeldmarschall;* commander-in-chief of Luftflotte 2.

KURUSU, SABURO: Japanese Ambassador to Germany, 1939–41.

LEEB, EMIL: *General der Artillerie;* chief of Ordnance, OKH.

LEEB, WILHELM RITTER VON: *Generalfeldmarschall;* commander-in-chief of Army Group C.

LEIGH-MALLORY, TRAFFORD: British Air Vice-Marshal; commanding officer of No. 12 Group, Fighter Command.

LOERZER, BRUNO: *General der Flieger;* commander of Fliegerkorps II.

LOSSBERG, BERNHARD VON: *Oberstleutnant;* chief of the Army Section of the OKW Operations Staff.

LUETJENS, GUENTHER: *Vizeadmiral,* later (Sept. 1, 1940) *Admiral;* commander of the High Seas Fleet (Flottenchef).

MANSTEIN, FRITZ ERICH VON LEWINSKI *gen.* VON: *General der Infanterie;* commander of the XXXVIIIth Army Corps.

MARCKS, ERICH: *Generalmajor;* chief of staff of the 18th Army.

MARTINI, WOLFGANG: *Generalleutnant;* chief of Luftwaffe signal communications.

MILCH, ERHARD: *Generalfeldmarschall;* Inspector-General of the Luftwaffe and Ministerial Secretary (*Staatssekretaer*) of the Air Ministry (RLM).

MOELDERS, WERNER: *Major;* group commander in and later commander of JG 51.

OSHIMA, HIROSHI: Japanese ambassador to Germany before and after Kurusu.

OSTERKAMP, THEODOR: *Generalmajor;* commander of JG 51, later Jagdfliegerfuehrer 1 (fighter-aircraft commander) in Luftflotte 2.

OTT, EUGEN: German ambassador to Japan.

PARK, KEITH RODNEY: British Air Vice-Marshal; commanding officer of No. 11 Group, Fighter Command.

PAULUS, FRIEDRICH: *Generalleutnant;* Oberquartiermeister I (Operations) of OKH.

PUTZIER, RICHARD: *Generalmajor;* acting commander of Fliegerdivision 7 (airborne troops).

RAEDER, ERICH: *Grossadmiral;* Commander-in-Chief of the Navy.

REICHENAU, WALTER VON: *Generalfeldmarschall;* commander-in-chief of the 6th Army.

REINHARDT, GEORG-HANS: *General der Panzertruppen;* commander of the XLIst Panzer Corps and of the Experimental Staff for Sea Lion.

RIBBENTROP, JOACHIM VON: German Foreign Minister.

RICHTHOFEN, WOLFRAM VON: *General der Flieger;* commander of Fliegerkorps VIII.

RUNDSTEDT, GERD VON: *Generalfeldmarschall;* commander-in-chief of Army Group A.

SAALWAECHTER, ALFRED: *Generaladmiral;* commander-in-chief, Naval Command West.

SCHMID, JOSEF "BEPPO": *Oberst;* chief of the Intelligence Section of the Luftwaffe General Staff.

SCHMIDT, PAUL OTTO: Principal interpreter in the German Foreign Office.

SCHNIEWIND, OTTO: *Vizeadmiral;* Chief of Staff, SKL.

SCHOBERT, EUGEN RITTER VON: *Generaloberst;* commander of the VIIth Army Corps.

SCHUSTER, KARLGEORG: *Admiral;* Commanding Admiral in France.

SPEER, ALBERT: Hitler's favored Nazi Party architect and successor to Todt in 1942.

SPERRLE, HUGO: *Generalfeldmarschall;* commander-in-chief of Luftflotte 3.

STAHMER, HEINRICH: German Foreign Office specialist in Far Eastern matters.

STAPF, OTTO: *Generalmajor;* OKH liaison officer at Luftwaffe headquarters.

STRAUSS, ADOLF: *Generaloberst;* commander-in-chief of the 9th Army.

STUMPFF, HANS-JUERGEN: *Generaloberst;* commander-in-chief of Luftflotte 5.

TELEKI, COUNT PÁL: Hungarian Minister-President.

THOMAS, GEORG: *General der Infanterie;* chief of the Military Economy Division of OKW.

TODT, DR. FRITZ: Reich Minister of Armaments, killed 1942 in an airplane accident.

UDET, ERNST: *Generaloberst;* chief of aircraft production and design (Generalluftzeugmeister) in the RLM.

WARLIMONT, WALTER: *Generalmajor;* chief of the Plans Section of the OKW Operations Staff, immediately subordinate to Jodl and superior to Lossberg and Falkenstein.

WATSON-WATT, ROBERT: British scientist, leading developer of radar.

WEIZSAECKER, ERNST FRH. VON: Ministerial Secretary (*Staatssekretaer*) of the German Foreign Office.

WEVER, WALTHER: *Generalmajor;* first Chief of Staff of the Luftwaffe, killed 1936 in an airplane accident.

WICK, HELMUT: *Major;* group commander in and later commander of JG 2.

APPENDIX C

COMPARATIVE TABLE OF GERMAN AND AMERICAN MILITARY RANKS

German Army and Air Force	U. S. Army	SS
Generalfeldmarschall	General of the Army	Reichsfuehrer SS
Generaloberst	General	Oberstgruppenfuehrer
General (der Inf., etc.)	Lieutenant General	Obergruppenfuehrer
Generalleutnant	Major General	Gruppenfuehrer
Generalmajor	Brigadier General	Brigadefuehrer
—	—	Oberfuehrer
Oberst	Colonel	Standartenfuehrer
Oberstleutnant	Lieutenant Colonel	Obersturmbannfuehrer
Major	Major	Sturmbannfuehrer
Hauptmann / Rittmeister	Captain	Hauptsturmfuehrer
Oberleutnant	Lieutenant	Obersturmfuehrer
Leutnant	Second Lieutenant	Untersturmfuehrer

German Navy	U. S. Navy
Grossadmiral	Admiral of the Fleet
Generaladmiral	—
Admiral	Admiral
Vizeadmiral	Vice Admiral
Konteradmiral	Rear Admiral
Kapitaen zur See	Captain
Fregattenkapitaen	Commander
Korvettenkapitaen	Lieutenant Commander
Kapitaenleutnant	Lieutenant
Oberleutnant zur See	Lieutenant (j.g.)
Leutnant zur See	Ensign

LUFTWAFFE RANK AND ASSIGNMENT LIST: AUGUST 1940*

Name	Seniority	Assignment
REICHSMARSCHALL		
1. Goering	19.7.40	C.-in-C., Luftwaffe
GENERALFELDMARSCHAELLE		
2. Milch	19.7.40	Inspector-General
3. Sperrle	19.7.40	Luftflotte 3
4. Kesselring	19.7.40	Luftflotte 2
GENERALOBERSTEN		
5. Stumpff	19.7.40 (1)	Luftflotte 5
6. Keller	19.7.40 (2)	Fliegerkorps IV; Luftflotte 1
7. Weise	19.7.40 (3)	Flakkorps I
8. Grauert	19.7.40 (4)	Fliegerkorps I
9. Udet	19.7.40 (5)	Generalluftzeugmeister
GENERALE		
10. Ruedel	1.10.37 (1)	Chief, Air Defense
11. Christiansen	1.1.39 (3)	Armed Forces Commander Netherlands
12. v. Witzendorf	1.2.39 (1)	Administration, RLM
13. Loehr	1.3.39 (1)	Luftflotte 4
14. v. Schroeder	1.4.39 (1)	Civil Air Defense
15. Kuehl	1.4.39 (3)	Chief, Training

* The list does not include Luftwaffe officers retired prior to this time and temporarily recalled to active duty during the war with the designation "z.V."

Name	Seniority	Assignment
16. Hirschauer	1.8.39 (1)	Air District XVII
17. v.d. Lieth-Thomsen	1.8.39 (2)	Science Section, RLM
18. Kitzinger	1.10.39 (1)	Western Air Defense
19. Wimmer	1.10.39 (4)	Acting c.o., Luftflotte 1; Air District Belgium-Northern France
20. Student	22.5.40	Fliegerdivision 7
21. Geisler	19.7.40 (1)	Fliegerkorps X
22. v. Greim	19.7.40 (2)	Fliegerkorps V
23. Loerzer	19.7.40 (3)	Fliegerkorps II
24. v. Richthofen	19.7.40 (4)	Fliegerkorps VIII
25. Jeschonnek	19.7.40 (5)	Chief, General Staff

GENERALLEUTNANTE[*]

Wenninger	1.3.38 (1)	Attached to Luftflotte 2
Bogatsch	1.1.40 (2)	Liaison with OKH
Bodenschatz	1.1.40 (4)	Personal assistant to Goering
Kastner-Kirdorf	8.1.40	Chief, Personnel
Martini	1.4.40 (3)	Chief Signal Officer
Coeler	19.7.40 (1)	Fliegerdivision 9
Dessloch	19.7.40 (2)	Flakkorps II
Speidel	19.7.40 (3)	Chief of Staff, Luftflotte 2
v. Seidel	19.7.40 (4)	Generalquartiermeister

GENERALMAJORE

Ritter	1.1.39 (7)	Liaison with OKM
Siburg	1.1.39 (8)	Air District Holland
Pflugbeil	1.1.39 (20)	Air District Belgium–North France; Fliegerkorps IV
Putzier	1.2.39 (4)	Deputy c.o., Fliegerdivision 7
v. Buelow	1.4.39 (4)	Air attaché, Rome
Feyerabend	1.4.39 (5)	C.o. Flak, Norway
Froehlich	1.12.39 (9)	KG 76
v. Wuehlisch	1.4.40 (3)	KG 77
v. Doering	4.7.40	Jagdfliegerfuehrer 2
Korten	19.7.40 (1)	Chief of staff, Luftflotte 3
Hoffmann v. Waldau	19.7.40 (2)	Chief of Operations Section, General Staff
Osterkamp	19.7.40 (3)	JG 51; Jagdfliegerfuehrer 1
Knauss	1.8.40 (1)	Chief of Staff, Luftflotte 1
Schwabedissen	1.8.40 (7)	Chief of staff, Armed Forces Commander Netherlands

[*] The balance of the list is selective. There were about 28 *Generalleutnante* and 93 *Generalmajore*, making some 150 general officers in all.

APPENDIX E

WEHRMACHT ORGANIZATION AND ORDER
OF BATTLE: SUMMER 1940

IN THIS APPENDIX, Charts 1 through 5 are intended to show the structure of and chain of command within the Wehrmacht in August 1940, at the time of the Battle of Britain and Sea Lion. Charts 6 through 10 portray the chain of command and order of battle for those operations. By "order of battle" (*Kriegsgliederung*) is meant the identity and subordination of the major field commands.

No effort has been made for completeness in every detail. In the interests of simplicity, numerous sections or subsections of secondary importance have been omitted.

For the most part, the names of the various offices have been rendered in English; German has been used where translation would be cumbersome or unclear. In German administrative terminology, the higher units are usually designated by the word *Amt* (department or office), and the lower by *Abteilung* (section).

During the course of the Battle of Britain, the location and subordination of individual Luftwaffe units were frequently shifted according to tactical requirements. It has been impossible to indicate every such shift; nevertheless, the charts should be of assistance in following the story told in the text.

CHART 1
Organization of the Wehrmacht: August 1940

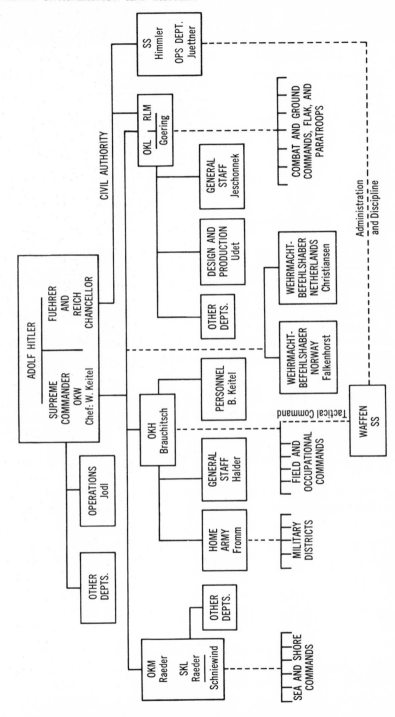

CHART 2
Oberkommando der Wehrmacht (OKW): August 1940

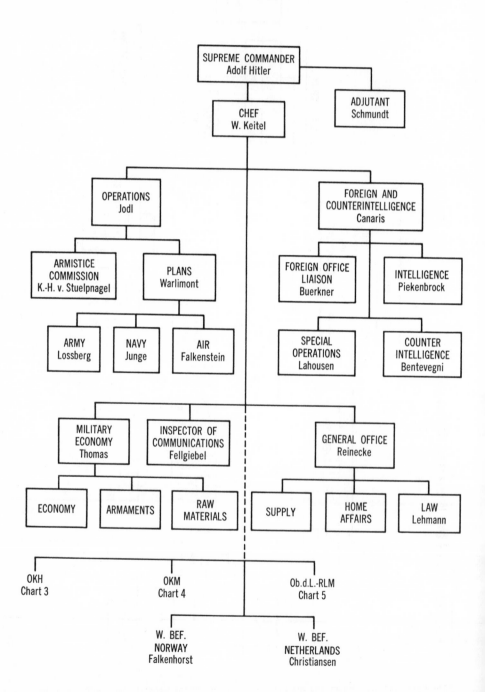

CHART 3
Oberkommando des Heeres (OKH): August 1940

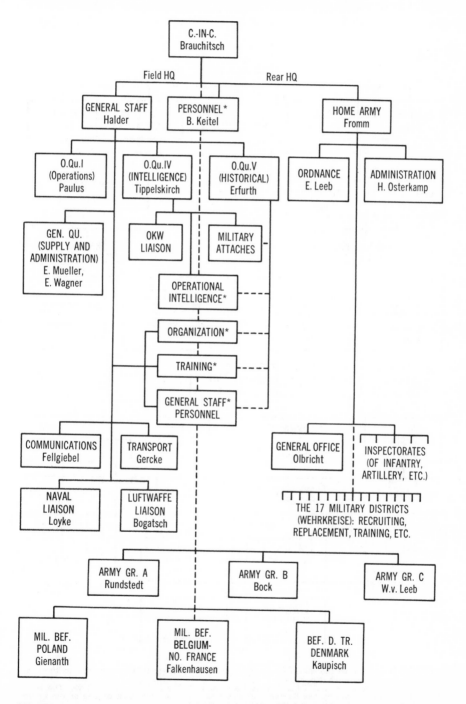

* The Personnel Department and the indicated branches of the General Staff were divided between the field and rear headquarters. The O.Qu.V exercised administrative command of the rear components of the General Staff. The positions of O.Qu.II (training) and O.Qu.III (organization) lapsed upon the outbreak of war; these functions were largely assumed by the Commander of the Home Army and his staff, but the General Staff retained small sections to handle the operational aspects.

CHART 4
Oberkommando der Kriegsmarine (OKM): August 1940

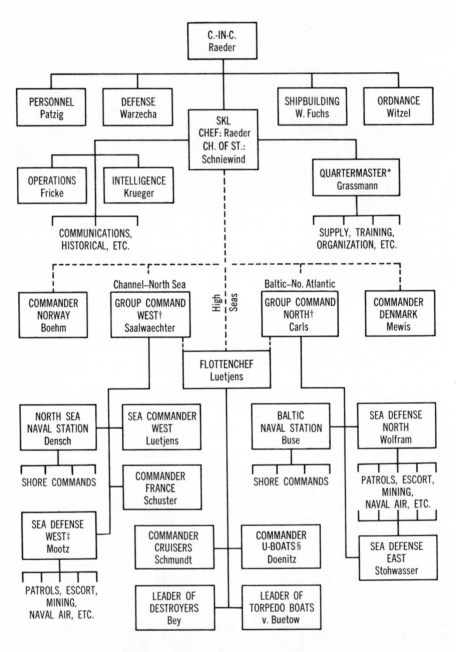

* This office was called the Marinekommandoamt, but its functions corresponded to those of a Quartermaster General's department.
† The boundary between Group Commands North and West was 53° north latitude. The High Seas Fleet (commanded by the Flottenchef) was under command of SKL or one of the group commands depending upon where the units were operating.
‡ The headquarters Sea Defense West was not established until October 1940; prior to that time the Flottenchef discharged these functions.
§ Commander U-boats was administratively subordinate to the Flottenchef until 1942, but operationally he reported directly to SKL.

CHART 5
High Command of the Luftwaffe (Ob.d.L. and RLM): August 1940

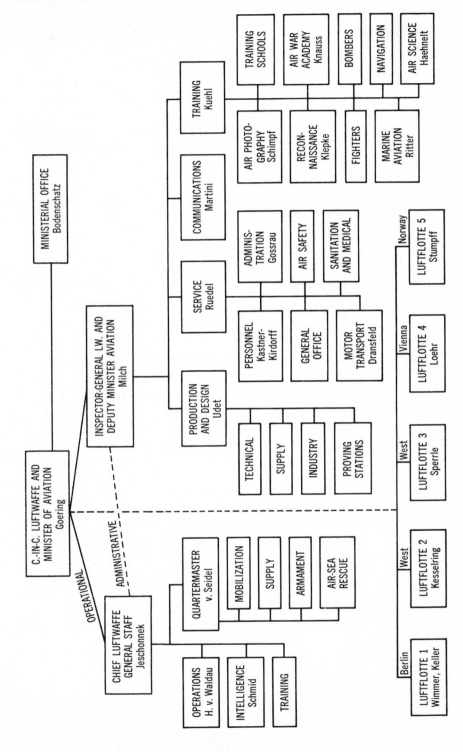

CHART **6**

Luftwaffe Order of Battle for the Adlerangriff: Early August 194C

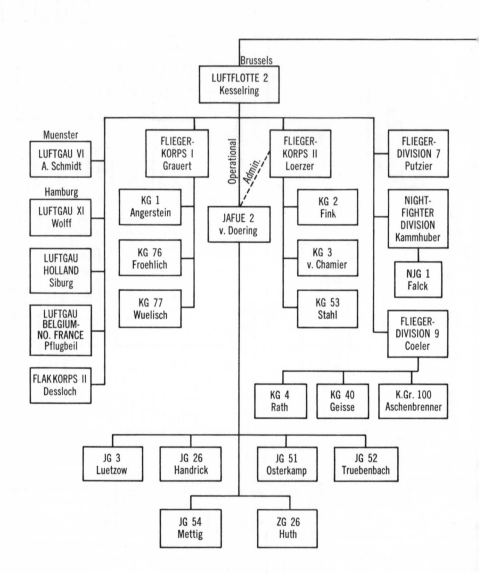

*The chart shows only major units, and omits separated *Gruppen*, reconnaissance and coastal units, etc.

†As explained in the text (*supra*, Page 93), the High Command of the Luftwaffe was not formally given that name (Oberkommando der Luftwaffe) until 1944. It is used here, as in the text, to designate Goering and his principal subordinates for operational command, including the General Staff under Jeschonnek. For detail see Chart 5.

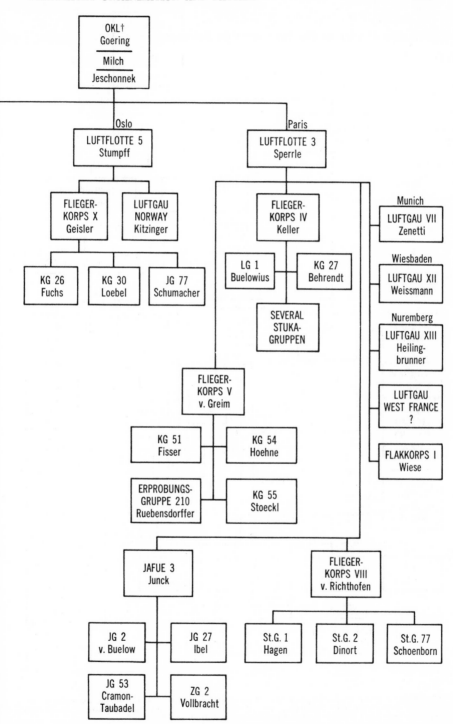

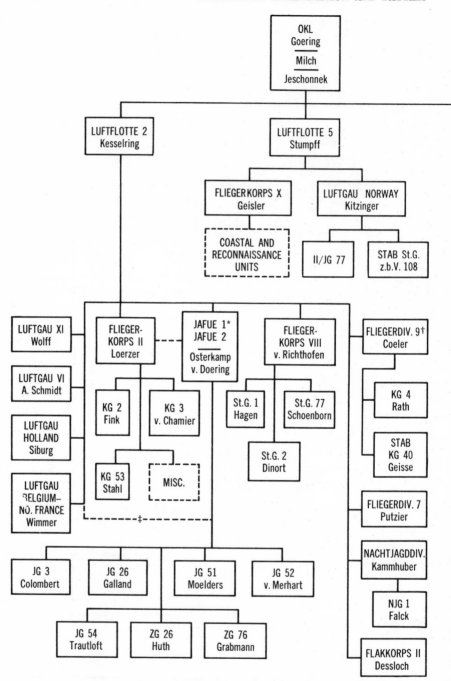

* Jagdfliegerfuehrer 1 was dropped, von Doering was transferred to the Air Ministry (RLM) as Inspector of Fighters, and Osterkamp, as Jagdfliegerfuehrer 2, assumed operational control of the fighter units in Luftflotte 2, sometime during the autumn of 1940.

CHART 7
Luftwaffe Order of Battle in the West: Late September 1940

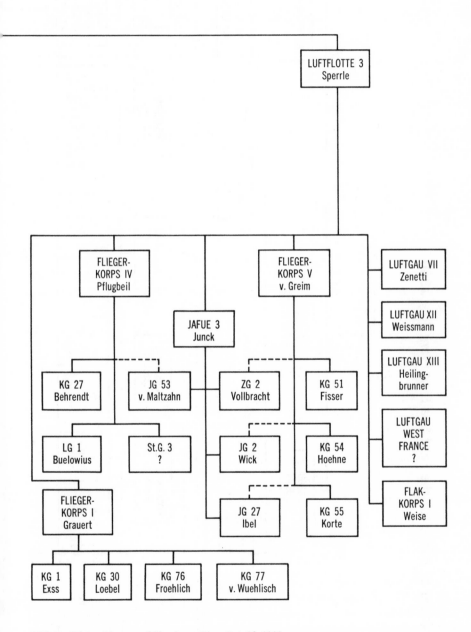

† Fliegerdivision 9 became Fliegerkorps IX on Oct. 16, 1940.
‡ Two *Gruppen* from JG 51 and JG 52, and six *Schwaerme* (four aircraft each) from JG 51, 52, and 54 were operationally subordinated to Luftgau VI, XI, and Holland.

CHART 8
Army Order of Battle for the First Sea Lion Plan: July 1940

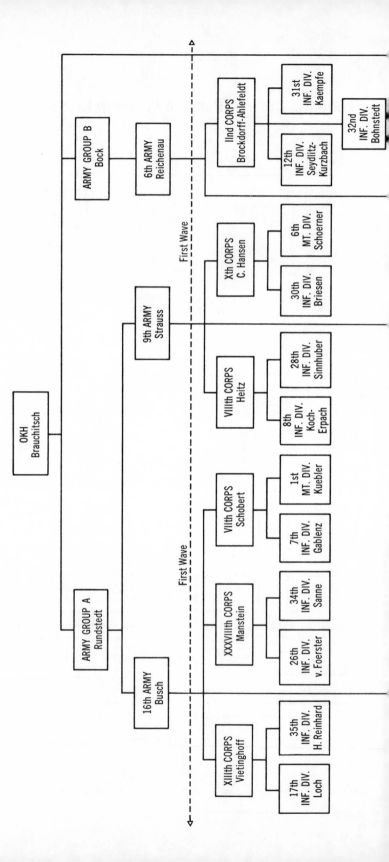

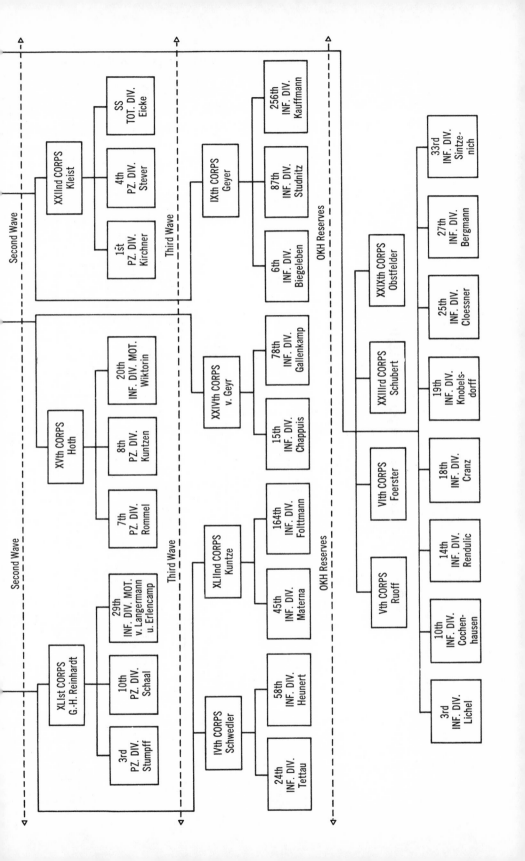

CHART 9
Army Order of Battle for the Second Sea Lion Plan: September 1940

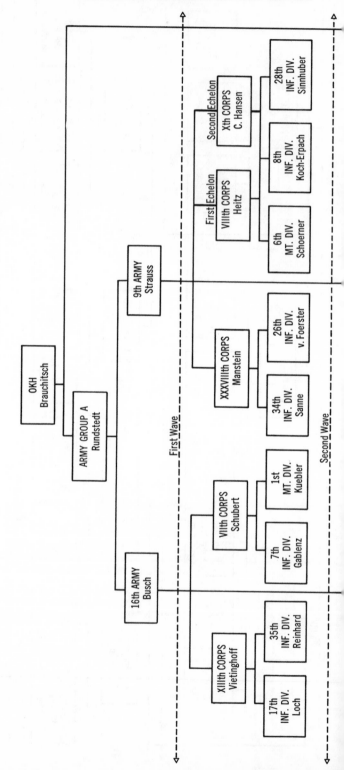

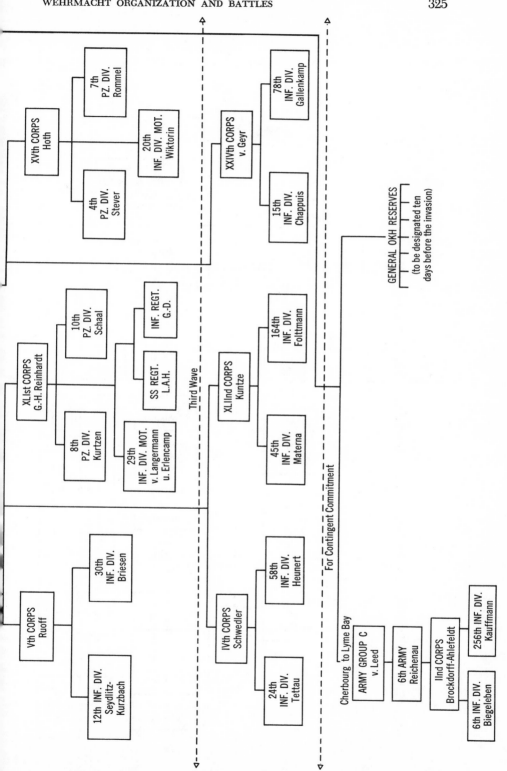

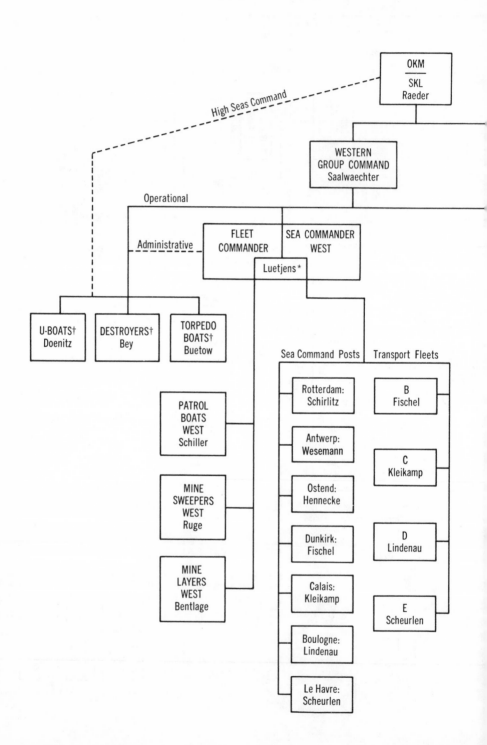

CHART **10**
Navy Order of Battle for Sea Lion

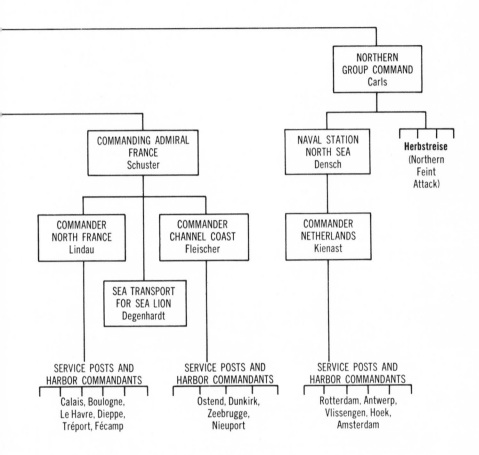

* Luetjens' regular assignment was Commander of the Fleet (Flottenchef); for tactical command of the invasion fleet he was given the additional title Seebefehlshaber West, which lapsed in October 1940, after Sea Lion had been indefinitely postponed.
† The submarine, destroyer, and torpedo-boat commands were administratively subordinate to the Flottenchef. For Sea Lion, operational command was to be exercised by the Western Group Command. On the high seas, beyond the command areas of the Western and Northern Group Commands, SKL took direct command of fleet operations.

Chapter Notes

IN THESE NOTES, the following abbreviations are used for some of the documentary sources cited.*

DGFP—*Documents on German Foreign Policy, 1918–1945.*

FCNA—*Fuehrer Conferences on Naval Affairs.*

Greiner KTB—*Kriegstagebuch des Oberkommandos der Wehrmacht* (the published OKW war diary, based on notes kept by Helmuth Greiner), Vol. I.

HD—Halder Diary, the shorthand diary kept by Generaloberst Franz Halder, Chief of the General Staff of the German Army.

MAB—Maxwell Air Force Base, Montgomery, Alabama, repository of captured Luftwaffe files.

KTB—Kriegstagebuch (war diary).

NCA—*Nazi Conspiracy and Aggression,* the "Red Book" series of Nuremberg documents, interrogations, etc.

N.D.—Nuremberg Documents.

SKL KTB—Seekriegsleitung Kriegstagebuch, war diary of the German Naval War Staff.

TMWC—*Trial of the Major War Criminals,* the "Blue Book" series of transcripts of testimony given and documents introduced at the first Nuremberg trial before the International Military Tribunal.

TWC—*Trials of War Criminals before the Nuremberg Military Tribunals,* the "Green Book" series of testimony and documents from the twelve subsequent Nuremberg trials.

---

* The sources are described more fully *infra,* pp. 355-58.

CHAPTER ONE

1. Bartz, *Als der Himmel brannte* (Hannover, 1955), p. 25; Taylor, *The March of Conquest* (1958), p. 357; von Hove, *Achtung Fallschirmjaeger* (1954), pp. 99-101; Ewan Butler and Gordon Young, *Marshal without Glory* (London: Hodder and Stoughton, 1951), p. 200.

2. Manstein, *Verlorene Siege* (Bonn, 1955), pp. 152-54, and *Lost Victories* (1958), pp. 152-54.

3. The memorandum is reproduced in English in *FCNA*, 1939, pp. 13-14, and is quoted in part in Taylor, *Sword and Swastika* (1952), pp. 348-49.

4. Churchill, *The Gathering Storm* (1948), p. 657; Taylor, *March of Conquest* (1958), pp. 153-54.

5. Doenitz, *Memoirs: Ten Years and Twenty Days* (1959), p. 31.

6. *Id.*, p. 47.

7. Richards, *Royal Air Force, 1939–1945* (1953), Vol. I, p. 152; Baumbach, *Zu Spaet?* (Munich, 1949), pp. 313-17; Suchenwirth, *Historical Turning Points in the German Air Force War Effort*, USAF Historical Studies, No. 189 (1959), pp. 66-67; Basil Collier, *The Defence of the United Kingdom* (London, 1957), p. 121; Churchill, *Their Finest Hour* (1949), p. 715.

8. Greiner *KTB*, Sept. 2, 1940.

9. *Id.*, Nov. 6, 1940; Richards, *op. cit. supra*, p. 410.

10. Capt. S. W. Roskill, *The War at Sea* (London: HMSO, 1954), Vol. I, pp. 61, 593-97; Marc' Antonio Bragadin, *The Italian Navy in World War II* (Annapolis: U.S. Naval Institute, 1957), pp. 3, 8-9.

11. *DGFP*, Vol. X (1957), No. 4.

12. These protocols are reproduced in English in *Nazi-Soviet Relations, 1939–1941* (Washington: U.S. Dept. of State, 1948), pp. 78, 107. The second protocol, by an attached map, indicated a small piece of Lithuanian territory which "should fall to Germany."

13. The diplomatic messages are reproduced *id.*, pp. 158-62. See also *DGFP*, Vol. X, Nos. 5, 8, 10, 13, 19, 25, 27.

14. *DGFP*, Vol. X, No. 156.

15. *Id.*, Nos. 162, 203-04, 251, 328.

16. *Id.*, Nos. 162, 332. See note 12, *supra*.

17. *Id.*, Nos. 317, 414.

18. *Id.*, Nos. 150, 182, 259.

19. Late in 1936 Germany and Japan concluded the Anti-Comintern Pact, and Italy adhered to it a year later, on Nov. 6, 1937. See *Ciano's Diplomatic Papers* (London, 1948), pp. 138-47.

20. HD, July 31, 1940.

21. *DGFP*, Vol. IX, No. 4 (Apr. 24, 1940).

22. *Id.*, No. 236 (May 11, 1940). See also, e.g., Sherwood, *Roosevelt and Hopkins* (1948), pp. 147-51.

23. *DGFP*, Vol. IX, No. 311 (May 24, 1940).

24. Churchill, *Their Finest Hour* (1949), p. 402; Sherwood, *op. cit.*, p. 149.

25. There is no reference to these American arms shipments in HD or FCNA.

26. Interview with Karl von Wiegand, reported in *Facts in Review*, Vol. II, No. 32 (Aug. 5, 1940), p. 378. This was a publication of the German Library of Information in New York during the period 1939–41.

27. HD, July 22, 1940; *FCNA, 1940*, p. 71 (July 21).

28. For the details of the negotiations see Sherwood, *op. cit.*, pp. 141, 175; Churchill, *op. cit.*, pp. 24-25, 398-416. Transfer of over-age destroyers was approved by the Attorney General, Robert H. Jackson, in an opinion which disapproved the transfer of "mosquito boats" then

under construction. 39 *Opinions of the Attorney-General* 411, 494-96.

29. HD, Aug. 23, 1940.

30. *FCNA, 1940*, p. 94 (Sept. 6).

31. The events in Japan and Japanese actions leading up to the Tripartite Pact are set forth in the *Judgment of the International Military Tribunal for the Far East* (Nov. 1, 1948), Vol. II, Part B, Ch. ɪᴠ, pp. 285, 314-17, 339, 369, 395-98, 410, 467, 501-03.

32. *Ciano's Diplomatic Papers*, pp. 242-46 (Oct. 28, 1938). For the course of negotiations with the Italians see also pp. 258, 281-87, 388-93, and Ciano, *Diario*, Vol. I, entries in 1939 for Jan. 1, 2, 7, Feb. 5, 8, Mar. 3, 6–8, Apr. 2, 25–28, May 5–7, 14, 17, 21, and in 1940 for Sept. 22–28.

33. There were two military Eugen Otts. This one had been military attaché in Tokyo and had retired from the Army upon his appointment as ambassador in 1938. The other was, at this time, a *General-leutnant* attached to OKH as infantry specialist.

34. The text is N.D. 2643-PS.

35. See the discussion of the merits of a "passive strategy" in Fleming, *Operation Sea Lion* (1957), pp. 305-09, and Taylor, *March of Conquest*, pp. 359-60.

36. Giulio Douhet, *The Command of the Air* (London, 1943), pp. 18-19. Douhet's book was first published in Italian in 1921. See the discussion of his doctrine in Theodore Ropp, *War in the Modern World* (Durham, N.C.: Duke Univ. Press, 1959), pp. 271-75.

37. In his speech in Parliament on June 4, 1940, quoted in Churchill, *Their Finest Hour*, p. 118.

38. See the discussions in Fleming, *op. cit.*, pp. 300-05, and Taylor, *March of Conquest*, p. 362.

39. *Infra*, pp. 72-75.

40. See Taylor, *March of Conquest*, pp. 363-65, and *infra*, pp. 72-75.

CHAPTER TWO

1. N.D. 1776-PS.

2. *Infra*, pp. 105-06.

3. N.D. L-79. See Taylor, *Sword and Swastika*, pp. 264-78.

4. *Infra*, pp. 201-04.

5. N.D. C-62, Oct. 9, 1939 (Directive No. 6).

6. N.D. L-52, Oct. 9, 1939. See the discussion of these documents in Taylor, *March of Conquest*, pp. 43-46, 158.

7. Directive No. 9 for the Conduct of the War. This and all the other major military directives issued by Hitler or by his authority from the outbreak of the war to Aug. 1, 1940, are listed and summarized in Appendix D of *March of Conquest*, pp. 433-36.

8. *FCNA, 1940*, pp. 50-51 (May 21).

9. Raeder, *Struggle for the Sea* (London, 1959), pp. 177-79. Raeder's account is generally confirmed by the official German naval historian, Assmann, *Deutsche Schicksalsjahre* (Wiesbaden, 1950), p. 171; see also Wheatley, *Operation Sea Lion* (London, 1958), p. 15. Raeder's minutes of the conference (*FCNA*) state only that Hitler and Raeder "discuss in private details concerning the invasion of England, which the Naval Staff has been working on since November."

10. See Taylor, *March of Conquest*, pp. 252-65.

11. Directive No. 13 for the Conduct of the War, May 24, 1940.

12. The order for the Somme-Aisne offensive was given by Directive No. 13 for the Conduct of the War, issued on May 24.

13. *FCNA, 1940*, p. 55 (June 4). The next day Raeder reported to the Naval War Staff that Hitler anticipated the defeat of France "within a few weeks" (SKL KTB, entry for June 5, 1940).

14. N.D. 2353-PS, p. 320.

15. Directive No. 15 for the Conduct of the War, June 14, 1940.

16. HD, July 15, 1940. The directive is quoted in part in Wheatley, *op. cit.*, p. 16, and J. R. M. Butler, *Grand Strategy* (London, 1957), Vol. II, pp. 265-66, 270.

17. Wheatley, *op. cit.*, p. 16, quoting an SKL war-diary entry dated June 18, 1940.

18. *Ciano's Diplomatic Papers*, pp. 372-75; Ciano, *Diario*, June 18-19, 1940; Paul Schmidt, *Hitler's Interpreter* (New York: Macmillan, 1951), pp. 177-78; *DGFP*, Vol. IX, No. 479. On June 17 Warlimont had told Fricke that the conditions for peace with Britain would be "the return of the German colonies and the renunciation of British influence in Europe." Wheatley, *op. cit.*, p. 17, quoting the SKL war diary.

19. Schmidt, *op. cit.*, pp. 178-79.

20 *FCNA, 1940*, pp. 58-60 (June 20). Goering had sent "a rude telegram" in response to Raeder's request that certain Luftwaffe units be left at Trondheim and Narvik. Hitler directed that "in the future his decision on such questions be sought through OKW." Early in August, Goering sent Raeder a letter of apology (*id.*, pp. 141-42).

21. HD, June 23, 1940; OKW/WFA notes on the conference, recorded the next day; Wheatley, *op. cit.*, p. 18.

22. Klee, *Das Unternehmen "Seeloewe"* (Goettingen, 1958), p. 61. The document is reproduced in Klee, *Dokumente zum Unternehmen "Seeloewe"* (Goettingen, 1959), No. 7, and is discussed *infra*, p. 207.

23. Greiner, *Die Oberste Wehrmachtfuehrung* (Wiesbaden, 1951), p. 110.

24. Lossberg, *Im Wehrmachtfuehrungsstab* (Hamburg, 1949), p. 86.

25. Kreipe, "The Battle of Brit-ain," in *The Fatal Decisions,* ed. Freidin and Richardson (1956), p. 13.

26. Greiner, *Oberste Wehrmachtfuehrung,* p. 110. One of Hitler's companions was Max Amann, who is believed to have been Hitler's company sergeant during the First World War, and who had since become a high Nazi Party official, with the title "Reichsleiter fuer die Presse" (MS. C-0656—Greiner memorandum on the OKW).

27. Lossberg, *op. cit.*, pp. 85-86. For a description of Leeb's assault on the Maginot Line see Taylor, *March of Conquest,* pp. 300, 304-05.

28. Lossberg, *loc. cit. supra.*

29. Ciano, *Diario*, June 30, 1940.

30. DGFP, Vol. X, No. 76.

31. Ciano, *Diario*, July 2, 1940.

32. *DGFP*, Vol. X, No. 73.

33. Unsigned memorandum dated June 28, 1940, entitled "Kriegsfuehrung gegen England," of which 9 copies were distributed within the high command.

34. N.D. 1776-PS, discussed *supra*, pp. 44-46.

35. The directive is reproduced in English in *FCNA, 1940,* pp. 61-62, and in German in Klee, *Dokumente zum Unternehmen "Seeloewe,"* No. 9.

36. Mueller-Hillebrand, *Das Heer,* Vol. II (Frankfurt-a.-M., 1956), p. 64; N.D. NOKW-1038 and NOKW-3437; *Die Hoeheren Dienststellen der deutschen Wehrmacht* (Munich: Institut fuer Zeitgeschichte, 1953), p. 30. Kuechler, whose headquarters was removed from France on July 5, became the highest military commander in the east until von Bock's arrival there in the autumn. Kuechler's divisions were grouped under six corps headquarters (III, XVII, XIX, XXVI, XXX, and XXXIV) transferred from France. For Kuechler's order to his troops to refrain from criticism of

Nazi racial policies in Poland, see Taylor, *March of Conquest*, pp. 74-75.

37. N.D. 1783-PS. Bock's Army Group B occupied the Biscay coast, with the 7th Army in the south (Bordeaux area) and the 4th Army in the north (Royan to Quimper). Rundstedt's Army Group A was deployed along the Channel coast and in Belgium and northern France, with the 6th Army in Brittany and Normandy, the 16th Army between Le Havre and Ostend, and the 9th Army in Belgium and northeastern France. Leeb's Army Group C was in the interior, with the 2nd Army in the Paris–Orléans area, the 1st Army around Strasbourg, Metz, and Nancy, and the 12th Army in southern Alsace and the Juras.

38. HD, June 24–July 6, 1940.

39. HD, July 1, 1940.

40. HD, July 6, 1940. Bockelberg was 66 years old, and had gone on the retired list in 1933. At the end of July 1940 he was relieved of his assignment, and went back to retirement.

41. For the development of the military occupational system in France and the other countries occupied by Germany in 1940 see Taylor, *March of Conquest*, pp. 324-36.

42. HD, June 22, 1940.

43. HD, June 30.

44. HD, July 1.

45. *Ibid.*

46. HD, July 2, 1940.

47. Wheatley, *op. cit.*, pp. 19-28; *infra*, pp. 204-07.

48. See, e.g., Doenitz, *Memoirs*, pp. 84-99, 110-12.

49. Frischauer, *The Rise and Fall of Hermann Goering* (1951), pp. 193-95.

50. The first mention of the projected Paris parade is in the OKW directive of June 19, *supra*, p. 51.

51. For a fuller account of the Paris project see Taylor, *March of*

Conquest, pp. 344-45. On July 14 Halder noted in his diary a "rumored threat to German parade by British Air Force."

52. HD, July 5, 1940.

53. HD, July 8.

54. *Ciano's Diplomatic Papers*, p. 375.

55. Ciano, *Diario*, Vol. I, p. 291 (July 7, 1940).

56. *FCNA, 1940*, p. 64 (July 11).

57. Schmidt, *Hitler's Interpreter*, p. 185.

58. The official English translation of Hitler's speech of July 19, 1940, is printed in *Facts in Review* (German Library of Information, New York), Vol. II, No. 32 (Aug. 5, 1940), pp. 362-75.

59. For a vivid eyewitness description and for an analysis of the military significance of the speech, see respectively Shirer, *Berlin Diary* (1941), pp. 452-57, and Taylor, *March of Conquest*, pp. 344-51.

60. Schmidt, *Hitler's Interpreter*, pp. 185-87.

61. Weizsaecker, *Memoirs* (1951), pp. 236-38. *Cf.* Ciano's observation (*Diario*, July 19, 1940) that the cold British press reaction to Hitler's speech spread an ill-concealed sense of disappointment among the Germans.

62. Churchill, *Their Finest Hour* (1949), pp. 260-61.

63. Ciano, *Diario*, entries for July 20 and 22, 1940; *Ciano's Diplomatic Papers*, p. 381.

64. *DGFP*, Vol. X, No. 129.

65. *Ibid.*; Ciano, *Diario*, July 7, 1940; *Ciano's Diplomatic Papers*, pp. 376-77.

66. *Ciano's Diplomatic Papers*, pp. 378-79.

67. *FCNA, 1940*, pp. 64-65.

68. HD, July 13, 1940.

69. *Ibid.* Actually, 17 divisions (infantry, largely second-line) were disbanded; some of the staffs were used to form local occupation head-

quarters in Poland (Mueller-Hillebrand, *Das Heer*, Vol. II, p. 63; HD, July 14, 1940). This left the Army establishment at about 140 divisions.

70. *DGFP*, Vol. X, No. 166; Ciano, *Diario*, July 16, 1940.

71. *DGFP*, Vol. X, No. 185.

72. N.D. 1781-PS, entitled "Erste Ueberlegungen ueber eine Landung in England"; Wheatley, *op. cit.*, pp. 34-35; Klee, *Das Unternehmen "Seeloewe,"* pp. 72-73.

73. N.D. 442-PS, reproduced in full in *FCNA, 1940*, pp. 67-69.

74. Kesselring, *A Soldier's Record* (1954), pp. 68-69; Bartz, *Als der Himmel brannte*, pp. 39-40.

75. Raeder's memorandum is quoted *in extenso* in *FCNA, 1940*, pp. 69-70.

76. *FCNA, 1940*, pp. 71-73; Wheatley, *op. cit.*, pp. 42-43; Klee, *Das Unternehmen "Seeloewe,"* pp. 80-81; HD, July 22, 1940.

77. *FCNA, 1940*, p. 73; Klee, *op. cit. supra*, p. 81.

78. *FCNA, 1940*, pp. 74-75.

79. *DGFP*, Vol. X, Nos. 233, 234, 244, 245, 248.

80. HD, July 28, 1940.

81. HD, July 29.

82. Wheatley, *op. cit.*, pp. 45-46, citing the SKL memorandum and war diary, July 29–30, 1940.

83. *Infra*, p. 129.

84. *FCNA, 1940*, pp. 76-81; HD, July 31, 1940; see also the notes made by Greiner for the OKW war diary ("Entwuerfe zum Kriegestagebuch des Wfst") on Aug. 1, 1940, based on information furnished by Jodl.

85. OKW directive dated Aug. 1, 1940, issued over Keitel's signature. It is set forth in full in *FCNA, 1940*, pp. 81-82.

86. Directive No. 17 for the Conduct of the War, Aug. 1, 1940.

87. "Vorbereitungen und Weisungen fuer Unternehmen 'Adler,'" issued by OKL Aug. 2.

88. *Supra*, pp. 64-65.

89. HD, July 22, 1940.

90. HD, July 30.

91. See Taylor, *Sword and Swastika*, pp. 36-42.

92. Greiner, *Oberste Wehrmachtfuehrung*, pp. 116-18; *TMWC*, Vol. XV, pp. 390-91 (testimony of Jodl).

93. *Supra*, pp. 70-71.

94. HD, July 31, 1940.

95. Greiner, *Oberste Wehrmachtfuehrung*, pp. 288-94.

96. *The German Campaign in Russia: Planning and Operations, 1940–1942*, U.S. Dept. of the Army Pamphlet No. 20-261a (1955), pp. 6-12.

CHAPTER THREE

1. See, e.g., Sir Arthur Bryant, *The Turn of the Tide* (New York: Doubleday, 1957), p. 162: ". . . the odds against the British fighters were at least two to one." As will appear, statistical comparisons are complicated, but the implication that German fighters outnumbered their British opponents by any such margin is demonstrably unsound.

2. Wheatley, *Operation Sea Lion;* Fleming, *Operation Sea Lion;* Klee, *Das Unternehmen "Seeloewe."*

3. See the bibliography, *infra*, pp. 358-61.

4. See Edward Warner's study of Douhet, Mitchell, and Seversky in *Makers of Modern Strategy*, ed. Edward Meade Earle (Princeton, N.J.: Princeton Univ. Press, 1948), pp. 485-503.

5. Harris, *Bomber Offensive* (London, 1947), pp. 53-54, 269-70.

6. Harris, *op. cit.*, p. 26; Spaight, *Bombing Vindicated* (London, 1944), pp. 37-38; Richards, *Royal Air Force, 1939–1945*, Vol. I (London, 1953), p. 20; Webster and Frankland, *The Strategic Air Offensive against Germany, 1939–1945* (London, 1961), Vol. I, pp. 65-81.

7. *TMWC,* Vol. IX, pp. 60-61 (testimony of Milch) and 203-06 (testimony of Kesselring); Suchenwirth, *Historical Turning Points in the German Air Force War Effort,* USAF Historical Studies, No. 189 (1959), pp. 40-44; Baumbach, *The Life and Death of the Luftwaffe* (1960), pp. 104-06.

8. The material in this section, unless otherwise noted, is based on Basil Collier, *The Defence of the United Kingdom* (1957), and Richards, *Royal Air Force, 1939–1945,* Vol. I (1953). Both are official accounts, published by Her Majesty's Stationery Office, London. See also Wykeham, *Fighter Command* (London, 1960).

9. M. N. Postan, D. Hay, and J. D. Scott, *Design and Development of Weapons* (London: HMSO, 1964), p. 123.

10. Watson-Watt, *Three Steps to Victory* (London, 1957); see also Sir Robert Watson-Watt's other account, No. 484 in the interview series of the Oral History Research Office of Columbia University, on deposit in the university's Butler Library.

11. Sir Robert Watson-Watt's two accounts (*supra,* note 10) are not identical; according to his book, the "culprit" was an assistant military attaché, Captain de Brantes.

12. Churchill, *Their Finest Hour,* pp. 12-15.

13. The material in this and the succeeding sections is based on a variety of sources, as indicated in the bibliography, *infra,* pp. 358-61. Where necessary, I have given specific citations.

14. According to a memorandum by Beppo Schmid (p. 31) in MAB file Western-V-3d, Luftschlacht-Ablauf.

15. *Cf.* Basil Collier, *The Battle of Britain* (London, 1962), p. 57. The Luftwaffe was not unique in this respect; throughout the Wehrmacht, staff intelligence was poor.

16. Collier, *Defence of the United Kingdom,* pp. 161, 452.

17. Richards, *op. cit.,* p. 410.

18. In Middleton, *The Sky Suspended* (1960), p. 40, the "over-all strength" of the Luftwaffe on Aug. 10 is given as "4,295 aircraft of which 3,242 were combat planes ready for action." These are apparently official conclusions of the British Air Ministry, as the constituent figures (though not the "over-all") are identical with those in Collier, *Defence of the United Kingdom,* p. 452, note 8.

19. Richards, *op. cit.,* p. 157; Lee, *The German Air Force* (London, 1946), p. 64; Lee, *Blitz on Britain* (London, 1960), p. 44.

20. A little on the high side are Churchill, *Their Finest Hour,* p. 523 (2,669 aircraft); Bryant, *The Turn of the Tide* (1957), p. 162 (2,700 aircraft); Goerlitz, *Der Zweite Weltkrieg* (Stuttgart, 1951), p. 159 (Churchill's figures); Kreipe, "The Battle of Britain," in *The Fatal Decisions,* ed. Freidin and Richardson (1956), p. 14 (2,830 aircraft). A little low is Tippelskirch, *Geschichte des zweiten Weltkriegs* (Bonn, 1951), p. 119 (2,200 aircraft). As accurate as circumstances permit is Collier, *Defence of the United Kingdom,* p. 452, with a figure of 2,355. The Luftwaffe Quartermaster General's records for Aug. 10 show 2,470 serviceable aircraft, excluding short-range reconnaissance planes; see "The Course of the Air War against England" (July 7, 1944), prepared by the OKL historical division and now at MAB. Bartz, *Als der Himmel brannte,* p. 50, gives a figure of 2,510 on the same basis. Excluding all reconnaissance planes and including only bombers, dive bombers, and single- and twin-engined fighters, Gen. Stapf reported the strength to

Gen. Halder on July 29 (HD) as 2,425 aircraft. At an OKW operational conference of Aug. 8, the Luftwaffe representative (on the same basis) reported that 2,422 aircraft were *"einsatzbare,"* ready for commitment (Greiner *KTB*, Aug. 8, 1940). The Luftwaffe Quartermaster General's figures for Aug. 3, as given in Suchenwirth, *op. cit.*, pp. 64-65, are roughly comparable.

21. Churchill, *Their Finest Hour*, pp. 715-16.

22. The figures broken down by Luftwaffe aircraft types are based on Greiner, Collier, and the Quartermaster General's records, all *supra*, note 20.

23. These attacks are described in Richards, *op. cit.*, pp. 161-64, 181.

24. *Infra*, pp. 151-58.

25. Richards, *op. cit.*, p. 156; Churchill, *Their Finest Hour*, pp. 716-17; Collier, *Defence*, pp. 162, 453-55.

26. For a somewhat romanticized but readable account of this remarkable aircraft see Gallico, *The Hurricane Story* (1960).

27. Bryant, *Turn of the Tide* p. 162; Lee, *Blitz on Britain*, p. 45.

28. Lee, *op. cit.*, p. 13.

29. Richards, *op. cit.*, p. 156.

30. *Id.*, pp. 152, 191; Churchill, *Their Finest Hour*, p. 715; Weber, *Die Luftschlacht um England* (1956), pp. 90-94; Baumbach, *Zu Spaet?* (Munich, 1949), pp. 313-17.

31. Richards, *op. cit.*, p. 156.

32. *Id.*, p. 176; Collier, *Defence*, pp. 154, 167, 200.

33. *The Rise and Fall of the German Air Force*, British Air Ministry Pamphlet No. 248 (1948), p. 33; Lee, *op. cit.*, pp. 29-40.

34. Wood and Dempster, *The Narrow Margin* (1961), pp. 345-48.

35. There is a vivid and rueful description of this most important feature of the Battle of Britain in

Galland, *The First and the Last* (1954), pp. 23-24, 27.

36. Knoke, *I Flew for the Fuehrer* (London, 1953), pp. 21-38, traces the author's training from his induction in November 1939 to his posting to a front-line unit in May 1941.

37. See Taylor, *Sword and Swastika*, pp. 40-41; Craig, *The Politics of the Prussian Army* (1955), pp. 410-24.

38. See Taylor, *March of Conquest*, pp. 138-41, 229-33.

39. Bross, *Gespraeche mit Hermann Goering* (Flensburg, 1955), p. 191.

40. Note, e.g., the paucity of reference to aviation in Hitler's recorded conversations: *Hitler's Secret Conversations* (1953), index, pp. 589-97.

41. N.D. L-79, quoted *supra*, p. 47.

CHAPTER FOUR

1. *TMWC*, Vol. IX, p. 281.

2. *Id.*, p. 205.

3. *Id.*, pp. 60-61.

4. Genlt. a. D. Andreas Nielsen, *The German Air Force General Staff*, USAF Historical Studies, No. 173 (1959), pp. 156-58.

5. These and other details of the prewar Luftwaffe studies are derived from an unpublished memorandum prepared at Hamburg in 1955 by Karl Klee, now in the archives at MAB, entitled "Operation 'Sea Lion' and the Role Planned for the Luftwaffe," and based on contemporaneous Luftwaffe documents, many of which are also available at MAB. Other pertinent Luftwaffe records are available at the Departmental Records Branch in Alexandria, Va. See also Gundelach, "Gedanken ueber die Fuehrung eines Luftkrieges gegen England," in *Wehrwissenschaftliche Rundschau*, January 1960, pp. 33-46.

6. See Taylor, *March of Conquest,* pp. 61-62. Testifying at Nuremberg (*United States v. List,* Nuremberg Case No. 7, mimeographed transcript, pp. 6892-96), Felmy attributed his dismissal in 1940 to Goering's lasting displeasure, caused by Felmy's 1938 memorandum.

7. See Taylor, *op. cit.,* pp. 75-76.

8. Lord Tedder, *Air Power in War* (London, 1947), p. 94.

9. See Taylor, *op. cit.,* pp. 41-64.

10. N.D. C-62.

11. N.D. L-52.

12. For the development of *Fall Gelb* through its various stages see Taylor, *op. cit.,* pp. 155-86.

13. *Jodl Diary,* Nov. 28, 1939; OKL Chef 1. Abt. memorandum Nov. 22, 1939, in the Von Rohden collection, series 4376, item 111. It was proposed that three *Kampfgeschwader* from Fliegerkorps X be used, with JG 27 as escort.

14. Quoted *supra,* pp. 47-48.

15. Directive No. 13 for the Conduct of the War, May 24, 1940.

16. Richards, *Royal Air Force, 1939–1945,* Vol. I, pp. 121-24; Webster and Frankland, *op. cit.,* Vol. I, pp. 144-49.

17. See *infra,* pp. 155-58.

18. According to Kesselring, Wever regarded Douhet as a "model" (*Vorbild*). Kesselring, *Soldat bis zum letzten Tag* [Bonn, 1953], p. 460. See also Baumbach, *Life and Death of the Luftwaffe,* pp. 21, 60.

19. *Supra,* p. 83.

20. *Over-all Report* (European War) of the United States Strategic Bombing Survey, Sept. 30, 1945, pp. 1, 3.

21. Adm. Sir Gerald Dickens, *Bombing and Strategy* (London: Sampson, Low, Marston & Co., 1946), pp. 3-5.

22. Webster and Frankland, *op. cit.,* Vol. I, pp. 86-106, and Vol. IV, pp. 99-102. Speaking in the House of Commons on June 21, 1938, Prime Minister Chamberlain declared that it was against international law deliberately to attack civilian populations, and that strategic air raids should be conducted so as to minimize civilian destruction; see Butler, *Grand Strategy,* Vol. II, *September 1939–June 1941* (London, 1957), pp. 567-68.

23. Spaight, *Bombing Vindicated* (1944), pp. 129-38.

24. The discussion of Guernica does not appear in the American edition of Galland's book, *The First and the Last* (1954), as it occurs in one of the omitted early chapters, to the typescript of which I was kindly given access by the publishers, Henry Holt and Co.

25. *Deutschland im Kampf: Die Berichte des Oberkommandos der Wehrmacht, 1. Sept. 1939 bis 31. Dez. 1940,* ed. Berndt and von Wedel (Berlin, 194?), p. 176.

26. The war diary of Army Group C includes the message from the 7th Army, dated May 11, 1940, and initialed by both von Leeb, commander-in-chief of Army Group C, and Felber, his chief of staff.

27. Fuller, *The Second World War* (1949), p. 222. Gen. Fuller's error was due in part to a misreading of passages in Spaight, *op. cit.,* pp. 40, 44, 68, 74, which reported, but did not accept, the German accusation.

28. For the story of the *Athenia* see Taylor, *Sword and Swastika,* pp. 343-53.

29. This story first appeared in a book by a former concentration-camp inmate, Isa Vermehren, entitled *Reise durch den letzten Akt* (Hamburg, 1946), and was based on the author's conversation with Gen. Halder at Dachau in April 1945. In 1947 Halder confirmed the conversation and explained that his sources of information had been Adm. Wilhelm Canaris (head of the

338

OKW intelligence service, who was executed in 1945) and a Luftwaffe general who knew of the report based on examination of the bomb fragments; the general, whom Halder did not name, was subsequently identified as Generalmajor Spruner von Merz, the senior air ordnance officer in the area. See *Dokumentation der Zeit*, Heft 84 (Dec. 15, 1954), p. 6161, a publication of the East German organization called Deutsches Institut fuer Zeitgeschichte in Berlin; *Stuttgarter Zeitung* for Dec. 6, 1947; *Die Neue Zeitung* for Dec. 5, 1947; *Marburger Presse*, Dec. 3 and 5, 1947; *Koelnische Rundschau*, Dec. 9, 1947.

30. In 1954, at the request of the Baden-Wuertemberg provincial government, an investigation was undertaken by the Institut fuer Zeitgeschichte in Munich. The report, upon which much of the account in the text is based, was published in the Institute's organ, *Vierteljahrshefte fuer Zeitgeschichte*, Heft 2 (April 1956), pp. 115-44, in the form of an article by Anton Hoch entitled "Der Luftangriff auf Freiburg am 10. Mai 1940." See also *The New York Times*, Apr. 5, 1956, pp. 1, 7.

31. Baumbach, *The Life and Death of the Luftwaffe* (1960), p. 70. The book is an abbreviated translation of Baumbach, *Zu Spaet?* (Munich, 1949).

32. *Facts in Review*, Vol. II, No. 22 (May 27, 1940), p. 217.

33. From the text of Hitler's speech in *Facts in Review*, Vol. II, No. 32 (Aug. 5, 1940), pp. 362-75.

34. The night attacks of June 5 and 6, 1940, are described in Richards, *Royal Air Force, 1939–1945*, Vol. I, p. 158, and Collier, *Defence of the United Kingdom*, pp. 156-57. Another source lists three, rather than two, raids: on the nights of June 4, 5, and 7 (Macmillan, *The Royal Air Force in the World War*,

Vol. II [London, 1944], p. 307). The official OKW communiqués (*Wehrmachtberichte*) reported bombing attacks on the nights of June 5 and 6, and armed reconnaissance on the night of June 7, in the course of which a few British airports and the harbor of Dover were attacked (Berndt and von Wedel, *Deutschland im Kampf*, Nos. 19-20 [June 1940]). The Luftwaffe liaison officer at OKM reported night attacks on June 5 and 6 and plans for renewed attacks on the night of June 7 (SKL KTB, Part D, Luftlage for those dates).

35. SKL KTB, Ops. Div., Part A, June 21, 1940, and Part D, Luftlage, same date.

36. Civilian casualties were also light, though 9 people were killed at Cambridge on the night of June 18 (Richards, *op. cit.;* Collier, *op. cit.*, pp. 157-59; Macmillan, *op. cit.*, p. 130). There were raids on the nights of June 18, 19, 21, and 24–29 inclusive.

37. Richards, *op. cit.*, pp. 198-201.

38. SKL KTB, Part D, Luftlage for June 23, 1940.

39. *"Ein Plan fuer die B. of B. existierte bei der deutschen Fuehrung nicht."* The quotation is at p. 5 of a memorandum written by Schmid in 1945, entitled "Der I-C Dienst der Luftwaffe und das Luftkrieg gegen England," in file G-Westen-V-3a, Luftschlacht um England (Vorbereitungen), at MAB.

40. OKL No. 5835/40, "Allgemeine Weisung fuer den Kampf der Luftwaffe gegen England." Copies are available at MAB.

41. Heinkel, *Stormy Life* (1956), pp. 125-27, 211.

42. Collier, *op. cit.*, pp. 163-64.

43. By Sir Edward Grigg, then parliamentary secretary to the Minister of Information. See Bishop, *The*

Battle of Britain (London, 1960), p. 18.

44. Churchill, *Their Finest Hour*, p. 321; Collier, *op. cit.*, p. 165; Middleton, *The Sky Suspended* (1960), p. 73.

45. "Weisung fuer der Verschaerfte Luftkriegsfuehrung gegen England," Fu/St 5841/40. No copy has come to light, but the document is listed and described in a "Combat Calendar" prepared by the historical section of the OKL staff at Karlsbad in 1944 (available as document 207 of series 4376 of the Von Rohden collection), and in Karl Klee's 1955 memorandum on Sea Lion (*supra*, note 5), p. 169a. See also Wheatley, *Operation Sea Lion* (1958), p. 59, quoting an order issued by Luftflotte 5 on July 13, based on the directive of July 11.

46. Osterkamp, *Durch Hoehen und Tiefen jagt ein Herz* (Heidelberg, 1952), pp. 328-40; Kesselring, *A Soldier's Record* (1954), p. 65.

47. Richards, *op. cit.*, Vol. I, p. 159; Collier, *op. cit.*, p. 170.

48. The official British figures vary slightly as between Churchill, *Their Finest Hour*, p. 339, and Collier, *op. cit.*, pp. 170-71, 450-51. The Germans' records of their own losses closely approximate those given in the text; see the chart, item 56 in series 4376 of the Von Rohden collection.

49. See the descriptions of the July and early-August fighting in Collier, *op. cit.*, pp. 167-74, and Osterkamp, *op. cit.*, pp. 318-24, 328-40.

50. Galland, *The First and the Last* (1954), pp. 19-30. JG 26 (Schlageter) was then commanded by Maj. Gotthardt Handrick. Galland regards July 24 as opening the "second phase" of the Battle of Britain, following the "first phase" of redeployment. But this date seems to be important only as the day on which

Galland's units became operational; other squadrons, such as Osterkamp's, had already been in action, and no doubt still others started later. JG 26 commenced operations at the Channel on July 21 (Priller, *Geschichte eines Jagdgeschwaders* [Heidelberg, 1956], pp. 66-70).

51. HD, July 11, 1940. See also KTB Fu. Abt. H.Gr. A, July 17, reporting Goering's prediction that air superiority would be achieved within 4 weeks after the beginning of the air battle.

52. Frischauer, *The Rise and Fall of Hermann Goering* (1951), p. 193.

53. The notes prepared for the conference by several sections of the OKL staff are included in the Von Rohden collection, series 4376, item 114. See also the memorandum of July 16 (apparently prepared for the same meeting), in file Westen-V-3g, Luftschlacht um England 1940, at MAB.

54. The Fuehrer's directive for Sea Lion (No. 16, of July 16, 1940) had come out less than a week earlier.

55. The Karinhall conference of July 21 is described in item 114, series 4376 of the Von Rohden collection, and in MAB file Westen-V-3g, Luftschlacht um England.

56. The Fliegerkorps VIII memorandum is available at MAB and is described in the chapter by Klee, "Die Luftschlacht um England, 1940," in Jacobsen and Rohwer (eds.), *Entscheidungsschlachten des zweiten Weltkrieges* (Frankfurt-a.-M., 1960), p. 72.

57. Deichmann's summary of the Fliegerkorps II study is set forth in Klee, "Luftschlacht um England, 1940," *loc. cit. supra*. Adm. Ansel states (*Hitler Confronts England* [1960], pp. 197-98) that he examined "the ideas submitted by I, II and III Fliegerkorps," but this cannot be correct, as there was no Flieger-

korps III. Furthermore, he declares that all three studies "concentrated on the purpose of air action for command to the absolute exclusion of invasion ideas." As shown in the text, this is not true of the study submitted by Fliegerkorps I.

58. The memorandum of Fliegerkorps I is available in MAB file G-Westen-V-3a, Vorbereitungen, and in the Von Rohden collection, series 4376, item 90.

59. Klee, *Das Unternehmen "Seeloewe,"* p. 169.

60. The text is available in MAB file Westen-V-3g, Luftschlacht.

61. *Supra,* p. 71.

62. Greiner *KTB,* Aug. 1, 1940.

63. Osterkamp, *op. cit.,* pp. 324-27. Osterkamp gives no date for the meeting, but Goering's new white uniform places it as after July 19, and all the other conferences during this period are recorded as taking place at Karinhall. An *Aktenvermerk* of Aug. 2, initialed by Jeschonnek, refers to a meeting between Goering and the *Luftflottenchefs* on Aug. 1 (MAB file *supra,* note 60, and Von Rohden series 4376, item 114). Bartz, *Als der Himmel brannte* (1955), p. 40, places the Osterkamp conference at the beginning of August. But it is possible that Osterkamp's memory of the white uniform was mistaken, and that the meeting took place earlier, perhaps in mid-July.

64. Von Rohden series 4376, item 114.

65. "Vorbereitungen und Weisungen fuer Unternehmen 'Adler' "—Fu/st 5881/40, Aug. 2, 1940. I have found no copy of this directive, which is referred to in the Von Rohden documents (series 4376, items 114, 207) and is described in Klee's 1955 memorandum on Sea Lion (*supra,* note 5), pp. 171-72, and in Wheatley, *op. cit.,* p. 63; Ansel, *op. cit.,*

p. 199; and Klee, *Das Unternehmen "Seeloewe"* (1958), p. 169.

66. Von Rohden (series 4376, item 114) and MAB file Westen-V-3g, Luftschlacht, contain copies of these instructions, issued through the OKL operations section.

67. Wheatley, *op. cit.,* p. 63, quoting the SKL war diary for Aug. 10, 1940.

68. SKL war diary for Aug. 5, quoted in Klee's memorandum, p. 179.

69. Von Rohden, series 4376, item 114; OKL Abt. 8 *Gefechtskalendar,* in MAB file G-Westen-V-3f, Luftschlacht.

70. Greiner KTB, Aug. 7, 1940.

71. OKW/L situation conferences, (Greiner MS. C-0651), Aug. 9, 1940.

72. HD, July 29, 1940.

73. Greiner *KTB,* Aug. 7.

74. Kesselring, *A Soldier's Record,* pp. 70-72.

75. Rieckhoff, *Trumpf oder Bluff?* (Geneva, 1945), p. 149; Feuchter, *Geschichte des Luftkriegs* (Bonn, 1954), p. 161; Suchenwirth, *Historical Turning Points of the German Air Force War Effort,* USAF Histor. Studies, No. 189 (1959), pp. 70-71; Lee, *Blitz on Britain* (London, 1960), pp. 33-35, 48, 55-56.

76. Rieckhoff, *loc. cit. supra.*

77. Lee, *op. cit.,* p. 53; Lee, *The German Air Force* (London, 1946), p. 261.

78. Collier, *Defence of the United Kingdom,* pp. 183, 451; Bishop, *Battle of Britain,* pp. 111-14.

79. Kesselring, *A Soldier's Record,* p. 73; Galland, *op. cit.,* pp. 21, 30; Richards, *op. cit.,* Vol. I, p. 164.

80. Collier, *op. cit.,* pp. 183, 451; Greiner *KTB,* Aug. 12, 1940.

81. Greiner *KTB,* Aug. 13.

82. It is so described in Richards, *op. cit.,* p. 164.

83. Bishop, *op. cit.,* pp. 119-20.

84. Collier, *op. cit.,* pp. 183-84, 451; Richards, *op. cit.,* pp. 164-65.

85. Collier and Richards, *loci cit. supra;* Watson-Watt, *Three Steps to Victory,* p. 234.

86. Richards, *op. cit.,* p. 165.

87. For the events of *Adlertag* (Aug. 13, 1940) see Collier, *op. cit.,* pp. 183-88, 456; Richards, *loci cit. supra;* Bishop, *op. cit.,* pp. 127-38; Greiner *KTB,* Aug. 13 and 14.

88. SKL KTB, Ops. Div., Part A, Aug. 14, 1940, and Part D, Luftlage, same date.

89. HD, Aug. 14, 1940.

CHAPTER FIVE

1. For the events of Aug. 14, see the Greiner *KTB* entries for that date and Collier, *Defence of the United Kingdom,* pp. 189-90, 456.

2. Greiner *KTB,* Aug. 14.

3. *Id.,* Aug. 15.

4. The account of these and subsequent daily developments in the Battle of Britain are based primarily (unless otherwise noted) on Collier, *Defence of the United Kingdom,* Chs. IX-XVI; Richards, *Royal Air Force, 1939–1945,* Vol. I, Chs. VI and VII; and Lee, *Blitz on Britain, passim.* German and additional English sources are specifically noted.

5. Greiner *KTB,* Aug. 16.

6. Von Rohden series 4376, document 205 (Karlsbad, 1944), p. 12.

7. Bishop, *Battle of Britain,* pp. 142, 149. These are not included in the RAF tabulation of losses during the Battle of Britain, which, as already noted (*supra,* p. 140), comprises only fighters.

8. Greiner *KTB,* Aug. 19, 1940.

9. Collier, *op. cit.,* pp. 203-04; Richards, *op. cit.,* pp. 178-79.

10. For the Karinhall conference of Aug. 15 see Von Rohden series 4376, items 114, 410; MAB file G-Westen-V-3a, F/st-1a, and -3g; Richards, *op. cit.,* pp. 171-72. For the attitude of Fliegerkorps VIII, see Seidemann, *Der Einsatz des VIII Fliegerkorps 1.7-1.10. 1940 an der Kanalküste Frankreichs* (Düsseldorf, 1953), unpublished monograph available at Maxwell Air Force Base.

11. SKL KTB, Ops. Div., Part A, Aug. 17, 1940, and Part D, Luftlage, same date.

12. Von Rohden and MAB sources as in note 10; Richards, *op. cit.,* p. 178.

13. Extracts from Milch's report ("Auszug aus dem Besichtungsbericht des Gen. Insp. der Luftwaffe bei der Verbaende der Luftflotte 2") are among the documents at MAB.

14. Galland, *The First and the Last,* pp. 35-36.

15. Osterkamp, *op. cit.,* pp. 340-43, 360; Bishop, *op. cit.,* pp. 93-94; Osterkamp, *Einsatz des Jagdfliegerfuehrers 2 an Kanal* (*Luftschlacht in England*), monograph written at Heidelberg in 1953, available at Maxwell Air Force Base.

16. Priller, *Geschichte eines Jagdgeschwaders* (1956), *passim.*

17. See the biography of Wick in *Deutsches Soldatenjahrbuch, 1965* (Munich: Schild, 1965), p. 31.

18. For the events of Aug. 24 and the withdrawal of the Defiants, see Collier, *op. cit.,* pp. 206-07, 210; Bishop, *op. cit.,* pp. 166-69.

19. McKee, *Strike from the Sky* (1960), pp. 197-209; Wood and Dempster, *The Narrow Margin* (London, 1961), pp. 316-25.

20. Bock Diary, Sept. 1, 1940.

21. Collier, *op. cit.,* p. 205; Wood and Dempster, *op. cit.,* pp. 332-33, 468-70; Churchill, *Their Finest Hour,* pp. 331-32.

22. HD, Aug. 30, 1940.

23. Greiner *KTB,* Sept. 3, 1940.

24. *Ciano's Diplomatic Papers,* p. 386.

25. OKW order Aug. 24, 1940, signed by Keitel, and quoted in MAB file G-Westen-V-3a.

26. *Supra,* p. 128 and note 57. In addition to the source quoted in

the text, see Lee, *Blitz on Britain*, p. 68 (attributing to Gen. Osterkamp the opinion that the attack on London "was part of the original German air plan of the attack on Britain"); Ansel, *Hitler Confronts England*, p. 247 (attributing advocacy of an attack on London to "Kesselring's staff" during the planning of *Adlerangriff*); Wood and Dempster, *op. cit.*, p. 330 (attributing like views to "many in the Luftwaffe command"). None of these writers cites a documentary source.

27. See, e.g., Osterkamp, *op. cit.*, p. 366 (*"Wir koennen abschiessen soviel wir wollen, es werden nicht weniger"*); Bartz, *Als der Himmel brannte*, p. 59.

28. Galland, *op. cit.*, pp. 40-41.

29. Wood and Dempster, *op. cit.*, p. 304. The general assumption in the postwar writings that the bombing of London was accidental seems entirely sound, as Hitler's ban was otherwise observed and had been reinforced by OKW order the very day before the bombing occurred.

30. For accounts of Bomber Command's operations in the summer of 1940 see Collier, *op. cit.*, pp. 141-42, 224-25; Richards, *op. cit.*, pp. 161-64, 181-82, 230-31; Webster and Frankland, *The Strategic Air Offensive against Germany* (1961), Vol. I, pp. 149-54, and Vol. IV, pp. 121-23, 431, 434, 455; Harris, *Bomber Offensive*, pp. 45-48.

31. Churchill, *Their Finest Hour*, p. 342; Richards, *op. cit.*, p. 182; Webster and Frankland, *op. cit.*, p. 215.

32. Greiner *KTB*, Aug. 29 and 31, 1940; SKL KTB, Part D, Luftlage, Aug. 28, 29, 30, and 31.

33. Shirer, *Berlin Diary* (1941), pp. 486, 490, 492-94.

34. Greiner *KTB*, Aug. 29: "The Fuehrer returns to Berlin in the evening on account of the British air attack of last night"; and: *"In Folge des Luftangriffs auf Grossberlin entschliesst sich der Fuehrer zur sofortigen Rueckkehr nach Berlin."*

35. Greiner *KTB*, Aug. 30: "... *dass der Fuehrer nunmehr bei guenstiger Wetterlage Vergeltungsangriffe gegen London mit zusammengefassten Kraefte durchfuehren lassen wolle."*

36. Wheatley, *op. cit.*, p. 102 and Appendix E; Klee, 1955 memorandum "Operation 'Sea Lion' and the Role Planned for the Luftwaffe," pp. 200-200a (MAB).

37. Greiner *KTB*, Aug. 30, 1940.

38. Wheatley, *op. cit.*, pp. 76-77. There also appears to have been a Hitler order for attacks on London issued Sept. 5. On Aug. 29 the OKL operations staff had noted that raids on London could best be carried out in the forenoon, with the sun behind the attackers (Von Rohden series 4376, item 114). The advice was disregarded, and the first several London attacks were launched late in the afternoon.

39. No record of this conference has come to hand. All the accounts seem to be based on information furnished after the war by the OKL intelligence chief, "Beppo" Schmid: MAB file G-Westen-V-3a, "Der I-C Dienst der Luftwaffe" (1945), p. 6; Wood and Dempster, *op. cit.*, pp. 115-17, 330-32; Ansel, *op. cit.*, p. 248.

40. See the eyewitness account in Shirer, *Berlin Diary*, pp. 495-97.

41. The text of the speech is available in Von Rohden series 4376, item 463, and extracts are given in Shirer, *loc. cit. supra*.

42. E.g., Bishop, *Battle of Britain*, pp. 156-59; Wilmot, *The Struggle for Europe* (1952), pp. 48-49.

43. *Supra*, note 28; see also Greiner *KTB*, Sept. 6: "Today's plans: Attacks on London combating the British fighter defense."

44. SKL KTB, Ops. Div., Part A, entry for Sept. 6, 1940.

45. SKL KTB, Part D, Luftlage, Sept. 6.

46. McKee, *op. cit.*, p. 125.

47. Collier, *op. cit.*, pp. 235-40; Wood and Dempster, *op. cit.*, pp. 334-39. For the Rotterdam raid see Taylor, *March of Conquest*, pp. 200-03.

48. For accounts of the fighting on Sept. 7 see Collier, *op. cit.*, pp. 235-40; Wood and Dempster, *op. cit.*, pp. 334-39. According to Galland (*op. cit.*, pp. 41-43) the Stukas were thrown back into the fray on Sept. 7 and were withdrawn after the first few London raids because their losses "could not be supported." But this appears to be an error. According to records of the *Quartiermeister OKL*, only two Stukas were lost on operations during the entire month of September, and there is no other evidence in the records that Stukas were used in the London raids. Rather, they were restricted to attacking convoys in the Channel. Seidemann's monograph (*supra*, note 10) on Fliegerkorps VIII's operations contains no reference to the use of Stukas in the Battle of Britain after August, and indicates that the combat headquarters at Landemer was abandoned and the Stuka aircraft left at their "rest" airfields south of Caen.

49. SKL KTB, Ops. Div., Part A, entry for Sept. 8.

50. For the operations during the week of Sept. 8–14, see Collier at pp. 240-42, Wood and Dempster at pp. 339-50, McKee at pp. 222-29, and SKL KTB, Part D, Luftlage entries for Sept. 9–15.

51. Greiner *KTB*, Sept. 7 and 9.

52. *Id.*, Sept. 14. See also HD, Sept. 13. According to Halder's account, the luncheon was attended by 14 Army and 5 Luftwaffe *Generalobersten*, Generaladmiral Carls (equivalent naval rank), Goering,

Brauchitsch, Keitel, Milch, Jodl, Buerckner, some adjutants, and Martin Bormann.

53. The fullest account of the meeting is in HD, Sept. 14.

54. Berndt and von Wedel (eds.), *Deutschland im Kampf*, August–September 1940.

55. See the account of this same meeting in FCNA, 1940, at p. 100.

56. OKW order (signed by Keitel) of Sept. 14, reproduced in English in FCNA, 1940, pp. 100-01.

57. Mr. Churchill described his visit to Uxbridge in *Their Finest Hour*, pp. 332-37; the visit of Gens. Strong and Emmons and Rear Adm. Gormley is mentioned in Wood and Dempster, *op. cit.*, at p. 351.

58. Greiner *KTB*, Sept. 16, 1940.

59. SKL KTB, Part D, Luftlage for Sept. 16 and 18.

60. *Id.*, Part A, Sept. 17.

61. Collier, *op. cit.*, p. 242.

62. A memorandum by "Beppo" Schmid in the MAB files (Westen-V-3d, Luftschlacht-Ablauf) shows (p. 31) Goering's forward headquarters at The Hague from Sept. 6 to Sept. 8, at Ronce (Belgium) from the 8th to the 15th, at Boulogne from the 15th to the 17th, and thereafter at Coudraix (near Beauvais) until March 20, 1941.

63. Hoffmann von Waldau's memorandum of the conference of Sept. 16 may be found in the MAB files (Westen-V-3g, Luftschlacht) and in Von Rohden series 4376, item 114.

64. Basil Collier, *Battle of Britain*, p. 108.

65. Greiner *KTB*, Sept. 23, 1940.

66. For the raids of Sept. 25 and 26 see Wood and Dempster, *op. cit.*, pp. 364-65, 462, and McKee, *op. cit.*, pp. 253-66.

67. Collier, *Defence of the United Kingdom*, pp. 491-92.

68. HD, Sept. 26, 1940.

69. Galland has given an account of his trip to Berlin and Rominten

in his book *The First and the Last,* at pp. 45-48.

70. A memorandum by Josef Kammhuber (the first commander of the postwar Luftwaffe of the Bundeswehr) on the Germans' use of fighter-bombers is in MAB file Westen-V-3g, Luftschlacht um England 1940.

71. Galland, *op. cit.,* pp. 51-56.

72. SKL KTB, Ops. Div., Part A, July 19, 1940.

73. Collier, *Defence of the United Kingdom,* pp. 499-500.

74. On Wick's death see McKee, *op. cit.,* p. 279; SKL KTB, Part D, Luftlage for Nov. 28 and 29. According to his biographer (*supra,* note 17), at the time of his death Wick had outstripped Moelders and Galland and, with 56 victories, "led all the rest."

75. Collier, *Defence,* pp. 156-59, 211-13, 458-60.

76. According to the contemporary German figures, during October 7,660 tons were dropped at night and 1,350 tons by day (SKL KTB, Part D, Luftlage, Nov. 8).

77. Wood and Dempster, *op. cit.,* p. 476.

78. Collier, *Defence,* pp. 251-59, 494-95.

79. Greiner *KTB,* Oct. 3 and Nov. 14, 1940.

80. Wood and Dempster, *op. cit.,* pp. 463, 470.

81. HD, Oct. 7.

82. Churchill, *Their Finest Hour,* p. 715.

83. Greiner *KTB,* Oct. 12.

84. Galland, *op. cit.,* pp. 36-37, 54.

85. McKee, *op. cit.,* p. 208.

86. Galland, *op. cit.,* p. 25.

87. Johnson, *Wing Leader* (1957), p. 24.

88. Rieckhoff, *Trumpf oder Bluff?* (Geneva, 1945), pp. 219-20; see also Weber, *Luftschlacht um England,* pp. 24-25. During the Battle of Britain, Oberstleutnant Rieckhoff was the operations officer (Ia) of Luftflotte 2.

89. The account of the *Graf Zeppelin* radar reconnaissance flights is taken from Wood and Dempster, *op. cit.,* pp. 17-20.

90. Wood and Dempster, pp. 345-46.

91. *Id.,* p. 288.

92. Notes, Aug. 29, 1940, Ia Fuehrungsstab, in Von Rohden series 4376, item 114.

93. *Supra,* p. 136.

94. Collier, *Eagle Day* (1966), p. 40. The author gives no source for this statement, but Deichmann is listed (at p. 278) as an "ever-present help" among those who gave valuable advice, so there seems to be little reason to question the statement.

95. Bross, *Gespraeche mit Hermann Goering* (Flensburg, 1950), pp. 191-92.

96. The totals include losses from all causes. The British figures are taken from the table in Wood and Dempster, *op. cit.,* pp. 472-73, and closely correspond to the combat-loss totals in Collier, *Defence,* pp. 451, 457, 492. The German figures are those of the Luftwaffe *Quartiermeister,* which are available in the captured German records and are set forth in part in Wood and Dempster, pp. 475-76. The figures in Collier, *loci cit. supra,* are a little lower, and apparently do not include nonoperational losses.

97. *Supra,* pp. 150-51.

98. Richards, *op. cit.,* pp. 190-91.

99. In August and September the British turned out 822 new Spitfires and Hurricanes, and about 120 other fighters (Wood and Dempster, p. 462).

100. Wood and Dempster, pp. 468-69, 472-73. From July 10 to Oct. 31 Fighter Command lost 414 pilots (Collier, *Defence,* p. 493).

101. From Aug. 1, 1940, to Mar.

31, 1941, the Luftwaffe lost 1,741 airmen killed and 2,537 taken prisoner, or 4,278 in all (Klee, "Luftschlacht um England, 1940," in *Entscheidigungsschlachten des zweiten Weltkrieges*, ed. Jacobsen and Rohwer, at p. 85).

102. Priller, *op. cit.*, pp. 73, 303-16.

103. Galland, *op. cit.*, p. 55.

104. *Supra*, p. 178.

105. *Ibid.*, and see Klee, *supra*, note 99.

106. Galland, *op. cit.*, pp. 55-56.

107. Precise figures on the damage and casualties on the ground during the Battle of Britain are not easily found. According to the *Encyclopaedia Britannica* (1953 ed., Vol. 14, pp. 367D-368), from September 1940 to July 1941 inclusive there were some 10,000 killed and 17,000 seriously injured in London alone. Of course, in the afterlight of what subsequently happened in Germany these figures are not impressive, but at the time they were by far the heaviest civilian casualties ever inflicted by bombing.

108. Ansel, *Hitler Confronts England*, p. 336.

109. *Ibid.*; Richards, *op. cit.*, p. 195.

110. *Supra*, p. 70.

111. Deichmann, "The Effects of Political Measures and Decisions on Logistical Planning" (unpublished MS. in the files at MAB), p. 8.

112. SKL KTB, Ops. Div., Part A, July 2, 1940.

113. Heinkel, *Stormy Life* (1956), p. 199.

114. Suchenwirth, *Historical Turning Points in the German Air Force War Effort*, USAF Hist. Studies, No. 189 (1959), pp. 73-75.

115. Galland, *op. cit.*, pp. 69-71.

116. Suchenwirth, *op. cit.*, p. 71.

117. See Klee, "Operation 'Sea Lion' and the Role Planned for the Luftwaffe" (Hamburg, 1955—unpub-lished MS. available at MAB), quoted *infra*, p. 292.

INTERLUDE

1. I. F. Clarke, "The Shape of Wars to Come," in *History Today*, XV (1965), pp. 108-16. This article reviews the relevant literature from 1900 to 1914. See also Barbara Tuchman, *The Proud Tower* (New York: Macmillan, 1966), pp. 380-81.

2. The author, who wrote under the pen name of Capitaine Daurit, was a Col. Driant who fell at Verdun.

3. In a letter to Edward Lee Childs dated Jan. 8, 1909. See *The Letters of Henry James*, ed. Percy Lubbock (London: Macmillan, 1920), Vol. II, pp. 124-25.

4. Subtitled *A Record of Secret Service*, and published by Sidgwick & Jacobson of London.

5. William Le Queux, *The Invasion of 1910* (London: Eveleigh Nash, 1906); naval chapters by H. W. Wilson, and introductory letter by Field Marshal Earl Frederick S. Roberts.

6. I. F. Clarke, *supra*, note 1.

7. Maj. Guy du Maurier, D.S.O., *An Englishman's Home* (New York: Harper, 1909). The scene of the action is a home in Wickham, Essex, and the German invaders are thinly disguised as from "Nearland."

8. Rudolf Meister, *Der Weltkrieg in den Luften*.

9. The same theme was recently exploited in an original drama in motion pictures by Kevin Brownlow and Andrew Mollo entitled *It Happened Here—The Story of Hitler's England*, produced by Lopert Pictures Corporation and exhibited in 1966.

10. Liddell Hart, *The Defence of Britain* (New York: Random House, 1939), pp. 129-34.

11. Churchill, *The Gathering Storm* (1948), pp. 516-17.

CHAPTER SIX

1. N.D. PS-442.
2. Wheatley, *Operation Sea Lion* (1958), p. 38.
3. *Id.*, p. 133.
4. Klee, *Das Unternehmen "Seeloewe"* (1958), p. 244.
5. Fleming, *Operation Sea Lion* (1957), p. 240.
6. Greiner *KTB*, Sept. 5, 1940.
7. See, e. g., Kreipe, "The Battle of Britain," in *The Fatal Decisions*, ed. Freidin and Richardson (1956), p. 27; Frischauer, *The Rise and Fall of Hermann Goering* (1951), pp. 195-96.
8. Blumentritt, *Von Rundstedt* (1952), pp. 85-87. Blumentritt (then an *Oberst*) was the staff operations officer (Ia) of Rundstedt's army group.
9. *Id.*, p. 86; Shulman, *Defeat in the West* (1948), pp. 49-51; Liddell Hart, *The German Generals Talk* (1948), p. 153; Klee, *Das Unternehmen "Seeloewe,"* pp. 244, 694 fn.
10. E.g., Kesselring, *A Soldier's Record* (1953), pp. 70, 77; Heinz Guderian, *Panzer Leader* (London: Michael Joseph, 1952), p. 138; Heusinger, *Befehl im Widerstreit* (Tuebingen, 1950), p. 101.
11. *Infra*, p. 254, quoting from the history of the 1st Mountain Division—Lanz, *Gebirgsjaeger* (1954), p. 90.
12. See Klee, "Die Luftschlacht um England, 1940," in *Entscheidigungsschlachten des zweiten Weltkrieges*, ed. Jacobsen and Rohwer (1960), p. 65.
13. The ensuing discussion of the early plans is based on Ansel, *Hitler Confronts England* (1960), pp. 42-50; Wheatley, *op. cit.*, pp. 4-13; Klee, "Luftschlacht um England, 1940," *loc. cit.*, pp. 53-57.
14. Its receipt is noted in Jodl's diary, Dec. 1, 1939 (N.D. 1809-PS).

15. *FCNA, 1940,* p. 51 (May 21). The SKL war diary contains a comparable entry.
16. Raeder, *Struggle for the Sea* (London, 1959), p. 178.
17. *Id.*, at p. 179.
18. Wheatley, *op. cit.*, pp. 19-22; Ansel, *op. cit.*, pp. 97-98.
19. Ansel, *op. cit.*, p. 112.
20. Directive No. 15, June 14, 1940; described in HD, June 15, and in Butler, *Grand Strategy*, Vol. II, pp. 265-66, 270.
21. Wheatley, *op. cit.*, p. 26.
22. SKL KTB, Ops. Div., Part A, Vol. 10, June 18, 1940.
23. Butler, *op. cit.*, at p. 270, citing *Hitler e Mussolini: Lettere e Documenti* (Milan, 1946), p. 54.
24. *FCNA, 1940,* pp. 58-60. (June 20).
25. Wheatley, *op. cit.*, p. 23.
26. Ansel, *op. cit.*, p. 103.
27. *Supra*, p. 52 and note 22.
28. N.D. 1776-PS, discussed in other connections *supra*, pp. 44-46.
29. *Cf.* Ansel, *op. cit.*, pp. 114-19.
30. The directive is set out in English in *FCNA, 1940*, pp. 61-62.
31. H.Gr. B KTB, June 23, 1940.
32. HD, June 28; H.Gr. B KTB, same date.
33. *Supra*, pp. 56-57; HD, July 1.
34. Halder's postwar recollection of the talk bears out the impressions conveyed by his diary. See Ansel, *op. cit.*, pp. 108-10.
35. *Supra*, p. 54 *et seq.*
36. OKW directive of July 10, signed by Keitel.
37. Chef WFA, "Erste Ueberlegung ueber eine Landung in England, Deckname: Loewe," July 12, 1940.
38. *Supra*, pp. 66-67.
39. SKL KTB, Ops. Div., Part A, Vol. 10, July 17, 1940.
40. Ansel, *op. cit.*, pp. 148-49; Wheatley, *op. cit.*, p. 147; Klee, "Luftschlacht um England, 1940," *loc. cit.*, p. 77. Fleming, *op. cit.*, pp.

48-52, restricts his criticism to the proposed location of the headquarters far inland, and the unnecessary disruption of staff work and communications which moving would have entailed.

41. See Taylor, *March of Conquest*, pp. 252-65.

42. *Id.*, pp. 92-94.

43. N.D. C-174.

44. Hitler directive of Mar. 14, 1940, set forth in *Fuehrer Directives* (U.S. Dept. of the Navy, 1948).

45. HD, July 3, 1940; Ansel, *op. cit.*, p. 136.

46. HD, July 3.

47. HD, July 5.

48. HD, July 11.

49. OKH Ops. Abt. 392/40, July 17, 1940.

50. HD, July 19.

51. SKL KTB, July 9.

52. *Id.*, July 18.

53. *Id.*, July 15.

54. Most of the memorandum is set forth in *FCNA, 1940*, pp. 69-70.

55. SKL KTB, July 21.

56. In addition to SKL KTB, see HD, July 22 (Brauchitsch's account to Halder the following day), and Raeder's memorandum in *FCNA, 1940*, pp. 71-73.

57. *FCNA, 1940*, p. 73; SKL KTB, July 25; Klee, "Luftschlacht um England, 1940," *loc. cit.*, p. 87.

58. *FCNA, 1940*, pp. 74-75; SKL KTB, July 25.

59. HD, July 28.

60. HD, July 29.

61. SKL KTB, July 29.

62. SKL memorandum "Betrachtungen [views] zur Durchfuehrung 'Seeloewe,'" July 29, described in Wheatley, *op. cit.*, pp. 169-70; Klee, "Luftschlacht um England, 1940," *loc. cit.*, pp. 94-95.

63. SKL KTB, July 30.

64. *Supra*, p. 73.

65. *FCNA, 1940*, pp. 76-81; HD, July 31.

66. SKL KTB, Aug. 1.

67. Greiner *KTB*, Aug. 1.

68. The directive is set forth in full in *FCNA, 1940*, pp. 81-82.

69. It still had not been received at OKH at noon on Aug. 4 (HD, Aug. 4). Apparently it came in at SKL on Aug. 5 (Ansel, *op. cit.*, p. 206, note 14).

70. HD, Aug. 2, 1940.

71. HD, Aug. 4.

72. Greiner *KTB*, Aug. 5.

73. SKL KTB, Aug. 5.

74. HD, Aug. 5.

75. HD, Aug. 6.

76. SKL KTB and HD, Aug. 7.

77. *FCNA, 1940*, p. 82; Ansel, *op. cit.*, p. 212 ("meat grinder"); Fleming, *op. cit.*, p. 252; Wheatley, *op. cit.*, p. 67.

78. Greiner *KTB*, Aug. 7.

79. HD, Aug. 5; Klee, "Luftschlacht um England, 1940," *loc. cit.*, p. 100.

80. Ansel, *op. cit.*, p. 221; Wheatley, *op. cit.*, pp. 66-68; Klee, *op. cit. supra*, p. 103.

81. Greiner *KTB*, Aug. 12.

82. Jodl heard about it orally on Aug. 12 and received the memorandum the next day (Greiner *KTB*, Aug. 12 and 13).

83. SKL KTB, Aug. 10 and 12.

84. The conference is described in *FCNA, 1940*, pp. 82-83, and in Greiner *KTB* and SKL KTB, Aug. 13.

85. Greiner *KTB*, Aug. 13.

86. Chef W Fst, Berlin, Aug. 13: "Beurteilung der Lage, wie sich nach den Auffassungen von Heer und Kriegsmarine fuer eine Landung in England ergibt," signed by Jodl and "noted" by Keitel.

87. This aspect of the problem is discussed *infra*, pp. 290-98.

88. SKL KTB, Aug. 14.

89. *Ibid.*

90. The account in Bock's diary (Aug. 14) is comparable; his record attributes to Hitler the oft-used expression *"ultima ratio"* and also describes the Fuehrer's ensuing com-

ments about Italy, Russia, Finland, Rumania, and the United States.

91. SKL KTB, Aug. 14.

92. Schniewind's memorandum, dated Aug. 14, is set forth in *FCNA, 1940*, pp. 83-85.

93. SKL KTB, Aug. 14.

94. Greiner *KTB*, Aug. 14.

95. *FCNA, 1940*, pp. 85-86.

96. HD, Aug. 18 and 20.

97. Klee, "Luftschlacht um England, 1940," *loc. cit.*, pp. 107-08.

98. *Id.*, pp. 108-09.

99. Greiner *KTB*, Aug. 22.

100. HD, Aug. 23.

101. Greiner *KTB*, Aug. 22, 23 and 24; Klee, "Luftschlacht um England, 1940," *loc. cit.*, pp. 109-11.

102. Greiner *KTB*, Aug. 25, 26 and 27.

103. HD, Aug. 26.

104. The document is reprinted as No. 25 in Klee, *Dokumente zur Unternehmen "Seeloewe"* (1959); see also Greiner *KTB*, Aug. 26.

105. HD, Aug. 26.

106. See Taylor, *March of Conquest*, pp. 190-205.

107. HD, Aug. 20.

108. Greiner *KTB*, Aug. 22.

109. HD, Aug. 23.

110. Greiner *KTB*, Aug. 30, Sept. 10, 14.

111. Greiner *KTB*, Sept. 4.

112. HD, Sept. 10.

113. Greiner *KTB*, Sept. 12.

114. Heeresgruppe A, "Heeresgruppenbefehl Nr. 1 fuer Durchfuehrung Seeloewe," Sept. 14, 1940.

115. HD, Sept. 17.

116. HD, Sept. 11.

117. AOK 16 KTB Ia Nr. 4, Anlage B, Sept. 12.

118. See Taylor, *op. cit.*, pp. 203-04.

119. AOK 16 KTB *supra*, Sept. 17.

120. Luftflotte 2/Ia, "Weisung fuer Einsatz der 7. Fliegerdivision in Fall 'Seeloewe,'" Sept. 18, 1940, found in AOK 16 file Ob.L.W.–Luft.

121. Anweisung Ob.d.H. Gen.St. Ia No. 480/40, reprinted in English translation in Wheatley, *op. cit.*, pp. 175-82. This order envisaged the use of paratroops at Brighton as well as at Dover; as stated above in the text, the Luftwaffe would not agree to this, and directed their commitment only near Folkestone.

122. OKM SKL Nr. 12040/40 v. 20.8.40 and OKM SKL/A VI Nr. 1506/4 v. 30.8.40. The first is described in Ansel, *op. cit.*, pp. 235-36, and the second in Klee, "Luftschlacht um England, 1940," *loc. cit.*, p. 146.

123. Ob.d.L. Fst. Ia Nr. 5944/40 v. 5.9.40. There appears to have been an earlier Luftwaffe order on Sea Lion, dated Aug. 27, but no copy has come to light.

124. AOK 6 Fu.-Abt. Zeitschrift des KTB Nr. 4 (West), entries for Aug. 25, Sept. 3, 9, 11, 12.

125. AOK 6 KTB *supra*, Sept. 3; 12th Inf. Div. KTB Nr. 3 (Ia) entries for Aug. 28, Aug. 29, Sept. 3; Friedrich Hossbach, *Infanterie im Ostfeldzug, 1941–42: Den Ueberlebenden und Toten der 31. Infanterie-Division* (Osterode: Giebel & Oelschlagel, 1951), p. 25; Schroeder and Schultz-Naumann, *Die Geschichte des pommerschen 32. Infanterie-Division* (1956), p. 72.

126. Xth A. K. Ia West VII entries for Aug. 29, Aug. 31, and Sept. 9, and Anlage Sept. 4.

127. Breithaupt, *Die Geschichte der 30. Infanterie-Division, 1939–1945* (1955), p. 71.

128. HD, Sept. 24, 1940.

129. Ob.d.L. Fu.St. Ia Nr. 5944/40, Sept. 5, 1940.

130. Operationsbefehl Nr. 1 Seebefehlshaber West B Nr. GKdos.-360/40-Al v. 14.9.40.

131. See the OKW instructions of Sept. 15, signed by Warlimont, reported as No. 34 in Klee, *Dokumente*.

132. See the OKH order dated Sept. 9, 1940 (Ob.d.H. Gen.St.d.H. /Gen.Qu. Nr. 2700/40) on the military administration of England; Fleming, *Operation Sea Lion*, pp. 260-67; Wheatley, *op. cit.*, pp. 122-24; Charles Wighton, *Heydrich* (Philadelphia: Chilton, 1962), pp. 207-11.

CHAPTER SEVEN

1. HD, July 1, 1940.
2. HD, July 3, 5, and 6.
3. XLI A.K.Activity Report, Abt. III (Judge Advocate), Feb. 5–Dec. 31, 1940; Merkblatt Nr. 5, Versuchsstab R (XXXXI A.K.) Ia/Pi. Ausb. v. 9.5.40 Berlin.
4. SKL KTB, July 10, 1940.
5. Ansel, *Hitler Confronts England*, pp. 159-60; Wheatley, *Operation Sea Lion*, p. 114.
6. HD, July 14.
7. OKH Ops. 392/40 of July 17.
8. July 17 entries, H.Gr. A/Ia KTB West Teil III; AOK 6 Fu. Abt. KTB Nr. 4 (West); AOK 16 Fu. Abt. KTB Nr. 4.
9. HD, notes July 26.
10. HD, July 19. The 2,000 barges are first mentioned in Halder's diary on July 16.
11. HD, July 26.
12. Christian von Lucke, *Die Geschichte des Panzer-Regiments 2.* (Kleve, 1953), p. 37.
13. Ansel, *op. cit.*, p. 209; Wheatley, *op. cit.*, p. 114 and fn. 1.
14. HD, Aug. 2.
15. SKL KTB, July 14.
16. *Id.*, July 23.
17. 20th Inf. Div. KTB Nr. 3 Qu. Abt., July 13; XVth A.K. KTB Qu. Abt., July 16; see also 17th Inf. Div. KTB Teil IV, July 18.
18. E.g., AOK 6 KTB Nr. 4, July 21; AOK 16 Ia 801/40 Armeebefehl Nr. 1 of July 21; VII A.K. order, July 24, referred to in 7 Inf. Div. KTB III for that date; H.Gr. A Ic

KTB West, Teil III, July 26; see also OKH (Gen.St.d.H. Op. Abt. [E]) 402/40 of July 27.
19. *Supra*, p. 200.
20. H.Gr. A KTB West Teil III, July 31, Aug. 3, 4, 6.
21. H.Gr. A Ia Heeresgruppenbefehl Nr. 1 of Sept. 14 provided that two days before the launching of Sea Lion the army group would establish a forward headquarters near Amiens and a command post (*Gefechtstand*) in the west, probably north of Boulogne.
22. The following records were among those consulted as basis for the text: H.Gr. A. Ia KTB West, Teil III, 25.6.40 to 17.10.40 and Anlagen 97–139; AOK 6 Fu.-Abt. KTB Nr. 4 (West), 28.6.40 to 31.12.40; AOK 16 KTB Nr. 4 Ia/01 Anlage B, 30.5.40 to 18.12.40; IV A. K. KTB Nr. ·8, 5.7.40 to 20.4.41; V A.K. Taetigkeitsbericht Ia, 26.6.40 to 31.3.41; VI A. K. KTB Nr. 6, 25.6.40 to 31.12.40; VII A. K. KTB Fu. Abt., Teil 4, 25.6.40 to 11.4.41; X A. K. Ia KTB West VI, 25.6.40 to 31.7.40, and West VII, 1.8.40 to 31.10.40, with Anlagen; XIII A. K. Qu. Abt. KTB Nr. 2, 25.6.40 to 21.2.41; XV A. K. Qu. Abt. KTB, 25.6.40 to 12.2.41, and Taetigkeitsbericht Abt. Ia, 5.7.40 to 14.2.41; XXII A. K. Taetigkeitsbericht Ia, 12.7.40 to 31.12.40; XXIII A. K. Ia KTB Nr. 6, 28.7.40 to 31.12.40; XXIV A. K. KTB 9.7.40 to 31.10.40 and Anlagen; XXXVIII A. K. Ia KTB Nr. 2, 25.6.40 to 31.10.40 and Anlagen; XLI A. K. Activity Report of Judge Advocate (Abt. III), 5.2.40 to 31.12.40; XLII A. K. KTB Nr. 1, 5.2.40 to 30.9.40 and Nr. 2, 1.10.40 to 15.4.41; 7 Inf. Div. Ia KTB II, 18.6.40 to 19.7.40, and III, 20.7.40 to 10.4.41; 8 Inf. Div. Ia KTB Nr. 5, 23.7.40 to 30.11.40; 12 Inf. Div. Ia KTB Nr. 3, 23.6.40 to 31.3.41; 17 Inf. Div. KTB, Teil IV, 1.7.40 to 30.5.41; 20 Inf. Div. (mot.) Qu.

Abt. KTB Nr. 3, 26.6.40 to 30.11.40; 26 Inf. Div. Fu.-Abt. KTB Nr. 3, 25.6.40 to 21.11.40 and Anlagen; 34 Inf. Div. KTB Nr. 3, 9.7.40 to 31.10.40 and Anlagen; 35 Inf. Div. Ia KTB Nr. 4, 9.5.40 to 31.7.40, and Nr. 5, 1.8.40 to 4.4.41; 1 Geb. Div. Ib KTB Anlagen, 15.7.40 to 30.3.41; 10 Pz. Div. Anlagenband I zum KTB Nr. 4, 30.6.40 to 18.12.40.

In addition, the text relies on several divisional histories published in Germany since the war, as noted. Some of these unit histories refer to war diaries which are not to be found among the captured documents, and it seems clear that a number of these diaries passed into private hands during or shortly after the war.

23. Schroeder and Schultz-Naumann, *Die Geschichte der pommerschen 32. Infanterie-Division*, p. 71.

24. Hubert Lanz, *Gebirgsjaeger: Die 1. Gebirgsdivision, 1939–1945* (Bad Nauheim, 1954), p. 90. During the summer of 1940 Lanz was chief of staff of the XVIIIth Corps, but before the war he had commanded a regiment of the division, and he became the divisional commander in October 1940, succeeding Gen. Ludwig Kuebler.

25. See, e.g., AOK 16 Ia 801/40, Armeebefehl Nr. 1, of July 21, 1940, so dividing the 16th Army, and designating the XIIIth, VIIth, and XXXVIIIth Corps for operations, and the Vth, XXIIIrd, IVth, and XLIInd Corps for occupation duties. The 6th and 9th Armies made similar arrangements.

26. HD, July 19.

27. HD, Aug. 3.

28. Ansel, *op. cit.*, pp. 104-05, 208-09. It is probable that the Army engineer colonel mentioned by Siebel (Ansel, pp. 104-05) was Strobl.

29. HD, Aug. 8.

30. *Karlsruhe als Garnison-Festschrift* (1956), p. 118.

31. HD, Aug. 16.

32. HD, Aug. 17; see also Ansel, *op. cit.*, pp. 229-30.

33. Bock Diary, Aug. 2–24; AOK 6 KTB Nr. 4, Aug. 2–Sept. 3; see also 12 Inf. Div. KTB Nr. 3 (Ia), June 23, 1940–Mar. 31, 1941, and two books by the then Ia of the division, Hermann Teske: *Bewegungskrieg* (Heidelberg, 1955), pp. 122-36, and *Die Silbernen Spiegel* (Heidelberg, 1952), pp. 90-95.

34. Bock Diary, Aug. 2–24; AOK 6 KTB Nr. 4, Aug. 2–Sept. 3.

35. HD, Aug. 20, 1940.

36. Bock Diary and HD, Aug. 24.

37. AOK 6 KTB Nr. 4, Aug. 25. Halder is there recorded as giving this order in conversation with Gen. Geyer, commander of the IXth Corps, who possibly was deputizing (as senior corps commander) for Reichenau. Halder's diary contains no such entry; on Aug. 25 he was on the Biscay coast, at Bayonne and Bordeaux. See also, however, in accordance with the 6th Army entry, VI A.K. KTB Nr. 6, Aug. 25.

38. The 7th Inf. Div. staff perceived this factor as early as Aug. 3; see also the 35th Inf. Div. war-diary entry for Aug. 23.

39. Merkblatt [pamphlet] 5 and Merkblatt 6 (the latter Aug. 25, 1940), issued by Versuchsstab R through the XLIst Corps headquarters, engineer training section, in Berlin.

40. XLIst Corps Activity Report of Judge Advocate, Feb. 5–Dec. 31, 1940. Parts of the *Versuchsstab* seem to have kept going, however, for on Oct. 16 it issued a pamphlet on troop leadership during the sea passage. By that time Sea Lion had been finally canceled.

41. Documentary records from the armored units are scanty; in addition to the sources in note 22 *supra*, see Schaub, *Aus der Geschichte Panzer-Grenadier Regiment 12* (Bergisch Gladbach, 1957), pp. 55-56; Brehm,

Mein Kriegstagebuch, 1939–1945: Mit der 7. Panzer-Division 5 Jahre im West und Ost (Kassel, 1953), p. 13.

42. HD, Aug. 18 and Sept. 2.

43. Wheatley, *op. cit.*, pp. 25, 114; Rudolf Lusar, *Die Deutschen Waffen und Geheim-Waffen des z. Weltkrieges* (Munich: J. F. Lehmanns, 1956), pp. 28-29.

44. Ansel, *op. cit.*, p. 216.

45. SKL KTB, Aug. 24, 1940.

46. *Id.*, Aug. 17, 21, 22.

47. AOK 16 report to H.Gr. A, Aug. 27, 1940.

48. SKL KTB, Aug. 31; Klee, "Luftschlacht um England, 1940," *loc. cit.*, p. 116; Ansel, *op. cit.*, p. 239. The figures given in the several sources are somewhat at variance.

49. OKW directive, signed "Keitel," Sept. 3, 1940. A translation is printed in *FCNA, 1940*, p. 88.

50. 17th Inf. Div. KTB, Teil IV, Sept. 5, 8–11.

51. HD, Aug. 31–Sept. 10.

52. HD, Sept. 10–12; see also H.Gr. A KTB West, Teil III, Sept. 8–11; AOK 6 KTB 4, Sept. 8–12.

53. HD, Sept. 13.

54. Greiner *KTB*, Sept. 14.

55. SKL KTB, Sept. 12 and 13.

56. HD, Sept. 14; *FCNA, 1940*, pp. 98-100.

57. HD, Sept. 15.

58. "Landing Staff England" was to be formed from Rear Army Command 584, under Generalmajor Kurt Spemann. It was initially authorized by the 16th Army's directive of Sept. 17, 1940.

59. Initially provided for by the 16th Army's directive of Sept. 13, 1940. The special staff leader, Oberstleutnant Goth, was to be subordinated to the chief of staff of the XXIIIrd Corps, commanded by Gen. Albrecht Schubert. See also XXIII A.K. Ia Taetigkeitsbericht entries for Sept. 14, 21, 28.

60. *Supra*, pp. 236-38.

61. 35th Inf. Div. KTB Nr. 4, Sept. 9.

62. VII A.K. Fuehr. Abt. KTB, Part 4, Sept. 6.

63. AOK 16 Ia Nr. 300/40. At the end of August, Fliegerkorps VIII sent to the 16th Army's headquarters at Tourcoing a small working staff (Arbeitsstab) headed by the Ia, Hauptmann von Heinemann. See Seidemann's monograph, *supra* note 10, chapter 5.

64. *Infra*, note 125.

65. 17 Inf. Div. KTB, Part IV, Sept. 17 and 18.

66. Wheatley, *op. cit.*, p. 106, quoting SKL teleprints to OKW and the Luftwaffe.

67. Ansel, *op. cit.*, p. 307.

68. Wheatley, *op. cit.*, p. 109.

69. As early as Aug. 31, the SKL war diary recorded 160 prahms available at Le Havre; only 175 were needed there for the first wave, and there was to be no second sailing from Le Havre. The same entry recorded a total of 168 steamers and 1,697 prahms on hand in Germany and the occupied countries.

70. VIIth A. K. KTB, Teil IV, Sept. 18, 20.

71. Richards, *Royal Air Force*, p. 186.

72. Wheatley, *op. cit.*, pp. 108-09.

73. VIIth A.K. KTB, Teil IV, Sept. 20.

74. *FCNA, 1940*, pp. 77-79.

75. *Supra*, p. 264.

76. Greiner *KTB*, Sept. 10. The Sea Lion draft directive bore the number 18; this number was eventually used for the Fuehrer directive of Nov. 12, 1940.

77. Greiner *KTB*, Sept. 14.

78. Greiner *KTB*, Sept. 14. Raeder (not present on the 13th but probably informed by Generaladmiral Carls, who was) also thought that on the 13th Hitler had planned to call off the operation (*FCNA, 1940*, p. 99).

79. HD, Sept. 14; *FCNA, 1940,* pp. 98-100.

80. HD, Sept. 5. This handful of submarines was, however, inflicting heavy losses.

81. Printed in *FCNA, 1940,* pp. 100-01.

82. Greiner *KTB,* Sept. 14.

83. SKL KTB, Sept. 17.

84. XXXVIIIth A.K. KTB, Sept. 6; Richards, *op. cit.,* p. 186.

85. Mil.Bef. Belg.–Nordfr. KTB, Sept. 8, 12.

86. SKL KTB, Sept. 8; VIIth A.K. KTB, Sept. 11.

87. Wheatley, *op. cit.,* p. 107.

88. H.Gr. A KTB, Sept. 15; AOK 16 KTB, Sept. 15, based on report from XLI A.K.; Mil. Bef. Belg.–Nordfr., Sept. 15, 16; VII A.K., Sept. 16; 35 Inf. KTB, Sept. 16; 8 Inf. KTB, Sept. 16; Richards, *op. cit.,* p. 187.

89. SKL KTB, Sept. 16.

90. KTBs of VII, XIII, and XXIII A.K., 17 Inf. Div., and 35 Inf. Div., Sept. 18.

91. SKL KTB, Sept. 18.

92. The OKW order of Sept. 19 is printed in *FCNA, 1940,* pp. 101-02.

93. Harris, *Bomber Offensive* (1947), p. 43.

94. *FCNA, 1940,* p. 102.

95. SKL KTB, Sept. 23; VII A.K. KTB, Sept. 23; Wheatley, *op. cit.,* pp. 111-12.

96. Richards, *op. cit.,* p. 189; Collier, *Defence,* pp. 227-29.

97. HD, Sept. 21, 24, 25, 26, 28.

98. XXXVIIIth A.K. KTB, Sept. 29, Oct. 1 and 30.

99. *FCNA, 1940,* p. 106.

100. *Ciano's Diplomatic Papers,* p. 390; Ciano, *Diario,* Sept. 19. Quite possibly Ribbentrop was unaware of Hitler's indefinite postponement order of Sept. 17.

101. Ciano, *Diario,* Sept. 27–28.

102. The OKH memorandum (from the operations section of the General Staff to the planning section of OKW, i.e. Warlimont) is described in Greiner *KTB,* entry for Oct. 2. In all probability it was initiated by Halder, whose disgust at the long period of indecision had been expressed on Sept. 28.

103. Greiner *KTB,* Sept. 30 and Oct. 1.

104. *Id.,* Oct. 20.

105. H.Gr. A KTB, Oct. 1 and 4.

106. IV A.K. KTB, Oct. 6; V and VII A.K. and 35 Inf. Div. KTBs, Oct. 5.

107. Greiner *KTB,* Oct. 8.

108. The OKW order of Oct. 12 is printed in *FCNA, 1940,* at p. 103; see also Greiner *KTB,* Oct. 12.

109. *Supra,* pp. 74-75 and 239.

110. VIIth AK KTB, Oct. 15, 16, and 17.

111. *FCNA, 1940,* p. 110 (Oct. 14); HD, Nov. 8.

112. Von Rohden series 4376, item 111.

113. *Supra,* pp. 268-69.

114. Document in AOK 16 file "Befehlstelle Festland."

115. HD, Nov. 4; N.D. 444-PS.

116. HD, Nov. 25.

117. HD, Dec. 5.

118. Fleming, *Operation Sea Lion,* pp. 296-97.

119. N.D. 874-PS (Mar. 9, 1941) and 876-PS (May 12, 1941).

120. OKH directives of Apr. 24, 1941 (*Haifisch*), Apr. 23, 1941 (*Harpune*), and Aug. 31, 1941 (discontinuing both).

121. *FCNA,* Feb. 13, 1942.

122. Wheatley, *op. cit.,* p. 98.

123. SKL war diary, Sept. 10 and 12, 1940.

124. Greiner *KTB,* Sept. 23, 1940.

125. As shown *supra,* p. , there had been conferences during the previous two weeks at the 16th Army and at corps level. Wheatley, *op. cit.,* pp. 118-21, points this out, and regards it as detracting from the accuracy of Warlimont's judg-

ment. But it is plain from the entries, as well as from Richthofen's comments, that the tactical plans for commitment of the Stukas were still in a fluid and unsettled condition, in no way suitable to an imminent prospect of invasion.

126. *Supra*, pp. 167-68.

127. Heusinger, *Befehl im Widerstreit*, p. 101.

128. Ansel, *op. cit.*, p. 316.

129. Fleming, *op. cit.*, pp. 158-64.

130. Manstein, *Lost Victories* (1958; German edition, 1955), pp. 164-71.

CONCLUSION

1. The quotation is from Klee's unpublished MS., "Operation 'Sea Lion' and the Role Planned for the Luftwaffe," in the files at MAB. Herr Klee is the author of *Das Unternehmen "Seeloewe"* (1958), the principal German study of Sea Lion. He is also the author of a short study of the Battle of Britain (presumably based on the cited MS.) published in *Decisive Battles of World War II*, ed. Jacobsen and Rohwer (1965), pp. 73-94, originally published in Germany in 1960. This study does not contain the sentence quoted in the text from the MS.

2. Warlimont, *Inside Hitler's Headquarters* (1964), pp. 107-09.

3. His recently published memoirs, written at Nuremberg during the last days of his confinement prior to his execution, give no indication that he either favored or opposed Sea Lion. See *The Memoirs of Field-Marshal Keitel* (London, 1965), pp. 116-18.

4. *Supra*, p. 274.

5. Gordon A. Craig, *The Politics of the Prussian Army, 1940–1945* (Oxford: Clarendon, 1955), pp. 299-341; Walter Goerlitz, *History of the German General Staff, 1657–1945* (New York: Praeger, 1953), pp. 143-203; Taylor, *Sword and Swastika*, pp. 13-16; Herbert Rosinski, *The German Army* (New York: Harcourt, Brace, 1940), pp. 140-65.

6. Taylor, *March of Conquest, passim*.

7. *Id.*, at pp. 344-51.

8. Blumentritt, *Von Rundstedt* (1952), pp. 87-95.

9. Heinz Guderian, *Panzer Leader* (London: Michael Joseph, 1952), pp. 135-39.

10. Lossberg, *Im Wehrmachtfuehrungsstab* (1949), p. 94; Taylor, *March of Conquest*, pp. 352-53.

11. Heusinger, *Befehl im Widerstreit* (1950), pp. 98-105.

12. At the Berghof conference of July 31 Hitler opined, "Submarine and air warfare may bring about a final decision, but this may be one or two years off." (*Supra*, p. 74.)

13. Klein, *Germany's Economic Preparations for War* (1959), pp. 188-93.

14. *DGFP*, Vol. X, Nos. 129, 166.

Sources
and Bibliography

MORE THAN TWENTY years have elapsed since the Second World War, and during this time the available documentation has grown to the point where, for the individual student, the pursuit of complete research is quite hopeless. This is especially true with respect to the records of the various German Army headquarters, most of which remained inaccessible to private historians until the last few years, and then were released in a veritable torrent. Extensive screening by teams working under institutional auspices appears to be essential for the full exploitation of this mountain of material.

Even for the few weeks covered by this book, I make no claim to have looked everywhere that one might find something useful. Especially with respect to interviews with surviving participants—a source which Admiral Walter Ansel has used to especially good effect in his able study of this same period—my work is regrettably deficient. On the other hand, I have found opportunity to examine a substantial amount of documentary material not heretofore covered, and have endeavored to make full use of the researches of others as well as my own in describing and analyzing the crowded events of this crucial summer.

For access to these documents and assistance in their use I am indebted to many persons, especially Rear Admiral E. M. Eller, the Director of Naval History, U.S. Department of the Navy; Philip Brower and Richard Bauer of the World War II Records Division of the National Archives; Detmar Finke of the Office of the Chief of Military History, U.S. Department of the Army; and Dr. Albert F. Simpson, Edwin P. Kennedy, Jr., and Harry B. Fletcher of the United States Air Force Historical Division at Maxwell Air Force Base, Montgomery, Alabama; and Herr Rudolf Absolon, of the West German State Archives (*Bundesarchiv*).

CONTEMPORARY DOCUMENTS

1. NUREMBERG TRIALS. This was the first collection of original documents made available to the public, and consists of those items thought to have possible significance for war crimes purposes, selected by re-

355

searchers from a great variety of military, diplomatic, economic, and Nazi Party sources. The documents introduced in evidence at the first Nuremberg trial before the International Military Tribunal are reproduced in the forty-two-volume *Trial of the Major War Criminals,* herein cited as *TMWC* (Nuremberg, 1947–49), the so-called Blue Book series. Selections from those introduced at the subsequent Nuremberg trials are contained in the fifteen-volume series *Trials of War Criminals before the Nuremberg Military Tribunals,* cited as *TWC* (Washington: U.S. Government Printing Office, 1949–52), the so-called Green Book series. Additional documents, affidavits, and interrogatories collected at Nuremberg are in the so-called Red Book series, *Nazi Conspiracy and Aggression* (cited as *NCA*), published 1946–48 by the U.S. Government Printing Office. Numerous other Nuremberg documents, unpublished, are on deposit in a few major libraries; they are designated herein "N.D." and individually identified by the designations then given them, e.g., the letters "PS," "L," "C," "NOKW," etc., plus a number.

2. GERMAN FOREIGN OFFICE. A generous but selective collection of the records of the Auswaertiges Amt (commonly referred to as "the Wilhelmstrasse") is comprised in the series *Documents on German Foreign Policy, 1918–1945* (Washington: U.S. Government Printing Office), cited herein as *DGFP.*

3. ARMED FORCES HIGH COMMAND (OKW). The "war diary" (*Kriegstagebuch*) of the Operations Staff of the OKW was kept to 1943 by Helmuth Greiner, and thereafter by Dr. Percy Schramm. Most of it was destroyed in May 1945, but Greiner had retained copies of certain portions, as well as some of the handwritten notes from which he had dictated the diary to stenographers. From these sources Greiner and Schramm (both of whom survived the war) have reconstructed much of the diary, and copies of the reconstructed text, both in German and in English translation, were prepared, duplicated, and given a limited distribution by the Historical Division of EUCOM (European Command) some years ago. These were assembled in two separate sequences: the diary itself, and notes on the daily "situation conferences" of the operations branch. The war-diary sequence begins August 1, 1940, and the situation-conference notes August 8, 1940; both extend through and beyond the remainder of the period covered by my book, subject to gaps owing to leave, illness, field trips, or other interruptions.

The two sequences have recently been merged, extensively annotated, and published in German under the title *Kriegstagebuch des Oberkommandos der Wehrmacht* (*Wehrmachtfuehrungsstab*) by Bernard & Graefe Verlag, Frankfurt-am-Main. Volume I, covering the period August 1–December 31, 1940, edited and annotated by Hans-Adolf Jacobsen, was published in 1965, and is the source of the OKW references and quotations in my book which are cited as "Greiner *KTB.*"

4. ARMY HIGH COMMAND (OKH). Apart from the many orders and memoranda of which copies have survived in multiple provenance, the principal source is the personal diary recorded in Gabelsberger short-

hand by Generaloberst Franz Halder, Chief of the Army General Staff. Annotated transcriptions in German and English were produced and mimeographed at Nuremberg in 1948, and copies were distributed to major libraries. In 1963 the diary, which covers the period August 14, 1939, to September 24, 1942, was published in three volumes (edited by Hans-Adolf Jacobsen) by W. Kohlhammer Verlag, Stuttgart, under the title *Generaloberst Halder: Kriegstagebuch.*

5.   NAVAL HIGH COMMAND (OKM). Minutes of the wartime conferences between Hitler and the Commander-in-Chief of the Navy—who, during the period covered by this book, was Grossadmiral Erich Raeder—were translated and circulated in photo offset in 1947 by the British Admiralty, under the title *Fuehrer Conferences on Naval Affairs,* cited as FCNA. The war diary of the Naval War Staff (SKL) was made available to me by the kindness of Rear Admiral Eller.

6.   HITLER's MILITARY DIRECTIVES (*Weisungen*). As Commander-in-Chief of the Wehrmacht, Hitler issued his general directives for the conduct of the war through OKW in a numbered sequence, beginning August 31, 1939. These were translated as *Fuehrer Directives,* duplicated, and given limited circulation in 1948 by the U.S. Department of the Navy. In 1962, annotated by Walther Hubatsch, they were published by Bernard & Graefe Verlag under the title *Hitlers Weisungen fuer die Kriegfuehrung, 1939–1945.* In 1964 they were edited by H. R. Trevor-Roper and published in English by Sidgwick and Jackson of London; the American edition of 1965, under the title *Blitzkrieg to Defeat,* was published by Holt, Rinehart and Winston.

7.   LUFTWAFFE. Surviving documents of the German Air Force are far scantier in quantity and sketchier in coverage than in the case of the other two services.[*] In the autumn of 1943 the bulk of the records by then accumulated in the military-science section of the Luftwaffe General Staff were moved from Berlin to Karlsbad, in the Sudetenland. Most of these were deliberately destroyed by burning in 1945, shortly before the end of the war. Less important documents that had been left in Berlin probably fell into the hands of the Russians.

However, a number of Luftwaffe documents (or copies) had been transmitted to the other services, and turned up in their files of incoming documents. Furthermore, a sizable collection of documents was preserved by the military-science section; these were taken by the United States Army in May 1945. Many of these are in the so-called "Von Rohden" collection (after Generalmajor Herhuth von Rohden, chief of the military-science section), and are maintained in the captured-military-documents archives of the Departmental Records Branch at Alexandria, Virginia. Still others are available at the Air University, Maxwell Air Force Base, Montgomery, Alabama.

[*] The information in this paragraph is drawn largely from a memorandum (dated July 31, 1963, at Freiburg-im-Breisgau) furnished to me by Oberstleutnant a.D. Greffrath, formerly of the Reichsluftfahrtministerium.

8. OTHER MILITARY DOCUMENTARY SOURCES. An enormous volume of captured German military documents—thousands of shelf feet—was deposited after the war in the Departmental Records Branch at Alexandria. Most of these are Army records, and they comprise war diaries of many of the higher headquarters, files of orders and memoranda dealing with specific operations, technical and training materials, and files based on a great profusion of other matters. Many if not most of the original documents have by now been "repatriated" to Germany after microfilming for deposit in the National Archives. Descriptive indices of these records have been published in the series entitled "Guides to German Records Microfilmed at Alexandria, Va.," published by the National Archives and Records Service of the General Services Administration.

9. MISCELLANEOUS. For security reasons (danger of capture, etc.) regulations against keeping personal diaries are general military practice. But these rules are frequently honored in the breach, and in this respect the Germans are no exception. The personal diary of Generalfeldmarschall Fedor von Bock has been transcribed, and was made available to me by the U.S. Army's Office of the Chief of Military History. There are others (by, e.g., Generalfeldmarschall Wilhelm von Leeb and Generalfeldmarschall Wolfram von Richthofen) to which I have not had access. In the diplomatic area, the best-known and most useful diary for this period is that of the Italian Foreign Minister and son-in-law of Mussolini, Galeazzo Ciano, published in two volumes as *Ciano: Diario* in 1946 by Rizzoli under the copyright of Doubleday, Doran and Co. of New York; other personal records by Ciano of his conversations as Foreign Minister are published in *Ciano's Diplomatic Papers* (London: Odhams Press, 1948). Many other Axis participants in the war, of high and low degree, kept diaries or "personal" sets of official papers, some of which have served as the basis for memoirs or for the numerous divisional unit histories which have been published in Germany since the war.

Bibliography

I. BATTLE OF BRITAIN

BALDWIN, HANSON B.: "The Battle of Britain," Ch. 2 of *Battles Lost and Won—Great Campaigns of World War II.* New York: Harper and Row, 1966.

BISHOP, EDWARD: *The Battle of Britain.* London: George Allen and Unwin, 1960.

COLLIER, BASIL: *The Battle of Britain.* London: Batsford, 1962.

COLLIER, RICHARD: *Eagle Day: The Battle of Britain.* New York: Dutton, 1966.

KLEE, KARL: "Die Luftschlacht um England, 1940," Ch. IV of *Entscheidungsschlachten des zweiten Weltkrieges,* ed. Jacobsen and Rohwer.

Frankfurt-am-Main: Bernard & Graefe, 1960. In the American edition of the book, published as *Decisive Battles of World War II* (New York: Putnam, 1965), Klee's chapter is entitled "The Battle of Britain."

KREIPE, WERNER: "The Battle of Britain," Part I of *The Fatal Decisions*, ed. Freidin and Richardson. New York: Sloane, 1956.

LEE, ASHER: *Blitz on Britain*. London: Four Square, 1960.

McKEE, ALEXANDER: *Strike from the Sky*. Boston: Little, Brown, 1960.

MIDDLETON, DREW: *The Sky Suspended*. New York: Longmans, Green, 1960.

WEBER, DR. THEO: *Die Luftschlacht um England*. Frauenfeld: Huber, 1956.

WOOD, DEREK, AND DEMPSTER, DEREK: *The Narrow Margin*. London: Hutchinson, 1961.

II. SEA LION

ANSEL, WALTER: *Hitler Confronts England*. Durham, N.C.: Duke University Press, 1960.

FLEMING, PETER: *Operation Sea Lion*. New York: Simon and Schuster, 1957.

KLEE, KARL: *Das Unternehmen "Seeloewe."* Goettingen: Musterschmidt, 1958.

————: *Dokumente zum Unternehmen "Seeloewe."* Goettingen: Musterschmidt, 1959.

WHEATLEY, RONALD: *Operation Sea Lion*. London: Oxford Clarendon Press, 1958.

III. GERMAN ARMED FORCES

Ehrenbuch der deutschen Wehrmacht/Weltkrieg 1939–1945. Stuttgart: Riegler, 1954.

GREINER, HELMUTH: *Die Oberste Wehrmachtfuehrung, 1939–1943*. Wiesbaden: Limes, 1951.

KEITEL, WILHELM: *The Memoirs of Field-Marshal Keitel*, ed. Walter Goerlitz. London: William Kimber, 1965.

LOSSBERG, BERNHARD VON: *Im Wehrmachtfuehrungsstab*. Hamburg: H. H. Noelke, 1949.

WARLIMONT, WALTER: *Inside Hitler's Headquarters, 1939–45*. New York: Praeger, 1964. Previously published in German as *Im Hauptquartier der deutschen Wehrmacht, 1939–1945* (Frankfurt-am-Main: Bernard & Graefe, 1962).

A. German Army[*]

BLUMENTRITT, GUENTHER: *Von Rundstedt*. London: Odhams, 1952.

BREHM, WERNER: *Mein Kriegstagebuch, 1939–1945: Mit der 7. Panzer-Division 5 Jahre im West und Ost*. Kassel, 1953.

BREITHAUPT, HANS: *Die Geschichte der 30. Infanterie-Division, 1939–1945*. Bad Nauheim: Podzun, 1955.

[*] Since only the Army High Command and the headquarters and units committed to Sea Lion are involved in the narrative, the bibliography is highly selective. For a fuller listing see Taylor, *The March of Conquest* (1958), p. 440.

ERFURTH, WALDEMAR: *Die Geschichte des deutschen Generalstabes von 1918 bis 1945.* Goettingen: Musterschmidt, 1957.

GROSSMANN, HORST: *Geschichte der rhenisch-westfalischen 6. Infanterie-Division, 1939–1945.* Bad Nauheim: Podzun, 1958.

HEUSINGER, ADOLF: *Befehl im Widerstreit.* Tuebingen: Rainer Wunderlich, 1950.

HUBATSCH, WALTHER: *61. Infanterie-Division.* Bad Nauheim: Podzun, 1952.

LANZ, HUBERT: *Gebirgsjaeger: Die 1. Gebirgsdivision, 1939–1945.* Bad Nauheim: Podzun, 1954.

LUCKE, CHRISTIAN VON: *Die Geschichte des Panzer-Regiments 2.* Kleve, 1953.

MANSTEIN, ERICH VON: *Lost Victories.* Chicago: Regnery, 1958. Previously published in German as *Verlorene· Siege* (Bonn: Athenaeum, 1955).

MARKER, LUDWIG, ED.: *Das Buch der 78. Sturmdivision.* Tuebingen.

METSCH, FRIEDRICH-AUGUST VON: *Die Geschichte der 22. Infanterie-Division.* Kiel: Podzun, 1952.

SCHAUB, OSKAR: *Aus der Geschichte Panzer-Grenadier Regiment 12.* Bergisch Gladbach, 1957.

SCHROEDER, JUERGEN, AND SCHULTZ-NAUMANN, JOACHIM: *Die Geschichte des pommerschen 32. Infanterie-Division, 1939–1945.* Bad Nauheim: Podzun, 1956.

TESKE, HERMANN: *Bewegungskrieg: Fuehrungsprobleme einer Infanterie-Division im Westfeldzug 1940.* Heidelberg: Vowinckel, 1955.

———: *Die Silbernen Spiegel.* Heidelberg: Vowinckel, 1952.

TETTAU, HANS VON, AND VERSOCK, KURT: *Geschichte der 24. Infanterie-Division, 1939–1945.* Stolberg, 1956.

ZYDOWITZ, KURT VON: *Die Geschichte der 58. Infanterie-Division.* Kiel: Podzun, 1952.

B. German Navy*

DOENITZ, KARL: *Memoirs: Ten Years and Twenty Days.* Cleveland: World, 1959. Previously published in German as *Zehn Jahre und zwanzig Tage* (Bonn: Athenaeum, 1958).

MARTIENSSEN, ANTHONY: *Hitler and His Admirals.* New York: Dutton, 1949.

PUTTKAMER, KARL JESKO VON: *Die unheimliche See.* Vienna: Karl Kuehne, 1952.

RAEDER, ERICH: *Struggle for the Sea.* London: William Kimber, 1959.

RUGE, FRIEDRICH: *Der Seekrieg 1939–1945.* Stuttgart: K. F. Koehler, 1954.

C. Luftwaffe

BARTZ, KARL: *Als der Himmel brannte.* Hannover: Adolf Sponholtz, 1955.

BAUMBACH, WERNER: *The Life and Death of the Luftwaffe.* New York: Coward-McCann, 1960. Previously published in German as *Zu Spaet?* (Munich: Richard Pflaum, 1949).

---

* The footnote on the Army bibliography applies, *mutatis mutandis,* to the Navy as well.

BEKKER, CAIUS (Hans-Dieter Berenbrok): *Angriffshoehe 4000: Ein Kriegstagebuch der deutschen Luftwaffe.* Oldenburg: Gerhard Stalling Verlag, 1964.

CONRADIS, HEINZ: *Forschen und Fliegen: Weg und Werk von Kurt Tank.* Goettingen: Musterschmidt, 1955.

FEUCHTER, GEORG: *Geschichte des Luftkriegs.* Bonn: Athenaeum, 1954.

GALLAND, ADOLF: *The First and the Last.* New York: Henry Holt, 1954.

HEINKEL, ERNST: *Stormy Life.* New York: Dutton, 1956.

HOVE, ALKMAR VON: *Achtung Fallschirmjaeger.* Starnberger See: Druffel-Verlag, 1954.

KENS, KARLHEINZ, AND NOWARRA, HEINZ: *Die deutschen Flugzeuge 1939–1945.* Munich: J. F. Lehmann, 1961.

KOCH, HORST-ADALBERT: *Flak: Die Geschichte der deutschen Flakartillerie.* Bad Nauheim: Podzun, 1954.

LEE, ASHER: *The German Air Force.* London: Duckworth, 1946.

NIELSEN, ANDREAS: *The German Air Force General Staff.* USAF Historical Studies No. 173. Research Studies Institute, Air University, 1959.

OSTERKAMP, THEO: *Durch Hoehen und Tiefen jagt ein Herz.* Heidelberg: Vowinckel, 1952.

PRILLER, JOSEF: *Geschichte eines Jagdgeschwaders: Das J.G. 26 (Schlageter), 1937–1945.* Heidelberg: Vowinckel, 1956.

RIECKHOFF, HANS: *Trumpf oder Bluff?* Geneva: Interavia, 1945.

Rise and Fall of the German Air Force, 1933 to 1945, The. British Air Ministry Pamphlet No. 218. London, 1948.

SUCHENWIRTH, RICHARD: *Historical Turning Points in the German Air Force War Effort.* USAF Historical Studies, No. 189. Research Studies Institute, Air University, 1959. An excerpt from this study, entitled "Abject Obedience to Hitler in the Luftwaffe," was published in the October 1965 issue of *Aerospace Historian* (Vol. XII, No. 4), pp. 124-31.

D. Compilations and Lists

BURKHART, MUELLER-HILLEBRAND: *Das Heer, 1933–1945,* 2 vols., published by E. S. Mittler & Sohn—Vol. I in Darmstadt, 1954, Vol. II in Frankfurt-am-Main, 1956.

FOLTTMANN, JOSEF, AND MOELLER-WITTEN, HANS: *Opfergang der Generale.* Berlin: Bernard & Graefe, 1952.

KEILIG, WOLF: *Das Deutsche Heer, 1939–1945.* Looseleaf. Bad Nauheim: Podzun, 1957 *et seq.*

———: *Rangliste des deutschen Heeres, 1944–45.* Bad Nauheim: Podzun, 1955.

LOHMANN, WALTER, AND HILDEBRAND, HANS: *Die deutsche Kriegsmarine, 1939–1945.* Looseleaf. Bad Nauheim: Podzun, 1956 *et seq.*

OBERMAIER, ERNST: *Die Ritterkreuztraeger der Luftwaffe, Band I, Jagdflieger 1939–1945.* Mainz: Verlag Dieter Hoffmann, 1966.

Order of Battle of the German Army. Military Intelligence Division, War Department, Washington, D. C., 1945.

SEEMEN, GERHARD VON: *Die Ritterkreuztraeger, 1939–1945.* Bad Nauheim: Podzun, 1955.

STAHL, FRIEDRICH: *Heeresinteilung 1939.* Bad Nauheim: Podzun, 1954.

IV. ROYAL AIR FORCE

BAKER, EDGAR C. R.: *The Fighter Aces of the R.A.F., 1939–1945.* London: William Kimber, 1962.

DIVINE, DAVID: *The Broken Wing—A Study in the British Exercise of Air Power.* London: Hutchinson & Co., 1966.

DOUGLAS, SHOLTO (LORD DOUGLAS): *Combat and Command.* New York: Simon and Schuster, 1966.

EMBRY, SIR BASIL: *Mission Accomplished.* London: Methuen, 1957.

GALLICO, PAUL: *The Hurricane Story.* Garden City, N.Y.: Doubleday, 1960.

HARRIS, SIR ARTHUR: *Bomber Offensive.* London: Collins, 1947.

JOHNSON, JOHN E.: *Wing Leader.* New York: Ballantine, 1957.

MACMILLAN, NORMAN: *The Royal Air Force in the World War,* 4 vols. London: Harrap, 1942–50.

RICHARDS, DENIS: *Royal Air Force, 1939–1945,* Vol. I, *The Fight at Odds.* London: HMSO, 1953.

SMITH, NORMAN DAVID: *The Royal Air Force.* Oxford: Basil Blackwell, 1963.

SPAIGHT, J. M.: *Bombing Vindicated.* London: Geoffrey Bles, 1944.

TEDDER, ARTHUR, LORD: *Air Power in War.* London: Hodder and Stoughton, 1947.

WYKEHAM, PETER: *Fighter Command.* London: Putnam, 1960.

V. GENERAL

ASSMANN, KURT: *Deutsche Schicksaljahre.* Wiesbaden: Eberhard Brockhaus, 1950.

BEWLEY, CHARLES: *Hermann Goering and the Third Reich.* New York: Devin-Adair, 1962.

BROSS, WERNER: *Gespraeche mit Hermann Goering waehrend des Nuernberger Prozesses.* Flensburg: Christian Wolff, 1950.

BULLOCK, ALVIN: *Hitler,* revised ed. New York: Harper and Row, 1962.

BUTLER, J. R. M.: *Grand Strategy, Vol. II, September 1939–June 1941.* London: HMSO, 1957.

CHURCHILL, WINSTON: *Their Finest Hour.* Boston: Houghton Mifflin, 1949.

COLLIER, BASIL: *The Defence of the United Kingdom.* London: HMSO, 1957.

DIRKSEN, HERBERT VON: *Moscow, Tokyo, London.* London: Hutchinson, 1951.

FRISCHAUER, WILLI: *The Rise and Fall of Hermann Goering.* Boston: Houghton Mifflin, 1951.

FULLER, J. F. C.: *The Second World War, 1939–45.* New York: Duell, Sloan and Pearce, 1949

GOERLITZ, WALTER: *Der zweite Weltkrieg, 1939–1945,* 2 vols. Stuttgart: Steingrueben, 1951.

HALDER, FRANZ: *Hitler as War Lord.* London: Putnam, 1950. Previously published in German as *Hitler als Feldherr* (Munich: Muenchener Dom, 1949).

HASSELL, ULRICH VON: *The Von Hassell Diaries.* New York: Doubleday, 1947. Previously published in German as *Vom andern Deutschland* (Zurich: Atlantis, 1946).

HILGER, GUSTAV, AND MEYER, ALFRED: *The Incompatible Allies: German-Soviet Relations, 1918–1941.* New York: Macmillan, 1953.

HINSLEY, F. H.: *Hitler's Strategy.* Cambridge, Eng.: Cambridge University Press, 1951.

JACOBSEN, HANS-ADOLF, AND DOLLINGER, HANS, EDS.: *Der Zweite Weltkrieg in Bildern und Dokumenten,* 3 vols. Munich: Kurt Desch, 1962.

KESSELRING, ALBERT: *A Soldier's Record.* New York: William Morrow, 1954. Previously published in German as *Soldat bis zum letzten Tag* (Bonn: Athenaeum, 1953).

KLEIN, BURTON H.: *Germany's Economic Preparations for War.* Cambridge, Mass.: Harvard University Press, 1959.

LIDDELL HART, B. H.: *The German Generals Talk.* New York: William Morrow, 1948.

MANVELL, ROGER, AND FRAENKEL, HEINRICH: *Goering.* New York: Simon and Schuster, 1962.

MENDELSSOHN, PETER DE: *Design for Aggression.* New York: Harper and Brothers, 1946.

NAMIER, SIR LEWIS: *In the Nazi Era.* London: Macmillan, 1952.

SCHMIDT, PAUL OTTO: *Hitler's Interpreter.* New York: Macmillan, 1951.

SEABURG, PAUL: *The Wilhelmstrasse.* Berkeley: University of California Press, 1954.

SHIRER, WILLIAM L.: *Berlin Diary.* New York: Knopf, 1941.

TAYLOR, TELFORD: *The March of Conquest.* New York: Simon and Schuster, 1958.

————: *Sword and Swastika.* New York: Simon and Schuster, 1952.

THOMPSON, LAURENCE: *1940.* New York: William Morrow & Co., 1966.

TIPPELSKIRCH, KURT VON: *Geschichte des zweiten Weltkriegs.* Bonn: Athenaeum, 1951.

WEBSTER, SIR CHARLES, AND FRANKLAND, NOBLE: *The Strategic Air Offensive against Germany, 1939–1945,* 4 vols. London: HMSO, 1961.

WEIZSAECKER, ERNST VON: *Memoirs.* Chicago: Regnery, 1951.

WUORINEN, JOHN: *Finland and World War II.* New York: Ronald Press, 1948.

INDEX

Aalborg, Denmark, 124, 142
Abbeville, 19, 48, 110, 204
Abe, Nobuyuki, 32
Adler (*-angriff*) [Eagle (Attack)], 70,
71, 75, 77–192 *passim*, 228, 231, 276;
historical and strategic importance
of, 14–15, 82; precursor plans, 44,
47–64 *passim*, 104, 107–12; "terror
attacks," 44, 113–18, 129, 130, 154,
157, 163, 207; strategy and tactics,
57, 71, 125, 127, 129–47, 167, 179,
184–85, 285, 291, 295–96; relation
to Sea Lion, 67, 68, 127–28, 167,
168, 220, 223, 228, 231, 263, 276,
284, 285, 287, 290–96; Luftwaffe
deployment, 90, 94, 95, 102, 103,
120–29, 246, 269; night-raid phase,
173–78; summary of success and
failure, 179–92; *see also* BATTLE OF
BRITAIN
Adlertag [Eagle Day], 71, 128–39, 142–
43, 228, 276
Alfieri, Dino, 54, 66fn.
Amsterdam, 57
Angola, 51
Ansel, Admiral Walter, 188, 204fn.,
209fn., 213, 214, 215, 287fn., 288
Anti-Comintern Pact, 29, 31
Antwerp, 243, 260, 265, 270, 271, 276,
279
Arita, Hachiro, 32
Army, German, 19–26 *passim*, 40, 55,
56, 215, 273, 279, 280; in Battle of
France, 19–20, 48, 49, 209, 214,
289; too big, reduction ordered, 21–
26, 36, 49–50, 52, 55–56, 65, 74;
lack of coordination with Luftwaffe,
24, 58, 71, 209, 214, 236–37, 269–

70, 295–96; projected invasion of
Russia, 42, 43, 55, 65, 73–75, 252;
invasion of Britain—plans, 54–59, 64,
67, 71, 202–3, 205, 208–44, 248;
—collaboration with Navy, 56–58,
67, 206, 212, 213, 219, 222–36, 238,
250, 251, 272; —preparations, deployment, training, 62, 224, 226,
238–41, 246–67, 278; —transportation needs, facilities, 67, 206, 220–
22, 235, 236, 242, 243, 246–49, 261–
67, 270, 271; —zeal for project,
209, 213, 226, 250, 254, 283, 293
Army, German, Command:
OKH (Oberkommando des Heeres—
High Command of the Army), 55–
57, 66, 73, 75, 202–3, 209, 216–19,
238, 247fn., 248, 249, 252, 261, 266,
269, 279–81, *passim; see also* BRAU-
CHITSCH; General Staff, 22, 46, 55,
59, 63, 66, 201, 202, 205, 219, 222,
246, 247, 294; *see also* HALDER
Army, German, Field Units:
Army Groups (*Heeresgruppen*):
A—218, 237, 238, 239, 244fn., 252,
258fn., 260, 266, 269, 278, 281
B—118, 209, 216, 218, 219fn., 239,
252fn., 253fn.
C—115, 239fn., 289
Armies (*Armeen*):
4th—239fn.
6th—218, 239, 241, 252fn., 255,
258fn., 259
7th—115
9th—218, 237, 240, 241, 244fn.,
251fn., 252fn., 253, 255, 259, 266,
267, 268, 278
11th—280

About the Author

TELFORD TAYLOR'S INTEREST in the German military machine dates from his experience as a wartime officer in the Army intelligence service, and later as chief counsel for the prosecution, with the rank of brigadier general, at the Nuremberg trials of war criminals. This volume is a sequel to *Sword and Swastika,* published in 1952, covering the story of the Nazis and the generals up to the fall of 1939, and to *The March of Conquest,* published in 1958, which analyzed the German victories in Western Europe in the spring of 1940.

Mr. Taylor held various government positions under Presidents Roosevelt and Truman. He has argued many cases before the United States Supreme Court, and is the author of *Grand Inquest: The Story of Congressional Investigations,*· published in 1955. He is now professor of law at Columbia University and a visiting lecturer at the Yale Law School.